PUBLIC MORALISTS

PUBLIC MORALISTS

Political Thought and Intellectual Life in Britain

STEFAN COLLINI

CLARENDON PRESS · OXFORD

This book has been printed digitally and produced in a standard specification in order to ensure its continuing availability

OXFORD
UNIVERSITY PRESS

Great Clarendon Street, Oxford OX2 6DP

Oxford University Press is a department of the University of Oxford.
It furthers the University's objective of excellence in research, scholarship,
and education by publishing world-wide in

Oxford New York

Auckland Bangkok Buenos Aires Cape Town Chennai
Dar es Salaam Delhi Hong Kong Istanbul Karachi Kolkata
Kuala Lumpur Madrid Melbourne Mexico City Mumbai Nairobi
São Paulo Shanghai Taipei Tokyo Toronto

Oxford is a registered trade mark of Oxford University Press
in the UK and in certain other countries

Published in the United States
by Oxford University Press Inc., New York

Reprinted 2003

ISBN 0-19-820422-1

Printed in Great Britain by

Antony Rowe Ltd., Eastbourne

CONTENTS

Now and then it is possible to observe the moral life in process of revising itself, perhaps by reducing the emphasis it formerly placed upon one or another of its elements, perhaps by inventing and adding to itself a new element, some mode of conduct or of feeling which hitherto it had not regarded as essential to virtue.

(Lionel Trilling, *Sincerity and Authenticity* (1972))

I shouldn't like anyone to call me an Intellectual, I don't think any Englishman would! They don't count really, you know; but still it's rather the thing to have them.

(George Bernard Shaw, *Fanny's First Play* (1911))

The life of nations no less than that of men is lived largely in the imagination.

(Enoch Powell, speech at Trinity College, Dublin (1946))

INTRODUCTION

This book is intended as a contribution to the intellectual history of modern Britain. It attempts to bring to life and to explore in sometimes unusual ways certain central themes in the development of English moral and cultural attitudes, and their bearing upon political argument from the mid-nineteenth to the early-twentieth century. In practice, the book largely concentrates on reconstructing the thought and sensibility of some of the leading members of the educated class of this period. But it does also express a conviction that our understanding of this aspect of our history, and still more the manner and tone in which we write about it, are consequential, albeit in a limited way, for our sense of identity and conduct in the present.

I began writing the book out of a desire to deepen, and in some respects to complicate, our understanding of the history of political thought in Britain by presenting a more thickly textured characterization of that activity as part of the public debate and wider intellectual life of the time. Although that accurately describes the book's genesis, and is the aspiration which the subtitle is intended to signal, the term 'political thought' may, in at least one respect, arouse misleading expectations. The book does not directly address what are conventionally regarded as the central questions of political theory—questions about democracy, authority, rights, and so on—nor is it written in the systematically analytical mode normally thought appropriate to such issues. Rather, the following chapters attempt, in different ways, to exercise the historical imagination—that is, to establish a balance between human familiarity and cultural remoteness—in exploring the reflective experience of a loose assortment of unusually articulate individuals. I discuss, sometimes in detail, sometimes only in passing, the writings of John Stuart Mill, Matthew Arnold, Herbert Spencer, George Eliot, Henry Maine, Walter Bagehot, Leslie and Fitzjames Stephen, John Morley, Charles Kingsley, T. H. Green, Henry Fawcett, James

Bryce, E. A. Freeman, A. V. Dicey, A. C. Bradley, Henry Sidgwick, Frederic Harrison, Mrs Humphry Ward, Bernard Bosanquet, John Churton Collins, Alfred Marshall, Benjamin Kidd, F. W. Maitland, and, more cursorily, such early twentieth century figures as Harold Laski, Arthur Quiller-Couch, T. S. Eliot, J. M. Keynes, Ernest Barker, and F. R. Leavis.

These authors are now commonly assigned, whether as founders, exemplars, or simple intellectual property, to a variety of disciplines—Politics, English, Philosophy, Law, History, Economics, Sociology. I return later in the book to some of the constraints imposed by taking such disciplinary categories for granted, but in practical terms this diversity of subject-matter has meant that in some places I have been unashamedly dependent on the work of other, more specialized scholars. Sometimes, indeed, my role has seemed to involve little more than taking research that is already relatively familiar in one subdiscipline—on, say, the growth of the legal profession or the establishment of a 'canon' of English literature—and juxtaposing it to the findings of scholars who have worked ostensibly distant fields, such as the study of Victorian periodicals or the history of education. I have tried to acknowledge these obligations in my footnotes, though I fear that the uses to which I have put other scholars' work may not always meet with their approval. Perhaps, here as elsewhere, one cannot hope to conjoin promiscuity with respectability.

The book's subject-matter can be approached from another angle by considering the juxtaposition of terms in my title. I choose the term 'public moralist' partly because the more conventional labels, such as 'social critic' or 'political theorist', while adequate for many purposes, may suggest misleading or inappropriately narrow connotations. But I also choose it because of the suggestive interplay between the two halves of the phrase. The figures I discuss may be seen as 'moralists' in their efforts to persuade their contemporaries to live up to their professed ideals and in their concentration on failings of character as the chief source of civic as well as private woe. They invoked a particularly strenuous ethic, and gave such moral considerations priority over other concerns, whether personal, political, or aesthetic. But the emphasis introduced by 'public' is helpful, too, because it directs attention to their relations with an audience, an audience, moreover, which could not be considered merely sectional or local. That, in turn, raises questions about their characteristic idiom and strategies of argument, and the opportunities available for deploying them.

'Public moralist' also suggests, in a way that 'social critic' may not, the intimacy of the relation between writer and audience. The moralist, I want to argue, does not speak from somewhere located, mysteriously, 'outside' society, nor should we assume that criticism requires the critic to be socially marginal, politically adversarial, or morally estranged. In the present case, as Chapter 1 below attempts to show, the figures I am dealing with were very much part of those overlapping political, social, and intellectual circles which might be loosely referred to as the 'governing' or 'educated' classes of their day (I try to give a little more precision to these labels in that chapter). For the most part, they were well-connected, conventionally educated, comfortably situated, professionally successful, intellectually inclined men. (Apart from passing mention of exceptional individuals like George Eliot or Mrs Humphry Ward, the cast includes no women, and the use of a male pseudonym by one of these writers and the 'correct' married form by the other may hint at some of the reasons for this.) In subtle as well as obvious ways, both their engagement in political debate and their more extended ruminations on human fate expressed the sense of identity this position conferred on them.

Recovering their sense (or, rather, senses) of identity is fundamental. Even when reading the works of these figures for some other or more specific purpose, I discover I have repeatedly been drawn to trying to discriminate the modulations of individual voice. I choose the metaphor of 'voice' (and use it in the heading of Part II) because it seems to capture something that talk about the 'thought' or 'views' or 'theories' of an author does not quite do. Most obviously, it focuses on the identity, in the broadest sense, which a particular writer chooses to present, while at the same time drawing attention to those characteristic patterns of tone and register which lie too deep for choice, but which reveal something quite fundamental about the relation in which an individual stands to his or her experience. But beyond that, it provides another reminder of the implied presence of an audience, whether addressed in a conversational or didactic or hortatory or other mode. It is not, therefore, as purely individualistic a focus as it may at first seem, since it presumes the use of shared linguistic and cultural resources, and insists upon the public nature of all but the most hermetic forms of writing (and even, more obliquely, of those too). Thus, the complement of a notion of individual 'voice' is that of a fabric or texture of arguments, assumptions, values, ideas, associations, and so on ('discourse' is currently the preferred abbreviation though it can bring with it some more specific assumptions about 'power' or 'hegemony' that would require extended discussion). These, it seems to me, can most helpfully be thought of as a range of available resources rather than as some all-explaining *Zeitgeist*, and much of this book is devoted to exploring the ways in which different individual public moralists made use of this common stock. In practice, this has involved a sustained attentiveness to the idiom and cadences of their prose, something more readily associated with the work of the literary critic than with that of the political theorist. One consequence of this is the copious quotation the book contains, a further advantage of which, in my view, is that it allows the past a better chance of escaping the vigilance of any one historian's necessarily procrustean categories and of striking up an acquaintance with other readers in its own right.

It should by now be clear that this book is far from being a survey of the chief political theories or 'isms' in this period, and not just because it omits or only indirectly discusses most of the topics that any such survey would be obliged to include. But there is at least one further way in which it does not conform to that model; in some respects, indeed, it even reverses the kinds of claims characteristically found in such accounts, and we here touch on a point that may be of more general significance. That is to say, the conventional explanatory relation tends to suggest that the political attitudes widely encountered in the records left by the educated class should be seen as evidence of the 'influence' of the most prominent theories of the period, such as Utilitarianism or Social Darwinism or philosophical Idealism. My initial assumption has been, rather, that those theories acquired their prominence partly because they gave a coherent form and foundation to attitudes and beliefs already widely, if unselfconsciously, entertained. In other words, political arguments, and their attempted systematization as bodies of theory, must, if they are to have any persuasiveness, deploy, re-work, or otherwise make use of the shared evaluative language of those to whom they are addressed, and hence must appeal to the ideals and aspirations which that language represents. In this sense, political theories are parasitic upon the less explicit habits of response and evaluation that are deeply embedded in the culture. Theories are, of course, never adequate abridgements of whole conceptions of the world, still less of an entire pattern of practices. Part of the interest of intellectual history lies in observing the ways in which successive theoretical constructions collapse or unravel as their inevitable loose ends are pulled by hostile critics, or, no less frequently, the ways in which they are simply bypassed by a shift of cultural attention to other aspects of the pattern. It is also true that attempting to reconstruct these deeper patterns can require the historian to focus, even within a single chapter or essay, on quite long stretches of time, since fundamental assumptions and responses change with almost geological slowness by comparison to the flighty world of systematic theory.

The structure and scope of the book reflect these general convictions. It is not constructed as a single linear narrative, nor as one sustained analytical argument. In part, no doubt, this expresses my scepticism about the adequacy of the tighter conceptual schemes to do anything approaching justice to the richness of past human activity, and in part, perhaps, it simply embodies my literary or temperamental taste for essayistic forms. Furthermore, the approach is unashamedly eclectic and the level of generality deliberately variable. Even within my given limits, other scholars would presumably have chosen to concentrate upon different topics and episodes, while the cast of figures discussed, though already pretty large, could certainly have been extended. One excuse for limiting the book in the way I have done is that I was conscious, in addressing again figures about whom I have written in other terms elsewhere, of the danger of simply repeating myself; I have therefore abbreviated the discussion in some places and provided cross-references to these fuller accounts. Similarly, I have deliberately eschewed one whole topic which might naturally have been dealt with in the present book—namely, the relation of philosophical Idealism to other currents in the political thought of the period—precisely because in this case an earlier set of essays I had written now seemed, unnervingly, both remote and right, two good reasons for not attempting to return to the subject.[1]

[1] 'Idealism and "Cambridge Idealism"', *Historical Journal*, 17 (1975), 170–8; 'Hobhouse, Bosanquet and the state: philosophical Idealism and political argument in England 1880–1918', *Past and Present*, 72 (1976), 86–111; 'Liberalism and the legacy of Mill', *Historical Journal*, 20 (1977), 237–54; 'Sociology and Idealism in Britain 1880–1920', *Archives européennes de sociologie*, 19 (1978), 3–50; 'Political theory and the "science of society" in Victorian Britain', *Historical Journal*, 23 (1980), 203–31.

The sequence of the chapters follows a thematic rather than a strictly temporal progression, since several chapters pursue their topics across the whole period; but the arrangement is loosely chronological, passing from a primary focus on the mid-Victorian period to a concentration on the late nineteenth and early twentieth centuries and beyond. In intellectual history, more perhaps than in many other kinds, defining a period by specific dates is artificial and may even suggest a misleading precision. In the present case, I have resorted to dates simply for want of a convenient label to cover the period as a whole. Indeed, I should not like to exaggerate the unity or distinctiveness of this span of time; its terminal date, in particular, might well be shifted a decade or so in either direction, though obviously a different implication about continuity and discontinuity would be entailed in each case. I briefly indicate in Chapter 1 some of the ways in which the world of the mid-Victorian intellectual differed from that of the first half of the nineteenth century, and many of the changes which contributed to the distinctiveness of that world, such as the flourishing of a new kind of periodical writing or the reform of the universities, largely date from the 1850s and 1860s. John Stuart Mill, doomed to be regarded as a transitional figure in almost any discussion, obviously belongs by formation and intellectual affinity to the earlier part of the century. Yet, as I argue in Chapter 4, there is a discernible alteration of role in the final phase of his career: in the last fifteen years of his life (he died in 1873) he became a commanding presence in public debate and a figure whom the next generation of intellectuals were forced to reckon with. Offering 1930 as a terminal date is an even more approximate and doubtful boundary marker, since it is the period before 1914, or even 1900, that receives the bulk of the book's attention; but several of the chapters extend substantively into the first couple of decades of the twentieth century, and the last two, in particular, pursue themes into the 1920s, and even gesture beyond. In addition, the unconventional pairing of these dates has a valuably disruptive effect on the accepted periodization, which in turn helps to support the larger suggestions I am making about some of the deeper continuities of English thought and sensibility. Perhaps I should also make clear at the outset that although for the most part (as in my subtitle) I follow what has become customary usage and speak of 'Britain' and its cognates rather than of 'England', I do sometimes employ the latter term deliberately where the more restricted entity is in question, and I may elsewhere have been led into inconsistency by the fact that, throughout the period I am dealing with, 'England' was unselfconsciously used to refer to a territory, a polity, and a culture that all contained much that was not, strictly speaking, 'English.' (I take up the historical significance of this more directly in Chapter 9 below.)

Part I explores the world of the Victorian public moralists in two ways. The first chapter sketches the basic conditions of their existence, their organizing institutions and forms of publication as well as their social position and sources of income. It looks at their place in the governing and cultural élites of the period, and raises the question of their relation to their audience. Chapters 2 and 3 then treat, in varying modes, some of the ostensibly non-political values and sensibilities which informed political argument in this period. I suggest that the cluster of ideals and responses represented by terms like 'altruism' or 'character' constitute the animating dynamic of much of the political thought of the period in ways neglected by concentration on the history of the more familiar theoretical 'isms.' Part II explores different aspects of the interplay between values and voice. Chapter 4 discusses John Stuart Mill's performance as a public moralist in some detail, since he most fully exhibited both the opportunities and the dangers of the role, and thereby provided his successors with something of a model. Chapter 5 moves on to look at some of these successors, and suggests that ideals of 'manliness' play an unexpectedly important part in defining their distinctive political attitudes. Part III then takes up the question of the identity of the moralist from a different angle. Chapter 6 examines the impact of increasing academic specialization upon the voices available for participation in public debate, while Chapter 7 addresses the interaction of these themes in a special case, that of jurisprudence, where claims to expert authority prove to be surprisingly subordinate to the persistence of certain common moral and political preoccupations. Finally, in Part IV I consider two different kinds of attempts to construct a genealogy for some part of modern British culture, the establishment of an intellectual or literary tradition intended to be no less enabling than the celebrated constitutional tradition had been. Since Mill had been the inescapable presence at the opening of this period, whilst also being regarded by many in polite society as unacceptably extreme and partisan, a special interest attaches to an examination of the growth of his posthumous reputation as the incarnation of the allegedly English virtues of moderation and fair-mindedness, which is the subject of Chapter 8. Questions of national identity are more straightforwardly involved in the celebration of the moral distinctiveness of English literature, and the final chapter explores some of the nationalist significance of this enterprise, and how it mutates into a form of cultural criticism in the twentieth century.

Over the years in which I have worked on the material dealt with in this book, I have incurred the usual range of scholarly, practical, and personal debts, but there would be something at once self-important and perfunctory in trying to discharge them all here in one consolidated list. In any event, it would pretty much be a case of 'round up the usual suspects', since I am dependent to the point of addiction on the encouragement and critical judgement of a few close friends, and they are doubtless tired of being saddled in print with responsibility for the errors and infelicities in what I write. So I shall confine myself to three specific acknowledgements. The first is to John Burrow, Peter Clarke, Geoffrey Hawthorn, Ruth Morse, Julia Stapleton, John Thompson, and Donald Winch, who read, criticized, improved, and profess to have enjoyed the final draft. The second is to the two unusual institutions where I have had the good fortune to teach while writing this book; both the Intellectual History Subject Group at Sussex and the English Faculty at Cambridge have, in their different ways, allowed me to feel at home while cultivating interests that elsewhere would have been regarded as disqualifyingly marginal. Where personal debts are so evenly distributed among the friends who have sustained me, the third acknowledgement risks appearing to make a selection which is invidious, but since the centre of my interests is now shifting towards twentieth-century cultural criticism, this may be the place to record that my education in nineteenth-century intellectual history, as in many other matters, owes more to John Burrow and Donald Winch than to anyone else. The evidence in the public domain of their own abundant talents as intellectual historians needs no commentary here; what has mattered most to me has been their affection, their loyalty, and their sometimes ill-rewarded generosity of spirit.

Parts of this book have already been published in different form, though the original may not always be easily recognizable here; I have revised, extended, or otherwise drawn upon these pieces principally in Chapters 3, 4, and 5. Shorter versions of Chapters 8 and 9 are due to appear in forthcoming volumes of essays. For permission to draw upon this material, I am grateful to the publishers and editors of the following books and journals: *Transactions of the Royal Historical Society*; *The Collected Works of John Stuart Mill*, ed. John M. Robson, vol. xxi (University of Toronto Press, and Routledge & Kegan Paul, 1984); *Utilitas*; Lawrence Goldman (ed.), *The Blind Victorian: Henry Fawcett and British Liberalism* (Cambridge University Press, 1989); Alan Diamond (ed.), *Sir Henry Maine: A Centennial Re-assessment* (Cambridge University Press, forthcoming); Michael Laine (ed.), *The Cultivated Mind: Essays on John Stuart Mill presented to J. M. Robson* (University of Toronto Press, forthcoming); Ciaran Brady (ed.), *Historians, Politics, and Ideology* (Gill & Macmillan, forthcoming).

I

Governing Values

I

Leading Minds
The World of the Victorian Intellectual

I

In the course of his biography of his brother, Leslie Stephen observed that, following his return to England in 1873 at the end of his period of service as Legal Member of the Viceroy's Council in India, James Fitzjames Stephen had reached the point of enjoying an established reputation. 'He was henceforward one of the circle—not distinguished by any definite label but yet recognized among each other by a spontaneous freemasonry—which forms the higher intellectual stratum of London society; and is recruited from all who have made a mark in any department of serious work.' Expanding on the point, the younger Stephen indicated some of the directions in which the reputation extended: 'He was well known, of course, to the leaders of the legal profession; and to many members of Government and to rising members of Parliament. . . . He knew the chief literary celebrities . . . whom he often joined in Sunday "constitutionals".' And to round off the observation, he cited the fact which conclusively set the seal on Fitzjames's standing in this world: 'His position was recognized by the pleasant compliment of an election to the "Athenaeum", "under Rule II", which took place at the first election after his return (1873).'[1]

In both its substance—a sketch of a social-cum-intellectual circle—and its tone—at once mildly detached and collusively self-satisfied—the whole passage provides a suggestive brief epitome of the world to be explored in this chapter. Of course, any one quotation, however rich, risks being a misleading or at best partial introduction to a book which ranges over the greater part of a century and over a

[1] Leslie Stephen, *The Life of Sir James Fitzjames Stephen* (London, 1895), 302.

wide variety of authors and issues. But since the purpose of this first chapter is to attempt to identify some of the preconditions for the kinds of public intellectual debate that went on in the first part of this period, and to connect those conditions to certain common features exhibited by so much of the political reflection of that period, there may be an advantage in starting with an example which emphasizes the typical and the central rather than the exceptional and the marginal.

The fact that my opening example is taken from a biography where author and subject were brothers may at first seem to suggest that this world was primarily defined in terms of family connection. But that, I think, would be to move in the wrong direction. Needless to say, a certain sort of social background was an advantage when embarking on an intellectual as on any other career in Victorian England, and a large enough number of those attaining some sort of distinction in this area have been shown to be linked by heredity and intermarriage to make it plausible to speak of an 'intellectual aristocracy.'[2] But this is at best a suggestive metaphor: family connection may have been important in more ways than the protagonists themselves would have acknowledged, but it was not, as in a true aristocracy, the qualification for membership in itself. What the members of Stephen's 'freemasonry' recognized in each other was a certain kind of publicly endorsed individual achievement, not the marks of a pedigree peculiar to the caste.

It is true that the terms in which Leslie Stephen characterized this group cannot help but seem complacent and even self-serving (he had himself been accepted into its ranks for at least two decades by the time he wrote this description in 1895). The reference to having made a mark 'in any department of serious work' rather too easily reproduces and colludes with the circle's own idiom. In practice, the criteria of what could count as 'serious work' were not necessarily as restrictive or merely cosy as hostile twentieth-century critics might suspect: the achievements of contentious or eccentric figures like Ruskin or Spencer were accorded their due. But 'serious work' undeniably suggests exclusions, and since the tone of the whole passage exudes such an untroubled confidence in the circle's ability to distinguish the meritorious from the meretricious, one begins, as

[2] The classic statement of this case was, of course, Noel Annan's fond charting of such links in his 'The intellectual aristocracy', in J. H. Plumb (ed.), *Studies in Social History: A Tribute to G. M. Trevelyan* (London, 1955), 241–87.

always when confronted by a self-described meritocracy, to want a more probing analysis of the cultural values and social assumptions embodied in this ostensibly straightforward recognition of individual intellectual achievement.

Stephen's observation does, however, gesture towards the social location of this 'circle': though not itself defined in terms of such sociological indices as family, class, or occupation, its members were largely drawn from the traditional genteel professions, particularly government, literature, and the law. In fact, even to suggest that these last were mutually exclusive activities would be seriously to understate the kinds of social and intellectual overlap characteristic of the world Stephen was referring to. Furthermore, it was definitely a metropolitan not a provincial élite, a stratum of *London* society. Its members mingled, albeit not on strictly equal terms, with those circles that could be typographically distinguished as 'Society.' And a rather more physical sense of location is suggested by the reference to the 'Athenaeum': encounters on its steps or in its corridors were one of the chief ways in which members of this freemasonry learned literally to recognize one another. Indeed, the phrasing of Stephen's sentence about his brother's election enacts the intimacy it refers to: it assumes not merely that its readers know the character of that particular institution—not in itself very recondite information, perhaps—but, more tellingly, that they will be familiar with the terms of election 'under Rule II' (which he nowhere explains). The allusions an author does not feel called upon to gloss provide one obvious way for the historian to reconstruct the assumed community of readers. Of course, it may have been a misjudgement on Stephen's part to presume that the biography's first readers in 1895 would be so intimate with the Athenaeum's categories of membership, especially since, as I shall argue below, the intellectual élite was becoming somewhat more segmented and dispersed by the end of the century than it had been when Fitzjames was making his mark within it. But Stephen certainly had some grounds for assuming that those of their contemporaries who would be most interested in a fairly lengthy narrative of his brother's life would hardly need to have 'Rule II' explained to them, for it was the nearest thing to a 'definite label' by which members of the 'freemasonry' were marked out.

The Athenaeum was (and to some extent still is) distinguished among London clubs by the fact that whereas most of these institutions primarily catered to those who inherited their wealth and social position, the membership of the Athenaeum included a far higher proportion of writers, bishops, judges, senior public servants, and such like. Ordinary members of the club were elected by the whole membership after having been nominated by existing members of their acquaintance, and the process was subject to the familiar clubland hazards of snobbery, 'blackballing', and waiting lists. Under Rule II, however, the committee could elect each year to immediate membership a certain number of men who were considered as being 'of distinguished eminence in Science, Literature, or the Arts, or for Public Service.' Most of the figures discussed in the first half of this book were members of the Athenaeum, the majority of them elected under Rule II. The 1860s and 1870s alone saw the election by this means of Maine, Spencer, Lecky, Seeley, Morley, Fitzjames and Leslie Stephen, Bagehot, J. R. Green, Bain, Bryce, Stubbs, Harrison, and Sidgwick, to cite only those names which will reappear with some frequency in the following chapters. (Had figures such as Mill, Arnold, Fawcett, and Dicey not, for different reasons in each case, already been elected as ordinary members, they would surely also have appeared in this list.[3])

This category of membership of the Athenaeum nicely captures some of the complexities of social status involved in trying to characterize the position in Victorian society of those who distinguished themselves by their intellectual achievements. Election did, needless to say, imply a kind of social acceptance, but that way of putting it reveals in turn that such figures may have been in need of this acceptance; it was not necessarily something to which they were born. At the extreme, it allowed a man of Herbert Spencer's decidedly humble origins to rub shoulders with the junior members of that hereditary landowning class his early works had denounced, just as it allowed T. H. Huxley, son of a modestly respectable schoolmaster, to fraternize with the bishops whose cosmological beliefs he was constantly challenging. In this respect the club was a microcosm of that 'ruling-class egalitarianism' some have detected at work in the upper reaches of English society as a whole.

At the same time, those of 'distinguished eminence in Science,

[3] Details of membership have been taken from F. G. Waugh, *Members of the Athenaeum Club from its Foundation* (privately printed (25 copies), n.d. [?late 1890s]); see also Humphry Ward, *History of the Athenaeum 1824–1925* (London, 1926), and Anon., *The Athenaeum: Club and Social Life in London 1824–1974* (London, 1975).

Literature, or the Arts' remained aware that, whatever their social origins, their intellectual activities themselves placed them at one remove from the chief possessors of wealth and power in their society. While not forming a socially excluded intellectual class, they were conscious that belonging to the fraternity of the reflective and the articulate set them apart from those more immediately involved in life's tasks and life's pleasures. Although the surviving photographs of these frock-coated worthies hardly suggest the rebel or radical who is banished to the margins of society, many of these figures were aware that they held views which were regarded with some suspicion in the best circles. Leslie Stephen's wry reflection on his own election in 1877 hints at this sense. It had been the publication in 1876 of his two-volume *History of English Thought in the Eighteenth Century* that had earned him this public recognition. Although historical in focus, this was a work which the discerning contemporary reader would have recognized as something of a polemical defence of free thought in religious matters.[4] Stephen confided to a correspondent that he was pleased at the 'indication of respect' that his election signified, though he professed to find it 'curious that a book of such a tendency should procure admission to a respectable haunt of bishops and judges'.[5] We must discount for Stephen's customary irony when talking of himself here; but irony is also a way of coping, and Stephen was signalling his awareness of the gulfs that still separated him from many of those he passed on the Athenaeum's steps.

For those members who could still loosely be described as 'men of letters' (itself an increasingly problematic term in this period), the Athenaeum functioned as hotel, restaurant, café, common room, library, office. Much of the surviving correspondence of the figures discussed in this book was written from there, and in some cases several of the books and articles that made them famous were composed in its library. In reporting the news of his election in 1856, Matthew Arnold declared that he 'look[ed] forward with rapture to the use of that library in London. It is really as good as having the books of one's own.' (And his friends thereafter relied upon seeing

[4] For a persuasive demonstration of this point, see John W. Bicknell, 'Leslie Stephen's "English thought in the eighteenth century": a tract for the times', *Victorian Studies*, 6 (1962), 103–20; for a fuller assessment, see Noel Annan, *Leslie Stephen: The Godless Victorian* (London, 1984), ch. VIII.

[5] Letter of 16 Mar. 1877 to Charles Eliot Norton, in F. W. Maitland, *The Life and Letters of Leslie Stephen* (London, 1906), 298.

him there: when T. H. Huxley wished to retrieve the umbrella he had left at Arnold's house, he simply asked him to 'bring it next time you come to the club'.[6]) Indeed, the club largely served as the base from which Arnold conducted his career as a writer. Having spent his mornings inspecting schools, he would commonly pass the afternoon in its library writing an article; during one week in November 1862, for example, he could be seen every afternoon from 2 to 6 seated in the library writing the article that was to become one of his celebrated *Essays in Criticism*.[7] It was in that year that Henry Maine was elected, largely on the strength of the great success of his *Ancient Law*, published the previous year, and after his return from being Legal Member of the Viceroy's Council in 1869 (in which post he was succeeded by Fitzjames Stephen), he, too, used to spend most of his afternoons at the club, and composed many of his subsequent writings there.[8] On many of those days he presumably acknowledged Herbert Spencer, who, following his election in 1868, used to go there daily ('The Club became more of a home to him than his own residence') to meet friends, to play billiards, and to scan the new books and periodicals, especially 'to notice adverse criticism of his views'.[9] And the club also provided a focal point for those few members elected 'under Rule II' who did not live in London (in the later part of the century several of them were resident professors at Oxford or Cambridge): Henry Sidgwick was representative in the way in which, following his election in 1879, 'he constantly used the club when in London during the remainder of his life'.[10]

This book is not a social history of Victorian men of letters, and I take membership of the Athenaeum to be merely a suggestive symbol of the relative homogeneity of the intellectual élite of this

[6] Letter of 8 July 1869, in Leonard Huxley, *The Life and Letters of Thomas Henry Huxley*, 3 vols. (London, 1900), i. 448.

[7] This was the article on Maurice de Guérin; *The Complete Prose Works of Matthew Arnold*, ed. R. H. Super, 11 vols. (Ann Arbor, Mich., 1960–77), iii. 407. For his pleasure at his election, secured through the good offices of his brother-in-law, the Liberal politician W. E. Forster, see his letter to his sister of 17 Feb. 1856 in *Letters of Matthew Arnold 1848–1888*, collected and arranged by George W. E. Russell, 2 vols. (London, 1901; 1st edn. 1895), 58. The very next letter in this collection was written from the Athenaeum, as are the majority of subsequent letters.

[8] George Feaver, *From Status to Contract: Sir Henry Maine 1822–1888* (London, 1969), 131, 134, 246.

[9] David Duncan, *The Life and Letters of Herbert Spencer* (London, 1908), 494–5.

[10] A. and E. M. S[idgwick], *Henry Sidgwick: A Memoir* (London, 1906), 341.

period, the metaphorical lodge of the 'freemasonry', rather than strictly a criterion for inclusion. It is revealing of the special circumstances of mid-Victorian intellectual life that this symbolism would be less appropriate both for the early nineteenth century and for the early twentieth. By the early twentieth century, the form taken by the segmentation of the intellectual circle to which Fitzjames Stephen had belonged was chiefly along the fault-lines of intellectual specialization (a development discussed at greater length in Chapter 6 below), whereas in the early nineteenth century the divisions had tended to be of a more partisan and sectarian kind. Social, intellectual, and educational historians have in their different ways remarked the growing homogeneity of the intellectual élite from the middle of the century: the redirected social ambitions which were involved in the revival of the public schools and ancient universities constituted a particularly significant feature of this change, and the enhanced centrality of the metropolis as against the province in English life formed another. (A comparison of the place of Scotsmen in British culture in the late eighteenth and early nineteenth centuries and their position a hundred years later is also instructive here, indicating a loss of distinctiveness and an example of what has to be termed the 'Oxbridgization' of the upper reaches of intellectual activity.) Put another way, those taking the lead in the public cultural debates of the 1820s and 1830s were less likely to have shared a common intellectual or educational formation than were their counterparts in the 1870s and 1880s, a fact which was related, arguably as both cause and effect, to the greater political and social antagonisms evident in the intellectual life of the earlier period. (I ought perhaps to emphasize that I am only talking here about the changed contours of the intellectual élite; this does not necessarily entail accepting larger claims about the growth of class harmony, the arrival of 'the age of equipoise', and so on.)

The centrality of the Athenaeum in the high Victorian period was one of the minor consequences of these changes. It had, after all, been founded as early as 1824, but a hint of the rather different assumptions prevailing at that time is provided in an improbable source, namely Alexander Bain's *Life of James Mill*. Bain recounts that James Mill had been one of the original members of the Club, and that when in 1830 they had been able to take possession of their present building, Mill was a member of the committee charged with electing 100 new members to mark the occasion. 'This would scarcely be worth mentioning', wrote Bain half apologetically,

> but that it recalls a curious remark that I heard John Mill make. He said that he was elected to the club by this Committee; and but for that would never have been admitted at all: having already excited a sufficient amount of personal dislike among some of the members to ensure his being blackballed. This would seem to show that mere party feeling went to greater lengths then, in excluding men from the Athenaeum, than it would do now. I am not aware of any offence that Mill can be supposed to have given to individuals in 1830, that would suffice to blackball a man in the present day.[11]

The slightly prissy, bloodless quality in Bain's prose serves to emphasize his point here: he sounds a little scandalized by the robust passions of the earlier period, and thankful to belong to a more tolerant and accommodating age. His reference to 'mere party feeling' sufficiently indicates his want of sympathy with what he is describing. After all, no very elaborate act of historical reconstruction would be required to suggest the kinds of objection that could have been brought against the young John Stuart Mill after the ferocity of his Philosophic Radical journalism of the 1820s and his savaging of Whig and Tory alike. But Bain, even if he seems an implausibly unworldly witness in this passage, was accurately reflecting the changed circumstances of the last three or four decades of the century. As I shall several times have occasion to argue or illustrate in the following chapters, Mill was in many ways a pivotal figure. In the last couple of decades of his life, and even in a sense for some time after his death, he was at the centre of the complex relations between political thought and intellectual life in this period, yet his own intellectual and political formation had taken place in a surprisingly different world: a world of greater social, regional, and educational diversity, perhaps; a world in which the periodicals were uninhibitedly partisan and where non-Anglicans were excluded from full participation in the national culture—where in fact 'national culture' may be an even more misleading abridgement than it usually is; a world in which men not only blackballed each other from clubs but challenged each other to duels. The figures dealt with in this book lived in a tamer world and paid allegiance, publicly at any rate, to common ideals which transcended 'mere party feeling.'

[11] Alexander Bain, *James Mill: A Biography* (London, 1882), 357.

It is also true, however, that the symbolism of the circle that nodded to each other across the reading room of the Athenaeum starts to lose its appropriateness as we move into the later part of the period covered in this book. This was partly because the intellectual, political, and fashionable circles of English society became less concentric by the early twentieth century, and partly because the cultural conditions of intellectual life itself changed in significant ways. In particular, the increasing 'professionalization' of intellectual activities within the newly expanding universities subtly altered the nature and opportunities of the role of public moralist (see the fuller discussion in Chapter 6 below). This change could be symbolized by shifting one's gaze from the expressively confident neo-classical grandeur of the Athenaeum's façade in Pall Mall, first to a room in the recesses of the British Museum which housed an unusual gathering of scholars on 28 June 1901, and then to the somewhat cramped quarters in Burlington Gardens occupied, after 1928, by the body that eventually resulted from the British Museum meeting—or, in other words, by taking as the representative institution not the Athenaeum but the British Academy.

Here, one is still dealing with a highly selected élite, of course, but one whose membership was required to display distinction in certain recognized scholarly disciplines. Actually, there was an interesting unsteadiness about the language used in the early stages of the scheme to characterize the activities the Academy was supposed to unite. The initial report from a committee of the Royal Society spoke of 'the exact literary studies'; the official account of the Academy's foundation referred to 'representatives of "literary" science', the quotation marks signalling that this traditionally broad sense of the term was straining against the pull of the increasingly standard restriction to 'imaginative literature.' The official title was finally fixed as 'The British Academy for the Promotion of Historical, Philosophical, and Philological studies', where the use of 'philological' to embrace all of classical learning as well as the specialized enquiry into the nature and development of language was by this date also on the verge of archaism.[12] More revealingly still, the Charter

[12] This sense of the word, defined in the *OED* simply as 'literary or classical scholarship', was rare in the second half of the 19th century, when it was increasingly supplanted by the modern sense, 'the study of the structure and development of language'. For further discussion of the implications of this change see J. W. Burrow, 'The uses of philology in Victorian Britain', in R. Robson (ed.), *Ideas and Institutions of Victorian Britain* (London, 1967), esp. 180; and Tony Crowley, *The Politics of Discourse: The Standard Language Question in British Cultural Debates* (London, 1989), ch. 1.

of Incorporation defined the objects of the Academy as 'the promotion of the moral and political sciences, including history, philosophy, law, politics and economics, archaeology and philology.' This may have represented the triumph of the local idiom ('the moral sciences') over attempts to import Continental European categories (the Academy had been founded in order to represent British scholarship in international gatherings and organizations); but what is most significant about this formulation is that it indicates the scope of the new institution by enumerating a list of 'disciplines.'[13] In this respect as in many others the new institution accurately, if conservatively, reflected the state of intellectual life at the beginning of the twentieth century.

It is, of course, hard to imagine such an Academy being founded in Britain in the early nineteenth century, so much did its character reflect the spread of (largely German-inspired) 'scientific' scholarship in the middle and later part of the century, and so it is a purely counterfactual exercise to try to imagine how its nature and membership would have been different. But it is at least clear that its membership would have been extremely miscellaneous in terms of both educational background and present employment. (The Royal Society of Literature, established in 1820 and incorporated in 1825, is hardly an adequate comparison, so different were its aims, though it bears out the point about the diversity and 'amateur' status of the membership of such societies in that period.) But those who were of sufficient eminence to provide the original Fellows of the British Academy in 1902 were mostly of an age to have been educated after the revived centrality in English life of the ancient universities which I mentioned earlier, and they were also the first generation among whom an academic career was at all common. As a result, among the original forty-eight Fellows, thirty-seven had been educated at Oxford or Cambridge, and, more significantly, twenty-nine of them held academic appointments there. (If one includes Trinity College, Dublin, in the calculations, which its position at this time might well justify, the proportions become still higher.) Not, of course, that at this point one would expect them to have largely been educated at

[13] There was some unsteadiness here, too: initially it was proposed to organize the Academy into seven sections—History, Classical Philology, Oriental Studies, Law and Politics, Metaphysics and Ethics, Economics, and Archaeology—but this was soon reduced to four—History and Archaeology, Philology, Philosophy, Jurisprudence and Economics; see Frederick G. Kenyon, *The British Academy: The First Fifty Years* (London, 1952), 10, 14.

other English universities, most of which were only establishing themselves, or evolving from local colleges, in the immediately preceding decades (one again has to remember that the situation had long been different in Scotland). It is rather that earlier in the century one would not have expected so many to be university educated at all, and certainly the proportion of private scholars or scholars with primarily non-academic employment would have been much higher. Intellectual distinction was becoming increasingly a matter of 'scholarship', and scholarship was becoming increasingly an academic activity.[14]

Moreover, although in the official account there is no mention of disagreements, the existence of at least one major conflict can be deduced even from the bare record of meetings and decisions. The proposal for an international association of Academies recognized a division between 'natural science' and 'literary science' (at least as reported in English), 'the term "literary" being used to indicate the sciences of language, history, philosophy, and antiquities, and other subjects the study of which is based on scientific principles.'[15] But this broad, and by now archaic, sense of 'literary' brought problems of its own in Britain. Was 'literature', in its narrower and increasingly dominant sense, susceptible to 'scientific' study? The recent debates at Oxford over the establishment of an Honours School in English there had indicated the strength of feeling this question could arouse: E. A. Freeman's dismissive remark that the proposed School would consist of 'mere chatter about Shelley' became something of a slogan among opponents of the proposal.[16] In the discussions that led to the founding of the Academy, the first list of seven sections drawn up in 1901 notably omitted all mention of literature (except so far as it fell under the chaste heading of 'classical philology'), and even the final scheme only modified this to the extent of including 'modern

[14] The list of founding Fellows of the British Academy is given in the 'Charter of Incorporation', attached to 'A brief account of the foundation of the Academy', in *Proceedings of the British Academy 1903–4*, pp. x–xii; I have calculated the numbers in the various categories on the basis of the details of education and academic position given in the *DNB*. In several cases, the categories of analysis overlap—for example, I have classified Bryce primarily as a politician though he had also been Regius Professor of Civil Law at Oxford for almost 23 years—and not all those who held 'academic posts' were necessarily practising professors (this applies particularly to some of the Oxbridge heads of house).

[15] 'Brief account', p. vii.

[16] See the account in D. J. Palmer, *The Rise of English Studies: An Account of the Study of English Language and Literature from its Origins to the Making of the Oxford English School* (Oxford, 1965), ch. VI, quotation at 96.

philology.' Moreover, the subcommittee charged with drawing up the initial list of members proposed at one point to add eleven further names to those already accepted, and at least seven of these were scholars whose work lay mainly in the field of English literature: Kenyon's account simply records that 'the General Committee decided to postpone these.' These discussions possibly became entangled with a question of strategy proposed by Israel Gollancz, a noted student of medieval literature and lecturer in English language at Cambridge, namely whether they could avoid all the difficulties involved in trying to obtain a Royal Charter, which might include stirring up public opposition, by amalgamating with the existing Royal Society of Literature which already possessed a charter. This scheme was soon squashed 'as likely to prejudice the prestige of the Academy by making it a mere appendage of a body which had no strong position of its own', but it may have aroused fears among many of the conservatively inclined scholars that the whole scheme might be compromised by too close an association with mere 'literature.'[17] Entry to the Academy was only to be secured by those 'subjects the study of which is based on scientific principles.'

That having been said, one immediately needs to guard against the pitfalls of exaggeration and anachronism. It is worth remembering, to begin with, that the impulse to found the British Academy was provided by the short-term need to have an organization to represent Britain at an international gathering of academies; its formation represented a conscious emulation of Continental models, and was entirely a private venture, not the result of initiative or funding from the state—indeed, it received no state grant until 1924. Moreover, it is clear that the chief movers of the project were not indifferent to the public standing of the proposed body, or even to questions of social prestige. The invitation to Lord Rosebery, scarcely the foremost scholar of the time, to be the first President (which he declined) indicates a shrewd sense of public relations, and it is also possible that the newer or more marginal subjects were very willing to profit from the respectability conferred by association with classical and philological learning.

Above all, the manner of its founding reveals just how much a certain familiarity between members of the intellectual élite still prevailed, since the first steps depended upon a chain of acquaint-

[17] Kenyon, *British Academy*, 5–14.

ance and even friendship. The Royal Society addressed its initial enquiry 'to certain selected persons'; the most active response came from Henry Sidgwick, who circulated a paper airing the idea of such an Academy to a few friends, and who then engaged in discussions with the Royal Society, his friend James Bryce acting as the chief intermediary. Sidgwick, Lord Acton, and Sir Richard Jebb were asked to propose a list of those who might be consulted. Negotiations with the Royal Society having broken down, 'certain persons who had received the original letter . . . in association with other persons', undertook to arrange the meeting at the British Museum referred to above. That meeting then suggested further names who might be approached. The rather bare official record in 'A brief account of the foundation of the Academy' does not altogether successfully disguise the extent to which the first organizers were already well known to each other. Kenyon merely remarks: 'I do not know who drew up the list of persons invited to attend the meeting on 28 June. Probably it was done at Cambridge.'[18]

The surviving correspondence between Sidgwick and Bryce indicates the kinds of considerations involved in assembling a list of possible candidates. 'I agree in your view that J. Morley belongs to "pure" literature rather than to Wissenschaft'; 'The list strikes me by the paucity of economists, yet I can't think of any others of mark'; 'I would suggest Bury of Dublin, esp as we have very few Irishmen.' The judgements could be brisk and uninhibitedly *ad hominem*: Sidgwick would exclude J. H. Round as 'he is rather an antiquarian than an historian is he not?', but would include Goldwin Smith, 'certainly one of the patriarchs of history.'[19] Sidgwick and Bryce, of course, shared personal and intellectual sympathies more closely than the generality of those eventually involved, and it is worth noting that not all these judgements were translated into the final list of founding fellows: Morley, for example, was elected and Goldwin Smith was not (the fact that the *DNB* entry for Goldwin Smith classifies him simply as 'controversialist' may indicate the

[18] Kenyon, *British Academy*, 8.

[19] Sidgwick's role in the early stages of the business can be partially reconstructed from his surviving correspondence for the period between the circulation of his initial paper in Dec. 1899 and the first meeting with the Committee of the Royal Society in May 1900. Letters on the subject to and from several correspondents are contained in the Sidgwick Papers, Trinity College, Cambridge; the correspondence with Bryce is in the Bryce MSS, Bodleian Library, Oxford, the quotations in the above paragraph being taken from Sidgwick's letter to Bryce of 5 Feb. 1900. See also his letter to Arthur Balfour of 9 Nov. 1899; Balfour Papers, British Library, Add. MSS 49832.

grounds of this exclusion). But the sense of a knowable community, with largely shared if implicit values and standards, is very strong.[20]

And although the dominance of the academics does mark something of a change from the first half of the century, such simple contrasts are always prone to mislead. The language used by Lord Reay, orientalist and former imperial administrator, in the first Presidential Address revealed the assumption that membership of the Academy would be far from coextensive with those engaged in university teaching when he assured the first Fellows that they were 'fortunate in having in the Academy many who are engaged in the actual work of higher education', and affirmed that 'the Universities will be largely represented in the Academy, and naturally a mutual connexion will be established between them'.[21] Certainly, what finally emerged was a less purely academic body than, say, its German counterpart, and there were still signs that the notion of 'literature' evoked in its founding retained its broader antique sense. The clearest indication that the new body was not intended to be a closed caste of professional scholars was the fact that at least eight of the founding Fellows were primarily distinguished as politicians, and several others were independent men of letters.

This sense of the continuities with the mid-Victorian world is at first sharpened by noticing that among those in the latter category was an author who had produced several more volumes of 'serious work' since his election to the Athenaeum twenty-five years earlier, but who by 1902 hardly represented the latest word in professional scholarship. As Sir Leslie Stephen cast his now watery eye down the list of original Fellows, the presence of such names as the Right Hon. James Bryce, MP, Professor A. V. Dicey KC, Sir Courtney Ilbert KCSI, the Right Hon. W. E. H. Lecky, MP, OM, and the Right Hon. John Morley, MP, would have been likely to suggest some gruff reflection about how damned distinguished his generation was becoming, at least as much as the far larger number of

[20] Political allegiances were shared to a considerable extent as well: of the 40 original Fellows whose politics have been identified, 34 had been Liberals before 1886, though 17 of those became Liberal Unionists thereafter; see Christopher Harvie, *The Lights of Liberalism: University Liberals and the Challenge of Democracy 1860–1886* (London, 1976), 274.

[21] Lord Reay, 'Presidential Address', *Proceedings*, 1 (1903), 14, 10. Some of Lord Reay's other expectations proved to be rather less well founded, for example his declaration that 'the claims of the leaders of thought in India and in the Colonies to be represented in this Academy will be readily admitted' (16).

professors in the list would have suggested the change that was coming over his world. But it was not a change to which Stephen was forced to accommodate himself: following his death in February 1904, his obituary appeared in the first volume of the Academy's *Proceedings*. Placing him in such company, even the devoted Maitland acknowledged the truth in Stephen's typically disparaging self-assessment, that he had 'scattered himself' too widely, 'not a scholar, not a philosopher, not an historian, only an amateur'.[22] Maitland loyally concluded that 'such an amateur, if that be the right term . . . is worth more to the world than many professionals', but the implicit charge as well as the terms of the defence were an acknowledgement that henceforth 'serious work' was to be largely the province of the professional.

II

In attempting to characterize the social position and cultural role of the figures mentioned in the previous section, the historian is faced with a range of categories furnished by modern social theory which are united above all by their inappropriateness. It may be that terms like 'bourgeois ideologues', 'alienated intelligentsia', 'professional knowledge-producers', and so on have their uses as analytical categories, especially when applied to the respective social milieux from which they originally arose. But these terms are positively misleading as a way of classifying those well-connected Victorian thinkers and men of letters whom I have been discussing up to this point. As a step towards a more fruitful vocabulary, it may be helpful to begin with the bland truism that any one individual can be classified in various ways, depending upon which aspect, analytically abstracted from the complex concreteness of a life, one chooses to concentrate upon. For example, a representative figure from this book might be simultaneously an editor, a graduate, a former Fellow of a college, a historian, a Liberal, a Germanophile, a free thinker, a gentleman, an employer of servants, a member of a club, as well, of course, as a man, a son, a father, a husband, and so on. Although each of these identities derives from a different scheme of classification, it is clear that several of them taken together do constitute what we conventionally recognize as a particular social position. Such a figure is clearly not, for example, a landowner or

[22] *Proceedings*, 1 (1903), 320.

hereditary peer, not an industrialist or financier, not a shopkeeper or farmer, not a skilled workman or agricultural labourer, and so on. Victorian usage supplied no single term with which to classify such a figure: 'man of letters' would probably have been the favoured term at the beginning of this period, though it was already too restrictive to do the work demanded of it; 'authors, editors, and journalists' was the nearest census category, but that was too inclusive in some directions (not discriminating types or levels of authorship or journalism), and too exclusive in others (not naturally embracing academic philosophers, economists, and so on who wrote for a wider audience).

Among such general categories of social analysis, the most inviting modern term is 'intellectual', and that is in fact the one which I shall use most frequently. But the term inevitably brings controversy and misconception in its train, especially when applied to a period before its usage to designate a social role was at all common.[23] Perhaps one way to defuse some of that controversy and avoid those misconceptions may be to emphasize just how heterogeneous were the possible identities I listed a moment ago, and hence to draw attention to the fact that 'intellectual' is not strictly an occupational category. Some occupations are no doubt more propitious than others for carrying on the activities to which the label applies, but just which occupations these are will vary with historical circumstances. Similarly, one should avoid defining the category of 'intellectual' in terms of particular substantive beliefs or attitudes towards society: it may be historically quite common for intellectuals to feel themselves determinedly antagonistic to their society, or socially excluded from its upper reaches, or politically allied to oppositional groups, but those are strictly contingent rather than constitutive features of the role. In the usage to be followed here, the term 'intellectual' refers to function and identity rather than occupation or belief. In this sense, most complex literate societies have their intellectuals, who are marked out by their involvement in the business of articulating reflections on human activities and exercising some kind of cultural authority acknowledged by the attentions of the wider society.

[23] There is now a large literature on the development of this term: for a recent survey, see Peter Allen, 'The meanings of "an intellectual": nineteenth- and twentieth-century English usage', *University of Toronto Quarterly*, 55 (1986), 342–58. There is also a useful discussion of the heightened collective self-consciousness involved in the increased use of the term in T. W. Heyck, *The Transformation of Intellectual Life in Victorian England* (London, 1982).

Approaching the matter in this way, it seems to me both appropriate and helpful to speak of John Stuart Mill as an intellectual, though he was for thirty-five years an employee of the East India Company, just as it is to speak of Matthew Arnold as one, though he was employed for the same number of years as a school inspector. Similarly, the term can be usefully applied to Leslie Stephen, who might be primarily classified as an editor, and equally to Walter Bagehot who was a banker as well as an editor; to Fitzjames Stephen, who was a barrister and eventually a judge, but also to Henry Sidgwick who was a professor; to John Morley, who had more than one occupation, and to Edward Freeman, who for the greater part of his life had none. As with all such categories, there will be demarcation disputes at the margins, and some figures the complexity of whose identities would make trouble for any classificatory labels; but for the working purposes of the historian, there is considerable practical utility and little danger of distorting anachronism in speaking of 'Victorian intellectuals.'

In a similar spirit, the term I shall most often use hereafter to refer to these writers and their audiences, taken collectively, is, simply, 'the educated classes.' I am aware that this is a slack phrase: it implicitly selects only certain forms of 'education',[24] and even then does not apply the criterion rigorously—a public school and university education was shared by the majority of those I refer to, but it was not absolutely universal (Mill, after all, scarcely attended an educational establishment of any kind). But it at least has the merit in this case of being a phrase from the vocabulary of the time, and I trust that in the contexts where I use the term it is helpful rather than mystificatory. The consequence of concentrating upon political argument as conducted within this class is, of course, to exclude large areas of Victorian culture and society from consideration. This book does not discuss political argument as conducted by, for example, Dissenting ministers, trade-union leaders, provincial journalists, or (apart from passing reference to a few exceptional

[24] One may recall here Raymond Williams's protest at the description of George Eliot, Thomas Hardy, and D. H. Lawrence as 'autodidacts', given that each enjoyed a level of education which was both high for their time and higher than that experienced by the majority of the population in the 20th century: 'The flat patronage of "autodidact" can then be related to only one fact: that none of the three was in the pattern of boarding-school and Oxbridge which in the late-nineteenth century came to be regarded not simply as a kind of education but as education itself. To have missed that circuit was to have missed being "educated" at all.' Raymond Williams, *The English Novel from Dickens to Lawrence* (London, 1970), 95–6.

individuals) women. In other words, I am trying not so much to bring new actors on to the historical stage as to deepen our understanding of those whose parts have in some ways long been familiar.

That understanding may be further aided by shifting our focus from social function to social status in the stricter sense. Here, contemporary usage possesses a special authority since status in modern societies is largely an ascribed quality, something constituted by the perceptions and attitudes of others. In these terms, the most sensitive dividing line in Victorian society was between those who were and those who were not recognized as 'gentlemen.'[25] Practically all the figures discussed at any length in this book would have been unhesitatingly awarded that cachet. Of course, there existed no single understanding of what this term was supposed to denote, and Victorian usage caught the label at a particularly delicate and confusing moment in its long journey from being strictly an indicator of social rank to being a term intended to pick out certain virtues of character or patterns of behaviour supposedly not tied to any one social position. A sense of this transition is nicely caught in Fitzjames Stephen's observation, made in 1862:

> In our own days, though the notion of some degree of rank—such an amount of it, at least, as raises the presumption of a good education—is still attached to the word 'gentleman', moral and social meanings connected with it are constantly assuming greater prominence, so that in course of time it may possibly come to be used simply as a term of moral approbation bearing no relation to the social rank of the persons to whom it is applied.[26]

It is an observation which may now seem to invite hostile scrutiny—the complacency about the nature and availability of the 'good education' would be one place to start—and it is not altogether clear what should be understood by 'social meanings' such that they could be so flatly contrasted with 'social rank.' But Stephen's contemporaries, however much they might have quibbled with the details of his remark, would have shared his assumption that the term was still a, perhaps the, central category of social discrimination. T. H. Green, a more radical moralist who cultivated a certain

[25] There is now a large literature on this subject; see the references cited in Shirley Robin Letwin, *The Gentleman in Trollope: Individuality and Moral Conduct* (London, 1982), ch. 1. Needless to say, many different questions would be raised in a discussion of the position of women.

[26] James Fitzjames Stephen, 'Liberalism', *Cornhill Magazine*, 5, (1862), 72.

distancing hostility to the complacencies of the comfortable classes, complained a few years later: 'The subtle distinction between those who claim to be a gentleman and whose claim is conceded, those who claim to be so but whose claim is not yet conceded, and those who do not claim to be gentlemen at all, is England's own. It embarrasses all the schemes of social reformers.'[27]

The other, partially overlapping, category which it was important to the established man of letters to be seen to occupy was that of the 'professional class', again a term which pointed to a never precisely defined combination of social position and cultural ethos. Summarizing a complex history briefly, one could say that in the century or so before the beginning of the period dealt with in this book, the 'liberal professions' consisted essentially of the Church, law, medicine, and possibly, though sometimes in conjunction with one of the other roles, government service and political life generally (a commission in the army or navy, though included in this list for some purposes, really belonged to a different category). These professions were closely intertwined with the landed classes, from whom they were still overwhelmingly recruited: younger sons of good social standing but no secure prospects turned to the professions as the least unacceptable way of sustaining an approximation to the leisured classes' way of life. In fact, it would not be too misleading to say that such professions were only looked upon as 'careers' to a limited extent: primarily, they were a means to affirming and protecting one's status as a gentleman, where their extensive leisure, independence, and freedom from direct market relations were symbolically of great importance. Interestingly, the chief argument advanced in favour of anonymity in contributions to periodicals in the first half of the century confirms this: it was precisely because contamination by the mere 'trade' of journalism was thought to be incompatible with the status of a gentleman that the identity of such contributors had to be protected. The shift from anonymity to signed articles reflected, and of course contributed to, a rise in the status of such 'higher journalism' as increasing numbers of undisputed 'gentlemen' engaged in it.[28] (Signature was not, of

[27] T. H. Green, 'Lecture on the grading of secondary schools' (1877), in *The Works of Thomas Hill Green*, ed. R. L. Nettleship, 3 vols. (London, 1885–8), iii. 403.

[28] See the summary of this episode in Walter Houghton, 'Periodical literature and the articulate classes', in Joanne Shattock and Michael Wolff (eds.), *The Victorian Periodical Press: Samplings and Soundings* (Leicester, 1982), 3–28, and esp. Oscar Maurer, 'Anonymity vs signature in Victorian reviewing', *University of Texas Studies*

course, the only issue which might touch upon a writer's social status: as a contributor to the *Fortnightly*, 'Frederic Harrison deeply resented any idea of editorial superiority as an intolerable affront both to his status as a gentleman and his principles as a Comtist'.[29])

The essence of the change that took place in the Victorian period was that many of the social connotations of the old 'status professionalism' were transferred to the new 'occupational professionalism.'[30] The ethic of work and the ethos of strenuousness which were making their mark on even the upper reaches of English society by the mid-nineteenth century endowed the energetic pursuit of a profession with additional respectability without forfeiting its traditional genteel status. As was widely remarked at the time, educational qualifications were assuming a new importance, though still as marks of general capacity or suitability (including social suitability) for the higher reaches of administrative and professional life and not simply as guarantees of a relevant expertise.[31] It was in these terms that a university education—which for the Georgian gentleman had been at best an irrelevance, at worst a positive handicap, an encouragement to monkish pedantry rather than polished sociability—became for members of the Victorian professional class a badge of both status and competence. Moreover, the

in English, 27 (1948), 1–27. Signed contributions also came to be seen as the franker and more 'manly' course of action, an interesting extension of the cluster of values discussed at greater length in Ch. 5 below.

[29] Christopher Kent, *Brains and Numbers: Elitism, Comtism, and Democracy in Mid-Victorian England* (Toronto, 1978), 114.

[30] This distinction was developed in Philip Elliot, *The Sociology of the Professions* (London, 1972); see the helpful discussion in Sheldon Rothblatt, *Tradition and Change in English Liberal Education: An Essay in History and Culture* (London, 1976), esp. 184: 'Status professionalism developed in a society where style and manners were co-determinants of prestige, and prestige was more important than career. . . . Unlike status professionalism, occupational professionalism, Victorian in origin, depends upon competence as validated by the diploma . . . merit as defined by the association [of professional men] and guaranteed by the university is more important than social standing.' Cf. Harold Perkin's remarks about 'the general rise in the status of the professional intellectual in society' in the mid-19th century; *The Origins of Modern English Society 1780–1880* (London, 1969), 255.

[31] Other historians have recently drawn attention to the ways in which the ideal of the well-educated but non-specialist mind strengthened the connection between the universities and the Civil Service: 'This model of leadership drew far more from the older ideal of the gentlemanly professional than from the occupational professionalism of the expert or specialist. It tended not to open the governing elite to the business and commercial classes, but to institutionalize the connection between the new professional classes and the older social elite.' Rosemary Jann, *The Art and Science of Victorian History* (Columbus, Ohio, 1985), 230.

spread of a more uniform educational pattern among the upper and professional classes not only helped to instil certain common values; it also facilitated subsequent access to those members of the political class with whom that education had so often been shared (at least as a social if not always as an intellectual experience).[32] Thus, doors were open to the successful Victorian intellectual as much on account of the social standing of the roles he and his peers characteristically occupied as for his individual achievement in some department of 'serious work.'

Some of these doors opened on to dinners and receptions at the houses of the wealthy and the powerful, where a sufficiently interesting man of letters might be cultivated or even lionized, both forms of treatment reminding him that this was not quite his natural habitat. Other, more metaphorical, doors might open on to opportunities for getting attention or exercising influence: as ever, the ideal of 'the career open to the talents' chiefly favoured those with a talent for furthering their own careers. But in Victorian England one door above all others beckoned the well-connected intellectual, promising access to an arena of unique significance.

'Nearly every Englishman with any ambition is a Parliamentary candidate, actual or potential.'[33] Morley's aside—for so it was, though time has almost made it an epigram—should remind us of the continuing centrality of Parliament in this period, the focus both of national political attention and of individual ambition. (A characteristically cooler observation by Bagehot hints at the mixture of motives involved in such aspirations: 'A man gains far more social standing, as it is called, by going into Parliament than he can gain in any other way.'[34]) Even if parliamentary oratory no longer exercised quite the imaginative command of late eighteenth- and early nineteenth-century eloquence, debates in the House were still

[32] See the figures cited in Harold Perkin, *The Rise of Professional Society: England since 1880* (London, 1989), 366–72 (though the argument of Perkin's book leads him to overemphasize the 'professional' character of this education). The social composition of the student body at Oxbridge may have been more exclusive in this period than at any time before or since; cf. the near-contemporary judgement of Albert Mansbridge that the period 'from 1854 to 1904 was the most difficult time for the poor scholar to make his way to Oxford and Cambridge'; quoted in Perkin, *Origins of Modern English Society*, 426.

[33] John Morley, *On Compromise* (London, 1886; 1st edn. 1874), 126.

[34] Quoted, without reference, in Norman St John Stevas, 'Walter Bagehot: a short biography' in *The Collected Works of Walter Bagehot*, ed. St John Stevas, 15 vols. (London, 1965–86), i. 69.

followed by the educated classes with the avidity and familiarity now more commonly reserved for the major televised sports.[35] Certainly, there were those who felt the importance of Parliament was declining: Leslie Stephen, for example, suggested in 1875 that 'the floor of the House has ceased to be the exclusive, or even the most effective, standing-point from which to address the true rulers of the country'.[36] For a great many of the intellectuals discussed here, however, the debating-chamber of the Commons remained the great stage upon which they dreamed of making an entrance. This sense of national theatre—the metaphor is inescapable—is present in, for example, Lecky's reference in 1871 to Parliament as 'that great stage, a stage upon which, I fear, it will never be my lot to mount', the wistful admission of the 'I fear' testifying to the way in which longing was tempered by a sober awareness of the obstacles.[37] The extent to which the authors of the major works of political thought in this period moved in circles in which parliamentary ambition was commonplace is amply indicated by the fact that of the list given on p. 16 above of sixteen prominent intellectual figures who were members of the Athenaeum in the 1860s and 1870s, five became MPs (Mill, Fawcett, Bryce, Morley, Lecky), three more contested at least one election (Bagehot, Fitzjames Stephen, Harrison), and a further five were approached as possible candidates (Arnold, Spencer, Seeley, Maine, Sidgwick).[38]

More would need to be said here about deference in Victorian politics, since 'social standing, as it is called', to use Bagehot's

[35] See John W. Burrow, *A Liberal Descent: Victorian Historians and the English Past* (Cambridge, 1981), 88–9, for examples of the fascination and even reverence elicited by the art of parliamentary eloquence in the earlier period.

[36] Leslie Stephen, 'The value of political machinery', *Fortnightly Review*, 24 (1875), 848–9. As his reference to 'the true rulers of the country' indicates, Stephen was here making a point about the power of public opinion in an enlarged franchise. On Stephen's increasing disaffection from politics, see Chapter 5 below, pp. 173–4.

[37] Quoted in Jeffrey von Arx, *Progress and Pessimism: Religion, Politics, and History in Late-Nineteenth-Century Britain* (Cambridge, Mass., 1985), 103. In fact, Lecky's ambition was eventually gratified: he sat as Member for Dublin University from 1895 to 1902.

[38] The overlap of these worlds is suggested from, at it were, the other end by the following observation, made in the course of emphasizing a different point about educated Victorians' saturation in the culture of Ancient Greece: 'In 1865 the major commentator on Homer as well as major translator of the poet, the chief critic and historian of Greek literature, the most significant political historians of Greece, and the authors of the most extensive commentaries on Greek philosophy either were or had recently been members of the House of Commons or the House of Lords'; Frank Miller Turner, *The Greek Heritage in Victorian Britain* (New Haven, Conn., 1981), 5.

phrase, was on the whole a precondition as well as a consequence of election to Parliament. But there was, of course, another, more tangible, condition of this as well as of all other public roles. We must turn, therefore, to the traditionally ungenteel question of money.

III

The successful Victorian intellectual commanded an income that enabled him to sustain the public identity of a gentleman, something that surely contributed to his sense of confidence in addressing those other gentlemen who ultimately disposed of power and wealth in that society. There is, unfortunately, no systematic analysis of the financial position of such people that one can readily turn to, but the following figures may at least help suggest the broad outlines of their situation. In considering these figures, one always needs to remember that the attempt to translate nineteenth-century sums into modern values is fraught with difficulties, and even were there an agreed index of inflation, the varying components of the cost of living in different periods, and the radically different social significance attached to apparently similar levels of income and expenditure, would still limit the value of the exercise. None the less, as an *extremely* rough guide one can multiply sums from the mid-Victorian period by approximately 30 to obtain late-twentieth-century values.[39]

The absolute minimum on which a single young man could live and still maintain appearances seems to have been around £250 a year in the mid-Victorian period. A guide for those intending to read for the Bar, published in 1879, suggested 'perhaps for a man who lived 40 weeks in London, as economically as would fairly be consistent with his position as a gentleman and a member of a learned profession, £150 a year would be the minimum on which he could do it with any pretence of comfort; probably the average student at the Bar spends about £200 a year'.[40] A similar figure is

[39] See the explanatory note to the facsimile reprint of the 1886 *Statistical Abstract of the United Kingdom* (London, 1986). One also has to bear in mind the general decline in prices in the late 19th century: as a guide, which is again extremely approximate, the average wholesale price index in the 1860s may be represented as 118, that for the 1890s as 82 (where 1913 = 100); B. R. Mitchell, *European Historical Statistics 1750–1950* (London, rev. edn., 1978), 389–91.

[40] Quoted in Raymond Cocks, *The Foundations of the Modern Bar* (London, 1983), 183.

suggested by the emolument attached to the kind of 'prize Fellowship' traditionally competed for within a year or two of graduation. Such Fellowships were at this time designed at least as much to tide a promising young man over the difficult period of making his mark in some sphere, such as law or politics, as to sustain the first stage of an academic career (an anachronistic concept which can only really be applied in the last two or three decades of the century): in the 1850s these Fellowships paid £250 on average, and the Royal Commission of 1877 proposed restricting them to £200 per annum for a limited tenure of seven years.[41]

The great financial commitment of a man's life came with marriage and the subsequent maintenance of an appropriate domestic establishment. Costs here varied enormously, of course, depending upon the style in which one chose to live: £500 a year was sufficient for those content to live modestly, while some got into debt on an income several times larger.[42] Leslie Stephen, who was notoriously and neurotically anxious about money, resolved in 1875 not to follow the same path as his brother, 'slaving to death to keep up an expensive house', but to try to live on £1,000 or £1,200 a year, adding, in a wildly inaccurate generalization about the economic conditions of Victorian society, 'for millions of people do it'.[43] Calculations by modern social historians about what constituted an 'upper middle-class' income in the mid-nineteenth century (the relevant level in terms of social aspiration) naturally vary, but a figure of £900 or £1,000 seems to be favoured.[44] In the late 1860s only

Given that reading for the Bar took three years, but that it might be as much as another five years before the young barrister earned enough to live on, this guide estimated that a young man needed access to a capital sum of about £2,400 before contemplating the Bar. Despite this, the numbers of those called to the Bar expanded significantly during the century: membership of the Bar in 1894 stood at 8,000, though only between 1,000 and 4,000 ever practised (ibid. 218).

[41] See Arthur J. Engel, *From Clergyman to Don: The Rise of the Academic Profession in Nineteenth-Century Oxford* (Oxford, 1983), chs. 3 and 4.

[42] Alfred Marshall suggested a little later that a family man pursuing an occupation where his 'brain has to undergo continuous great strain' (such as, we may presume, a teacher of political economy) needed at least £500 a year; *The Principles of Economics*, 9th (variorum) ed., with annotations by C. W. Guillebaud, 2 vols. (London, 1961; 1st edn. 1890), i. 59. Cf. the judgement in Zuzanna Shonfield, *The Precariously Privileged: A Professional Family in Victorian London* (Oxford, 1987), 134: 'Somewhere between £1,000 and £2,000 a year lay the line between middle-class comfort and gentlemanly ease for a professional man with a wife and three adult children to his charge.'

[43] Quoted in Annan, *Leslie Stephen*, 74.

[44] See the sources cited in Sheldon Rothblatt, *The Revolution of the Dons: Cambridge and Society in Victorian England* (London, 1968), 201. This income,

some 30,000 families in Britain (that is to say, 0.5 per cent of the total) enjoyed incomes of this level or higher.[45] At the end of the century (when prices had, on the whole, dropped slightly) it was considered possible for 'a professional man' and his wife to live in an acceptable if not 'fashionable' neighbourhood of London, employ two servants, and generally 'keep up appearances' on £800 a year.[46] How do these figures compare with what a successful Victorian intellectual might earn?[47]

In very general terms, we are dealing with a period which was bounded on one side by the last stages of a system of aristocratic or other private patronage for writers and savants of various kinds, and on the other by the beginnings of that modern situation in which the state is the chief employer of intellectuals, especially through institutions of higher education. In the early nineteenth century the gently bred young man of mildly scholarly or literary tastes could still follow the traditional path that led to a country rectory without experiencing a disabling conflict between his private preoccupations and his public rôle. But for the more troubled generation coming to maturity in the middle of the century this conventional accommodation ceased to seem natural or even, eventually, possible. Thus, in mid-Victorian England, the young man of gentlemanly standing and secular intellectual inclinations who did not enjoy a substantial private income tended to look to one of four main sources of employment: public service, higher journalism, the universities, or

course, bought a far higher level of comfort, and especially of domestic service, not to mention social status, than would £30,000 a year in 1990, a further reminder of the difficulties of directly translating from a society with a very different economic and social structure.

45 See the table from R. D. Baxter's *National Income* (London, 1868) reproduced in Harold Perkin, *Origins of Modern English Society*, 420; Perkin's accompanying commentary indicates the grounds for caution in interpreting these statistics. In the same period, £150–200 constituted a very respectable lower middle-class income, while a manual labourer in regular employment might earn £40 to £80 per annum.

46 G. Colmore, 'Family budgets III: eight hundred a year', *Cornhill Magazine*, NS 10 (1901), 790–800. 'Such a couple have usually to consider, to a certain extent, what is vaguely called keeping up appearances; that is to say they belong to a society, a large number of the members of which are much wealthier that they themselves are, and the general level of whose social usages and demands they must, in so far as they mix in it, maintain' (790).

47 The following discussion is confined to *earned* income: several of the individuals mentioned also had varying amounts of unearned income in the form of allowances from fathers or inherited capital; Frederic Harrison, probably one of the best provided-for in this way, had £700 a year from his stockbroker father by 1875 (Martha S. Vogeler, *Frederic Harrison: The Vocations of a Positivist* (Oxford, 1984), 108), and in 1881 he inherited £40,000 (165).

the law. Schoolmastering might be regarded as a fifth possibility, though often only as a temporary measure. Certainly, senior masters at the major public schools enjoyed a very comfortable standard of living, and the not uncommon movement in both directions between headmasterships of such schools and Fellowships and even headships in Oxbridge colleges indicates a closer comparability between those two occupations than might be suggested by late twentieth-century conventions. But for the young man ambitious to make a mark in public debate, schoolmastering appeared all too likely to offer a route into comfortable obscurity.

At the beginning of this period, personal connections could still secure a remunerative bureaucratic niche. John Stuart Mill had been introduced into the East India Company by his father in 1823 at the age of 17; by 1836 he had been promoted to third Examiner at a salary of £1,200 a year, rising eventually to be, like his father, Chief Examiner, earning a salary of £2,000 by the time the company was wound up in 1858.[48] Through the patronage of Lord Lansdowne, the 29-year-old Matthew Arnold found a gentlemanly post as school inspector in 1851, which provided him with a sufficient salary upon which to marry. Arnold in fact never enjoyed early promotion at any stage of his career, but by the early 1880s his salary was £1,000 a year.[49] In 1887, after retiring as a Chief Inspector of Schools, his *income* from all sources (including his pension, a Civil List pension of £250, his royalties, and the proceeds of a lucrative American lecture tour) was £1,655.[50] It has also to be remembered that for the most part such posts only involved gentlemanly hours of attendance at the office, leaving ample time for writing and other public pursuits.

As competitive examinations increasingly replaced patronage, the now-familiar incremental salary-scales appeared: in the late Victorian period Upper Division civil servants could progress up three scales, running from £200–600 a year to £1,000–1,200 a year, while individual senior appointments could pay more handsomely still.[51] At the same time, the hours of work tended to become more demanding, and it became correspondingly harder to combine a

[48] M. St J. Packe, *The Life of John Stuart Mill* (London, 1954), 204, 388.

[49] Lionel Trilling, *Matthew Arnold* (New York, 1939), 391–2.

[50] Park Honan, *Matthew Arnold: A Life* (London, 1981), 412.

[51] Perkin, *Rise of Professional Society*, 92; see his observation that 'top civil servants, though they earned only from £1,000 to £1,200 a year, mixed socially with the rich perhaps more readily than today' (91). Senior legal appointments, especially overseas, paid several times this sum.

successful Civil Service career with significant literary or intellectual achievements, quite apart from the increased sensitivity on the question of public servants engaging in public political debate. None the less, in the later part of this period intellectually outstanding graduates with strong political interests, like Hubert Llewellyn Smith in 1887 or J. M. Keynes in 1906, continued to regard the Home Civil Service as an attractive and eventually well-paid career.[52] (Keynes in fact returned to an academic post at Cambridge two years later, where his earnings from various sources, including a lot of private tuition, were to total £600 a year by the end of 1909.[53])

The 'higher journalism' was the most easily available occupation, and certainly offered a possible, if somewhat precarious, living in the first part of this period. John Morley expressed the point bluntly many years later: 'The young graduate, born with a political frame of mind, who towards 1860 [the year in which Morley himself left Oxford] found himself transported from Oxford in pursuit of a literary calling, had little choice but journalism'.[54] In the 1860s both Morley and Leslie Stephen supported themselves for a few years almost entirely by this sort of writing, above all for the *Saturday Review*. The great success of the *Cornhill* in the early 1860s had raised the rates for the longer articles that appeared in the monthly magazines. For the periodical publication of each of the more substantial of the essays that were to appear in *Essays in Criticism*, Arnold received on average £20; for 'The literary influence of academies', which appeared in the *Cornhill* in 1864, he was paid £25—'the most I have yet received'.[55] (This was still small beer by comparison to what a successfully serialized novelist could make: Trollope's carefully itemized literary earnings revealed him to have earned over £3,000 a year at his peak.) For most of the writers mentioned in this book, the higher journalism was not their sole

[52] Keynes entered the India Office in 1906 having come second in the Home Civil Service examination; his starting salary was £200 a year; Robert Skidelsky, *John Maynard Keynes, i: Hopes Betrayed 1883–1920* (London, 1983), 175.

[53] Roy Harrod, *The Life of John Maynard Keynes* (Harmondsworth, 1972; 1st edn. London, 1951), 174; Skidelsky, *Keynes*, 212. In addition, his father, John Neville Keynes, made him an allowance of £100 a year out of his own substantial private income.

[54] John Morley, *Recollections*, 2 vols. (London, 1917), i. 31. For further discussion of the mid-Victorian periodicals, see below, Ch. 1 s.iv.

[55] One of the many admirable features of R. H. Super's edition of Arnold's prose is that full financial details are given of each of his publications where possible; in this case see the 'Critical and explanatory notes' to *Complete Prose*, iii, quotation at 463.

source of income, but there were periods in the lives of many of them when it made a crucial contribution to sustaining their social position, quite apart from giving them a public platform. Arnold, for example, explained to his publisher, George Smith, 'I make literature put my boys to school', and he complained that his work on a report on foreign schools meant 'I have been able to earn nothing for the last 8 or 10 months'.[56] For those with an established reputation, the financial rewards in the middle of this period were on a quite different scale from those familiar in the late twentieth century. When the *Nineteenth Century* was launched in 1877, it deliberately set out to capture big names with big fees: a star contributor in the late 1870s could expect £50 for an article, the equivalent of three or four months' salary for a lower middle-class clerk at the time.[57]

Needless to say, things could be very different at the other end of Grub Street. Consider this description of the so-called 'Bohemians of Fleet Street' in the 1850s, a group who were certainly not at the bottom of the journalistic ladder: 'As lower-middle-class writers with neither private incomes nor university educations, they took to bohemianism out of necessity. They could not afford the luxury of writing for the *Quarterly Review*: they relied upon daily or weekly journalism for their income and could only snatch odd moments to work on novels or poems.'[58] All of the people I have been discussing so far began their careers with some advantages of connection and education, but for every contributor to a major journal who might merit the term 'successful Victorian intellectual', there were dozens of lesser penny-a-liners whose scribblings for a variety of publications have not released them from historical obscurity.

Once successfully launched in the higher journalism, the metropolitan man of letters might hope to secure the editorship of a major monthly or weekly magazine, which, though usually only a part-time

[56] Letter to Smith, 1 Mar. 1867, negotiating with him a loan of £200 to be repaid over two years with the condition that Arnold write for no other periodical but the *Cornhill* during that time; William E. Buckler, *Matthew Arnold's Books: Towards a Publishing Diary* (Geneva, 1958), 19.

[57] Gladstone and Tennyson received higher rates still: for an article in 1887 Gladstone was paid 100 guineas; Priscilla Metcalf, *James Knowles: Victorian Editor and Architect* (Oxford, 1980), 285.

[58] Nigel Cross, *The Common Writer: Life in Nineteenth-Century Grub Street* (Cambridge, 1985), 94–5. Even so, their position could be comfortable: G. A. Sala reported living for four years in the 1850s by writing one article a week for Dickens's *Household Words*, which at about 6 guineas per article gave him 'a tolerably certain income' of around £300 a year.

job in practice, paid relatively well. The *Cornhill* again set the pace: in its boom years in the early 1860s it paid Thackeray £2,000, though by the time Leslie Stephen was offered the editorial chair in 1871 sales had dropped to the point where the salary offered was reduced to £500 a year.[59] This seems to have been fairly standard at the time: James Knowles was paid £500 as editor of the *Contemporary* in the early 1870s, and in his novel *The Way We Live Now* Trollope had his character Professor Booker receive £500 for editing a literary review, though Trollope himself, as a famous novelist, was offered £1,000 to take on the new *St Paul's* in 1867.[60] In the 1860s, Bagehot was paid £400 a year as editor and manager of *The Economist*, plus ordinary contributor's rates for whatever he wrote for the paper and half the profits over £2,000 a year whenever they rose above that sum; in 1873 he calculated that he had received an income of £780 a year from the paper since 1862.[61] In the mid-1870s John Morley received £800 as editor of the *Fortnightly*, which, together with his other literary activities, gave him an annual income of around £1,300.[62] Of course, the conjunction of a big name and a demanding editorial role on a daily paper could produce a higher figure still: in 1880 Morley was lured to the *Pall Mall Gazette* by a salary of £2,000 per year.[63]

Although these figures relate to the heyday of the general reviews from the 1860s to the 1880s, more regular kinds of journalism continued to offer handsome rewards for those intellectuals with talent and inclination for this now respectable activity. As editor of the most successful Edwardian political weekly, the *Nation*, H. W. Massingham received £1,000 a year apart from any additional earnings, and he paid his contributors well.[64] The famous *Nation*

[59] John Sutherland, 'The *Cornhill*'s sales and payments: the first decade', *Victorian Periodicals Review*, 19 (1986), 106–8; Annan, *Leslie Stephen*, 66; Barbara Quinn Schmidt, 'In the shadow of Thackeray: Leslie Stephen as editor of the *Cornhill Magazine*', in Joel H. Wiener (ed.), *Innovators and Preachers: The Role of the Editor in Victorian England* (Westport, Conn., 1985), 77–96.

[60] Metcalf, *James Knowles*, 236; R. H. Super, *The Chronicler of Barsetshire: A Life of Anthony Trollope* (Ann Arbor, Mich., 1988), 221–2.

[61] Bagehot, *Collected Works*, i. 65. Less austere publications could afford even higher salaries: by the time *Punch* became a national institution in the 1860s, its editor was paid £1,500 a year, 'at that time the highest income earned by any weekly editor'; Cross, *Common Writer*, 107.

[62] Kent, *Brains and Numbers*, 111.

[63] Stephen Koss, *The Rise and Fall of the Political Press*, 2 vols. (London, 1981, 1984), i. 231.

[64] See A. F. Havighurst, *Radical Journalist: H. W. Massingham (1860–1924)* (Cambridge, 1974), 143.

weekly lunch, at which Massingham brought together leading politicians and writers, was still a gathering of gentlemen of comfortable means. Similarly, when L. T. Hobhouse became political editor of the new *Tribune* weekly in 1906, he was paid £1,000.[65] The higher reaches of daily journalism could be no less lucrative. While C. P. Scott was editing the *Manchester Guardian*, he liked to recruit his leader-writers from among the outstanding recent 'Greats' men: though they might start at only £300 a year, once established they could quickly progress to £1,000, and a few outstanding individuals could receive considerably more ('If St Loe Strachey, whom I know, be worth £1,500 a year to the *Spectator*, certainly [W. T.] Arnold ought to be worth as much to us. . . . [T]o attract and secure men of the calibre we require we shall have to pay these high salaries', commented John Taylor, the paper's proprietor in 1895).[66] In none of these cases were the attendance requirements those of a full-time job, so, given sufficient intellectual stamina, one could continue to write books and contribute to public debate in other ways, or even to cultivate one's scholarly interests: Hobhouse used his mornings while a *Guardian* leader-writer to pursue his researches into animal psychology, while W. T. Arnold, Matthew Arnold's nephew, who had been recruited by Scott in 1879, four years after he had taken 'Greats', continued his studies in Roman history alongside his writing duties until his death in 1904.[67]

The third chief occupation followed by intellectuals in mid- and late Victorian Britain was that of don, though in the early part of this period, as I have already remarked, it was scarcely possible to pursue an academic career as such. Fellowships at Oxford and Cambridge were then still confined to bachelors, and usually held only for as long as it took to be appointed to a good living; few of them entailed any teaching duties, and fewer still were likely to lead to any kind of more senior position, either as a head of house or as a professor. At the beginning of this period, the 'customary value' of a Fellowship in

[65] Alan J. Lee, 'Franklin Thomasson and the *Tribune*: a case-study in the history of the Liberal press', *Historical Journal*, 16 (1973), 341–60.

[66] David Ayerst, *'Guardian': Biography of a Newspaper* (London, 1971), 254, 243, 238.

[67] For Hobhouse, see S. Collini, *Liberalism and Sociology: L. T. Hobhouse and Political Argument in England 1880–1914* (Cambridge, 1979), 147; for Arnold, see Ayerst, *'Guardian'*, 259, and particularly the list of publications in Mrs Humphry Ward and C. E. Montague, *William Thomas Arnold, Journalist and Historian* (Manchester, 1907), 127–8.

Cambridge was £300; the (eventually abortive) proposal of the 1852 Commission to establish a kind of university lectureship assumed that the salary and fees combined would bring the holder at least £450 a year.[68] The unofficial 'coaches', who did most of the actual teaching at this time, could earn anything between £250 and £800 a year depending upon reputation and hours taught.[69]

Various reforms in the 1860s and 1870s, above all the removal of the celibacy restriction on Fellowships, together with the enhanced status of the universities nationally, made being a don more attractive, and successive Royal Commissions attempted to deploy some of the wealth of the colleges to finance a proper teaching career. None the less, even thereafter there remained wide variation in the financial position of those who could broadly be classed as academics. In most cases, a head of house received a very comfortable income indeed—on average (there were significant contrasts between individual colleges of course) approximately £1,500 a year plus a good house.[70] At Cambridge, the Tutor (in the local sense, i.e. the senior college officer apart from the Master) might receive anything between £700 and £2,000 a year, with an average of £1,000 plus substantial perks; at Oxford in the early 1870s, a Tutorial Fellow (i.e. a teaching Fellow in a particular subject) might have an income of between £500 and £800 a year.[71] The salaries of established chairs varied according to the generosity of their endowments; the Lady Margaret's Professor of Divinity was the highest-paid Cambridge professor, with a salary of over £1,000 per annum, while £900 a year was the figure which the 1877 Commissioners tried to bring all professorial salaries up to in Oxford.[72] Those who, from the 1870s and 1880s, taught at the newly established provincial universities tended to be rather less well paid: as the Professor of Political Economy and first Principal of Bristol's new University College in the late 1870s, the salary of the economist

[68] Rothblatt, *Revolution of the Dons*, 206.

[69] Ibid. 68, 200–1.

[70] Engel, *Clergyman to Don*, 92–7.

[71] Rothblatt, *Revolution of the Dons*, 242; Engel, *Clergyman to Don*, ch. 3. There is still some controversy about the effect on college finances of the depression in agricultural prices after 1873; Engel, for example, emphasizes how badly college revenues were hit, but a less gloomy picture emerges from J. P. D. Dunbabin, 'Oxford and Cambridge college finances 1871–1913', *Economic History Review*, 2nd ser., 28 (1975), 631–47.

[72] Rothblatt, *Revolution of the Dons*, 201; Engel, *Clergyman to Don*, 218.

Alfred Marshall was £700.[73] One estimate of the average provincial professorial salary in the 1890s, when general prices were low, is £300 plus two-thirds of student fees, which had risen to £600 without fees by 1910, though in some civic universities, such as Leeds, professors could earn £1,000 before 1914.[74] As ever, there were various supplementary payments and other 'perks' to be taken into account in calculating actual whole incomes, and someone without any kind of academic position might still make a fair amount of money from other fees. Coaching at Oxford and Cambridge declined in the later part of the century as the colleges increasingly provided effective tuition, but the need for examiners at all levels grew; Frederic Harrison, for example, received 120 guineas a year as examiner for the new Oxford School of Jurisprudence from 1872, and £250 a year as examiner at the Inns of Court.[75]

Less can be said about the income to be earned by practising as a barrister simply because the Bar's traditional discretion in financial matters means that very few figures are available. Moreover, there are at least three reasons for treating all quoted figures with caution. First of all, it was a profession in which the financial rewards varied hugely, all the way from those whose income ran to several thousands down to those who needed to subsidize their pretensions to the Bar from other sources. Secondly, the earnings were irregular from year to year unless one attained the relative eminence and security of a salaried appointment. According to the most reliable estimates, the large majority of barristers earned 'very few hundreds' of pounds, but for those with talent and connections who devoted their energies to practice the rewards could be considerable: the average income among 'successful' barristers at mid-century was calculated at £3,000 a year, and in 1874 19 out of 20 of those doing 'second or third rate business' earned between £500 and £1,500 a year.[76]

The third reason for treating such figures with caution is that the group I am most interested in here, namely those barristers who continued to pursue their independent intellectual and political

[73] Shonfield, *Precariously Privileged*, 136–7.

[74] Stuart Wallace, *War and the Image of Germany: British Academics 1914–1918* (Edinburgh, 1988), 246.

[75] Vogeler, *Frederic Harrison*, 108.

[76] A. H. Manchester, *A Modern Legal History of England and Wales 1750–1950* (London, 1980), 73–4; Manchester prefaces his discussion by warning that 'accurate details of the average lawyer's income are hard to come by' (73).

aspirations, might well earn more from other sources, such as writing for periodicals, than from a languishing legal practice. Frederic Harrison was called to the Bar in 1858, but his radical political activities and a private income meant that he never really applied himself to building up an orthodox practice, and by 1873 he reflected that he could not earn £200 a year from his nominal profession.[77] This was true of even an exceptionally energetic and relatively successful barrister such as Fitzjames Stephen: three years after embarking on the Midland Circuit, he was still only earning £50 a year from it. Three years later, his fee income from the circuit rose to £100, yet even when he had what he described as 'a wonderful circuit', his income only rose to £200. Commenting upon the irregular appearance of remunerative briefs for his brother, Leslie Stephen sighed: 'Now and then a puff of wind filled his sails for the moment, but wearying calms followed, and the steady gale which propels to fortune and to the highest professional advancement would not set in with the desired regularity.'[78] Not until he was appointed as Legal Member of the Viceroy's Council in 1869 (at the age of 40) did his profession alone bring him a reliable income, and only his prodigious journalistic output had enabled him to maintain a growing domestic establishment. After his return from India, he received various further official appointments, and it was these rather than practice as such that brought him prosperity, his annual earnings in the late 1870s rising to around £4,000.[79] Stephen was one of the few who eventually made a financial success of his legal career; an insecure period as a barrister followed by gaining a niche in some related profession was the more common pattern. Thus, A. V. Dicey was called to the Bar in 1863, but he later reported that until he was appointed Junior Counsel to the Commissioners of the Inland Revenue in 1876, 'the Bar was never anything but a loss to me. I should long ago have starved had I depended upon my briefs for food.'[80] His two chief forms of income in this period were his

[77] Vogeler, *Frederic Harrison*, 108.

[78] Stephen, *Fitzjames Stephen*, 173–4, 148.

[79] K. J. M. Smith, *James Fitzjames Stephen: Portrait of a Victorian Rationalist* (Cambridge, 1988), 269. This meant he was 'sufficiently prosperous to be able to retire altogether from journalism'. Even so, it was only with his appointment as a judge in 1879 that he feels he is 'out of all my troubles'; Stephen, *Fitzjames Stephen*, 381, 401.

[80] Quoted in Richard A. Cosgrove, *The Rule of Law: Albert Venn Dicey, Victorian Jurist* (London, 1980), 29.

Fellowship of Trinity College, Oxford, relinquished upon his marriage in 1872, and his journalism; only with his appointment to the Vinerian Chair at Oxford in 1882 did he obtain financial security. The Bar played a comparable role in the career of his friend James Bryce. As his biographer put it: '[His] Fellowship at Oriel, aided by the emoluments to be derived from teaching, examining, and writing for the papers, made it possible for him to enter for the bar, then as now the easiest avenue into political life for a young man of scanty means and high ambition. The bar however was an instrument rather than an end.'[81] Bryce entered Parliament, at his second attempt, in 1880; he gave up his practice at the Bar, such as it was, in 1882.

Separating these four occupations for the purpose of analysis risks making them appear more distinct and self-contained than they actually were. It was very common for a man with his way to make to engage in more than one of them, often simultaneously. Sir Henry Maine's career provides a particularly telling illustration of this, though it has to be borne in mind that he was recognized as unusually resourceful in securing well-paid congenial appointments and even his contemporaries were on occasion a little scandalized by his pluralism. In a letter to a mutual friend in 1879, Fitzjames Stephen remarked of Maine that 'in nothing has he shown more ability than in his wonderful economy of labour for many years', and yet, added Stephen, with a mixture of fondness and asperity, 'he somehow manages to do just as much and just as well as if he did work, and he is at the top of the tree of respectability and splendour'.[82] The son of a Scottish doctor, Maine had none of the advantages of family wealth or connection to ease his passage into society. Following graduation from Cambridge in 1844, he became a Fellow of Trinity Hall, and in 1847, at the age of 25, was appointed to what Fitzjames Stephen called 'an ill-paid sinecure, worth perhaps £100 a year or a little more', the Regius Chair of Civil Law (the Commission of 1852 was to raise the stipend to £320 p.a.).[83] In the same year he married, the financial demands of his new state driving him to attempt legal practice for some years thereafter, never with any great success. More remunerative were his first steps in journalism: he contributed leaders to the *Morning Chronicle* in the late 1840s, where

[81] H. A. L. Fisher, *James Bryce*, 2 vols. (London, 1927), i. 61–2.

[82] Quoted in Feaver, *Status to Contract*, 306.

[83] Ibid. 19, 22.

the pay was regarded as 'very high', £3 10*s*. per article. In 1855 Maine was closely involved in establishing the new *Saturday Review*, writing for it very regularly during the next three years.[84] Meanwhile, appointment to the newly established Readership in Jurisprudence and Civil Law at the Middle Temple in 1852 (though he did not resign his Cambridge chair until 1854) had improved his financial position; his salary and fees from this post yielded £600 a year.[85]

The success of *Ancient Law* in 1861 may only slightly have boosted his income, but it was decisive for his career. It certainly influenced his appointment as Legal Member of the Viceroy's Council in India in 1862, among the inducements of which post was what his biographer refers to as a 'handsome salary'.[86] He was soon investing some of that salary in Indian railway shares, and received some dividend income for the rest of his life. Following his return from India at the end of 1869, Maine was appointed to the newly established Corpus Professorship of Jurisprudence in Oxford, a non-resident post which only required one overnight stay in Oxford during term. His real interests were in politics and public service in London, and for the rest of his life he toyed with, or attempted to secure the offer of, various official positions, including Clerk of the House of Commons and Permanent Secretary at the Home Office. In 1871 he was appointed to a permanent paid post on the India Council in London, which particularly gratified his desire for an influential advisory role, while allowing him plenty of time to pursue his other interests.[87]

These continued to include journalism, since for much of the 1870s he wrote 'two or three leaders a week at special rates of pay' for the *Pall Mall Gazette*.[88] Always alert to the prospect of substantial income without substantial duties, he accepted election as Master of Trinity Hall in 1877 (Fitzjames Stephen's views of Cambridge posts

[84] See the analysis of contributors in M. M. Bevington, *The Saturday Review 1855–1868: Representative Educated Opinion in Victorian England* (New York, 1941), 331–91.

[85] Cocks, *Modern Bar*, 98.

[86] Feaver, *Status to Contract*, 62.

[87] For a glimpse of his London way of life, see the materials quoted in Feaver, *Status to Contract*, 132, 134.

[88] J. W. Robertson Scott, *The Story of the 'Pall Mall Gazette'* (Oxford, 1950), 154. For a more extensive list of Maine's contributions in the course of the 1870s, see William N. Coxall, '"The use and misuse of internal evidence in authorship attributions": some further thoughts', *Victorian Periodicals Review*, 20 (1987), 93–102.

hardly seem to have improved in the interim: the Mastership he described as 'a sinecure of £600 a year and a good house').[89] He resigned his Oxford chair the following year, though he remained an active member of the India Council, spending most of the time in London. He also continued his journalism: when the *Pall Mall Gazette* moved in a more Liberal direction, the refugees from it set up a new evening paper of Tory persuasion, the *St James's Gazette*. Maine wrote the (anonymous) leading article in its first number of 31 May 1880, and contributed at least 180 articles in the following eighteen months.[90] When the Whewell Professorship of International Law at Cambridge became vacant early in 1887, Maine lobbied the electors: he recognized that they might be uneasy at his holding the post simultaneously with his seat on the India Council in London and the Mastership of Trinity Hall, and promised to resign the former if elected, though it would involved 'some sacrifice of income.' In fact, once elected he pleaded special interest in current Indian business and retained his seat, arousing much unfavourable comment in Cambridge.[91] Such pluralism had been not uncommon earlier in the century when academic posts were often little more than honorific; the criticism of Maine's behaviour indicated the more exigent standards which accompanied the newly enhanced sense of professionalism in academic life (this is discussed more fully in Chapter 6 below). Maine died early in 1888, leaving an estate worth over £46,000, a sum approaching £1½ million at late twentieth-century prices.[92] He can hardly be regarded as a typical figure, but his carefully managed career does illustrate some of the possibilities for economic as well as social advancement open to the successful Victorian intellectual.

Although each of these four occupations—the Civil Service, the higher journalism, the universities, and the law—could yield a comfortable upper middle-class income for those intellectuals who successfully pursued them, only the really outstanding barrister was ever likely to exceed this. One encounters a different scale of financial reward altogether if one looks at, say, the incomes of the

[89] Feaver, *Status to Contract*, 174.

[90] Robertson Scott, '*Pall Mall Gazette*', 256; Feaver, *Status to Contract* 214.

[91] See Maine's correspondence with Sidgwick in 1886 and 1887, Sidgwick Papers, Trinity College, Cambridge: Add. MSS c.94.102–5, some of which is quoted in Feaver, *Status to Contract*, 255–7.

[92] I am grateful to Professor George Feaver for supplying me with a copy of Maine's will and an account of its probate.

most fashionable London doctors, some of whom could earn anything from £5,000 to £12,000 a year,[93] and of course even this affluence was dwarfed by the great concentrations of inherited wealth. Moreover, the situation was not stable across the whole period: as I have already remarked, prices fell in the late nineteenth century and rose sharply in the second decade of the twentieth, though it is not clear that the scale of professional earnings fluctuated correspondingly.[94] But the sums mentioned in the previous paragraphs should give some indication of the position in the economic structure of Victorian society of the individuals whose names will recur in this book. That economic structure has been represented as a steeply sloping pyramid founded on an extremely broad base: in the 1860s the 30,000 families with incomes over £1,000 came above the 600,000 families with incomes over £100, beneath whom were 5.5 million families with a 'working-class' income.[95] That world which contemporaries referred to as 'the upper ten thousand' constituted the very apex of this pyramid, and historians have calculated that apart from some 8,000 of the titled and wealthy it included 'perhaps 2,000 other members of the élite—bishops, judges, leading barristers, fashionable physicians, editors, writers, artists, academics, and so on—with the entrée to London "society"'.[96]

This last figure tallies intriguingly with an assessment by a far from disinterested contemporary observer. Sidney Webb represented a new class coming to the fore in radical politics at the end of the century.[97] The son of London shopkeepers of radical inclinations (his father had worked for John Stuart Mill in the 1865 election), in 1875 Webb became a clerk in the City of London at the age of 16, and thereafter pursued self-improvement through evening classes.[98]

[93] See Shonfield, *Precariously Privileged*, 133.

[94] In 1911 Frederic Harrison, grumbing about the declining value of his investments and the difficulties his sons had in securing financial independence, declared that 'the day of the middle-class and professional man of £1,000 p.an. is ended' (Vogeler, *Frederic Harrison*, 282). However, he estimated his own income as £2,000 a year, and we should bear in mind that the Harrisons kept four indoor and four outdoor servants at this point.

[95] See Perkin, *Origins of Modern English Society*, 420. A different kind of statistic helps bring home the reality of late Victorian class relations: in 1891, one in six of the total labour force was employed in domestic service; Perkin, *Rise of Professional Society*, 79.

[96] Perkin, *Rise of Professional Society*, 63.

[97] See the classic discussion of this 'nouvelle couche sociale' in Eric Hobsbawm, *Labouring Men: Studies in the History of Labour* (London, 1964).

[98] Details of Webb's early life are taken from *The Letters of Sidney and Beatrice*

Exceptionally talented and wearyingly industrious, he won his way through the maze of late Victorian competitive examinations. Averse to a commercial career, and wishing to 'have time for his own intellectual work', he sat the entrance exams for the Lower Division of the Civil Service in 1881, and then those for the Upper Division (recently established as the entry route for university graduates) in 1882, meanwhile taking a London external law degree, being called to the Bar in 1886. His fellow resident clerk in the Colonial Office was Sydney Olivier, fresh from a First in Greats at Oxford, who introduced him to his college friend Graham Wallas, who, after a disappointing Second and an estrangement from his clergyman father, was making a living as a schoolmaster. This was the nucleus of the Fabian Society. Thus, it was from a particular perspective that Webb declared, while writing in 1886 to his fellow Fabian, Edward Pease: 'Nothing is done in England without the consent of a small intellectual yet political class in London, not 2,000 in number. We alone could get at that class.'[99] The exaggeration of the first sentence is matched by the self-serving quality of the second in this statement, which thus provides a nice epitome of both the ambition and eventual failing of Fabianism. But for all its hyperbole, the remark is testimony to the contemporary sense of the smallness of that 'intellectual yet political class in London.' The intellectuals who belonged to this élite thus carried on public debate from a social and cultural position of indisputable centrality. But by what means did they largely contribute to that public debate? Here we have to turn to what historians, in a term expressive of craft pride, like to refer to as 'the sources'.

IV

To begin by observing that different kinds of history characteristically rely upon different kinds of sources risks conferring undue prominence on what is at best a truism. The slightest acquaintance with the diversity of modern historiography makes us aware of the different kinds of problems posed (and opportunities offered) for historical reconstruction by, say, manorial rolls, the membership

Webb, ed. Norman Mackenzie, 3 vols. (Cambridge, 1978), i. 72–5; and from Willard Wolfe, *From Radicalism to Socialism: Men and Ideas in the Formation of Fabian Socialist Doctrines 1881–1889* (New Haven, Conn., 1975), 185–8.

[99] *Letters of Sidney and Beatrice Webb*, i. 101.

lists of guilds, or the private correspondence of politicians. But it may be worth repeating this truism if only to call attention to the fact that the intellectual historian of the modern period also works with 'sources', which, as the term immediately suggests, have their own characteristic problems of interpretation and exploitation. This point is not, thus stated, open to reasonable dispute, but the fact that the intellectual historian mostly works with that most readily accessible and reassuringly recognizable form, the published book, means that the peculiar properties of the sources as such rarely receive explicit scrutiny. After all, the chief collection of 'primary sources' for the historian of Victorian political thought is that familiar shelf-ful of books which begins with Mill's *Utilitarianism*, and includes Bagehot's *English Constitution*, Arnold's *Culture and Anarchy*, Fitzjames Stephen's *Liberty, Equality, Fraternity*, Maine's *Popular Government*, and similar tomes. Whether handling them in their original gilt-lettered cloth-bound form or in some recent paperback reprint, the modern political theorist seems scarcely to need to be troubled by issues of *Quellenkritik*: the object studied so resembles the form in which the results of the research will themselves see the light of day that a special effort is needed to regard the form of the sources with anything like the same kind of reflective distance which we inevitably bring to more remote or more alien materials.

Though this point may be worth making in a general way, it may still not seem to be particularly consequential; at most it reminds us of the cultural and material differentness hiding behind the appearance of familiarity. But the point can be given a more telling turn in relation to the material dealt with in this book. For in fact none of the titles mentioned in the previous paragraph were originally published as books: they all first appeared as articles in periodicals, and in the case of these five books they appeared in five different periodicals, each with its own character and intended audience.[100] It is true that references to articles in Victorian periodicals

[100] The articles that make up *Utilitarianism* (1863) appeared in *Fraser's Magazine* Oct. to Dec. 1861; those that make up *The English Constitution* (1867) in *Fortnightly Review* between May 1865 and Nov. 1866; those that make up *Culture and Anarchy* (1869) in *Cornhill Magazine* between July 1867 and Aug. 1868; those that make up *Liberty, Equality, Fraternity* (1873) in *Pall Mall Gazette* between Nov. 1872 and Jan. 1873; and those that make up *Popular Government* (1885) in *Quarterly Review* 1883–5. In nearly all of these and the many other cases one might cite, the original articles were to a greater or lesser extent revised and extended for eventual book publication.

now appear with some frequency in the footnotes of the more contextually minded historians of political thought as of various other students of the period. But even in these cases no real attention is given to them *as sources*: after all, they present no real textual problems, no complexities of translation from foreign languages, no arcane technical vocabularies, none of the complications which attend unpublished or private materials. Accordingly, these articles, too, can be ransacked for evidence of their authors' 'views' and 'theories', and they can usefully supplement the standard book sources. But in their periodical form even more than in their book form these sources should give us pause. If, instead of merely extracting some reconstructed doctrinal content from such writings, we concentrate on the genre itself, its preconditions and presuppositions, we shall be better able to identify some of the distinctive characteristics of Victorian intellectual life.

Once again, a very brief historical retrospect is required to provide the necessary perspective. In terms of polemical writing, the seventeenth and eighteenth centuries may be considered the great age of the pamphlet. Those periodicals which do figure at all significantly in the intellectual history of that period tend to be in effect vehicles for a single programme or single author, as in the case of Addison and Steele's *Spectator* or Johnson's *Rambler*. Thus, the first great age of the general cultural periodicals is that initiated by the founding of the *Edinburgh Review* in 1802 and the *Quarterly Review* in 1809, which, together with their subsequent imitators and rivals, dominated the polemical literature of the first half of the nineteenth century. But by the 1850s the old quarterlies came to seem expensive, slow-moving, and overly partisan.[101] In fact, some of their rivals seemed to wear rather better than the originals. After a somewhat scurrilous early period, *Fraser's Magazine* became extremely respectable and carried articles by most of the leading intellectual lights, especially during the years of J. A. Froude's editorship (1860–74), while the *Westminster Review*, once the house-organ of the Philosophic Radicals, was successfully refounded in mid-century as a platform for 'advanced' opinion ('it is now a review

[101] Both the *Edinburgh* and the *Quarterly* had sold for 5*s*. or 6*s* an issue, a huge sum for all but a tiny fraction of the population. At their peak (the 1810s and 1820s) they had a combined circulation of some 20,000 copies; Halévy calculated that they may have reached a combined readership of 100,000 (see John Gross, *The Rise and Fall of the Man of Letters* (London, 1969), 2).

that people talk about, ask for at the clubs, and read with respect', recorded G. H. Lewes in 1852[102]). But the reformed public schools and ancient universities were beginning to supply a new kind of contributor as well as reader, and the mid-Victorian decades thus saw the flourishing of a new style of periodical, which was meant to be something more than the literary form of the party struggle.

A crucial material precondition for this flowering was the abolition of the stamp tax in 1854, making papers of all kind much cheaper. One of the first publications to exploit this new opportunity, and at the same time to reveal the changed nature of the educated readership, was the *Saturday Review*, which began publication in 1855. The *Saturday* self-consciously presented itself as the paper written by the clever 'university man'; it offered serious and well-informed judgement in a tone of deliberately hard-headed detachment. It presupposed a certain level of education, but as a weekly largely devoted to comment on current politics and literature, it was in no sense 'academic'.[103] The paper had a decidedly metropolitan character, offering topical comment on the public doings of the political and intellectual élite (typically by the kind of able young barrister or author who wished to join it). Fitzjames Stephen was, inevitably, one of its most prolific and characteristic contributors.

But the great expansion in numbers and prestige of the new kind of periodical really dates from the founding of the shilling monthly magazines, beginning with *Macmillan's* in 1859 (described on its appearance as 'a review of political affairs, from the philosophical rather than from the partisan point of sight'), and the *Cornhill* in 1860.[104] These were deliberately more popular than their quarterly predecessors: they carried (and, financially speaking, were carried by) fiction and other 'lighter' pieces, often illustrated, as well as

[102] Quoted in Gordon S. Haight, *George Eliot and John Chapman* (London, 1940), 63.

[103] See the dated but still useful Bevington, *The Saturday Review*. For the general theme see Christopher Kent, 'Higher journalism and the mid-Victorian clerisy', *Victorian Studies*, 13 (1969), 181–98, and Houghton, 'Periodical literature', 3–27. The *Saturday* claimed a circulation of 20,000 by 1870, and was described by Ellegård as 'far above other political-literary Reviews of the time, both in terms of quality of writing, and importance as an organ of opinion'; Alvar Ellegård, 'The readership of the periodical press in mid-Victorian England', *Göteborgs Universitets Årsskrift*, 63 (1957), 24.

[104] Charles Morgan, *The House of Macmillan (1843–1943)* (London, 1943), quotation at 58. Ellegård calculated a circulation of 15,000 for the magazine in its first year, but only half that figure by 1868; Ellegård, 'Readership of the periodical press', 34.

extended articles on politics, history, literature, and so on. The early success of the *Cornhill*, in particular, with Thackeray as its first editor, suggested there was indeed a large market to be tapped: 109,274 copies of the first number were sold.[105] Inevitably, this success could not be sustained: when Leslie Stephen became the editor in 1871, the regular circulation stood at 25,000 copies per month, and by the time he resigned in 1882 it had declined further to 12,000.[106]

That decline may indicate, among other things, that by then the *Cornhill's* identity was uncomfortably stretched across what were becoming two different categories of journal. On the one hand there were the avowedly light and popular productions, such as *Temple Bar* (1860), with a circulation of around 12,000 by the late 1860s, the *Argosy* (1865), *Tinsley's Magazine* (1867), or *St Paul's* (1867) where Trollope was the first editor (and where the circulation never rose above 10,000).[107] On the other hand, there were the general cultural periodicals which aimed to sustain a more seriously intellectual level, like the *Fortnightly*, founded in 1865 (and, perversely, a monthly), the *Contemporary*, founded in 1866, and the *Nineteenth Century*, started in 1877. In these cases, circulation was not the only test of success: the *Fortnightly* was soon recognized as the leading organ of 'advanced' opinion and counted many of the most distinguished figures of the day among its contributors, but its confirmed circulation only seems to have reached 2,500 by 1872. By 1873, Morley, its editor, proudly claimed that it had 30,000 readers 'of the influential class'.[108] The *Contemporary*, an unimpeachably respectable

[105] Sutherland, '*Cornhill's* sales and payments', 106.

[106] Annan, *Leslie Stephen*, 83.

[107] Circulation figures are taken from the *The Wellesley Index to Victorian Periodicals 1824–1900*, ed. Walter E. Houghton, 5 vols. (Toronto, 1966–89) and Super, *Chronicler of Barsetshire*, 236–7, 273. The *Wellesley Index*'s description of *Temple Bar* roughly applies to all this group: it catered for 'the comfortable, literate, but ill-educated middle class which read magazines for pure entertainment and easy instruction' (*Wellesley Index*, iii. 387).

[108] Letter from Morley to Joseph Chamberlain, 11 Aug. 1873, quoted in Kent, *Brains and Numbers*, 115. There appears to be some uncertainty about the circulation of the *Fortnightly*: the figure of 2,500 was Morley's, repeated by Ellegård ('Readership of the periodical press', 27) and the *Wellesley Index*, but Heyck, without citing other evidence, gives a figure of 14,000 (*Transformation of Intellectual Life*, 33). For general studies of the *Fortnightly*, see E. M. Everett, *The Party of Humanity: 'The Fortnightly Review' and its Contributors, 1865–1874* (Chapel Hill, London, 1939), and F. W. Knickerbocker, *Free Minds: John Morley and his Friends* (Cambridge, Mass., 1943). The *Fortnightly* was explicitly intended to emulate *La Revue des deux mondes*, which in turn had been founded in 1829 on the model of the *Edinburgh* (the French journal's circulation had gone from an initial 1,000 to 25,000 by 1868; Christophe Charle, in *Histoire de l'édition française*, iii (Paris, 1986), 133–5).

and Anglican production ('the *Fortnightly* of the Established Church'), was selling 10,000 copies monthly at that point. Its take-over by a more narrowly evangelical group led its editor, James Knowles, to resign and found a new periodical, the *Nineteenth Century*, which was ambitiously intended to recruit the most famous names of Victorian culture ('the Metaphysical Society in print' might be an apt label), partly by being determinedly unsectarian, partly by paying unprecedentedly handsome rates. By 1884 it claimed a circulation of 20,000.[109]

The 1860s and 1870s were the heyday of these periodicals of general culture; by the 1890s, 'the active warfare of opinion' was beginning to be conducted elsewhere.[110] Some complex and still puzzling aspects of the economics of periodical publishing may have been one important cause of this change; the development of more specialized academic and professional journals, to be discussed in Chapter 6 below, was another. But these changes need to be seen as the modulation of the forms of public debate rather than as some fatal fragmentation of a once healthily organic culture.[111] The best antidote to the nostalgia implicit in such accounts of an irrecoverable common culture may be, as with the similarly ideological laments for a lost 'organic community', to recognize how each generation has projected the same yearnings on to a succession of earlier periods. Victorian reviewers frequently grumbled about the narrowness and superficiality which had overtaken periodical literature in their own time, in contrast to the virtues ascribed, according to taste, to the early years of the quarterlies or even to the original practitioners of the art in the Augustan age. None the less, the period which

[109] There is no separate study of the *Contemporary*, but see the introduction to its entry in the *Wellesley Index*, i, (1966), quotation at 210. For the connection with the Metaphysical Society see Alan Willard Brown, *The Metaphysical Society: Victorian Minds in Crisis 1869–1880* (New York, 1947), ch. 10. For Knowles's editorship see Metcalf, *James Knowles*, ch. 8 (circulation figure on 285). For the role of editors in these developments generally, see Joanne Shattock, 'Showman, lion-hunter or hack: the quarterly editor at mid-century', *Victorian Periodicals Review*, 16 (1983), 89–103.

[110] The quoted phrase comes from Mark Pattison's observation of the way the previous generation of periodicals displaced their predecessors: 'Those venerable old wooden three-deckers, the *Edinburgh Review* and the *Quarterly Review*, still put out to sea under the command, I believe, of the Ancient Mariner, but the active warfare of opinion is conducted by the three new iron monitors, the *Fortnightly*, the *Contemporary*, and the *Nineteenth Century*'; Mark Pattison, 'Books and critics', *Fortnightly Review*, NS 22 (1877), 663, quoted by Houghton, 'Periodical literature', 16–17.

[111] A tendency to depict the changes in such over-dramatic and putatively exhaustive terms mars Heyck's otherwise useful *Transformation of Intellectual Life*, for example.

stretches, at its longest, from the mid–1850s to the late 1880s can be seen as a distinctive phase in the development of periodical writing, and without representing subsequent changes as a decline, we have to recognize them as marking a significant alteration in the conditions of public debate.

More than many other forms of writing, the periodical essay is an excerpt whose full intelligibility depends upon a fairly intimate acquaintance with the larger cultural conversation from which it is taken. To adapt a phrase from a quite other context, it may be helpful to speak of the 'imagined community' of a journal's readers.[112] The notion of such an imagined community can be posited as a kind of transcendental deduction from the very act of writing for periodicals: more specific inferences can be made from noting which topics are assumed to be of interest, or identifying which allusions and references a writer does or does not feel called upon to explain, and so on. Contemporaries have a great deal of tacit knowledge with which to answer these questions were they ever to be put explicitly. The correspondence of Victorian editors and contributors shows them constantly assuming certain characteristics or tastes in their readers, constantly adjusting the contents of their publications to try to accommodate or appeal to the relevant market.[113] Scholars are now very familiar with the activities of Dr Bowdler's heirs as far as serially published fiction is concerned, but similar if subtler efforts to adjust to the assumed convictions of the subscribers went on in other sections of these journals too.

An alertness to the form in which so much of the writing now classified as 'political thought' first appeared in this period should not entail slack notions about such writings expressing 'the Victorian consensus.' But they were written to persuade a particular audience, and persuasion, as I have already suggested, presupposes an appeal to shared values and criteria of argument. There is a way of writing—academics embittered by *Kulturpessimismus* have often cultivated it in the twentieth century—which implies that readability is a sign of culpable collusion with a corrupt culture and that posterity is the only audience one can responsibly address. The figures discussed in this book do not belong in that company: their writing was not

[112] I take the phrase from Benedict Anderson, *Imagined Communities: Reflections on the Origin and Spread of Nationalism* (London, 1983).

[113] See the examples discussed in Laurel Brake, 'Literary criticism and the Victorian periodicals', *Yearbook of English Studies*, 16 (1986), 92–116.

hermetic, technical, clandestine. Once again, both halves of the term 'public moralist' are apt. Furthermore, and in rather more critical vein, a deepened sense of the habitual perspective and felt identity of such writers can be helpful when confronting the pretensions of the Victorian moralist to speak 'from the point of view of the universe',[114] a topic which will recur in succeeding chapters. Of course, some of the more extended writings to be considered here did not address merely topical or local issues: they aspired to call across the canyons of time to moralists and political thinkers of distant ages and cultures. Something of this has no doubt contributed to the continued currency even of those works by Mill, Bagehot, Arnold, Fitzjames Stephen, and Maine mentioned earlier which first appeared as articles in the general periodicals. Such texts may quite properly be analysed from several points of view, not all of them historical. But for the historian, puzzling over the mixture of strangeness and familiarity encountered in such writings, one way to bring into focus, out of the limitless expanse of what they do not say, the historical specificity of the assumptions sheltering beneath their confident abstractions is to imagine the closely packed columns of type on the original servant-ironed page as held in the hands of a conventionally educated, comfortably situated, male reader sitting in his club, at the social and political heart of the most important city in the world.

V

Coming to inhabit a social status furnishes part of a sense of identity, fostering one range of attitudes and preoccupations and discouraging others. One hardly needs to emphasize, for example, the extent to which the social experience I have been sketching encouraged a fairly intimate engagement with the practical concerns of the Victorian governing class. (Some judged it too intimate, even at the time: Morley was not alone in protesting against what he termed 'the House of Commons' view of human life', in which 'the coarsest political standard is undoubtingly and finally applied over the whole realm of human thought'.[115]) Perhaps a little less obvious is the way in

[114] Bernard Williams takes this phrase (from Sidgwick's *Methods of Ethics*) as his cue in criticizing the whole project of Sidgwick's Utilitarian moral philosophy in 'The point of view of the universe: Sidgwick and the ambitions of ethics', *Cambridge Review*, 103 (1982), 183–91.

[115] Morley, *On Compromise*, 117, 14.

which it made it easy, even damagingly easy, for these intellectuals to believe that they were not expressing the views of any merely partial or sectional interest, but spoke rather from a vantage-point that combined reflective disinterestedness with judicious realism, a belief which contributed to the distinctively high tone of much Victorian political argument. Beyond this, the assumptions upon which their status rested made them particularly responsive to a sense of paternalistic obligation to the less fortunate members of society. This was partly a consequence of their having inherited some of the self-justifications of a traditional genteel class, partly because their professional occupations enabled them to feel exempt from direct economic or social competition with those below them in the social hierarchy. Not identifying themselves as a sectional economic or political interest (though of course as a social group they did have distinctive economic interests as well as characteristic political allegiances), well-connected Victorian intellectuals persuaded themselves they had a special duty to remind their more self-interested contemporaries of the strenuous commitments entailed by the moral values embedded in the public discourse of their society.

This was the role of the public moralist. It was a role predicated upon a degree of intimacy between critic and criticized which had social and practical as well as cultural foundations. Such intimacy, the degrees of which in different cases need to be delicately calibrated, could be expressed in a tone which was now didactic, now reproachful, now cajoling, but was always in some sense confident—confident of having the ear of the important audience, confident of addressing concerns and invoking values which were largely shared with that audience, confident of an easy, intimate, even conversable, relationship with both Reason and History. There is a significant difference in tone between defending one's views and being defensive; Victorian moralists for the most part did not fall into the latter stance in their writings. Though nearly all of them experienced misgivings about the workings of democratic politics, they did not indulge in the affectation of complete withdrawal from public debate; and though they might on occasion be fiercely critical of the tendencies of the times, they never entirely yielded to the seductions of cultural pessimism. Yet recognizing their integration into the governing élites of their society should not entail treating their social criticism as an example of the narcissism of small differences. Rather, it allows a more nuanced characterization of their activities as social critics, a way of exploring their complacencies as well as their strengths, their limitations as well as their advantages.

2

The Culture of Altruism
Selfishness and the Decay of Motive

I

The coining of a new term may not always be a significant landmark in the history of thought and sensibility. Many such coinages, or attempted coinages, are unsuccessful after all, and even some of those that do manage to insinuate themselves into the company of the established vocabulary may only limp along after the main idiom, tolerated for certain special or technical purposes. But when a new term is so quickly and generally domesticated that within a few years its users treat it as an old familiar and exhibit no sign of remembering that it was once a gauche neologism, then the intellectual historian would usually do well to pause and reflect upon what is revealed by this linguistic success story.

The term 'altruisme' was coined by Auguste Comte, and, as the *OED* informs us, it was 'introduced into English by the translators and expounders of Comte.' The first recorded use occurs in G. H. Lewes's exposition of the *Cours*, *Comte's Philosophy of Science*, published in 1853. In rehearsing Comte's elaborate taxonomy, he declared that 'in the higher animals' there were two categories of affective life, '*Egoism* and *Altruism*', and that in this respect Comte's scheme challenged 'the old psychology' which 'reduced all our emotive actions to a principle of Selfishness'.[1] Subsequent uses of the term and its derivatives by other authors initially signalled their recognition of its origin, as in James Hinton's aside to a correspondent in 1862: 'The word *altruistic* I borrow from Comte. Is it not a capital word? I am resolved to naturalise it.' The more general needs the word was to meet were briskly indicated by Hinton's continuing:

[1] G. H. Lewes, *Comte's Philosophy of Science* (London, 1853), 216–17.

'We want it. It is the antithesis to "self"; self-being = deadness; altruistic being = life, and so on.'[2] Though its Comtist associations lingered, the term was soon established in its own right. By the time Spencer, for example, was using the contrast between egoism and altruism to structure his account of the 'the principles of ethics' in the mid-1870s, the word clearly no longer needed to carry its identity papers with it (though the more cautious Sidgwick still hedged it with quotation marks as late as 1874).[3]

For my purposes, there is no need to trace the further proliferation of uses in any detail. I begin with this minor philological enquiry because it draws attention to the way in which the cluster of values I discuss in this chapter acquired a new prominence in the middle of the nineteenth century. I have already made clear that this book does not address those 'foundational' questions which have been the traditional concern of moral and political philosophy. But in this and the following chapter, I do attempt to excavate some deep patterns of assumptions which, while they did not serve to provide any kind of theoretical grounding for the specific beliefs and attitudes which recur in the following chapters, none the less shaped the contours and informed the tone of that larger public conversation engaged in by writers who may have disagreed sharply at the level of explicit doctrinal allegiance. For this reason, the argument in this chapter will initially be conducted at a higher level of abstraction than elsewhere in the book, though still without, I suspect, coming at all closely to resemble those accounts of this period to be found in the standard histories of political theory. Even the more nuanced versions of those accounts suggest that nineteenth-century political thought (which is often rather selectively reduced to 'liberalism') was distinguished above all by its emphasis upon the egoism and rationality of individual agents, and while it would be absurd to deny that those are central elements in many of those models of 'liberalism' we construct for various quite legitimate theoretical

[2] Letter of Sept. 1862 (to an unnamed correspondent) in Ellice Hopkins (ed.), *The Life and Letters of James Hinton* (London, 1878), 194. Hinton, described as 'philosopher and aural surgeon', was one of the earliest members of the Metaphysical Society; its historian records that he 'placed great store' by the idea of altruism, which he construed as 'the moral unity, "myself in and for others"'. See Alan Willard Brown, *The Metaphysical Society: Victorian Minds in Crisis 1869–1880* (New York, 1947), 123–5.

[3] Spencer used the word from at least the early 1870s; it plays a particularly important part in *The Data of Ethics* (London, 1879), esp. chs. XI and XII; for Sidgwick, see *The Methods of Ethics* (London, 1907; 1st pub. 1874), 439.

purposes, I want to suggest that the texture of moral response among the most prominent Victorian intellectuals was marked at least as much by an obsession with the role of altruism and a concern for the cultivation of feelings as it was by any commitment to the premisses of self-interest and rational calculation.

It will immediately be evident that this is a widely ramifying theme, discussion of which must inevitably be open-ended and somewhat untidy; a close look at one or two concrete examples may be more revealing than either a set of generalizations or a compendium of isolated quotations taken from the whole range of possible sources. I am dealing with an aspect—or, more precisely, a set of characteristics together with their implied assumptions—of the moral sensibility of the Victorian educated classes. As a result, the pursuit of this theme will lead, in later sections of this chapter, into areas rarely visited by historians of political theory, ranging from ruminations on the insidious power of self-absorption in sapping individual energy to the kinds of justifications offered for the teaching of English literature. For, as one reads beyond the few canonical works of political thought from the period, one becomes increasingly aware not just of the distinctive tone and idiom of the Victorians' sense of moral seriousness, but, less obviously, of a recurring pattern of assumptions about the relations between selfishness, altruism, and human motive. At first it may be hard to identify this *as* a pattern, precisely because assumptions are something which their bearers tend not to articulate in explicit and systematic form. But, as with any such pattern, once one is alerted to its existence the danger may lie rather in exaggerating its pervasiveness than in overlooking possible examples.

II

Adopting for the moment the schematic idiom of rational reconstruction, I shall begin with some stipulative definitions. First of all, I am assuming that for certain purposes it can be helpful to talk holistically about 'Victorian culture' as something analytically distinguishable from 'Victorian society', and also that among the plurality of symbolic patterns that make up a complex culture we can, in the interest of any given discussion, choose to designate one selection from that plurality as a 'dominant' one.[4] (There seems to me

[4] There is a useful discussion of the distinctions involved here, and one which is helpfully concrete rather than merely programmatic, in Daniel Walker Howe, 'American Victorianism as a culture', *American Quarterly*, 27 (1975), 507–32.

more loss than gain in attempting to characterize that dominant pattern as an 'ideology': it is something less systematic than that, something that does not presuppose such a tight 'fit' with the social and economic structure of the society, and something that is not necessarily geared to facilitating the dominance of a particular class.) By talking of a 'dominant' Victorian moral sensibility, therefore, I mean to suggest, rather than to deny, that there were some who did not share it and that there were degrees of sharing it, but also to suggest that its dominance would be acknowledged by the fact that those who did not share it necessarily stood in some defensive, deferential, or antagonistic relation to it.

Secondly, I am assuming that while in some general sense values are central to and partly constitutive of any culture, what is now commonly termed 'morality', understood as a set of rules of conduct or obligations towards others, is only one subset of those values. Furthermore, it seems reasonable to assume not only that the content of such values may vary in different cultures, but that what may be termed 'the hierarchy of priority' of one subset over another may vary also. In these terms, it would not be startlingly revisionist to suggest that Victorian culture was marked by what I want to call 'the primacy of morality', or in other words that in their more extended reflections on the political, religious, aesthetic, and other dimensions of human life, Victorian intellectuals gave evaluative priority to 'morality' in this sense (though their usage did not consistently discriminate morality from 'ethics' in the widest sense).

With these boundary markers in place, I want to go on to construct something like an ideal-type of the notion of morality characteristic of dominant Victorian culture (I call it an ideal-type to emphasize its deliberately heuristic status). First of all, morality was understood very much as a system of obligations in which, to adapt a suggestive phrase from a quite different context, 'only an obligation could beat an obligation',[5] and in which, consequently, there was a tendency to extend the category of 'duty' as widely as possible. Secondly, the characterization of the alternative to performimg one's duties stressed giving in to temptation or being seduced by one's inclinations, and these inclinations were regarded as inherently selfish. (It is to this feature, above all, that I am pointing when I refer in the following chapter to the 'unreflective Kantianism of Victorian moral commonplaces';[6] it should not be taken to mean that there was

[5] Bernard Williams, *Ethics and the Limits of Philosophy* (London, 1985), 180.

[6] See below, Ch. 3, p. 98.

necessarily any historical link with Kant's philosophy, and, as we shall see, in some ways, such as the emphasis on the positive role of feeling in moral action, it was very un-Kantian). Thirdly, it was assumed that in any given situation there was always one moral right answer: all ultimate values are presumed to be compatible, and obligations, when clearly understood, cannot conflict. Fourthly, the 'others' whose welfare was the object of one's duties were coextensive with humanity as a whole; no 'thick description' of the identity of these others was required, and the partiality involved in privileging the claims of any more restricted group tended to be castigated as another form of selfishness.

This notion of morality obviously includes certain substantive beliefs as well as purely formal properties, and so I next want to suggest, more controversially, that within this ideal-typical moral system there was in fact rather little substantial moral dispute among the educated classes in this period (I leave open the larger question of whether there may in fact be less actual *moral* disagreement in most periods than we casually assume, which does not mean that there are not all kinds of disputes over moral issues). There was, of course, a great deal of moral theorizing: indeed, the volume of production of books on ethics may even have been measurably higher than at other periods.[7] This partly followed from what I am calling 'the primacy of morality': this gave a privileged position to philosophical and other reflection about morality as opposed to about other topics. But the disputes in this voluminous literature were essentially *theoretical* disputes, disputes about the foundations of morality, and it is evident that the sequence of disputes in ethical theory largely reflected developments in the culture as a whole. That is to say, new intellectual fashions such as Social Darwinism or philosophical Idealism stimulated fresh attempts to theorize a set of moral practices and intuitions which were not thereby subject to fundamental revision. In particular, anxiety about the possible consequences of a terminal decline in belief in Christianity directed attention to the question of the grounding of the claims of moral obligation (and there is here an interesting connection with moral psychology and the sources of motivation that I shall return to later). But within the dominant culture, the actual obligations were only rarely contested.

[7] For a, somewhat hyperbolic, characterization of the period as 'the ethical epoch', see Ian MacKillop, *The British Ethical Societies* (Cambridge, 1986), ch 1.

Of course, the literature of Victorian moral reflection, including novels, is full of a sense of conflict and of moral perplexity, but this conflict was essentially of two kinds. There was, first, that kind of moral perplexity that comes from an apparent clash of obligations: for example, was one obliged to resign one's living or one's Fellowship if one could no longer subscribe in good faith to the Thirty-nine Articles?. But this is not the same thing as a challenge to the standing of any of the obligations or the counter-assertion of considerations other than obligations. Second, there is a great deal of *psychological* conflict, and especially an abundance of testimony to the strains of the struggle between duty and inclination, between will and appetite. Again, the standing of the duty was not here being contested, nor even for the most part being criticized for making unrealistic demands on human frailty: weakness of will was regarded as recurrent, reprehensible, and remediable.

The characteristic preoccupations and assumptions of the leading intellectuals I am chiefly dealing with may be seen as intensifications of aspects of this more general moral framework. These assumptions, too, may be cast into baldly propositional form as follows. First, Victorian moralists exhibited an obsessive antipathy to selfishness, and consequently their reflections were structured by a sharp and sometimes exhaustive polarity between egoism and altruism. The ramifications of this exhaustive polarity are the central concern of this chapter. Secondly, they were intensely preoccupied with the question of arousing adequate motivation in the moral agent. Thirdly, they accorded priority to the emotions over the intellect as a source of action, and so addressed themselves particularly to the cultivation of the appropriate feelings. Fourthly, they tended to assume that our deepest feelings, when aroused, would always prove to be not just compatible with each other, but also productive of socially desirable actions. And finally, they betrayed a constant anxiety about the possibility of sinking into a state of psychological malaise or anomie, a kind of emotional entropy assumed to be the consequence of absorption in purely selfish aims.

The one feature of this pattern that may require further preliminary clarification is the exhaustiveness of the dichotomy between selfishness and altruism. As I have suggested, 'selfishness' came to be regarded as the Mark of the Beast morally speaking, the category which contained the root of all moral failing. By an intelligible, though obviously not a necessary, extension this encouraged a tendency to look upon altruism as the heart of all moral virtue. The most extreme version of this tendency (embraced, characteristically, by Comte and some of his more faithful followers) involved making it an obligation that *all* our actions should benefit others. But the structuring, or distorting, effect of the scheme is seen in other, not quite so extreme, ways, most importantly in the extended sense given to the terms 'selfishness' and 'altruism' themselves. Victorian usage here frequently blurred what has come to be thought of as an important distinction in each case. In the first case, the distinction I am referring to is between, on the one hand, actions which, in benefiting the agent, also harm, or neglect an obligation towards, others (what we would now tend to call 'selfishness', strictly speaking), and, on the other, actions which simply have one's own interests as their end. In the second case, the corresponding distinction is between positively directing our actions so that they benefit others rather than ourselves (the common usage of 'altruism' today), and simply taking the interests of others into account when framing our actions. I am suggesting, in other words, that Victorian moralists tended to assimilate the second of each of these two senses to the first, and then to see the polarity between them as exhaustive of the moral possibilities. As a consequence, given that the evaluative vocabulary was so heavily tilted towards the altruism end of the scale, it could be difficult to frame a morally positive description of purely private or non-collaborative forms of self-cultivation or self-assertion.

Obviously, many of the elements of this structure were not peculiar to this period; the distinctiveness, if any, lies in the particular shape of the pattern as a whole, and in its relation to other aspects of the culture (the same is true of the discussion of 'character' in the following chapter). In fact, despite the temptation to label this pattern 'Victorian', my general argument suggests, though without attempting to substantiate the claim here, that it persists much later into the twentieth century than we conventionally suppose, imparting a distinctive tone to English culture still discernible in some quarters as late as the middle of the century. The more obvious historical comparison which requires mention, even though I shall hereafter largely neglect it, is with the eighteenth century. At the level of moral philosophy, as distinct from more substantive ethical concerns, the continuity is obviously strong. For example, the project of rebutting systematic egoism had arguably been on the agenda of English and Scottish moral philosophy since the time of Hobbes and certainly since Mandeville. But given that moral philosophy is, eventually, responsive to substantive moral change as well as to more purely intellectual developments, even this apparent continuity can be misleading. It is hard to be precise about what other changes were involved in the transposition of the eighteenth-century debate about 'Self-Love' versus 'Benevolence' into the nineteenth-century idiom of 'egoism' versus 'altruism', though one would certainly have to include the legacy of the Protestant revival in intensifying the sense of inner struggle, as well as the effect, in different ways, of both Romanticism and the spread of religious agnosticism in raising the spectre of inadequate motivation. But whatever its sources, the change is undeniable, if subtle: 'living for others' was less likely to be trumpeted as an ideal in the eighteenth century, 'rational self-love' had a harder time of it in the nineteenth. A certain worldly tolerance of the imperfections inherent in rubbing along was perhaps lost, a more exigent notion of individual strenuousness and social harmony certainly became more prominent. Adam Smith had expressed the more relaxed requirements of the eighteenth century when he observed that perfect coincidence of feeling among members of society was rare: 'Though they will never be unisons, they may be concords, and this is all that is wanted or required.' But Buckle spoke with the voice of the mid-nineteenth century when, in explaining that in his *Theory of the Moral Sentiments* Smith 'investigates the sympathetic part of human nature' while in the *Wealth of Nations* 'he investigates its selfish part', he declared: 'This classification is a primary and exhaustive division of our motives to action.'[8] Even without pursuing the possible contrasts systematically, it is surely reasonable to assume that both senses of the pun or ambiguity present in the phrase 'the culture of altruism' find readier application in the nineteenth than in either of the adjoining centuries.

III

If the general scheme outlined above is to be recognized as identifying a pattern of moral assumptions fundamental to the

[8] H. T. Buckle, *The History of Civilization in England*, 2 vols. (London, 1861), ii. 432–3. The exhaustiveness of the selfishness/altruism dichotomy in Victorian thought may in this way have played its part towards creating *Das Adam Smith Problem*; see the editors' comments on Buckle in Adam Smith, *The Theory of the Moral Sentiments* (Oxford, 1976), pp. xxx–xxxii.

thought of Victorian intellectuals, it must show itself able to illuminate the work of John Stuart Mill. It is not just his obvious prominence that invites this test. It is also that his work may seem likely to be awkwardly resistant to being accommodated within this scheme. After all, as the author of *On Liberty* he is remembered for his protest, in the name of ideals such as 'individuality' and 'self-cultivation', against the coercive power of Victorian moralism, whether exercised by law or by opinion. It seems unlikely, therefore, that he would have been willing, even implicitly, to endorse those features of the dominant morality whose tendency may appear to have been, potentially, to threaten to stifle the free development of individual capacity. Moreover, as we shall see in more detail in Chapter 4 below, Mill stood at a somewhat oblique angle to High Victorian culture in several ways: not only was he a critic of many of the cherished commonplaces of his time, especially in matters of religion and politics, but it was an important part of his rhetorical strategy to exaggerate his isolation and his unpopularity.

The evidence which Mill's case provides is thus all the more telling, for what his partly self-created reputation as the embattled champion of individuality has helped to obscure is the extent to which a fierce antipathy to selfishness, and a correspondingly intense commitment to altruism, structured his substantive moral views. I say 'substantive' to indicate that it is not his Utilitarian *justification* for morality that is in question here, but rather the range of human actions he actually favoured and recommended. In fact, even in a primarily theoretical work like *Utilitarianism*, the argument depended to a considerable extent on the premiss that 'selfishness [is] the principal cause which makes life unsatisfactory', and on his optimistic belief that with the advance of civilization 'a fellow-feeling with the collective interests of mankind' would largely supplant 'selfishness'. Not only, he asserted, 'does all strengthening of social ties, and all healthy growth of society, give to each individual a stronger personal interest in practically consulting the welfare of others; it also leads him to identify his *feelings* more and more with their good'. The tone suggests the dispassionate recorder of social fact, but the claim was, of course, both tendentious and highly disputable: it would have been at least as plausible to claim that the increasing individualism of modern societies diminished rather than increased the forces making for unselfishness. But Mill had built the opposite assumption into the terms of his argument: '*healthy* growth' brooked no nonsense on that score.[9]

The extent to which Mill's moral ideal involved an extraordinarily close coincidence of *feelings* among all members of the human race can also be documented from *Utilitarianism*. In its milder form, the ideal may seem bland enough: 'In an improving state of the human mind, the influences are constantly on the increase which tend to generate in each individual a feeling of unity with all the rest; which feeling, if perfect, would make him never think of, or desire, any beneficial condition for himself, in the benefits of which they are not included.' Even here, a rather demanding standard of harmony was involved: the 'never' suggests an austere exclusion of all private goods. Mill recognized that this happy state was some way off, yet the form of the concession seems to set the stakes even higher. 'In the comparatively early state of human advancement in which we now live', he lamented, 'a person cannot indeed feel that entireness of sympathy with all others, which would make any real discordance in the general direction of their conduct in life impossible.' The language here surely betrays an unnervingly intense yearning for total harmony: that there should be 'an *entireness* of sympathy' with '*all* others', so that '*any real* discordance, would not just be unlikely but would be '*impossible*', is to set a very stiff requirement indeed. It is, for example, stronger than the claim (itself already pretty strong) that conflicts of interests can all be resolved by an appeal to some overarching criterion: it is saying that there will not be conflicts of interest because individuals will come to have the desires that further rather than clash with the desires of others. Thus, when Mill went on to refer casually to 'any mind of well-developed feelings', he was taking for granted that this meant one in which the 'selfish feelings' have been overcome by the 'social feelings'; selfish feelings, in other words, were defined as somehow primitive and excluded by a proper 'development' of the feelings.[10]

In this example, we have Mill explicitly endorsing the relevant pattern of assumptions in a work of self-conscious moral theorizing.

[9] John Stuart Mill, *Utilitarianism* (1863), *The Collected Works of John Stuart Mill*, ed. John M. Robson, 31 vols. (Toronto and London, 1965–91) (hereafter *CW*), x. 215, 231. It is worth remarking that the chief charge against which Mill was defending the Benthamite doctrine was that of being 'the selfish philosophy'; what is interesting here is not so much the accuracy of the charge, as the fact that these were the terms which the dominant moral sensibilities made available for critical purposes.

[10] *Utilitarianism*, *CW*, x. 232–3.

But in some ways, the centrality to his thought of this pattern is best indicated by the ways in which its components surfaced almost as asides while he was addressing some other point. Perhaps the most revealing source for my purposes is the section of *Auguste Comte and Positivism* in which Mill discussed Comte's moral thought. Comte propounded, in his obsessively prescriptive *Système de politique positive*, what could be seen as the limiting-case of an altruism-centred moral theory. Having come to regard devotion to others as the only acceptable motive to action, he tried to devise ways of punishing all actions that were not altruistic in inspiration. Mill, of course, objected to so vastly extending the domain of coercion, whether exercised by legal or moral means, and he charged Comte with making the classic Calvinist mistake of decreeing everything that is not a duty to be a sin. But although he was sharply critical of Comte about the means, he revealed a very marked sympathy with the ends, and the evidence is all the more telling for coming in the course of a discussion whose explicit purpose is to establish the rather narrow limits to his agreement with Comte in matters of doctrine.

Mill was, needless to say, deeply sympathetic to the idea of the Religion of Humanity, shorn of the excesses of the later Comte's religiosity, and in defending it against potentially sceptical objections, he spoke of 'the majesty' of 'the idea of the general interest of the human race, both as a source of emotion and as a motive to conduct.' That 'the general interest of the human race' provided an adequate theoretical basis for morality he did not here question; his attention was directed to its efficacy as a source of the feelings needed for moral action. For this reason he was willing to accept Comte's restriction of 'Humanity' to 'those who, in every age and variety of position, have played their part worthily in life.' It is perhaps a sign that Mill and his contemporaries were not in practice bothered by anxieties about moral relativism that he could so unblinkingly endorse the circularity implicit in this formulation. But it was also because his main preoccupation was with the pragmatic question of effects, with ensuring that 'the ennobling power of this grand conception may have its full efficacy'.[11]

Mill, of course, was not willing to countenance Comte's programme to extirpate all personal (or, in Comte's binary classification, 'egoistic') motives to action, but he did allow to pass without

[11] *Auguste Comte and Positivism*, *CW*, x. 333–4.

comment Comte's claim that 'the grand duty of life [is] . . . to strengthen the social affections by constant habit and by referring all our actions to them.' '*Constant* habit' and '*all*' our actions was again pitching the demand high, and again Mill's concern was with behaviour, character, and motive, not with the content of the actual moral code. And when he cited Comte as saying that 'all moral discipline should have but one object, to make altruism . . . predominate over egoism', he commented, as if sifting the unobjectionable platitude from Comtean excess: 'If by this were only meant that egoism is bound, and should be taught, always to give way to the well-understood interests of enlarged altruism, no-one who acknowledges any morality at all would object to the proposition.'[12] Now, clearly a sense could be given to this sentence whereby it would seem to represent something on which most moral systems have placed some weight, though even then the implication that this was an exhaustive pair of alternatives would still raise problems. But it is hard to know quite how to construe a phrase like 'well-understood interests of enlarged altruism'; though the modifying adjectives at first seem to suggest a harmlessly anodyne sentiment, they may also be a way of smuggling in some rather more coercive premisses. And again, the 'always' may seem to exclude any possibility of actual moral conflict: if the individual does experience some conflict, it is because he has yet to be 'taught' the overriding nature of altruism.

The celebration of 'enlarged altruism', and the corresponding presumption that conflict must represent the expression of selfishness, recurs in Mill's writings at all levels, often colouring his views in a surprising way. For example, when deploring the self-interested attitudes fostered by much commercial competition, he declared: 'Until labourers and employers perform the work of industry in the spirit in which soldiers perform that of an army, industry will never be moralized, and military life will remain, what, in spite of the anti-social character of its direct object, it has hitherto been—the chief school of moral cooperation.'[13] This is hardly the voice of the text-book stereotype of liberal individualism. Or in different vein, when in his *Inaugural Address* he took up the question of aesthetic education, he glancingly observed that 'there are few capable of feeling the sublimer order of natural beauty . . . who are not, at least temporarily, raised by it above the littleness of humanity and made

[12] Ibid. 337–41. [13] Ibid. 341.

to feel the puerility of the petty objects which set men's interests at variance, contrasted with the nobler pleasures which all might share.' 'Petty' and 'nobler' pre-empt objections here: no room is left for the thought that the unavoidable clash of legitimate values might 'set men's interests at variance'. His residual Wordsworthianism is visible in such sentiments, albeit inflected with the language of Victorian 'enthusiasm'.[14]

The insistent emphasis among Victorian moralists upon the central polarity between altruism and egoism was, I suggested, inseparable from a concern with questions of motivation, with ways of arousing what Leslie Stephen was to refer to as 'enduring motives to noble action'.[15] In Mill's case, one feature of this pattern that made the question of motivation particularly intriguing was that the 'others' with whom we are to identify have, ideally, to be seen as coextensive with humanity at large (or at least with Humanity in its Comtean sense), and not with any of those smaller units of kinship or locality to which the feelings more naturally attach themselves. Though Mill was willing to allow that such lesser groups might provide valuable education in the identification of one's feelings with something larger than oneself, not even one's country was considered to be sufficiently extensive ultimately to constitute a morally worthy object of attachment. One striking illustration of this was provided by another passing remark, this time from his essay on 'Nature'. Having established that there is a basis for sympathetic as well as selfish feelings in what we may conjecturally regard as man's 'natural state', he went on to say that in their untutored form these natural feelings of sympathy are really selfish. 'The difference is in the *kind* of selfishness: theirs is not solitary but sympathetic selfishness; *l'egoïsme à deux, à trois*, or *à quatre*', which may go along with being 'grossly unjust and unfeeling to the rest of the world'.[16] The awkwardness of his oxymoronic 'sympathetic selfishness' sufficiently indicates the curious extremism of Mill's position here: it is not only that the natural affections are limited in their scope, but also that they are partial in the other sense—they are not sufficiently disinterested, and therefore (and Mill does lay claim to the full logical force of that connective) they can be stigmatized as 'selfish.'

For the moralist anxious about motive this undifferentiated global

[14] *Inaugural Address Delivered to the University of St Andrews* (1867), *CW*, xxi. 255.

[15] See below, p. 77.

[16] 'Nature' (1854; 1st publ. 1874), *CW*, x. 394.

solidarity raises a difficult question: is it plausible to think of universal, disembodied humanity as capable of stirring the feelings strongly enough to act against the selfish inclinations? In effect, Mill addressed this question in his essay on 'The utility of religion'. There, he defined 'the essence of religion' as 'the strong and earnest direction of the emotions and desires towards an ideal object recognized as of the highest excellence, and as rightfully paramount over all selfish objects of desire'. (It is noticeable that, like so many agnostics in the nineteenth and other centuries, he thought of religion primarily in pragmatic terms, that is, in terms of how it shapes our behaviour, and hence in terms of how this function might be otherwise fulfilled; the believer usually talks in other terms.) Again, we see that the antithesis is between ideal objects of emotion and 'all selfish objects of desire': religion is seen as essentially a corrective to selfishness. He maintained that in fact the conception of humanity does 'offer to the imagination and sympathies a large enough object to satisfy any reasonable demand for grandeur of aspiration'. Moreover, he was optimistic that 'if human improvement continues', everyone will be 'capable of identifying their feelings with the entire life of the human race'. Ancient patriotism showed what could be done by way of being inspired by such an impersonal ideal, and he believed, with sublime disregard for sociological conditions, that such emotion and commitment could be effective on behalf of 'that larger country, the world'.[17]

The animating power of these assumptions in Mill's thought was further indicated by the way in which, in the same essay, he went on to make the case for the superiority of the Religion of Humanity over traditional theisms (where superiority was again judged in terms of its effects). The chief basis for this claim was that the Religion of Humanity is 'disinterested': 'It carries the thoughts and feelings out of self, and fixes them on an unselfish object, loved and pursued as an end for its own sake.' Mill always attacked Christianity for relying on, indeed encouraging, 'selfish motives', by making the prospect of personal immortality the inducement to virtuous action: as a criticism, it is an interesting example of turning the prevailing evaluative hierarchy against the established religion. And here he maintained that this was 'a radical inferiority' of the supernatural religions,

17 'The utility of religion' (1854; 1st publ. 1874), *CW*, x. 422, 420–1.

since the greatest thing which moral influences can do for the amelioration of human nature is to cultivate the unselfish feelings in the only mode in which any active principle in human nature can be effectively cultivated, namely by habitual exercise; but the habit of expecting to be rewarded in another life for our conduct in this, makes even virtue itself no longer an exercise of the unselfish feelings.[18]

This was, arguably, unfair (to Christianity) and, as a result, hectoring; but the moral priority assigned to 'the cultivation of the unselfish feelings' is beyond doubt. For all his self-conscious antagonism to many of the religious and political prejudices of the educated classes of his day, Mill surely shared some of their most fundamental moral assumptions with untroubled conviction. We shall see in more detail in Chapter 4 below how the presence of such shared assumptions crucially determined the direction and tone of so much of Mill's writing as a public moralist.

IV

Although Mill engaged with the question of how to stimulate individuals to act morally, he did not, once his youthful 'mental crisis' had been resolved, appear to suffer from any debilitating paralysis of the will himself. But the next step in my argument is to suggest that one of the sources of the hold on Victorian intellectuals of the pattern of moral assumptions I have been describing was that it appeared to address the problem of motivation as they actually experienced it. Their public pronouncements were spiced with personal testimony about the enervating effect of the absorption in purely 'selfish' aims. Much of their commitment to the ideal of altruism derived from the felt need to stimulate the will to rise above the listless despondency that was assumed to accompany the pursuit of strictly individual satisfactions.

In all this, they may be represented as acting out their own form of the Romantic malaise, Victorian Werthers trying to find in work and duty an antidote to the ever-threatening perils of languid *Welt-schmerz*. Certainly, Carlyle, who gave most memorable expression to this movement of feeling, brooded over the early reading of a whole generation of troubled souls. But the public preoccupation with the 'nobler' purposes of altruism gave a more peculiarly English and

[18] 'The utility of religion' (1854; 1st publ. 1874), *CW*, x. 422.

mid-nineteenth-century inflection to this larger European phenomenon. Moreover, the framing preoccupation in this setting was provided, as I have already indicated, by anxieties about the decline of orthodox Christian belief. Intellectual historians have explored in some detail those various late nineteenth-century attempts to develop an alternative creed, whether in the form of the Religion of Humanity with its explicit attempts to replace the rites of Christian worship as well as the content of Christian beliefs, or in the form of those various ethical societies, fellowships of the new life, and so on that particularly flourished in London in the 1880s and 1890s.[19] But the framework of assumptions outlined earlier also suggests a different perspective here, one which focuses on Victorian attempts to deploy largely familiar cultural resources to stimulate the kinds of sympathetic feelings needed to overcome the enervating impasse of selfishness. Above all, literature, construed didactically, could be made to meet this need, a development exemplified by the appropriation of Wordsworth to serve the purposes of Victorian moralism.

The interplay of these themes, once identified in this way, is discernible in much mid- and late nineteenth-century moral reflection. A convenient epitome is provided by Leslie Stephen's essay 'Wordsworth's ethics', first published in 1876. A prominent part in Stephen's literary criticism was played by the metaphor of moral or spiritual 'health', a standard of judgement that expressed his emotional affinity with the ethos of 'muscular Christianity' (to which I shall return in Chapter 5) as well as his intellectual allegiance to Darwinian naturalism. This combination is insistently present in the declaration of critical principle with which he opens his essay on Wordsworth.

> The highest poetry must be that which expresses not only the richest but the healthiest nature. Disease means an absence or want of balance of certain faculties, and therefore leads to false reasoning or emotional discord. The defect of character betrays itself in some erroneous mode of thought or baseness of sentiment. And since morality means obedience to those rules which are most essential to the spiritual health, vicious feeling indicates some morbid tendency, and is so far destructive of the poetical faculty.[20]

[19] See, among others, T. R. Wright, *The Religion of Humanity: The Impact of Comtean Positivism in Victorian Britain* (Cambridge, 1986); Warren Sylvester Smith, *The London Heretics 1870–1914* (London, 1967); MacKillop, *British Ethical Societies*.

[20] Leslie Stephen, 'Wordsworth's ethics' (1876), *Hours in a Library*, ii (London, 1876), 254.

As critical credos go, this is at least succinct, almost pungent. 'Morbid' was a favourite critical term for Stephen, suggestive both of what does not make for health and survival, and of that listless, paralysed state of the will that comes from excessive introspection or moral slackness. The implied contrast, and the premiss of the position, is the possibility of that complete harmony of feelings that issues in the actions of the genuinely virtuous. On Stephen's showing, neither Byron nor Shelley, for example, could resolve the moral dilemmas their own characters presented them with, 'and therefore neither can reach a perfect harmony of feeling'.[21] Wordsworth, by contrast, can, and can therefore help to cultivate this harmony in his readers. The key to this achievement Stephen locates in Wordsworth's capacity to find in our positive feelings towards others an effective substitute for the natural energies that impelled us to action when young. Like many of the poet's Victorian admirers, Stephen was particularly taken by the lines: 'We live by admiration, hope and love;/ And even as these are well and wisely fused,/ The dignity of being we ascend.' And, like Mill (and indeed Arnold and the majority of Victorian commentators), his judgement here rests partly on a pragmatic basis: both selfishness and despair deprive us of this one effective stimulus to action, and are thus self-defeating.[22]

On Stephen's reading of Wordsworth's ethical teaching, the next step is to answer the question: 'How can we build up our moral being?' The criteria for discriminating this from our non-moral or immoral being are tacitly assumed, and throughout Stephen takes for granted that our strongest feelings are invariably benevolent. For example, when defending Wordsworth's celebration of the value of solitude as ultimately nourishing the human sympathies rather than withdrawing from them, he writes: 'The value of silent thought is so to cultivate the primitive emotions that they may flow spontaneously upon every common incident, and every familiar object becomes symbolic of them.' Less positive outcomes of cultivating the 'primitive emotions' do not intrude. Wordsworth, needless to say, took Nature to be the soundest moral educator, a claim with which Stephen's language seems willingly to collude. Even the sounds of

[21] Leslie Stephen, 'Wordsworth's ethics' (1876), *Hours in a Library*, ii (London, 1876), 261.

[22] Arnold's somewhat similar treatment of Wordsworth is discussed in Stefan Collini, *Arnold* (Oxford, 1988), 105–7.

Nature are alleged to have a part to play in this process, for they have, as Stephen typically puts it, 'a spontaneous affinity for the nobler emotions'.[23] This may be true of Wordsworth's response to a gurgling Lakeland beck, and may even be a fair report of what a thunderstorm in the Alps meant to Stephen; but one might, at the very least, want to murmur something about nobility lying in the ear of the beholder.

In effect, Stephen's account of 'Wordsworth's ethics' is a discussion not of actual ethical ideals or their grounds, but of moral psychology. This is particularly evident in his long discussion of why Wordsworth is the only poet who enables us to turn sorrow to positive account (Stephen's first wife had just died, and Maitland treats this as pretty straightforwardly autobiographical[24]). None of the usual platitudes are consoling when one is faced with the death of a loved one, but Wordsworth suggests the one source of comfort: 'There is some consolation in the thought that even death may bind the survivors closer, and leave as a legacy enduring motives to noble action.' And if we ask why suffering should stimulate this high-minded reaction rather than bitterness and despair, we come back to the question of the pragmatic superiority of 'living for others'. If, claims Stephen, you are already someone who has cultivated 'the higher motives', then you

> will be prepared to convert sorrow into a medicine instead of a poison. Sorrow is deteriorating so far as it is selfish. The man who is occupied with his own interests makes grief an excuse for effeminate indulgence in self-pity . . . [whereas] the man who has learnt habitually to think of himself as part of a greater whole, whose conduct has been habitually directed to noble ends, is purified and strengthened by the spiritual convulsion.[25]

Perhaps Stephen's need of the moment to persuade himself of some such truth may be allowed to excuse the insufferable preachiness of this, but it makes explicit an assumption implicitly present throughout. Good moral habits are their own reward: the prime requirement is to avoid selfishness, and thus to cultivate 'enduring motives to noble actions'.

23 'Wordsworth's ethics', ii. 273, 269.

24 F. W. Maitland, *The Life and Letters of Leslie Stephen* (London, 1906), 270–1.

25 'Wordsworth's ethics', ii. 279. Quentin Bell's account of the effect of Stephen's grief on his family after the death of his second wife suggests a larger than usual gap between aspiration and achievement here; Quentin Bell, *Virginia Woolf: A Biography*, 2 vols. (London, 1972), i. 40–1.

So, Wordsworth's argument, as abstracted and stated in a prosier idiom by Stephen, is that there is a potential natural harmony and natural virtue in us as children—'the instrument in fact finds itself originally tuned by its Maker'—and that it then depends which pattern of life we follow whether we maintain and develop this harmony or destroy it. And what destroys it is selfishness, which withers the powerful emotions: 'The old emotions dry up at their source . . . ' and so on. Stephen's conclusion is thus that 'in this way the postulate justifies itself by producing the noblest type of character'. He recognizes that the sceptic will claim that he has been given no conclusive grounds for following the path of virtue, but here Stephen falls back upon his metaphor of 'health'. How is the doctor to answer when asked why should health be preferred to disease? 'The moralist is in the same position when he has shown how certain habits conduce to the development of a type superior to its rivals in all the faculties which imply permanent peace of mind and power of resisting the shocks of the world without disintegration.'[26]

Stephen's vocabulary here should remind us that his theoretical allegiance was given to a form of evolutionary naturalism, and that he did actually attempt to provide some systematic grounding for these views in that monument to mistaking where one's talents lie, his large and largely unread treatise *The Science of Ethics*. But at this level, too, the dichotomy between selfishness and altruism is assumed as an axiom. In that work he argued that 'altruism is . . . the faculty essentially necessary to moral conduct. Were it not a reality, virtue would be a name and society an impossibility.' But it requires that through sympathy we should 'feel' the needs of others, and this feeling should override our 'selfish' calculations. How this may come about is never made altogether clear, despite the length of the work, but identification with 'the social organism' emerges as the essential condition. Stephen's treatise was yet another of those late nineteenth-century attempts to ground ethics in the requirements of evolution, and so 'the needs of the social organism' play a large and cloudy role. But what brings about this identification on the individual's part remains a little under-explained (partly because 'the social organism' is such a forbiddingly abstract entity which seems unlikely to have the hold on the emotions a more concretely specified community would). At a general level, the explanation is teleological:

[26] 'Wordsworth's ethics', ii. 281–2.

morality is 'a statement of the conditions of social vitality', and the social organism expects every healthy individual to do his duty. In detail, the prescription is the same as that given in his informal essays: only by attempting to 'live for others' will the individual be able to partake of this 'vitality'.[27] Again, we return to the question of how to stimulate the imaginative sympathy necessary to provide 'enduring motives to noble action', for as Stephen said when addressing one of those 'Ethical Societies' that grew up in the last two decades of the century:

> You no more teach men to be moral by giving them a sound ethical theory, than you teach them to be good shots by explaining the theory of projectiles. . . . To convert the world you have not merely to prove your theories, but to stimulate the imagination, to discipline the passions, to provide modes of utterance for the emotions and symbols which may represent the fundamental beliefs.[28]

It was to fulfil this purpose that Stephen and many of his contemporaries increasingly looked to imaginative literature. In general terms, of course, this had been regarded as part of the office of literature down the ages. But here, too, we can discern an inflection characteristic of this generation, an inflection which reveals the presence of this same pattern of moral preoccupations. As an indication of the extent to which this pattern habitually presented itself in discussions of this topic, consider the phrases which that very busy man, John Morley, fell back upon when, despite more pressing demands on his time, he agreed to address a gathering of the University Extension movement in 1887 on the topic of 'The study of literature'. Among the generalities we might expect from that conjunction of speaker, topic, and audience, we find Morley emphasizing the special modern need 'to find some effective agency for cherishing within us the ideal'. This, he could declare without fear of being inappropriately controversial, 'is the business and function of literature'. And in spelling out the manner in which it might discharge this function, he reached for a similarly uncontentious litany of phrases: literature acts by 'the cultivation of the sympathies and imagination, the quickening of the moral sensibilities, and the enlargement of the moral vision'.[29] Morley could take for

[27] Leslie Stephen, *The Science of Ethics* (London, 1882), 264, 257, 265.

[28] Leslie Stephen, *Social Rights and Duties*, 2 vols. (London, 1896), i. 43.

[29] John Morley, 'On the study of literature' (1887), in *Studies in Literature* (London, 1890), 201.

granted, in other words, that the most persuasive grounds upon which the teaching of literature could be recommended were to be found in its value as a stimulus to sympathetic feeling. The underlying conviction had been stated some thirty years earlier, in terms which did not yet seem quite so hackneyed or second-hand, by that writer whom so many intellectuals of this generation revered as the most effective moral teacher of the age because of the unrivalled effectiveness with which her novels educated the feelings against the self-destructive perils of selfishness: 'The greatest benefit we owe to the artist is the extension of our sympathies . . . a picture of human life such as a great artist can give, surprises even the trivial and the selfish into that attention to what is apart from themselves which may be called the raw material of moral sentiment.'[30]

It is arguable, of course, that the very needs that led mid- and late Victorian intellectuals to place this burden on literature constrained both the selection and interpretation of the works they thereby promoted. This surely contributed to that mid-nineteenth-century construction of 'Romanticism' as a benign, pastoral, almost Anglican, celebration of simplicity of feeling and English rural nostalgia. Less obviously, these moral attitudes may have helped to account for a noticeable thinness in the Victorian understanding of tragedy as a literary genre. The kind of pre-emptive commitment to harmony, both harmony among members of society and harmony among the impulses of the individual, that I have been exploring here was hardly a promising basis for a profound understanding of the irresolvable conflicts which must be at the heart of tragedy. This habit of feeling made it too easy to assume that where values appeared to clash, there was a presumption of selfishness at work somewhere. Even Arnold, for all his immense regard for the Greek tragedians, was a little too prone to emasculate the bleak savagery of their art, and lesser critics readily drew uplifting and familiar moral lessons from the most unpromising classical texts.[31] (Was E. M. Forster, for example, thinking of the influence of Arnold-inspired schoolmasters when some twenty years later he had a character in

[30] George Eliot, 'The natural history of German life' (1856), in *The Essays of George Eliot*, ed. Thomas Pinney (London, 1963), 270.

[31] Was this, perhaps, the kind of emollient interpretation ironized in advance in Schiller's epigram: 'Oedipus tears out his eyes, Jocasta hangs herself, both guiltless: the play has come to a harmonious conclusion'? Quoted in Richard Jenkyns, *The Victorians and Ancient Greece* (Oxford, 1980), 99. For Arnold's exaggeration of the harmony and serenity of Greek art, see Collini, *Arnold*, 82–5.

The Longest Journey say: 'You know, the Greeks aren't Broad Church clergymen. . . . Boys will regard Sophocles as a kind of enlightened bishop, and something tells me they are wrong.'[32]) We are also touching here on the ways in which this widely shared moral sensibility helped to shape the formation of a 'canon' of works of English literature at the time when its study was first being established as an academic discipline, a topic discussed more fully in Chapter 9 below.

By this point, we may seem to have moved far from politics and political thought. However, it is part of the argument of this book that these journeyings are not deviations, but, rather, an essential way of exploring the informing dynamic of the public sensibility of the period. A helpful marker to the next stage of the route is provided by the fate of one of the emblematic fictional characters of the late nineteenth century, the eponymous hero of Mrs Humphry Ward's best-selling novel *Robert Elsmere*.[33]

The novel has become a *locus classicus* for discussions about the struggle between those two great warring engines, Faith and Doubt, and it is taken as showing quite accurately that historical criticism of the Bible, rather than the findings of Darwinian biology, played the chief part in undermining religious belief among the educated class. Without attempting to displace those characterizations, I want to suggest that the novel also provided its first readers with a recognizable parable about the need to 'live for others'. What it portrays as being so fatal in such figures as Langham, the aetiolated don, or Wendover, the free-thinking squire, is not their lack of religious belief, but their selfishness. For all their intellectual and worldly advantages, neither manages to find sufficient purposes to sustain life. The contrast is with Elsmere himself (a Daniel Deronda inside whom a Charles Kingsley is struggling to get out), who, though he loses his faith in Christianity, continues to identify his feelings with the interests of others.

The final section of the novel, where Elsmere finds peace and satisfaction working among the uneducated inhabitants of the East End, pointed the moral for those primed to see. Elsmere tells his

[32] Quoted in Jenkyns, *Victorians and Ancient Greece*, 91.

[33] For a wealth of detail on both the composition and reception of the novel (including the statistic that it had sold one million copies within twenty years), see William S. Peterson, *Victorian Heretic: Mrs Humphry Ward's 'Robert Elsmere'* (Leicester, 1976).

new audience stories, using literature for the purposes of secular sermons: 'In these performances Elsmere's aim had always been twofold—the rousing of moral sympathy and the awakening of the imaginative power pure and simple.' Another character is used to voice the obvious sceptical question of the point of this surrogate preaching: 'What will you gain? A new sect?'

> 'Possibly. But what we *stand* to gain is a new social bond', was the flashing answer—'a new compelling force in man and in society. Can you deny that the world wants it? What are you economists and sociologists of the new type always pining for? Why, for that diminution of the self in man which is to enable the individual to see the *world's* ends clearly, and to care not only for his own but for his neighbour's interest, which is to make the rich devote themselves to the poor, and the poor bear with the rich. If man only *would*, he *could*, you say, solve all the problems which oppress him. It is man's will which is eternally defective, eternally inadequate.'[34]

At the level of explicit statement, the novel emphasizes the role of Elsmere's example in encouraging in others an enthusiasm for unselfish purposes; but at the level of enacted experience, it is the animating effect of this 'diminution of self' on Elsmere's *own* will with which its first readers could imaginatively identify.

Mrs Ward's writing involved a sustained attempt to combine the legacy of Matthew Arnold, whose niece she was, with that of T. H. Green, to whose memory *Robert Elsmere* was dedicated (arguably, A. C. Bradley should be seen as attempting a similar synthesis at the level of criticism). In this particular novel, the balance appears to have been strongly tipped in Green's direction—indeed, it contains a very favourable portrait of him, thinly disguised as 'Mr Grey'—and this enables us to take a further step towards re-connecting these concerns with more familiar forms of political thought. The considerable reputation which Green's arcane teachings had achieved at the time of his death in 1882 suggested how the message about altruism could, when delivered in this specific context, be taken to yield a political conclusion. For, Green's moral philosophy was an exceptionally systematic expression of the sensibility which found something repugnant in even the hint of self-regarding actions; in his scheme, private goods simply had no standing. Faced with the pressing needs of others less fortunate than ourselves, sacrifice was strictly an obligation. As Green had memorably declared at one point:

[34] Mrs Humphry Ward, *Robert Elsmere* (London, 1889; 1st ed., 1888), 473, 572.

It is no time to enjoy the pleasures of eye and ear, of search for knowledge, of friendly intercourse, of applauded speech or writing, while the mass of men whom we call our brethren . . . are left without the chance, which only the help of others can gain for them, of making themselves in act what in possibility we believe them to be. . . . Interest in the problem of social deliverance . . . *forbids* a surrender to enjoyments which are not incidental to that work of deliverance.[35]

In this morally demanding theory, no legitimate conflict with the demands of the common good is even *possible*.[36] But those historians who have tried to see the 'rise of collectivism' or the dominance of ideas of 'duty' in the English administrative class in terms of the influence of Green's philosophy are guilty of that misplaced individualism in explanation that is an occupational hazard of a certain kind of history of ideas.[37] We need to approach the question from the other end and to recognize that Green theorized more fully and consistently than anyone else the assumptions of the anti-selfishness sensibility: it was because these assumptions were so widespread that his philosophy enjoyed the success it did, and not vice versa.

In Green, as in *Robert Elsmere*, we also see a feature that became more common in the 1880s and 1890s, namely the explicit concentration upon the duties of altruism to those below one in the social scale. Several of the forms of what was regarded at the time as 'collectivism' were in this respect very much the beneficiary of this emphasis on the duty of altruism.[38] This was, moreover, a commitment which enjoyed a long life among 'progressive' members of the educated class: the slightly patronizing tone and somewhat aggressive personal austerity that often accompanied it remained distinctive features of many of the Labour Party's intellectuals, for example, until at least the 1950s.[39] Turning in the other direction, it is

[35] T. H. Green, *Prolegomena to Ethics*, ed. A. C. Bradley (London, 1883), para. 270 (my emphasis).

[36] For a helpful analysis of Green's thought along these lines, see Melvin Richter, *The Politics of Conscience: T. H. Green and his Age* (London, 1964), 255–7.

[37] For some striking examples of claims of this sort, see A. B. Ulam, *The Philosophic Foundations of English Socialism* (Cambridge, Mass., 1951), and Craig Jenks, 'T. H. Green, the Oxford philosophy of duty, and the English middle class', *British Journal of Sociology*, 28 (1977), 481–97.

[38] This claim is more fully documented, though not in terms of the larger pattern of assumptions discussed here, in Stefan Collini, *Liberalism and Sociology: L. T. Hobhouse and Political Argument in England 1880–1914* (Cambridge, 1979), ch. I.

[39] The political consequences of this persistence are sharply characterized in Gareth Stedman Jones, *Languages of Class: Studies in English Working-Class History 1832–1982* (Cambridge, 1983), ch. v. Dennis and Halsey illustrate this continuity in

evident that the dominance of this moral sensibility is one of the things that distinguished Victorian liberalism from the Whiggism of the earlier part of the nineteenth century. Whiggism conducted its politics in a cooler and morally less demanding idiom, and its worldliness could tolerate more of a gap between public pronouncement and private conviction than was acceptable in 'the politics of conscience'.[40] As the rigid scaffolding of Duty stretched further across the edifice of ethical life, it became harder to present a whole range of public issues as, morally speaking, matters indifferent. Gladstone's career was conspicuously parasitic upon this development.

This emphasis on 'social duty' suggests an intriguing connection with the whole issue of the social and political consequences of the widespread loss of religious faith among mid- and late Victorian intellectuals. In dealing with this, historians have on the whole taken their cue from Beatrice Webb's classic formulation. 'I suggest', she wrote in her autobiography, 'it was during the middle decades of the nineteenth century that, in England, the impulse of self-subordinating service was transferred, consciously and overtly, from God to man.'[41] This obviously points towards a large truth, and the reference to 'subordinating' the self catches the authentic flavour of the idiom. Yet the conventional construal of this passage still leaves the psychological mechanism involved somewhat obscure. The suggestion is that, while the beneficiaries changed, the impulse to serve remained constant. Yet, other difficulties aside, this depends upon a play on the sense of 'service': in 'serving' God one was essentially obeying a superior, doing His will, whereas in 'serving' the poor and needy one was helping them, doing them good, often whether they liked it or not. At the risk of inflating a small point into a large claim, I think the argument of this chapter suggests a mild revision of Beatrice Webb's phrase. The constant, one could say, was the need for purposes—the kind of purposes which, when supported by the appropriate feelings, are sufficient to motivate to action. The representative Victorian intellectual, whether believer or sceptic, did

another way by beginning their celebration of 'the tradition of English ethical socialism' with an endorsement of its 'consistent principles of responsibility and altruism'; Norman Dennis and A. H. Halsey, *English Ethical Socialism: Thomas More to R. H. Tawney* (Oxford, 1988), 1.

[40] This contrast is illuminatingly explored in J.W. Burrow, *Whigs and Liberals: Continuity and Change in English Political Thought* (Oxford, 1988). See also below, Ch. 3 s. III.

[41] Beatrice Webb, *My Apprenticeship* (London, 1926; repr. Cambridge, 1979), 143.

not have a constant impulse to serve: he (or, here, she) had a constant anxiety about apathy and infirmity of the will. The prevailing moral scheme, when internalized, meant that 'selfish' purposes, whether religious or secular, could not sustain the necessary load. Thus, it was *because* altruistic aims were assumed to motivate that Victorian intellectuals found social work an antidote to doubt, and not that, already having the motivation, they 'transferred' its direction from God to man.

V

When dealing with so extensive a theme as the character and shape of one of the central elements in the moral sensibility of a period, or at least of the most articulate members of the educated class of that period, even a longish chapter can only gesture towards some of the possible ramifications of the topic. For example, it seems possible that the exaggerated hostility to selfishness helped to legitimate the claims of the professions in their great phase of expansion in the mid- and late nineteenth century (a topic discussed from a different perspective in Chapter 6 below). Historians of the professions in this period have remarked the implausibility of these bodies' claims to represent 'altruistic' motives or an ethic of 'service', and have often treated these claims as merely cynical.[42] But a more complex intelligibility is restored to these claims when they are seen as part of the pattern I have been describing. Similarly, one does not need to assume that ordinary commercial practice was as unmitigatedly 'selfish' as the propagandists for the professional ethic tendentiously described it; the caricature of all non-altruistic actions as 'selfish' was readily and perhaps inescapably available in the moral vocabulary of the period.

A more tantalizing connection suggests itself between these moral assumptions and the casual universalism of much Victorian political language. The logic of moral argument, to consider it in general terms for a moment, suggests that the 'thinner' the specification of

[42] See, for examples, Daniel Duman, 'The creation and diffusion of a professional ideology in nineteenth-century England', *Sociological Review*, 27 (1979), 113–38; Harold Perkin, *The Origins of Modern English Society 1780–1880* (London, 1969); id., *The Rise of Professional Society: England since 1880* (London, 1989). But for a more discerning treatment, see Thomas L. Haskell, 'Professionalism vs. capitalism: R. H. Tawney, Emile Durkheim, and C. S. Peirce on the problem of self-interest', in Haskell (ed.), *The Authority of Experts* (Bloomington, Ind., 1984).

the social texture of which individuals form a part, the stronger has to be the emphasis on the work of reason or something similarly universal, such as instinct, to supply adequate motives to action (in another idiom this might be described as the illusion of universalism typical of bourgeois society). Yet the more that Victorian intellectuals emphasized the subordination of intellect to emotion, the more they were faced with the difficulty of finding an adequately powerful motor to action in feelings for a generalized 'humanity'. As my analyses of Mill and Stephen suggested, this dilemma was not squarely faced largely because fundamental human feelings were construed as benign and harmonious: they thus operated as a covert universal. In this way, some of the demands and constraints of living in a particular, historically specific and geographically limited, community were lost sight of in the extension of the relevant 'others' to embrace universal humanity. Making explicit the claims of one's actual, limited (and hence exclusive) personal, local, or national attachments always threatened to call up more tribal or aggressive emotions. The rhetoric of late nineteenth-century imperialism, at once local in its attachments but still universal in its purported significance, offered to move the emotions more effectively, but, revealingly, most of the older generation of intellectuals recoiled from the belligerent and 'irrational' passions it aroused.

A whole variety of other points suggest themselves more briefly still. For example, this pattern perhaps throws some light on the ethical (as opposed to scientific) appeal of Comte to so many mid- and late Victorian intellectuals which can otherwise seem rather baffling: his 'elevating' conception of the centrality of altruism may have helped many to ignore the fatuity of so much of the actual programme of the Religion of Humanity. Consider, for example, the terms in which the young Sidgwick confided to his journal in 1861: 'The strongest conviction I have is a belief in what Comte calls "*altruisme*" . . . it may be that my philanthropy has its root in selfishness . . . but surely if this profound and enlightened selfishness be a vice, and I sometimes fear that it is, in me, no other regimen could be applied to it than that suggested by itself, namely devotion to society.'[43] Or, not altogether unconnected to this, there might be more to be said about the terms of the Victorian

[43] Sidgwick Papers, Trinity College Cambridge: Add. MS d.70. This interesting passage was not included in A. and E. M. S[idgwick], *Henry Sidgwick: A Memoir* (London, 1906).

idealization of a particular conception of womanhood. The ascription to women, especially in the roles of wives and mothers, of special gifts for 'feeling' and 'concern for others' fed into the sentimentalized rhapsodies to the role of feminine influence as an antidote to 'selfishness' that were particularly common in the autobiographies of some of the more self-critical literary and intellectual figures in the period. Or, finally, the connections could be explored between this moral scheme and the 'sociology' of the period, where theorists as otherwise diverse as Spencer, Kidd, and Hobhouse all concentrated on an increase of altruism as one of the chief indicators of social progress.[44]

One of the hazards of this kind of historical reconstruction of an aspect of the intellectual life of the past, especially where it involves drawing attention to implicit sensibilities and assumptions, is the possibility of so drastically re-describing its leading preoccupations that they would cease to be recognizable to those who, it is alleged, expressed them. One useful corroboration of the interpretation, however, may be provided by the response of the next generation. While the belligerent frenzy of Oedipal revolt may not be the best vantage-point from which to arrive at a balanced assessment of the whole pattern of views held by one's predecessors, it sometimes has the merit of starkly highlighting and isolating one particular aspect which might otherwise escape the attention of later and less impassioned observers. In the present instance, it is particularly striking how salient the mid-Victorian emphasis upon the duty of altruism and sacrifice to others was in the hostile portraits of the beliefs of that age penned by the first generations of its critics, in the reaction against 'Victorianism' at the very end of the nineteenth and beginning of the twentieth centuries.

A few selective quotations can never be more than illustrative in such cases, but the repetition of the same note may suggest a larger pattern. If, for example, mid-Victorian culture had in fact been marked by the unadorned commitment to rational egoism often ascribed to it by historians of political thought in particular, the nature of these reactions would have been imcomprehensible.

[44] For Spencer, see the discussion in J. D. Y. Peel, *Herbert Spencer: The Evolution of a Sociologist* (London, 1971), esp. 125, 139, 153; for Kidd, see D. P. Crook, *Benjamin Kidd: Portrait of a Social Darwinist* (Cambridge, 1984), esp. 57–66, 148–9, 255 (where Kidd is described as 'the apostle of altruism'); for Hobhouse, see Collini, *Liberalism and Sociology*, esp. 173–4, 183–4.

Shaw's *Quintessence of Ibsenism* would be one obvious source of evidence for the sense that the demands of an altruism-centred morality had become oppressive. 'The lesson of the plays', in this provocative account, was that 'the real slavery of today is slavery to ideals of goodness'.[45] As Shaw put it later in the preface to his ironically entitled *Three Plays for Puritans*, the self-assertive creed of what he called 'Diabolonian ethics' had had a particularly hard time of it in the Victorian period. 'All seemed lost when suddenly the cause found its dramatist in Ibsen, the first leader who really dragged duty, unselfishness, idealism, sacrifice, and the rest of the anti-diabolic scheme to the bar at which it had indicted so many excellent Diabolonians.'[46] Much of the impact of Wilde's paradoxes depended upon hitting the same target—what he called 'the sickly cant about Duty' and that 'sordid necessity of living for others'.[47]

Above all, the vogue for Nietzsche in England at the turn of the century related directly to this response. As one observer remarked at the time: 'The present furore over Nietzsche' should be seen as 'simply a part of the reaction against "psychological" and "romantic" literature and against foolish "altruism" and foolish "philanthropy"'.[48] It is interesting that this remark not only linked altruism with 'philanthropy', but also saw these as in turn related to a certain sort of literature. A similar, if more hostilely expressed, observation lay behind the characterization by Nietzsche's translator in the 1890s of why an English audience might be in need of works like *The Genealogy of Morals*: 'By intoxicating themselves with phrases like altruism, charity, social justice, equality before the law, freedom and right to labour and happiness, the majority of English-speaking people do not feel that they live in a world in which these things are by no means self-evident or fundamental to society.'[49] Nietzsche himself, of course, started from radically different premisses: 'An "altruistic" morality, a morality under which egoism *languishes*—is under all circumstances a bad sign . . . To choose what is harmful to *oneself*, to be *attracted* by "disinterested" motives, almost constitutes

45 George Bernard Shaw, *The Quintessence of Ibsenism* (London 1891; repr. 1913), 181.

46 Quoted in David S. Thatcher, *Nietzsche in England 1890–1914* (Toronto, 1970), 177.

47 Oscar Wilde, *The Soul of Man under Socialism* (1891), repr. in *The Artist as Critic: Critical Writings of Oscar Wilde*, ed. Richard Ellmann (New York, 1970), 255.

48 W. Caldwell, 'Schopenhauer and present tendencies', *New World*, 9 (1900), 643.

49 A. Tille, quoted in Thatcher, *Nietzsche in England*, 26.

the formula for *décadence*.' And elsewhere: 'Bad conscience, the desire for self-mortification, is the wellspring of all altruistic values.'[50] Not surprisingly, the dominant response to Nietzsche's ideas in late-Victorian England mixed hostility and incomprehension in almost equal parts.

As that response suggests, however, such outspoken critics of these moral assumptions were still very much minority voices. Many of the generation who were formed by the 'culture of altruism' that particularly flourished between the 1850s and the 1880s retained a commitment to these ideals through later decades. It is revealing, for example to see the terms in which L. T. Hobhouse reflected, in 1915 when he was in his fifties, on recent cultural changes. Reacting against the 'immoralism' of early Modernism in the arts, he looked back nostalgically to George Eliot, the best of whose novels, he claimed, provided a 'justification for all that it was then usual to sum up in the word altruism'. The same cluster of values is evident in his remark thirteen years later: 'The unmitigated selfishness with which Shaw has indoctrinated his generation isn't going to make them happier. It's probably going to lead to the final world catastrophe which a generation bent on pleasure will never take the trouble to avert.'[51] Even allowing for Hobhouse's characteristic apocalyptic moodiness, his making 'selfishness' the chief charge, and then exaggerating it to being 'bent on pleasure', indicates the persistence of an older moral sensibility into the less friendly atmosphere of the 1920s.

Possible explanations of the deep hold of these moral assumptions about selfishness and altruism during this period would have to be explored in other ways (and by other authors), but from the standpoint of late twentieth-century knowingness it is hard not to hypothesize about the ways it may have been related to a kind of distancing of the sexual instincts. Something of the kind may be implicit in Freud's remark that altruism is to be contrasted not just with egoism, in terms of which person's advantage the actions are directed to securing, but more revealingly with *all* attempts at 'libidinal object-cathexis': altruism 'is distinguished . . . by the absence of longings for sexual satisfaction'.[52] Comte, when coining the

[50] Friedrich Nietzsche, *Twilight of the Idols* (1889) (Eng. trans., Harmondsworth, 1968), 87; *On the Genealogy of Morals* (1887) (Eng. trans., New York, 1956), 221.

[51] Quoted in Collini, *Liberalism and Sociology*, 246, 251.

[52] Sigmund Freud, *Introductory Lectures on Psychoanalysis* (1917) (Eng. trans., Harmondsworth, 1973), 466–7.

term '*altruisme*', had perhaps been alive to this negative connection, since he 'never ceased to deplore the sexual instincts as the most disturbing of the egoistic propensities, "the least capable of being usefully transformed", one of "the chief imperfections of human existence"'.[53] Recent work may have fleshed out—the verb seems inescapable—our picture of the varieties of sexual expression in nineteenth-century societies, but in the aspects of the moral sensibility discussed here one can surely still discern the influence of what might be called (adapting a phrase of Matthew Arnold's) the Victorian 'quarrel with the body and its desires'.[54] And, looking in a different direction, we must also allow that there was an element of a more general truth in T. S. Eliot's waspish jibe at his great predecessor: 'Like many people the vanishing of whose religious faith has left behind only habits, [Arnold] placed an exaggerated emphasis on morals. Such people often confuse morals with their own good habits, the result of a sensible upbringing, prudence, and the absence of any very powerful temptation.'[55]

For a final, and even more general, concluding reflection one may turn to yet another remark by Nietzsche, the incomparable diagnostician of nineteenth-century moral thought. It is not necessary to endorse his sweeping dismissal of modern moral *décadence*, or his bitter denunciation of Christianity as its source, to recognize the truth of his perception that Victorian moralists were too prone to take the moral harmony posited in the dominant culture of their time as a universal ethical condition. 'If the English really do believe they know, of their own accord, "intuitively", what is good and evil; if they consequently think they no longer have need of Christianity as a guarantee of morality; that is merely the *consequence* of the ascendancy of Christian evaluation and an expression of the *strength* and *depth* of this ascendancy: so that the origin of English morality has been forgotten, so that the highly conditional nature of its right to exist is no longer felt. For the Englishman morality is not yet a problem . . .'[56]

[53] Wright, *Religion of Humanity*, 31–2.

[54] *Culture and Anarchy* (1869), in *The Complete Prose Works of Matthew Arnold*, ed. R. H. Super, 11 vols. (Ann Arbor, Mich., 1960–77), 165. For recent work on 19th-century sexuality, see the comprehensive account in Peter Gay, *The Bourgeois Experience: Victoria to Freud*, vols. i and ii (New York, 1984, 1986).

[55] T. S. Eliot, *The Use of Poetry and the Use of Criticism: Studies in the Relation of Criticism to Poetry in England* (London, 1933), 114. We are invited to make what we will of the phrase Eliot appended to this harsh judgement: 'But I do not speak of Arnold or of any particular person, for only God knows.'

[56] *Twilight of the Idols*, 70.

3

The Idea of Character
Private Habits and Public Virtues

I

When in the summer of 1902 Helen Bosanquet published a book called *The Strength of the People*, she sent a copy to Alfred Marshall. On the face of it, this might seem a rather unpromising thing to have done. Mrs Bosanquet, an active exponent of the Charity Organization Society's 'casework' approach to social problems, had frequently expressed her dissatisfaction with what she regarded as the misleading abstractions of orthodox economics, and in her book she had even ventured a direct criticism of a point in Marshall's *Principles*.[1] Marshall, then Professor of Political Economy at Cambridge and at the peak of his reputation as the most authoritative exponent of neo-classical economics in Britain, was, to say the least, sensitive to criticism, and he had, moreover, publicly taken issue with the COS on several previous occasions. But perhaps Mrs Bosanquet knew what she was about after all. In her book she had taken her text from the early nineteenth-century Evangelical Thomas Chalmers on the way in which character determines circumstances rather than vice versa, and, as the historian of the COS justly remarks, her book 'is a long sermon on the importance of character in making one family rich and another poor'.[2] It was a theme which she and her husband, the Idealist philosopher Bernard Bosanquet, had addressed in a series of books and essays published in the preceding decade, where they had argued that 'characters or dispositions react altogether differently to circumstances that are

[1] Helen Bosanquet, *The Strength of the People: A Study in Social Economics* (London, 1902), iv, 120, 129.

[2] C. L. Mowat, *The Charity Organisation Society 1869–1913: Its Ideas and Work* (London, 1961), 125.

quantitatively and materially the same', and thus 'the skilled observer becomes aware that circumstance is modifiable by character, and, so far as circumstance is a name for human action, by character alone'.[3]

Although Marshall can hardly have welcomed the general strictures on economics, he was able to reassure Mrs Bosanquet that 'in the main' he agreed with her: 'I have always held', he wrote to her, 'that poverty and pain, disease and death are evils of greatly less importance than they appear, except in so far as they lead to weakness of life and character.'[4] It may now seem hard not to detect a tone of wilful moralism here: one would scarcely have to be an abandoned materialist to feel that the evil of death, in particular, was being somewhat underrated by this remark. But we can confidently exonerate Marshall from any charge of having disingenuously adopted the language of his correspondent just for the occasion. For in both his theoretical work and in his more direct contributions to the economic and political debates of the previous twenty-five years he had displayed a pervasive concern with the role of character under modern industrial conditions. What, he had declared in the opening pages of the *Principles*, made economics more than just 'a study of wealth', what made it 'part of the study of man', was that it dealt with the strongest of the forces shaping 'man's character', and elsewhere he insisted it was an integral part of the economist's task to enquire 'whether the desires which prevail are such as will help to build up a strong and righteous character'. Thus, 'the ultimate aim' of economic studies was to understand 'the progress of man's nature', and as Marshall told the story of that progress so far, its highest point had been reached in the development of the English character, which exhibited 'more self-reliant habits, more forethought, more deliberateness and free choice', than any of its historical rivals.[5] When, in his correspondence with Mrs Bosanquet, Marshall expressed his anxiety about those forms of state action

[3] Bernard Bosanquet (ed.), *Aspects of the Social Problem, by Various Writers* (London, 1895), vii–viii; iv. See also Bernard Bosanquet, *The Civilisation of Christendom and Other Studies* (London, 1893).

[4] The correspondence is reprinted in the preface to the 2nd edition of *Strength of the People* (1903), quotation at viii.

[5] Alfred Marshall, *The Principles of Economics*, 9th (variorum) edn., with annotations by C. W. Guillebaud, 2 vols. (London, 1961; 1st edn. 1890), i. 1, 723–5, 740–4; ii. 17. For fuller discussion of Marshall's views on the scope of economics, see Stefan Collini, Donald Winch, and John Burrow, *That Noble Science of Politics: A Study in Nineteenth-Century Intellectual History* (Cambridge, 1983), 309–37.

which 'risk injury to self-reliance and wholesome independence', he balanced this with a reference to those surroundings which could themselves 'undermine the springs of strength and independence of character'; but the larger concern, the concern to understand how 'the forces of human character' provided the key to 'the reasoned history of man', remained constant.[6]

In seeking to understand this exchange, we shall not, I think, get very far if we explain away our two correspondents' affirmation of the crucial importance of character simply as the coincidence of peculiarly personal preoccupations, and yet it is hard to know quite where to turn for further enlightenment. Such limited notice as historians have taken of the role of character in Victorian political argument has tended to suggest that it should be understood as an ideological device for imposing middle-class values upon a potentially disruptive working class.[7] Whatever truth this description may contain, it surely cannot be very near to the whole truth. Socialists, too, justified their preferred economic arrangements on the grounds that they would produce 'a higher type of character', and even members of the Fabian Society could be found arguing that 'the end of the State . . . is, in fact, the development of character'.[8] Indeed, the stated 'Object' of the Fellowship of the New Life out of which the Fabian Society had grown in 1883 was 'The cultivation of a perfect character in each and all'.[9] As one Socialist commentator put it in the 1890s: 'Today the key word . . . in economics is "character". . . . [The reason] why individualist economists fear socialism is that they believe it will deteriorate character, and the reason why socialist economists seek socialism is their belief that under individualism character is deteriorating.'[10] Moreover, although invocations of the ideal of character undeniably possessed a special polemical force in

[6] *Strength of the People* (2nd edn.), p. xi; Alfred Marshall, 'The present position of economics' (1885), repr. in J. M. Keynes (ed.), *Memorials of Alfred Marshall* (London, 1925), quotation at 299–300.

[7] For the most sophisticated discussion along these lines, see Gareth Stedman Jones, *Outcast London: A Study in the Relationship between Classes in Victorian Society* (Oxford, 1971), part III.

[8] W. P. D. Bliss (ed.), *The Encyclopaedia of Social Reform* (London, 1898), 1271; Sidney Ball, 'The Socialist ideal', *Economic Review*, 9 (1899), 437. Although Ball, founder of the Oxford branch of the Fabian Society, was not by this date a typical Fabian, his testimony is particularly relevant here because he had taken issue with the Bosanquets' 1895 volume: see esp. his 'The moral aspects of Socialism', *International Journal of Ethics*, 6 (1896), 291–322.

[9] Edward R. Pease, *The History of the Fabian Society* (London, 1916), 32.

[10] *Encyclopaedia of Social Reform*, 895.

the arguments about the role of the state which dominated political debate in the late nineteenth century, it would be a mistake not to recognize the privileged place occupied by that ideal in the political thought of the previous half-century. Even if we confine ourselves to the established canon of Victorian liberal political theorists, we find Spencer urging that 'the end which the statesman should keep in view as higher than all other ends is the formation of character', or Mill that 'the problem of character is the determining issue in the question of government', or Green, in typically more tortured prose, that the state must secure those 'powers . . . necessary to the fulfilment of man's vocation as a moral being, to an effectual self-devotion to the work of developing the perfect character in himself and others'.[11]

Naturally, each of these authors, as well as the many others one could cite to the same purpose, was deploying the term to suit his own requirements, but *that* only raises the larger question. The very fact that these politically and theoretically diverse declarations should take this common form points to the extraordinary status and centrality of the cluster of assumptions and values which the term denoted. It would, of course, be naïve to assume that it always involved an appeal to exactly the same values or to an identical ideal of human life: on this subject, John Stuart Mill's writings are most vulnerable to having representative status thrust upon them, so we would do well to remember that his famous plea for individuality was couched as a *protest* against what he called 'the pinched and hidebound type of character' which he took to be enjoying an insidious popularity in the moral reflection of the time.[12] But such differences may be taken as providing further testimony to the standing of the category itself: it represented a prize worth fighting for. In other words, I am suggesting that the ideal of character, in a sense of the term that I shall analyse in this chapter, enjoyed a prominence in the political thought of the Victorian period that it had apparently not known before and that it has, arguably, not experienced since. Here I shall explore the ramifications of that centrality and enquire into the psychological and cultural assump-

[11] Herbert Spencer, *The Principles of Ethics*, 2 vols. (London, 1893), ii. 251; Mill as paraphrased in L. T. Hobhouse, *Liberalism* (London, 1911; repr. New. York, 1964), 62; T. H. Green, *Lectures on the Principles of Political Obligation*, with preface by Bernard Bosanquet (London, 1895), para. 21.

[12] John Stuart Mill, *On Liberty* (1859), *The Collected Works of John Stuart Mill*, ed. John M. Robson, 31 vols. (Toronto and London, 1965–91) (hereafter *CW*), xviii. 265.

tions which conferred such authority on the moral ambitions it represented. This involves attending once again to some of the ways in which this concentration on the political importance of forming character accorded with various non-political aspects of Victorian sensibility and belief, and of considering how these correspondences affected some of the more general political preoccupations of the period.

II

As a prelude to attempting to isolate the distinctiveness of this subject, we should acknowledge that there is presumably some, albeit often implicit, conception of human nature in any body of professedly systematic political thinking, and in several cases we can find an explicit concern with the ways in which the moral formation of citizens may be effected by the political arrangements and practices of their communities. The example of ancient Sparta provided an unfailing source of reflection for those who entertained the most ambitious aspirations of this kind, while a more restrained and less specific commitment to fostering the moral qualities appropriate to a citizen in a free state was a constitutive element in the long tradition of civic republicanism which derived from Aristotle, was renewed by Machiavelli, and which featured significantly in European, and particularly Anglo-American, political thinking down to at least the end of the eighteenth century.[13] It is not so much that, by contrast to such traditions, the Victorian concentration on character introduced a radically new conceptual element, as that it gave a new form to an old concern, and did so in a way that traded upon certain distinctive nineteenth-century cultural resonances. Tom Brown, though he had to learn to defend himself, was not trained to be a member of a landholding militia, and Samuel Smiles, though Shaw called him 'that modern Plutarch', portrayed other qualities than those needed to keep a republic from succumbing to the temptations of luxury.

Part of the elusiveness of this subject arises from the fact that the dominant Victorian sense of the term 'character' embraced what we may for expository purposes distinguish as a descriptive and an

[13] E. D. Rawson, *The Spartan Tradition in European Thought* (Oxford, 1969); J. G. A. Pocock, *The Machiavellian Moment: Florentine Political Thought and the Atlantic Republican Tradition* (Princeton, N. J., 1975).

evaluative element.[14] The nineteenth-century compilers of the *OED* attempted to capture this complexity by discriminating two senses of the term. In the first, it was said to mean 'the sum of the mental and moral qualities which distinguish an individual or race viewed as a homogeneous whole; the individuality impressed by nature and habit on man or nation; mental or moral constitution.' This definition refers us to an individual's settled dispositions (and suggests something about their formation to which I shall return) but does not in itself involve a judgement on the goodness or otherwise of these dispositions. The definition of the second sense, however, suggests just this evaluative use of the term when it refers to 'moral qualities strongly developed or strikingly displayed'. There is, of course, a potential ambiguity here, in that the term 'moral' itself can be used in two different senses: in the more inclusive, neutral sense the vices as well as the virtues are classified as moral qualities, while in the narrower affirmative sense 'moral' qualities are confined to those which meet with ethical approval, and there can be no doubt that 'character' was used to refer to the possession of certain highly valued moral qualities in just this way. Those familiar secular homilies calling for 'the development of character' were, after all, doing more than recommending merely that a man (rarely a woman, for whom the public ideal was in many ways different) get on with the business of establishing his identity whatever it was.

At the same time, the cogency of these recommendations depended upon the very large causal role the Victorians assigned to character in the purely descriptive sense. For it was, notoriously, the favoured explanatory element in the analysis of different human fates, just as, the *OED* definition reminds us, national character enjoyed a special status in accounting for the variety of historical outcomes on a larger scale. In the classic late nineteenth-century discussion of the most celebrated literary representation of human fate, A. C. Bradley's *Shakespearean Tragedy*, it is taken for granted that tragedy follows from the deeds of men 'and that the main source of these deeds is character'. Indeed, Bradley praised Shakespeare for not allowing extraneous or accidental elements to weaken 'the sense of the causal connection of character, deed, and catastrophe', and he

[14] Cf. Anthony Quinton's similar point about the two 20th-century senses of having a 'personality', though there was perhaps no 19th-century equivalent to 'the alleged usage of Hollywood press agents . . . "this girl has a terrific personality" being a euphemistic formula for conveying the fact that she had large and well-shaped breasts'; *Thoughts and Thinkers* (London, 1982), 21–2.

clearly found a congenial moral vision at work in the way that 'the concentration of interest, in the greater plays, on the inward struggle emphasizes that [the action] is essentially the expression of character'.[15]

The transition from this descriptive or explanatory sense to the evaluative sense—or, better, the blurring of the distinction between them—was facilitated by the assumption that the possession of settled dispositions indicated a certain habit of restraining one's impulses. The contrast was with behaviour which was random, impulsive, feckless; and where the impulses were identified, as they so often were, with the 'lower self' (conceived as purely appetitive and hence selfish), then a positive connotation was conferred on the habit of restraint itself. A residue of this surfaces explicitly in the definition of 'character' given in the self-consciously 'value-free' language of social science at the end of this period:

> An enduring psychophysical disposition to inhibit instinctive tendencies in accordance with regulative principles. . . . Some other phrase, such as 'prepotent impulses' or 'firmly ingrained habits' may be substituted for 'instinctive tendencies', but the implication remains that the more resistance there is to overcome in order to achieve a desirable end, the more character is to be ascribed to the successfully inhibiting individual.[16]

Where cultural attitudes accord a higher standing, or even priority, to the gratification of impulse, this movement between the two senses is bound to appear more strained or contrived. One may be in danger of labouring the obvious here, but it would certainly be a more serious failing to neglect the particularly strong hold exercised over the moral and political thought of the period by the Manichaean view of the self.

The relations between habit and the will premissed by the local version of this view are particularly crucial for my theme. A long tradition of political theorists had pondered the paradoxes of trying to contrive that citizens should pursue aims which were only of value if pursued voluntarily. Speaking very generally, we may say that the nineteenth century's distinctive preoccupation with the shaping

[15] A. C. Bradley, *Shakespearean Tragedy* (London, 1965; 1st edn., 1904), 7, 9, 13. (The book was based on lectures Bradley had been giving for some years previously.) For a discussion of Bradley's book which concentrates on its relations with the Idealist moral philosophy of the period, see G. K. Hunter, *Dramatic Identities and Cultural Traditions: Studies in Shakespeare and his Contemporaries* (Liverpool, 1978), 270–85.

[16] *The Encyclopaedia of the Social Sciences* (New York, 1930), 335.

power of time, with the slow, sedimentary processes of development, be it of geological layers or of linguistic forms or of legal customs, produced an intensified awareness of the role of habit. This could, of course, be taken in a determinist direction, as several notable nineteenth-century social theorists took it. But when married to the unreflective Kantianism of Victorian moral commonplaces,[17] it issued in a concern with the long-term determinants of the will which particularly took the form of anxiety about the insidiously corrosive power of habit. The note of anxiety is well caught in this passage from William James cited by Mrs Bosanquet:

> The hell to be endured hereafter, of which theology tells, is no worse than the hell we make for ourselves in this world by habitually fashioning our characters in the wrong way. Could the young but realise how soon they will become mere walking bundles of habits, they would give more heed to their conduct while in the plastic state. We are spinning our own fates, good or evil, and never to be undone. Every smallest stroke of virtue or of vice leaves its never-so-little scar.[18]

If occasionally Victorian political commentators seem to be concerned with what look like the implausibly distant consequences of proposed measures, we must remember the prevalence of a psychological model that predisposed discussion towards indirect effects and long-term results. What gave added force to this sort of anxiety about cumulative damage to an individual's moral psychology was the suggestion that it might have a physiological basis. Those mid-Victorian psychologists and physiologists who obtained a wide non-professional readership, such as Bain, Spencer, Carpenter, and Maudsley, all toyed with the notion that habit could modify or leave a deposit in the nervous system itself. This needs to be seen in the context of that more general appeal of a diluted Lamarckianism to a scientifically semi-educated audience, which nurtured a fascination with the idea that in properly exercising the muscles of the will the individual might be acquiring a new capacity that could operate instinctively on future occasions and, through the related Lamarckian belief in the inheritance of acquired characteristics, could determine the behaviour of future generations. And even where no physiological basis for this was fully elaborated, as for the most part it was not, this concern still shifted the analytical focus away from—

[17] See above, Ch. 2, pp. 63–4.

[18] William James, *The Principles of Psychology*, 2 vols. (London, 1890), i. 127; cited in Bosanquet, *Strength of the People*, 32–3.

perhaps 'behind' is the appropriate preposition—the situation in which the individual found himself in the present. As Maudsley put it in 1867, with the air of one summarizing the current state of scientific knowledge on the subject: 'The strong or well-formed character which a well-fashioned will implies is the result of good training applied to a well-constituted original nature; and the character is not directly determined by the will, but in any particular act determines the will.'[19]

There was clearly an unresolved tension between voluntarism and determinism in all this. It was an unclarity which surfaced most famously in John Stuart Mill's repudiation of the Owenite doctrine that 'our characters are made *for* us, not *by* us.' Mill, anxious to be free of what he saw as the fatalistic implications of this, argued that man's character is not simply formed by *external* circumstances (including therein the influence of other people), for 'his own desire to mould it in a particular way is one of those circumstances'. Subsequent critics have always seen a vicious regress here, in that the very desire to mould our own character may itself be regarded as a product of circumstances beyond our control, and so on. I do not wish to suggest that Mill makes a satisfactory escape from this regress; but it is revealing that he accepts, and indeed insists upon, the premiss that 'our actions follow from our characters', and that he perpetuates the basic ambiguity. For he proceeds by denying that other people have been directly able to mould our character: 'They made us what they did make us, by willing not the end but the requisite means; and we, when our habits are not too inveterate, can, by similarly willing the requisite means, make ourselves different.'[20] Mill is not, therefore, challenging determinism by asserting our freedom at any given moment to act differently from the way we in fact choose to act; he accepts, in other words, that character determines the will. He also accepts that character can only be shaped indirectly. His sticking-point is that the individual's own desire to be different must be seen as an effective force in this shaping process. But it is so, note, only when (in a phrase which Mill did not subject to further analysis) his 'habits are not too inveterate.' The spectre of habit as a prison from which there is no escape still

[19] Quoted in Bruce Haley, *The Healthy Body and Victorian Culture* (Cambridge, Mass., 1978), 44; cf. Alexander Bain, *The Study of Character* (London, 1861), esp. ch.7.

[20] John Stuart Mill, *A System of Logic* (1843), *CW*, viii. 840–1.

haunts the discussion. And this basic unclarity constantly cropped up in the political uses of the language of character. On the one hand, each individual is regarded as the ultimate author of his own fate: overwhelmingly unfavourable social circumstances are an inadmissible plea. On the other hand, political proposals are constantly challenged on the grounds that they will weaken character, by presenting temptations which the individuals in question will be *unable* to resist, and thereby warping the habits that will ineluctably govern their actions in the future.

There is no great obscurity about the basic core of qualities invoked by the evaluative sense of character: self-restraint, perseverance, strenuous effort, courage in the face of adversity. What is perhaps less obvious is the intimate dependence on a prior notion of duty. Samuel Smiles is a witness whom it would be unthinkable not to call at this point, if only because he published one book called *Duty* and another called *Character* and it is more or less impossible to tell without looking at the title-page which is which. Both books tirelessly urge that 'the abiding sense of duty is the very crown of character', and whereas Smiles's earlier work had come in for some criticism on the grounds that it might seem to have been encouraging the pursuit of merely material gain, these later books were praised for inculcating 'that honest and upright performance of individual duty which is the glory of character'.[21] What all this indicated, I would suggest, was that the constant invocations of the virtues of character in fact presupposed an agreed moral code.[22] The fear was not moral relativism but weakness of will. For the most part it was not even suggested that the dictates of conscience were obscure or internally inconsistent, but rather that the required moral effort might not be

[21] Samuel Smiles, *Character* (London, 1871), 189; Kenneth Fielden, 'Samuel Smiles and self-help', *Victorian Studies*, 12 (1968), 165. *Duty* was published in 1880. Even in *Self-Help*, published in 1859, Smiles had insisted that 'elevation of character' was more important than mere 'getting-on'.

[22] Cf. the remark of a historian of 19th-century America, which he describes as a 'culture of character': 'It is significant in this context to call attention to all the other key words most often associated with the concept of character. A review of over two hundred such items reveals the words most frequently related to the notion of character: citizenship, duty, democracy, work, building, golden deeds, outdoor life, conquest, honor, reputation, morals, manners, integrity, and above all manhood. The stress was clearly moral and the interest was almost always in some sort of higher moral law. The most popular quotation—it appeared in dozens of works—was Emerson's definition of character: "Moral order through the medium of individual nature".' Warren I. Susman, '"Personality" and the making of twentieth-century culture', in John Higham and Paul K. Conkin (eds.), *New Directions in American Intellectual History* (Baltimore, 1979), 214.

forthcoming were the will once allowed to fall into disrepair. Smiles's favourite hortatory device was the exemplary life, and his books celebrate a succession of worthies with the manners of an ironmaster and the morals of the corps. A particularly monotonous feature of his stylized portraits was the emphasis upon his subjects' unselfishness and even altruism, a reminder that the accepted understanding of character in this period was more complex than the stereotype of the resolutely self-interested or callously indifferent figure of subsequent criticism. Here we have again that moral tissue that was assumed to provide the flesh on the otherwise abrasively bare skeleton of the Individualist idea of the state (a topic I return to below in Chapter 5).

Of course, the somewhat narrow vision of human potential displayed in such literature, and in much else written at the same level, was not without its critics. I have already remarked how Mill's famous essay *On Liberty* was a protest against that 'pinched and hidebound type of human character' which he saw being promoted in the chapels and meeting-houses of provincial England, and this in turn reminds us of Arnold's no less celebrated denunciation of a narrow Hebraism in the name of a Goethian ideal of classical harmony and roundedness. But although both Arnold and Mill looked to aspects of German Romanticism for their inspiration here, the subtle contrasts between their ideals suggest different ways in which the insufficiencies of the ideal of character could be insisted upon by some of the more discriminating mid-Victorian minds. Both were, in effect, adapting a notion of *Bildung* for the purpose of criticizing the shortcomings of their countrymen, but they responded to different strains in that complex notion. For Arnold, it was the unrecognized narrowness and idiosyncrasy, the adversarial small-mindedness, of contemporary political and religious attitudes which required the antidote of 'culture'. To his critical eye, the glorification of character was, above all, one-sided: it over-valued 'self-conquest' and 'right conduct', elevating the psychological type of Hebraism into a sufficient human life. But his classically inspired vision tended to supply a corrective which could, in its turn, be seen as one-sided, leading him, as I have observed elsewhere, 'to overvalue balance, achieved form, and the perfect proportion of the finished object, and to undervalue the untidy but possibly creative experience of searching and struggling'.[23] In Arnold's plea for the

[23] Stefan Collini, *Arnold* (Oxford, 1988), 92.

'harmonious expansion of all the powers which make the beauty and worth of human nature', it is just this yearning for a Goethian serenity that obscures from him the possible tensions between the aspirations to harmony and to development in this ideal.[24]

Interestingly, just as he was meditating the composition of *On Liberty* Mill confided to his diary (though did not publish) an observation which very sharply expressed his dissatisfaction with this ideal, indicating how he came at the deficiencies of character-talk from, as it were, the other side.

> To me it seems that nothing can be so alien and (to coin a word) antipathetic to the modern mind as Goethe's ideal of life. He wished life itself, and the nature of every cultivated individual in it, to be rounded off and made symmetrical like a Greek temple or a Greek drama. . . . Not symmetry, but bold, free expansion in all directions is demanded by the needs of modern life and the instincts of the modern mind. Great and strong and varied faculties are more wanted than faculties well proportioned to one another.[25]

Fearing social uniformity, Mill was uneasy with the element of 'self-abnegation' (Arnold's 'self-conquest') fostered by the popular ideal of character, yet, as I have already suggested, he profoundly shared many of the beliefs upon which that ideal rested. Faced with 'the cramped and dwarfed' models of human excellence promoted by 'Christian self-denial', Mill recommended 'experiments in living' and the deliberate expansion of experience in terms that could appear alien to the moral assumptions built into character, even though, like Arnold, he in fact shared those assumptions more thoroughly than his reputation as a critic of Victorian moralism might suggest. He invoked the Humboldtian ideal of 'human development in its richest diversity', without ever seeming to fear that this might pose a threat to 'the better development of the social part of [the individual's] nature' which he simultaneously held up as the goal.[26] For my purposes, it is particularly revealing that the feature of *On Liberty* to which contemporary critics took strongest exception was its perceived glorification of individual caprice and selfish indulgence at the expense of the stern demands of duty which were,

[24] Matthew Arnold, *Culture and Anarchy* (1869), in *The Complete Prose Works of Matthew Arnold*, ed. R. H. Super, 11 vols. (Ann Arbor, Mich., 1960–77), v. 94. For further discussion of this ideal, see Collini, *Arnold*, ch. 5.

[25] John Stuart Mill, diary entry 6 Feb. 1854; *CW*, xxvii. 651.

[26] Mill, *On Liberty*, *CW*, xviii. 261, 266. The quoted passage from Humboldt served, of course, as the epigraph for the book (215).

it was indignantly affirmed, 'the true school of character'.[27] And this serves to underline the very considerable distance between the dominant Victorian ideal of character and notions of *Bildung* to which it may at first seem comparable. *Bildung*, at least in its purest Romantic forms, suggests an openness to experience, a cultivation of the subjective response, an elevation of the aesthetic, and an exploratory attitude towards one's own individuality and potential, all of which carry a different, perhaps more self-indulgent, certainly more private, message and political bearing. Dilettantism may, it has been suggested, be 'a possible parody of *Bildung*',[28] but it is clearly the very antithesis of character.

John Morley, Mill's representative on earth, voiced a rather different kind of dissatisfaction with the coerciveness of popular character-talk when advancing the case for systematic and clear-sighted reasoning—essentially agnosticism and radical Liberalism in parade uniform—as a necessary form of mental hygiene. He began with a concession: 'Character is doubtless of far more importance than mere intellectual opinion.' Suitably glossed, this was an assertion Morley could genuinely endorse, yet the 'doubtless' here betrays, perhaps, a certain impatience with a too-constantly reiterated commonplace. Certainly, 'persons of weak purpose or low motives'—an interesting epitome of the antithesis of character—could not be redeemed by mere intellectual brilliance, 'yet it is well to remember the very obvious truth that opinions are at least an extremely important part of character'. In *On Compromise* Morley acknowledged that there were times when it might be injudicious, especially for the 'advanced' politician, to exhibit all his convictions to public gaze, but even in those cases the habit of thinking them through was valuable as leading him to 'acquire a commanding grasp of principles.' 'And a commanding grasp of principles, whether they are public or not, is at the very root of coherency of character.'[29] This is the rationalist politician's version of the critique of contemporary Hebraism. Morley was evidently tired of having the unintellectual 'sound man' held up as the model public figure. Yet at the same time, he was unwilling simply to cede all claim to the crucial term:

[27] See J. C. Rees, *Mill and his Early Critics* (Leicester, 1956), now reprinted in John C. Rees, *John Stuart Mill's 'On Liberty'*, ed. G. L. Williams (Oxford, 1985).

[28] See 'Editor's introduction' to Wilhelm von Humboldt, *The Limits of State Action*, ed. J. W. Burrow (Cambridge, 1969), p. xxii.

[29] John Morley, *On Compromise* (London, 1886; 1st edn. 1874), 120–1.

his very attempt at redefinition was, as it always is, testimony to the deep centrality of the contested notion in the thought of the period.

By the beginning of the twentieth century, imaginative literature furnishes hints of the change in sensibility which would eventually displace this preoccupation even from the public language of political thought. In his self-consciously iconoclastic novel *The New Machiavelli*, published in book form in 1911, H. G. Wells put several speeches in the mouth of Richard Remington, his fictional *alter ego*, railing against 'the cant about character'. Himself the embodiment of the briefly fashionable 'tough-minded' dedication to efficiency and to government by the 'New Samurai', trained in modern science, Remington is impatient with the shibboleths of a Victorian moralism now coming to seem dated. These pieties are upheld in the novel by Dayton, an unreconstructed Individualist who still guards the flame of Gladstonian Liberalism. Remington mocks these values at every opportunity: 'Just to exasperate Dayton further, I put in a plea for gifts as against character in educational, artistic, and legislative work. "Good teaching", I said, "is better than good conduct. We are becoming idiotic about character."' Searching for a suitably scornful simile, he compares Britain to a brontosaurus: '"It sacrifices intellect to character; its backbone, that is to say—especially in the visceral region—is bigger than its cranium."'[30] Perceptive contemporaries could recognize the force of Wells's criticism even if they were made uncomfortable by it, and once the Owl of Minerva takes wing in these matters, in however unlikely a form, the vultures of intellectual history cannot be far behind.

III

Tracing the aetiology of this idea of character and the cluster of values it embraced, and, what might be of greater interest, charting the ways in which concepts long available came to acquire a new prominence and resonance, partly in response to the rise of new

[30] H. G. Wells, *The New Machiavelli* (Harmondsworth, 1970; 1st edn. London, 1911), 268, 259, 266. The novel enjoyed a certain *succès de scandale*, with its easily recognizable portrayals of leading political figures such as Balfour and the Webbs as well as its implicit justification of Wells's own affair with Amber Reeves. The whirligig of time may have been turning with particular relish in the case of the Dayton figure, since internal evidence suggests he may have been intended as an unflattering version of John Morley who, as we saw in the previous paragraph, had himself protested 35 years before against 'sacrific[ing] intellect to character'.

political preoccupations, would require a major effort of intellectual history which will be a constitutive part of the task facing any future historian of the Making of the English Respectable Class. But even the much more limited enterprise of identifying the place of this idea in the political thinking of Victorian intellectuals demands that we have an eye to the more general intellectual currents of which it was a part, to moral and social developments which may be regarded as preconditions rather than sources. One could not, for example, go very far into this subject without mentioning the wider cultural impact of Evangelical Christianity, though it must be said that the most directly relevant feature of that legacy—the vision of life as a perpetual struggle in which one's ability to resist temptation and overcome obstacles needed to be subject to constant scrutiny—was, with only minor changes of emphasis, a feature shared by otherwise theologically diverse groups who also left their mark on the early Victorian educated classes, such as the Tractarians and the Arnoldians.[31] Of particular consequence for the present theme was the way in which an essentially Evangelical moral psychology penetrated the discussion of economic life early in the century (a point to which I return in Chapter 5 below). In Evangelical social thought economic activity was portrayed as a proving-ground of moral discipline where the existence of the possibility of debt and bankruptcy, or, lower down the social scale, of unemployment and destitution, operated as a check on that financial imprudence which was only the outward sign of moral failure.[32] Mrs Bosanquet was acknowledging a genuine affinity in taking her text on the economic power of character from Thomas Chalmers, however far apart they would have been on other matters.

In exploring this issue, we also need to note a significant shift away from eighteenth-century ideas of the moral and cultural primacy of leisure. For the Georgian gentleman, and thus for all those who aspired to that status, the most prized human qualities could only be developed in the enjoyment of 'society' in the older meaning of the term; mechanics were rude and scholars monkish precisely because, whether from necessity or choice, they spent so little time cultivating the virtues of sociability.[33] By contrast, for the respectable Victorian

[31] For a general account, see the still useful Walter E. Houghton, *The Victorian Frame of Mind 1830–1870* (New Haven, Conn., 1957), esp. 233–4.

[32] See the authoritative account by Boyd Hilton, *The Age of Atonement: The Influence of Evangelicalism on Social and Economic Thought 1795–1865* (Oxford, 1988).

[33] For some perceptive remarks on this ideal, see Sheldon Rothblatt, *Tradition and*

—who might, of course, belong to a much larger and less leisured class—work was the chief sphere in which moral worth was developed and displayed. It is not hard to see, for example, how the virtues of character spoke to the economic experience of those groups who made up the urban middling rank. That experience was above all of individual ventures under conditions of uncertainty with no financial safety-net. Stories of businesses which had 'gone down' and of modest fortunes lost in speculations which were imprudent or worse furnished the moralist with particularly telling illustrations. It was, at all levels, an economic world in which reputation played a powerful part: to be known as a man of character was to possess the moral collateral which would reassure potential business associates or employers. Victorian lexicographers assigned a correspondingly prominent place to reputation in their definitions of character: 'good qualities or the reputation of possessing them' was how *The Century Dictionary* (1889) laconically and revealingly put it, while the *OED* suggested 'the estimate formed of a person's qualities; reputation; when used without qualifying epithet, implying "favourable estimate, good repute"'. (A less inhibited commentator on the language observed: 'Character is like an inward spiritual grace of which reputation is, or should be, the outward and visible sign.'[34]) Although the classic scenes of character-testing are essentially private—facing the discouragement of an empty order-book, coping with the failure of one's inventions and projects, studying deep into the night to acquire by hard labour what seemed to come so easily to the expensively educated—it was also true that character was an ascribed quality, possessed and enjoyed in public view.

The increased circulation of the language of character also represented part of a wider reaction against the alleged vices and indulgences of the territorial aristocracy, especially in their metropolitan form. At its most general this involved a revolt against convention, artificiality, and mere outward polish, a post-Romantic assertion of authenticity as well as a puritan taste for austerity. More specifically, this repudiation of the ethics of the salon fed into a protest against the politics of patronage, in which the long-

Change in English Liberal Education: An Essay in History and Culture (London, 1976), and Nicholas Phillipson, 'Culture and society in the eighteenth-century province: the case of Edinburgh and the Scottish Enlightenment', in Lawrence Stone (ed.), *The University in Society*, 2 vols. (Princeton, NJ, 1975), ii. 407–48.

34 R. G. White, *Words and Their Uses* (London, 1870), 99.

celebrated value of 'independence' acquired a new force. It is noticeable how often—Smiles could again be called to the witness-stand, but so could many others—the mid-Victorian panegyrics on character occur in the context of homilies on how true worth is unrelated to social position, or, conversely, how the justifiable pride of the man of noble character is contrasted with, even provides the criterion for criticism of, the tawdriness of wealth and station and the snobbery of that sham gentility which pretended to them. Here we are beginning to back into the larger question of the sources of Victorian liberalism, for accompanying the self-assertion of new groups in the political nation there developed something of a vogue for candour and manliness, a revulsion from the degrading nature of dependence and the social pretences which dependence demanded.

I shall return to the political form taken by these emotions, but first I want to draw attention to a very different strand in the fabric, to a tradition of political reflection in which the relevant contrast to talk of 'character' was not a moral posture of dependence or inauthenticity, or even just a state of chronic weakness of will, but such terms as 'political machinery' and 'paper constitutions'. It was, that is to say, part of a vocabulary of political analysis, with a very wide currency among the educated classes in post-Napoleonic Britain, which insisted on the inadequacy of merely constitutional or legal changes when unaccompanied by the necessary qualities and habits in the people. In practice, this usually slid into a celebration of England's good fortune by contrast to the unhappy experiences of politically less gifted nations (the French, needless to say, provided the main source of cautionary tales), and there was certainly a congratulatory element in the way 'national character' acted as the chief explanatory concept in these meditations on comparative political fortunes.[35] Such assumptions were not confined to those who wished to conserve existing arrangements: by 1868 one also finds the likes of John Morley insisting that merely institutional change must be subordinate to 'the multiplication and elevation of types of virtuous character'.[36] Mill, in self-consciously scientific vein, maintained that 'the laws of national character are by far the most important class of sociological laws', even insisting that national

[35] For examples, see Collini, Winch, and Burrow, *That Noble Science of Politics*, 151–9, 170–4, 185–205, 317–29.

[36] Quoted in Jeffrey von Arx, *Progress and Pessimism: Religion, Politics, and History in Late-Nineteenth-Century Britain* (Cambridge, Mass., 1985), 136.

character was 'the power by which all those of the circumstances of society which are artificial, laws and customs for instance, are altogether moulded'.[37] (It is worth noting that character is being regarded as the very bedrock of explanation when even 'customs' are classed as 'artificial'.) But Mill, too, raised his glass to that 'point of character which beyond any other, fits the people of *this* country for representative government', and Alfred Marshall was simply one of many who extended this analysis from political stability to economic prosperity: 'The same qualities which gave political freedom gave [the English] also free enterprise in industry and commerce'.[38]

We have here again that blending of descriptive and evaluative elements: progress is analysed in terms of the causal power of national character, and at the same time the development of a certain type of character is itself an index of progress, a specification of modernity where what Bagehot described as the 'cake of custom' has been broken. Lecky generalized the point in a way which flattered the self-esteem of the political class: 'In the long run, the increasing or decreasing importance of character in public life is perhaps the best test of the progress or decline of nations.'[39] Progress, after all, was still regarded as a rarity in world history, a fragile achievement born of countless acts of initiative, acts which shape that character which in turn becomes the chief, perhaps the only, guarantee of future progress. Here is the anxiety about the long term once more. The fear of returning to a 'Chinese stationariness' was more than just a cultural cliché.

One way to bring out the distinctiveness and interdependence of the elements in the Victorian language of character is to contrast that language very briefly with comparable strands in the political discourse of the preceding century. The two strands that could most plausibly be seen as comparable are the language of virtue and the language of sociability or politeness, for unlike, say, political thinking which remained in the austere language of natural law or pressed one of the various radical or Utopian cases in the language of rights, these two dealt primarily with a comparable kind of concern and level of analysis—the moral qualities of the citizen and the habits and manners of a member of civil society. In making such a

[37] Mill, *System of Logic*, *CW*, viii. 904–5.

[38] John Stuart Mill, *Considerations on Representative Government* (1861), *CW*, xix. 421; Marshall, *Principles*, i. 744.

[39] W. E. H. Lecky, *Democracy and Liberty*, 2 vols. (London, 1896), i. 370.

contrast, I do not mean to preclude the possibility of tracing survivals and mutations of these languages into the nineteenth century, but I take it that this is just what they would be—survivals and mutations rather than the chief structuring vocabularies of the political reflection of the age.

In both the language of virtue and the language of character there is a similar emphasis on the moral vigour of the citizens as the prime requirement for the health of the body politic, though the civic humanist tradition tended to portray this as instrumental to the maintenance of political liberty whereas in the nineteenth century the cultivation of character could more readily be represented as an end in itself.[40] But the simplest way to bring out the chief contrast between them is to look at their different visions of nemesis. Putting it in a single phrase, one might say that the politics of virtue was haunted by the fear of corruption, while it was stagnation that figured as the chief threat in the politics of character. As this suggests, the former was primarily concerned with maintaining an existing balance and was essentially backward-looking, in that it understood its political fate in terms of a well-established cycle, frequently enacted in the relevant ancient history, of liberty, opulence, corruption, loss of liberty; a cycle it was doomed to repeat if the valour and public spirit of its freeholding, militia-serving citizenry should once be sapped. By contrast, the striving, self-reliant, adaptable behaviour endorsed by the imperatives of character is inherently tied to movement and progress, to a future which must be regarded as to some extent open-ended (another point I shall return to below). Both, of course, are strenuous ideals, containing a generous dash of asceticism, yet they stand in an interestingly different relation to the private pursuit of wealth. In the civic humanist tradition, it is a precondition of political liberty that those classed as citizens should be able to devote their energies to participation in public affairs, and hence should be at least partly free of the need to engage directly in productive activity, while at the same time luxury is an agent of decay precisely because it diverts men's concerns from the public to the private sphere. In character-talk, the

[40] For my understanding of 'the language of virtue' I am primarily indebted to Pocock, *Machiavellian Moment*: for its relation, particularly relevant to my theme, to political economy, see Istvan Hont and Michael Ignatieff (eds.), *Wealth and Virtue: The Shaping of Political Economy in the Scottish Enlightenment* (Cambridge, 1983), esp. the essays by Robertson and Pocock himself.

individual is not primarily regarded as a member of a political community, but as an already private (though not thereby selfish) moral agent whose mastering of his circumstances is indirectly a contribution to the vitality and prosperity of his society. Here, the getting of wealth, even in quite substantial quantities, is a salutary moral experience, provided the emphasis is placed on the getting; the civic humanist ideal of an *assured* independence would from this perspective figure rather as a temptation to indulgence than as a guarantee of political commitment. Furthermore, for the civic humanist, uniformity of material conditions is conducive to the practice of virtue, whereas the growth of character is inherently tied to a situation of diversity. In both traditions there is an abhorrence of apathy: it is the obverse of their common strenuousness. But whereas in the civic humanist eschatology apathy is what leads to a decline from public to private, in Victorian individualism apathy, in the form of lack or weakness of character, is more likely to figure as the force propelling the otherwise self-maintaining individual into a state of dependence and in *that* sense into the public sphere.

Somewhat similar contrasts can be made between the eighteenth-century language of politeness and sociability and the nineteenth-century language of character.[41] In this case we are dealing with a cultural or moral ideal which coloured political discussion without issuing in a systematic programme in the way that civic humanism did, but this arguably brings it nearer to the role of character in Victorian political thought. In general terms, of course, there is an obvious contrast between the emphasis the ideals of the two periods respectively placed on the outer and the inner man (though, as I have mentioned, character was also bound up with reputation). This is evident even where the same term is invoked, as in the praise for the way in which the founding of the Poker Club of Edinburgh in 1762 not only served 'national purposes' by bringing together representatives of different social groups, but also had 'Happy Effects on Private Character by Forming and polishing the Manners which are suitable to Civilis'd Society'.[42] Here, 'private' means 'individual' as contrasted with 'national', but it clearly involves social qualities far removed from character as the Victorians celebrated it. Where the

[41] For 'the language of sociability' see the sources cited in n. 33 above, and Nicholas Phillipson, 'Adam Smith as civic moralist' in Hont and Ignatieff, *Wealth and Virtue*.

[42] Quoted in Rothblatt, *Liberal Education*, 73.

autodidact, for example, was the archetypal Smilesian hero, Georgians deplored him as likely to be obtuse or crotchety, lacking the urbanity and moderation imparted by extensive experience of sociability. Similarly, where 'getting on' suggested to the Victorian the overcoming of adverse circumstances and engaging in wholesome competition, for the Georgian 'getting along' required more attention to the arts of winning esteem and cultivating connections. The Georgian fear of isolation or eccentricity as a sign of a rude, uncivilized way of life can be contrasted with the Victorian anxiety about the way in which the pressures of opinion in a commercial society made for conformity and lack of enterprise. 'Independence', to be sure, was highly valued in both traditions, but even here its ramifications differed somewhat. In eighteenth-century England, as one historian has well put it, 'the sinecure was the favourite mode of achieving independence in the heyday of the patronage system',[43] whereas the holding of a 'place' came to be treated with opprobrium by Victorian moralists, scenting in the lack of fair competition damning evidence of both dependence and deceit.

These contrasts are clearly part of much larger developments: both of my chosen eighteenth-century languages were, for example, addressed to a smaller class than any nineteenth-century political idiom could plausibly be. Although none of these languages was exclusively the possession of a party, it is already evident that I am trenching on the larger question of the development of Whiggism into Liberalism.[44] The language of character encapsulated a substantial passage in this development. As a body of political thought, Whiggism had been formatively and enduringly shaped by a view about the nature, and certainly by a conviction about the importance, of the constitution, and in the course of the nineteenth century many of these matters inevitably lost their political immediacy. An increasingly attenuated Whiggism still spoke to the one great recurrent constitutional issue, namely the extension of the franchise, yet even here it is interesting to see that the language of 'interests' and 'balance', which still occupied the centre of the stage in 1832, had by 1867 ceded considerable ground to the language of character. Discussion of the Second Reform Bill, both in and out of Parliament, turned to a considerable extent on the question of

[43] Ibid. 28.

[44] See the very perceptive treatment of this theme in J. W. Burrow, *Whigs and Liberals: Continuity and Change in English Political Thought* (Oxford, 1988).

whether the moral qualities of the respectable urban artisan were such that he should be entrusted with the vote.[45] Proponents of reform argued that his exclusion could no longer be justified because he had revealed—whether in his regular contributions to Friendly Societies or in what Gladstone termed 'that magnificent moral spectacle', his supposed support against his own economic interest of the North in the American Civil War—that he had now developed that strength of character which would prevent him from misusing the vote in recklessly short-sighted or self-interested ways.[46] 'Self-command and the power of endurance' had been among the desirable qualities of a potential elector enumerated by Mr Gladstone in the debate on Baines's Bill, and it is an indication of the hold of the language of character that so much of the discussion in 1867 was not about the respectable workman's rights but about his habits.

Approaching the same transition from a different angle, one of G. M. Young's remarks supplies, as so often, a helpful provocation to thought: the Whigs, he wrote, 'came from the eighteenth century where privilege was taken for granted'.[47] Although in the history of political thought Liberalism is mostly treated as a theory of the priority of liberty or of the defence of the rights of the individual, its expression in the political culture of mid-nineteenth-century England suggests that its fundamental emotional dynamic was something more like hostility to unreflective and unjustified privilege and a related hatred of being patronized. That somewhat prickly touchiness which characterized several leading Liberals—Bright is a particularly conspicuous example—was an expression of this resentment of unmerited superiority and a fear of being slighted. A generation ago we were persuasively urged to see a vehicle for the expression of such emotions in the electoral Liberalism of the bootmakers of Rochdale and the shipwrights of Whitby,[48] but

[45] For examples, see Stefan Collini, 'Political theory and the "science of society" in Victorian Britain', *Historical Journal*, 23 (1980), esp. 217.

[46] Quoted in Ian Bradley, *The Optimists: Themes and Personalities in Victorian Liberalism* (London, 1980), 154–5. The fullest account of the educated classes' views of reform in 1867 is Christopher Harvie, *The Lights of Liberalism: University Liberals and the Challenge of Democracy 1860–1886* (London, 1976), but for some reservations about Harvie's interpretation see Collini, 'Political theory and the "science of society"', 212–18.

[47] G. M. Young, *Victorian England: Portrait of an Age* (1936), annotated edn. by George Kitson Clark (London, 1977), 31.

[48] John Vincent, *The Formation of the British Liberal Party 1857–1868* (London, 1966), and *Poll-Books: How Victorians Voted* (Cambridge, 1967).

something similar remains to be said, I think, due allowance being made for differences of register, about the theories of the likes of Spencer and Green. From one point of view, the lofty stoic ideal of self-command inculcated by the language of character may seem very far removed from that spirit of self-righteous, mean-minded *ressentiment* which marked much of provincial dissenting Liberalism. But for many of those who read Smiles and admired Bright the language of character could produce a certain *frisson*; it allowed a vicarious form of self-assertion, a public affirmation of one's own worth in the face of a daily experience of the condescension of the well-born and well-connected. Further up the social scale, the vogue among the professional and preaching classes for 'manliness' (discussed more fully in Chapter 5 below) expressed a not altogether dissimilar political aesthetic. That mingling of ethical and physiological properties which character-talk always involved was particularly pronounced here: bodily and moral vigour could be cultivated by the same means, expressed by the same actions. Weakness of will, of which sentimentalism was a variety, could be walked or climbed out of the system, an attitude which in many cases found expression in what, to coin a necessary label, can only be called 'Muscular Liberalism'.

IV

By the late nineteenth century the sectarian resonances of character were drowned out by the swelling chorus of politicians of all parties who professed to stand in the same relation to any scheme which might be said to weaken character as the preacher did to sin. One feature of the framework of assumptions which gave vitality and persuasiveness to these repeated invocations of character, a feature I have left implicit so far, was that it was an ideal peculiarly suited to a future of unknown circumstances. This applied with felt power to economic life as the individual member of the middle and working classes might experience it; it was part of the anxiety of those contemplating an extension of the franchise, as all the catchphrases about 'shooting Niagara' and 'a leap in the dark' remind us; and it seemed to be almost a defining characteristic of the many forms of colonial experience towards which so much of late nineteenth-century character-training was directed. In travelling to these unknown futures, well-maintained habits and a breakdown-free will were essential. Victorian intellectuals were self-consciously members of a society in the van of progress: the first arrivals in the future cannot be sure what to expect, and no particular technical expertise can be guaranteed in advance to be relevant. Where circumstances are known or can reliably be predicted (possibly a more common frame of mind before the nineteenth century's historicizing of all experience, or in a society of more stable roles and statuses), then particular substantive virtues tend to figure more prominently among the moralist's desiderata. Seen thus, character may be said to represent a set of 'second-order' virtues, or even an acquired form of what a later age would call a 'personality-type', which would provide the best chance of first-order virtues being upheld in unknown circumstances.[49] It is perhaps a little misleading to represent the Victorian emphasis on character-formation, as at least one distinguished cultural historian has done, as indicative of 'a society without a consensus of values'.[50] It is surely nearer the mark to speak of a society which paradigmatically envisaged the individual—often an isolated individual, whether literally so, in a remote hill station, or only subjectively so, surrounded by those who seemed to have succumbed to various forms of temptation—confronting the task of maintaining his will in the face of adversity. 'When England's far and honour a name', the temptation is to duck the obligation to 'play up and play the game'; but the obligation itself is not actually called into doubt.

In a fuller account, one would need to say much more here about those great ateliers for turning out well-made characters, the late Victorian public schools.[51] The potential anti-intellectualism and philistinism which Mill, Arnold, and others had protested against in the ideal of character cherished among the dissenting provincial commercial classes was realized here in a new form, especially once

[49] Cf. Alasdair MacIntyre's remark about Adam Smith's moral philosophy: 'On Smith's view knowledge of what the rules are, whether the rules of justice or of prudence or of benevolence, is not sufficient to enable us to follow them; to do so we need another virtue of a very different kind, the Stoic virtue of self-command which enables us to control our passions when they distract us from what virtue requires'; *After Virtue: A Study in Moral Theory* (London, 1981), 218.

[50] Rothblatt, *Liberal Education*, 135.

[51] There is now an extensive literature on this subject: see particularly J. R. de S. Honey, *Tom Brown's Universe* (London, 1977), and J. A. Mangan, *Athleticism in the Victorian and Edwardian Public School: The Emergence and Consolidation of an Educational Ideology* (Cambridge, 1981).

the cult of organized games got under way from the 1870s onwards. The ethic of this cult has been summarized in the following terms:

> The imposed moral imperatives of the game are few and simple: one does not cheat, take unfair advantage, shirk, or give up. Although this represents a type of seriousness, it is nothing like Arnold's 'high seriousness'. The player who lives by these lights on or off the field does not need the developing vision, the mental receptivity, or the imaginative or philosophic grasp—qualities most Victorian intellectuals considered necessary for a healthy mind. Those qualities he does need—tenacity, daring, and moral decisiveness—are not so much mental traits as traits of the mind-body, constitution, or 'character'.[52]

Adopting the terminology of the younger Arnold, this was very much a case of the Barbarians taking over an idol of the Philistines and re-making it in their own image.

Part of the function of organized games was, of course, the artificial provision of adversity. Edward Lyttleton (classified in the *DNB* as 'schoolmaster, divine, and cricketer') insisted on this point even in a game like cricket: the removal of the element of pain which came with the development of smooth pitches made the game, he announced, 'comparatively worthless'.[53] As one might expect, the specification of the moral contribution of sport could be adapted to fit various value-hierarchies. For example, the *Pall Mall Gazette* treated the Eton and Harrow match of 1866 as the occasion for reading a lesson on some quintessentially *mid*-Victorian values:

> Cricket is a game which reflects the character—a game of correct habits, of patient and well-considered practice—the very last game in the world in which any youth without the power of concentrativeness—nine-tenths of education but voted a bore at Eton—is ever likely to excel. To any lover of education the play of Harrow was a treat, and that of Eton a disappointment. In Harrow we saw care and discipline, and patient labour; in Eton a wild erratic performance, no sign of training or mental effort.

Over a quarter of a century later, Hely Hutchinson Almond, fresh-air fanatic and Headmaster of Loretto, eulogized rugby football in terms more expressive of *late*-Victorian preoccupations:

> Games in which success depends on the united efforts of many, and which also foster courage and endurance, are the very life-blood of the public

[52] Haley, *Healthy Body*, 260–1.

[53] Quoted in Mangan, *Athleticism*, 187; the cult of organized games is treated in very similar terms in Haley, *Healthy Body*, chs. 6–9.

school system. And all the more self-indulgent games or pursuits contain within themselves an element of danger to school patriotism and might, if they permanently injured the patriotic games, cause public schools to fail in their main object, which we take to be the production of a grand breed of men for the service of the British nation.[54]

Character was not, it perhaps needs to be said, merely a weapon fashioned to suit the purposes of middle-class moralists frightened by the possible consequences of the poor's apparent indifference to respectable values. It was an expression of a very deeply ingrained perception of the qualities needed to cope with life, an ethic with strong roots in areas of experience ostensibly remote from politics. Where cricket or rugby could be spoken of in these terms without the slightest hint of irony or defensiveness, it would be surprising if the implied reservoir of cultural values were not tapped by various forms of political argument as well.

By the end of the century, the imperial and military resonances of this ethic were widely recognized, as Almond's reference to 'the service of the British nation' suggests. The ideal-type of heroism underwent corresponding changes. A concise way to represent the core of these changes would be to say that the nature of the relevant loneliness altered. The emblematic mid-Victorian moral hero, as we have seen, struggled above all with his own weaknesses and seductive impulses; the greatest spiritual isolation was experienced when stranded on the battlefield of the self, even though the unseen drama had to be acted out in full view of family, friends, and colleagues. The imperial hero, typically a soldier or explorer, knew, and in some cases courted, an isolation that was at once more obvious and more exotic. Lost, beyond the reach of courier or telegraph; up country, days from the nearest white man; surrounded, the last officer still on his feet—in these situations the measure of a man (the maleness was more emphatic than ever) lay in not 'cracking' under the pressure, or, in a sporting metaphor which helped to disguise the tensions between the individual and collective components of the ethic, in 'not letting the side down'. This latter language provided the stuff of which many an Edwardian prize-day address was made, in which the potentially conflicting values of teamwork and self-reliance, of concentration and courage, of

[54] Both quoted in Mangan, *Athleticism*, 69–70, 56; see also Almond's article on 'Football as a moral agent', in *Nineteenth Century* for 1893, discussed in Haley, *Healthy Body*, ch. 8.

obedience and initiative, were presented as unproblematically compatible. No doubt it contributed to the portrayal of 1914 as one big away match, where *homo Newboltiensis*, his character moulded by those early experiences of 'a bumping pitch and a blinding light', displayed the loyalty, bravery, narrowness, and unquestioning commitment which the situation demanded.[55] There would be a satisfying neatness in being able to say that the games-playing ethic of Harrow was lost on the battlefields of the Somme, but cultural change has happened more slowly than that even in twentieth-century Britain.

Quite how far such change *has* gone in this matter in the course of the twentieth century, and what the main agents of it have been, are questions beyond the scope of this book. Clearly, deeper diggings by psychology into the ego's early career, and the diffusion of profoundly sociologized notions of 'society' and its powers, have both proved inhospitable to the explanatory power of character; the will has been effectively disenfranchised in political discussion, and habit dissolved into the less voluntarist language of complexes and conditioning. It is also true that the growth of security for all classes has given the qualities represented by character less purchase in everyday economic life. And as a political ideal it was naturally less congenial to a Labour Party committed to remedying structural defects in the distribution of wealth and power, and less central to a political debate dominated by concern about mass unemployment and the establishment of a welfare state. When the National Insurance Act was passed in 1911, C. S. Loch, the secretary of the Charity Organization Society and Mrs Bosanquet's closest political ally, remarked that it indicated a great change of social principles: 'The fear of moral injury which state dependence may cause is decreasing.'[56] Underlying this remark was the ideal of moral health and its priority which I have been exploring in this chapter, an ideal which had itself to be in a pretty rude state of health if the language

[55] For the term *homo Newboltiensis*, see Patrick Howarth, *Play Up and Play the Game: The Heroes of Popular Fiction* (London, 1973), 14. For the understanding of the First World War in sporting terms, see Paul Fussell, *The Great War and Modern Memory* (New York, 1975), ch. 1, which also cites (p. 26) Lord Northcliffe's explanation of why the German soldier cannot be capable of acts of individual initiative like his British counterpart: 'He has not played individual games. Football, which develops individuality, has only been introduced into Germany in comparatively recent times.'

[56] Quoted in Mowat, *Charity Organisation Society*, 170.

of character was to have a more than merely decorative function in political argument. The ignorant and tendentious nonsense talked about 'reviving Victorian values' in the 1980s was perhaps the most telling indication that this ideal and its supporting assumptions had long since ceased to occupy a genuinely animating and central role in such argument.[57]

[57] This point is argued more fully in Stefan Collini, 'Victorian values', *Cambridge Review*, 109 (1988), 31–2; repr. in *Oxford Magazine*, 33 (1988), 3–4.

II

Public Voices

4

Their Master's Voice
John Stuart Mill as a Public Moralist

I

Any discussion of Victorian political and intellectual life, especially one primarily concerned with the relation between the moral assumptions exhibited in public debate and the kinds of voice available for addressing the relevant audience, must accord a special degree of attention to John Stuart Mill. It would be an exaggeration to say that he 'dominated' the higher reaches of political argument in the mid-nineteenth century; no one writer did that, though Mill's was as inescapable a presence at the intellectual level as Gladstone's was in the practical sphere. More particularly, Mill was, especially in the later part of his life, an adroit and conspicuous controversialist, vigorously exploiting his special role and the opportunities it offered to tax his opponents with their failure to measure up to the moral values to which allegiance was so frequently, at times piously, expressed in the public discourse of the Victorian educated classes. There is still a tendency among historians and political theorists to treat Mill as a detached, Olympian figure, who held himself above the fray of current politics, a tendency easily encouraged by the equable serenity of his prose in his larger treatises and by his unusually strenuous commitment to an ideal of open-mindedness. There is, of course, an element of truth in this picture, but it needs to be complemented by an exploration of the ways in which Mill engaged more directly in public debate on topical issues, where he revealed himself to be avowedly partisan and, when roused to a pitch of moral outrage, violently polemical.

This was especially true of the last fifteen years or so of his life (he died in 1873), the period which will be the focus of this chapter.

These years marked the peak of Mill's reputation and influence as a public figure, and he quite deliberately set about exploiting his acknowledged intellectual authority to promote certain social and political views as they related to the leading public issues of the day, utilizing all those means of addressing the relevant audiences which become available to an established public figure—pamphlets and manifestos as well as books, formal lectures and addresses to national organizations as well as testimony to Royal Commissions, and, above all, articles, reviews, and letters in the periodical press. In addition, he was able for three years to explore the opportunities, and experience the constraints, that came from being a Member of Parliament in a period when speeches from the floor of the House were still a prime means of engaging the attention of the political nation.

No one reading this book will need to be told that some phases of Mill's career and certain aspects of his writing have been subjected to intensive, or at least repeated, study and are now comparatively familiar. Works expounding and criticizing his major theoretical writings in philosophy, politics, and economics exist in industrial quantities, and of course the earlier stages of his intellectual development have come to constitute one of the best-known identity-crises in history. But neither his less extended mature writings nor the final, and in some ways quite distinct, phase of his career have received anything like such close attention. Here I shall first attempt to characterize Mill's performance in the role of public moralist and to place him in that world of High Victorian polemical and periodical writing to which he was such a notable contributor. As throughout this book, my concern is not primarily the set of doctrines which could be extracted from the essays and articles of his later years. As a practitioner of the higher moralizing, Mill exemplified a particular tone and level of discussion and employed certain characteristic modes of argument and other rhetorical resources in ways that, taken together, both provided something of a standard for his successors to emulate, and did much to earn him a reputation as an extreme and partisan controversialist. That, however, was only one of his reputations, the one most widely put about in Tory circles, certainly, but hardly the whole story. We must therefore begin with a larger view.

II

> With his reputation will stand or fall the intellectual repute of a whole generation of his countrymen. . . . If they did not accept his method of thinking, at least he determined the questions they should think about. . . . The better sort of journalists educated themselves on his books, and even the baser sort acquired a habit of quoting from them. He is the only writer in the world whose treatises on highly abstract subjects have been printed during his lifetime in editions for the people, and sold at the price of railway novels. Foreigners from all countries read his books as attentively as his most eager English disciples, and sought his opinions as to their own questions with as much reverence as if he had been a native oracle.[1]

It is, no doubt, difficult to write the obituary of an oracle, and John Morley's prose here betrays the strain. Yet his studied hyperbole, or at least his apparent need to resort to it even when writing for a sympathetic audience, indicates the quite extraordinary public standing that Mill achieved in the last decade or so of his life. We must be careful not to let the development of his reputation during the earlier stages of his career be either obscured by or assimilated to its final remarkable apotheosis: in the 1830s he was best known as a leading representative of an extreme and largely unpopular sect; in the 1840s and into the 1850s his double-decker treatises on logic and political economy won him a reputation that was formidable but restricted in scope and limited in extent. After all, up until 1859 these were the only books he had published (apart from the rather technical and commercially never very successful *Essays on Some Unsettled Questions of Political Economy*), and although he continued to publish occasional articles and reviews during his period of comparative withdrawal from public life in the 1850s, he did not, before his retirement from the East India Company and his wife's death in 1858, deliberately and consistently seek the limelight by publication or any other means. It is interesting to reflect how different the obituaries would have been had Mill died in the mid-1850s, as seemed to him very likely at the time. Not only would his place in the history of political thought, for example, be comparatively negligible, but he would be seen as one of those distinguished figures in the history of ideas who never achieved full recognition in their lifetimes, and whose subsequent reputation partly derived from incomplete or posthumous works, a fate which always indicates a

[1] John Morley, 'The death of Mr. Mill', *Fortnightly Review*, NS 13 (1873), 670.

rather different relation to one's contemporary audience. Nor, of course, would he have served his term in Parliament, the extraordinary manner of his election to which was both a symptom of his peculiar standing and a cause of its further growth. 'Whatever were the intermediate steps by which Mr Mill's reputation was brought to bear upon the electors' votes', observed Leslie Stephen shortly afterwards, 'that reputation really caused his election.'[2]

Mill himself was well aware of the influence this lately acquired reputation gave him. Referring to his spate of publications after 1859, he remarked to an American correspondent in 1863: 'They have been much more widely read than ever [my longer treatises] were, & have given me what I had not before, popular influence. I was regarded till then as a writer on special scientific subjects & had been little heard of by the miscellaneous public,' but, he added with evident satisfaction, 'I am in a very different position now.'[3] The triumphant note of realized ambition is even clearer in his reflection recorded during his Westminster candidacy of 1865: 'I am getting the ear of England.'[4] He did not hesitate to bend that ear, and although he did not exactly pour honey into it, he was keenly aware of the persuasive arts needed to hold its attention. There may well be figures who conform to the stereotype of the theorist, working out ideas on abstract subjects heedless of the world's response, but Mill cannot be numbered among them. Nor should his justly celebrated defence of the ideals of toleration and many-sidedness obscure the fact that on nearly all the issues of his time, intellectual as well as practical, he was rabidly partisan; as 'a private in the army of Truth'[5] he frequently engaged in hand-to-hand combat, offering little quarter to the unhesitatingly identified forces of Error.

A revealing statement of Mill's own conception of his role as a public moralist can be found in a letter written during the period in which he and Harriet had largely withdrawn from active participa-

[2] Leslie Stephen, 'On the choice of representatives by popular constituencies', in *Essays on Reform* (London, 1867), 112.

[3] Letter of 23 Feb. 1862 to Charles A. Cummings, *The Later Letters of John Stuart Mill 1849–1873* (hereafter *LL*), *The Collected Works of John Stuart Mill*, ed. John M. Robson, 31 vols. (Toronto and London, 1965–91) (hereafter *CW*), xv. 843. Cf., for further 'proof of the influence of my writings', Mill's letter of 7 Feb. 1860 to Helen Taylor, *LL*, *CW*, xv. 673.

[4] Letter of 30 May 1865 to Max Kyllmann, *LL*, *CW*, xvi. 1063 n. (Mill may have felt uneasy with the tone of this passage since he cancelled it from his draft).

[5] The phrase is John Sterling's, recorded by Caroline Fox in her *Memories of Old Friends*, ed. Horace N. Pym, 2 vols. (London, 1882), ii. 8.

tion in public life. In his reply in 1854 to the secretary of the charmingly named Neophyte Writers' Society, which had invited him to become a member of its council, Mill explained at some length his reasons for declining:

So far as I am able to collect the objects of the Society from the somewhat vague description given of them in the prospectus, I am led to believe that it is not established to promote any opinions in particular; that its members are bound together only by the fact of being writers, not by the purposes for which they write; that their publications will admit conflicting opinions with equal readiness; & that the mutual criticism which is invited will have for its object the improvement of the writers merely as writers, & not the promotion, by means of writing, of any valuable object.

Now I set no value whatever on writing for its own sake & have much less respect for the literary craftsman than for the manual labourer except so far as he uses his powers in promoting what I consider true & just. I have on most of the subjects interesting to mankind, opinions to which I attach importance & which I earnestly desire to diffuse; but I am not desirous of aiding the diffusion of opinions contrary to my own; & with respect to the mere faculty of expression independently of what is to be expressed, it does not appear to me to require any encouragement. There is already an abundance, not to say superabundance, of writers who are able to express in an effective manner the mischievous commonplaces which they have got to say. I would gladly give any aid in my power towards improving their opinions; but I have no fear that any opinions they have will not be sufficiently well expressed; nor in any way would I be disposed to give any assistance in sharpening weapons when I know not in what cause they will be used.

For these reasons I cannot consent that my name should be added to the list of writers you send me.[6]

It could be argued that almost his entire mature career is a gloss on this letter; with an eye to the themes discussed in Chapter 1 above, I shall concentrate on just three aspects of it.

First of all, Mill was no tiro as far as the means for diffusing his opinions were concerned. Morley called him the best-informed man of his day: certainly he was one of the most attentive readers of the great reviews in their heyday. His correspondence is studded with references to the latest issue of this or that journal, the political and intellectual character of each being duly noted; a more than casual interest in the medium is revealed when a man spends several weeks

[6] Letter of 23 Apr. 1854 to the secretary of the Neophyte Writers' Society, *LL*, *CW*, xiv. 205.

systematically catching up on back issues of a periodical, as Mill did in 1860 with the *Saturday Review* despite the fact that it was largely a journal of comment on the inevitably ephemeral preoccupations of current politics. The exercise was no labour of love: he observed at the end, after grudgingly conceding the quality of much of its writing, that the review 'is among the greatest enemies to our *principles* that there now are'.[7] While in Avignon for part of the year, as he was throughout the 1860s, he arranged to receive (as far as Napoleon III's censors would permit) the *Daily News* as well as weeklies such as the *Spectator* and the *Saturday Review*, reserving weightier, or perhaps just more censorable, periodicals like the *Fortnightly Review* for his return to London.[8] Moreover, he was always alive to the nature of the different audiences he could reach by contributing to these journals. He cultivated his connection with the *Edinburgh Review* for example, despite the defects of its increasingly hidebound Whiggism, because appearing in its pages conferred greater authority and respectability than any of its lesser rivals could offer; on the other hand, particularly contentious or merely slight pieces were seen as needing more congenial company. Thus, to do justice to Austin's reputation nothing less than the *Edinburgh* would do (and the subject was anyway a 'safe' one), but the *Westminster* was a better platform from which to issue a timely puff in favour of Cairnes's controversial work, *The Slave Power*. As Bain tersely put it: 'He chose the *Westminster* when he wanted free room for his elbow.'[9]

The importance Mill attached to the maintenance of 'an organ of really free opinions' shows clearly his belief, whether justified or not, that it would otherwise be difficult to get a hearing for 'advanced' views.[10] When coaching the young Lord Amberley on how best to put

[7] See his letters to Helen Taylor for Jan. and Feb. 1860, *LL*, *CW*, xv. 660–87, quotation at 687.

[8] Letter of 11 Jan. 1866 to Thomas Hare, *LL*, *CW*, xvi. 1138–40.

[9] Alexander Bain, *John Stuart Mill: A Criticism; with Personal Recollections* (London, 1882), 118. For an interesting example of Mill's wishing to use the *Edinburgh* in this way and agreeing to 'put what I have to say in a form somewhat different from that in which I should write for another publication', see his correspondence in 1869 with its editor, Henry Reeve, about a proposed review of *On Labour*, by his friend W. T. Thornton; eventually Mill was unwilling to meet Reeve's stipulations, and his review of Thornton, which contained his famous recantation of the 'wages-fund' doctrine, appeared in the *Fortnightly* instead (see *LL*, *CW*, xvii. 1574–82).

[10] See, e.g. *LL*, *CW*, xiv. 62, 72.

a shoulder behind the wheel of Progress, he remarked: 'The greatest utility of the Westminster Review is that it is willing to print bolder opinions on all subjects than the other periodicals: and when you feel moved to write anything that is too strong for other Reviews, you will generally be able to get it into the Westminster.'[11] For this reason Mill remained willing, long after he had relinquished ownership of the paper, to sink money in its never very promising battle against low circulation figures, and in this he was only one among several contemporary public men to whom the prestige or accessibility of a review of a congenial temper justified often quite substantial subsidies.[12] When in the last decade of his life the *Fortnightly Review* got under way, it fulfilled this role more successfully, especially while edited by his self-proclaimed disciple John Morley, and several of Mill's later pieces were written for it. Testimony of a different kind about the importance Mill attached to such a review is provided by the fact that he should have offered, at the age of 64 and with numerous other claims on his time, to occupy the editor's chair during Morley's threatened absence rather than have the *Fortnightly* fall into the wrong hands or suffer a break in publication.[13] The same concern surfaced in a later letter to Morley expressing the hope that the latter would not stand for the Chair of Political Economy at University College, London, 'lest the undertaking of additional work might possibly affect either your health or the time you can give to the Fortnightly. I am very desirous that the F. shd continue, & increase rather than diminish in importance & I think you exercise a wider influence through it than you could do through the Professorship.'[14]

Although he was predictably censorious of 'professional excitement-makers',[15] Mill's mastery of his role also extended to that other important requirement, a sense of timing. In writing to the editor of the *Westminster* about a proposed article by another contributor, Mill reported: 'He does not like the idea of its not appearing till April, and I should certainly think January would be a better time, as giving it a chance of helping to shape the speeches in Parliament or at

[11] Letter of 8 Mar. 1865 to Lord Amberley, *LL*, *CW*, xvi. 1007.

[12] See the essays in Joanne Shattock and Michael Wolff (eds.), *The Victorian Periodical Press: Samplings and Soundings* (Leicester, 1982), esp. the essay by Sheila Rosenberg on the period of John Chapman's proprietorship of the *Westminster*.

[13] Letter of 28 Nov. 1870 to John Morley, *LL*, *CW*, xvii. 1785.

[14] Letter to Morley of 11 May 1872; *LL*, *CW*, xvii. 1892.

[15] Letter of 5 May 1865 to John Elliot Cairnes, *LL*, *CW*, xvi. 1003.

public meetings, and the newspaper articles, by which alone any impression can be made upon unwilling Finance Ministers.'[16] In issuing his own work, Mill calculated the moment for making the maximum 'impression': he delayed full expression of his unpopular views on the American Civil War until there was a 'chance of getting a hearing for the Northern side of the question', and later congratulated himself that his article on 'The contest in America' had appeared at just the right moment to influence opinion.[17] Similarly, he delayed publication of *The Subjection of Women* (which was largely written in 1861) until the campaign for the suffrage, which he helped to orchestrate, had created a more receptive audience.[18] Judicious distribution of offprints of his articles was intended to increase this impact, just as the pamphlet form of many of his public and Parliamentary speeches, as well as of his evidence to the Royal Commission on the Contagious Diseases Acts, gave his views greater publicity and currency at the right time. And of course he was no less careful in judging the occasion for publishing further Library Editions of his earlier writings, as well as the cheap People's Editions that, beginning in 1865, gave wide circulation to his major works.[19] Having got 'the ear of England', Mill did not intend to let it go.

The second aspect of Mill's performance in the role of public moralist that requires comment here is the fact that many of his views were always likely to be unpopular with the majority of the educated classes, or at least—what may be rather more interesting—Mill always thought of himself as the holder of unpopular views, despite the success of his writings. In very general terms it is true that Mill's beliefs on 'most of the subjects interesting to mankind' were those of an 'advanced Radical'—secular, democratic, egalitar-

[16] Letter of 12 July 1861 to John Chapman, *LL*, *CW*, xv. 733.

[17] Letter of 20 Jan. 1862 to Cairnes, *LL*, *CW*, xv. 767. For his later reflection about its timing, see *Autobiography*, *CW*, i. 268.

[18] *Autobiography*, *CW*, i. 265. Cf. letter of 14 July 1869 to Alexander Bain, *LL*, *CW*, xvii. 1623, on how the strategy of *The Subjection of Women* was now appropriate in a way it would not have been 'ten years ago'.

[19] In fact, 1865 marked, as J. M. Robson has noted, an extraordinary peak of simultaneity in the publication of Mill's work: in addition to two editions of *Representative Government*, 'the fifth editions of both the *Logic* and the *Principles*, the People's Editions of *On Liberty* and the *Principles*, the periodical and first book editions of *Auguste Comte and Positivism*, and the first and second editions of the *Examination of Sir William Hamilton's Philosophy*' all appeared in that year; see J. M. Robson, 'Textual introduction', *Essays on Politics and Society*, *CW*, xviii, p. lxxxix.

ian, actively sympathetic to Socialism and the emancipation of women, yet more actively hostile to privilege and injustice and to the moral callousness he took to underlie these evils—and these views hardly commanded immediate assent in the smoking-rooms of mid-Victorian England. But it may have become important to Mill to exaggerate the extent to which he was a lonely crusader, lacking a supporting army (a few white knights aside), sustained only by the righteousness of the cause and the kinship of a scattering of rare spirits in other countries. Certainly, it is an identity which a self-described 'radical' thinker is always likely to find comforting, since it simultaneously flatters the intellect, provides a sense of purpose, and explains away failure. Occasionally there is an almost paranoid note in Mill's writing—it is part of what gives *On Liberty* its somewhat shrill tone in places—and although it is true that Mill was frequently reminded of the unpopularity of many of his causes, it is also true that magnifying the strength of the Forces of Darkness in his typically Manichaean vision of the world was essential to his polemical strategy. There are numerous instances of this in the writings of this last period: to take but one, it is noticeable how often in the opening paragraphs of *The Subjection of Women* he depicts his task as 'arduous', emphasizing the great 'difficulty' of 'contend[ing] against . . . a mass of feeling', and leading up to the subtly self-flattering, self-excusing statement: 'In every respect the burthen is hard on those who attack an almost universal opinion. They must be very fortunate as well as unusually capable if they obtain a hearing at all.'[20] The first two editions of the book, it might be noted, sold out within a few months.

As the metaphor of 'advanced' or 'progressive' opinion suggests, Mill projected his differences with the majority of his contemporaries into a reassuring historical dimension. Mankind were strung out in an enormous caravan, slowly and often unwillingly trudging across the sands of time, with the English governing classes, in particular, reluctant to move on from their uniquely favoured oasis. Mill, some way in advance of the main party, could see distant vistas hidden from their view: the task was to convince the more susceptible among them to move in the right direction, and crucial to this task was showing that the recommended route was but an extension of the path successfully followed so far. The following

[20] *The Subjection of Women* (1869), *CW*, xxi. 261.

characterization of his views, given to the electors of Westminster in 1865, is revealing here:

> Believing as I do that society and political institutions are, or ought to be, in a state of progressive advance; that it is the very nature of progress to lead us to recognize as truths what we do not as yet see to be truths; believing also that by diligent study, by attention to the past, by constant application, it is possible to see a certain distance before us, and to be able to distinguish beforehand some of these truths of the future, and to assist others to see them—I certainly think there are truths which the time has now arrived for proclaiming, though the time may not yet have arrived for carrying them into effect. That is what I mean by advanced Liberalism.[21]

Mill, unlike several of the most prominent nineteenth-century social thinkers, did not elaborate a fully teleological account of history, but he frequently resorted to the claim that there had been a discernible line of moral improvement, not dissimilar to what T. H. Green was to call 'the extension of the area of the common good',[22] whereby the circle of full moral recognition was gradually being extended to all those hitherto neglected or excluded, whether they were English labourers or negro slaves or—the argument was used to particularly good effect here—women. It is always an advantage to portray one's opponents as committed to defending a quite arbitrary stopping-place along the route of progress, and the argument had a particular resonance when addressed to an audience of mid-nineteenth-century English liberals who regarded such moral improvement as the chief among the glories of their age.

As this account reveals, Mill did not in fact stand in such a purely adversarial relation to his culture as he sometimes liked to suggest, since he was constantly appealing to certain shared values when berating his contemporaries for failing either to draw the right inferences from their professed moral principles in theory or to live up to their agreed standards in practice. Mill—it is one of the few things about him one can assert with reasonable security against contradiction—was not Nietzsche. He was not, that is, attempting fundamentally to subvert or reverse his society's moral sensibilities, but rather to refine them and call them more effectively into play on public issues (further examples are discussed below). In these circumstances, the moralist runs the risk of priggishness, as he

[21] Speech to the electors of Westminster, 5 July 1865, in *Public and Parliamentary Speeches*, *CW*, xxviii. 23.

[22] T. H. Green, *Prolegomena to Ethics*, ed. A. C. Bradley (Oxford, 1883), 217.

contrasts the consistency of his own position and the purity of his own motives with the logical confusions and self-interested prejudices that he has to impute to those who, sharing the same premisses, fail to draw the same conclusions.

This consideration brings us to the third aspect of Mill's performance as public moralist to be discussed here, his characteristic style and manner of argument. Coleridge's dictum, '*Analogies* are used in aid of *Conviction*: *Metaphors* as means of *Illustration*',[23] catches and at the same time explains one of the most characteristic features of Mill's style. His prose, typically, is didactic and forensic, conducting the reader through the logical deficiencies of arguments like a severe, slightly sarcastic, and not altogether patient tutor dissecting a pupil's essay. He wrote to convince and, where he could not convince, to convict. No one has ever doubted the power of sustained analysis that he could command, but many of his lesser-known occasional pieces also display his mastery of the blunter weapons of controversy. One would be wise to respect an opponent who could begin a paragraph with a bland enquiry into the nature of Confederate society and then move smoothly to the conclusion: 'The South are in rebellion not for simple slavery; they are in rebellion for the right of burning human creatures alive.'[24] The invention of imaginary opponents underlined the gladiatorial nature of Mill's dialectic, and he could be as unfair to them as Plato often is to Socrates' stooges (in the examples of the genre Mill admired above all others), as when in *The Subjection of Women* we are told what a 'pertinacious adversary, pushed to extremities, may say', only to discover a few lines later that this 'will be said by no one now who is worth replying to'.[25]

But perhaps his most common rhetorical strategy is the *reductio ad absurdum*, and this fact underlines the earlier point about Mill's reliance on a certain community of values between himself and his readers: without such common standards, the reductions would seem either not absurd or else simply irrelevant. Similarly, the use of analogy requires that the characterization of one term of the analogy be beyond dispute: if it is not, the alleged extension will have no

[23] Quoted in John Holloway, *The Victorian Sage: Studies in Argument* (London, 1953), 13–14, from Coleridge's *Aids to Reflection* (London, 1825), 198 (aph. 104 in other editions).

[24] 'The contest in America', *CW*, xxi. 136.

[25] *The Subjection of Women*, *CW*, xxi. 292; cf. also 310–11.

persuasive force. Arguments about equality are particularly likely to involve appeals to analogy; indeed, the whole of *The Subjection of Women* could be regarded as one long elaboration of the basic analogy between the historical position of slaves and the present position of women. And finally, the gap between profession and practice, to which Mill was constantly calling attention, invites the use of irony, though it must be said that his efforts at irony often sailed close to mere sarcasm and ridicule; his own highly developed sense of being, and having to be seen to be, 'a man of principle' did not, perhaps, leave much room for that more generous and tolerant perception of human limitation which sustains the best forms of irony.

As a medium for addressing the reader of the periodicals of general culture, Mill's prose was certainly not without its drawbacks. Carlyle's ungenerous description of Mill's conversation as 'sawdustish'[26] could also be applied to some of his writing. He was aware, Bain tells us, that he lacked that facility of illustration which would have mitigated the overly abstract texture which characterizes almost all his work, and a compendium of Mill's wit would be a slim volume indeed. His scorn for the mere 'literary craftsman' quoted above was of a piece with his own avoidance of those arts common among the more winning essayists and reviewers in the nineteenth century. He never quite hits off the ideal tone for such writing in the way in which, say, Bagehot or Leslie Stephen did: he never manages to create that sense of intimacy between reader and author, that warming feeling of sharing a sensible view of a mad world. But in some ways the achievement of this effect would have been foreign to Mill's purpose, for the sense of complicity it nurtured was to him only a subtler form of that complacency which he saw as the chief danger of modern society, the *fons malorum* that, above all else, required constant criticism: and here we come to the heart of his role as a public moralist.

Behind the particular issues to which the topical pieces of this last period were addressed there runs a common theme: the moral health of society is the highest good, calling, as the metaphor suggests, for constant care and sustenance if decay is not to set in.[27] Mill is here

[26] Quoted in Bain, *John Stuart Mill*, 190.

[27] Cf. his reply of 6 Dec. 1871 to a correspondent who had asked him if he thought France was 'en décadence': 'A mon sens, la décadence morale est toujours la seule réelle' (*LL*, *CW*, xvii. 1864).

acting as moral coach, keeping the national conscience in trim, shaming it out of flabbiness, urging it on to yet more strenuous efforts. In some ways this is an ancient role, and he sometimes hits a surprisingly traditional note: when, in defending the military action of the Union in the American Civil War, he declared that 'war, in a good cause, is not the greatest evil which a nation can suffer. . . . [T]he decayed and degraded state of moral and patriotic feeling which thinks nothing worth a war, is worse,'[28] it is the language of Machiavelli and civic *virtù* which echoes more resonantly rather than that of Cobden and Bright and the age of pacific commercialism. But, for the most part, the conception of morality to which Mill appealed appears unambiguously Victorian, both in its emphasis upon the active shaping of 'character', that constantly self-renewing disposition to form virtuous habits of conduct, and in its focus on the welfare of others as the object of moral action—in its insistence, indeed, on the duty of altruism. What Mill was trying to do, beyond keeping this conception of morality in good repair, was to mobilize and make active its power in areas too easily given over to complacency and self-interest. In assessing England's foreign policy he made questions of moral example paramount; in discussing attitudes towards the American Civil War, the moral tone of opinion in England was his chief concern; in opposing the Contagious Diseases Acts, it was their public endorsement of vice he most objected to.

As prompter of the national conscience, Mill derived certain advantages from his deliberately nurtured position as an outsider among the English governing classes. Where the aim is to make one's readers morally uncomfortable, too great an intimacy can be an obstacle; Mill seems to have felt that his avoidance of 'Society' helped to provide the requisite distance as well as to preserve a kind of uncorrupted purity of feeling (he, though not he alone, attributed the allegedly superior moral insight of the labouring classes to the same cause). More obviously, he claimed a special authority on account of his familiarity (his unique familiarity, he sometimes seems to imply) with the main currents of Continental, and especially French, thought. Reproaches to his countrymen for their insular prejudice and ignorance are a staple ingredient in Mill's writing, whether he is castigating them for their aversion to theories

[28] 'The contest in America', *CW*, xxi. 141.

of history or upbraiding them for their unresponsiveness to the beauties of art. This is a further aspect of the didactic voice: tutor and pupil are not equals. An interesting complication emerges, however, where the comparative moral achievements of the English are concerned, for he repeatedly asserted that England had been the superior of other nations in its 'greater tenderness of conscience' (though characteristically he could not resist the censorious warning, 'I am not sure that we are not losing . . . the kind of advantage which we have had over many other countries in point of morals').[29] As far as individual conduct was concerned, he could still maintain that its tendency to harden into a narrow 'Hebraizing' called for correction from larger views of life that needed, on the whole, to be imported. But where national policy was at issue, Mill conceded England's superior reputation, only to treat it as the source of an enlarged duty: as 'incomparably the most conscientious of all nations' in its 'national acts', England had a special responsibility for maintaining and improving standards of international morality.[30] In either case there was no rest for the virtuous. Since the English, according to Mill, were perpetually liable to complacency, a critic who could keep a more strenuous ideal before their minds would never want for employment.

It may help us to place that role as Mill's practice defined it if we contrast it with two others, which were certainly no less available in mid-Victorian England, and which may, for convenience, simply be labelled the role of 'the Sage' and the role of 'the Man of Letters'.[31] Claims to both these titles could be made on Mill's behalf, yet their ultimate inappropriateness as descriptions of the author of the occasional pieces dating from his last period (and, I think, of most of Mill's mature *œuvre*) is revealing of his position in the intellectual life of his time. The Sage (to construct a highly simplified ideal-type) trades in wisdom and new visions of experience as a whole. Typically, he is not so much attempting to *argue* his readers out of

[29] *Inaugural Address delivered to the University of St Andrews* (1867), *CW*, xxi. 253.

[30] 'A few words on non-intervention' (1859), *CW*, xxi. 115. This was a theme he returned to in several of his Parliamentary speeches (on which see below pp. 159–60) and especially in his contributions in 1868 to the Commons Select Committee on Extradition; see Appendix B in *CW*, xxix. 542–71.

[31] For suggestive uses of these terms, which I have drawn upon but not strictly followed, see Holloway, *Victorian Sage*, George P. Landow, *Elegant Jeremiahs: The Sage from Carlyle to Mailer* (Ithaca, NY, 1986), and John Gross, *The Rise and Fall of the Man of Letters* (London, 1969).

false beliefs as to reveal to them—or, better still, to put them in the way of discovering for themselves—the limitations of that perception of the world upon which they purport to base all their beliefs. The ineffable constantly looms, and the Sage frequently employs a highly idiosyncratic vocabulary in an effort to disclose those dimensions of experience which the conventional categories are said to distort or obscure. Coleridge, Carlyle, and Newman might be taken as obvious nineteenth-century examples of this type, their very heterogeneity ensuring that it will not be understood to imply a set of common doctrines.

Now, for all his Coleridgean and Carlylean flirtations in the late 1820s and early 1830s, I think it is clear that Mill does not belong in this *galère*. The *Logic* is hardly attempting to awaken in us a sense of the mysteries of the universe, and none of the essays in the volumes of *Dissertations and Discussions* leaves us feeling that we now possess our experience in a quite new way. Nothing in Mill's philosophy strains at the limits of the plainly expressible, and if this restriction gives his prose a rather pedestrian quality by comparison with that of the Sages, we might remember that it is part of the definition of the pedestrian that he has his feet on the ground. After all, when a few years earlier Mill had clashed directly with Carlyle over 'the Negro Question',[32] it was not obvious that the latter's esoteric vision yielded the more appealing view, still less that it provided the more persuasive basis for action.

As one who wrote so extensively for the great Victorian reviews and on such a diverse range of subjects, Mill might seem to have a better claim to be included in the more capacious category of Man of Letters. His literary essays of the 1830s could be cited as one qualification for membership, his later reviews on historical and classical subjects, more dubiously, as another, and in any inclusive survey of the type Mill ought arguably to find a place. But even then he seems to be at most a kind of honorary member, too important to be entirely left out, too individual to be comfortably conscripted, and his reply to the Neophyte Writers' Society again provides the clue which helps us to pin down his distinctiveness. It is not only that Mill aimed to instruct rather than to delight, though it is worth recalling the disdain he entertained for what he dismissively termed 'the mere faculty of expression'; he could never have subscribed to

[32] 'The Negro Question' (1850), *CW*, xxi. 85–96.

the view expressed in Francis Jeffrey's defence of the lively style of the early *Edinburgh Review*: 'To be learned and right is no doubt the first requisite, but to be ingenious and original and discursive is perhaps more than the second in a publication which can only do good by remaining Popular.'[33] But Mill is not divided from the best practitioners of literary journalism in his day only by a difference of tactics: there is the far deeper difference that he was not sufficiently interested in the variousness of literary achievement, not drawn to those exercises in appreciation, discrimination, and evocation that bulked so large in the reviews of the time. Where others collected their essays under such titles as 'Hours in a Library', 'Literary Studies', or simply 'Miscellanies', Mill quite accurately called his 'Dissertations and Discussions'.

Interestingly, he never wrote that kind of extended meditation on and appreciation of the work of a single figure which is among the chief essayistic glories of, say, Macaulay or Bagehot or Stephen, or even, more revealingly, of Morley—'more revealingly' because Morley was close to Mill in both doctrine and temperament. It is hard to imagine Mill, had he lived another ten years, contributing to Morley's 'English Men of Letters' series (discussed more fully in Chapter 9 below). Of the two books which Mill did devote to individual figures, that on Hamilton is a massive display of destructive criticism and dialectical overkill, while even the briefer and more general assessment of Comte remains firmly tied to an analytical discussion of the strengths and weaknesses of Comte's *theory*. The nearest Mill had earlier come to this genre was in his famous essays on Bentham and Coleridge, yet even these were thinly disguised instalments in Mill's own philosophical progress, less essays in appreciation than occasions for further synthesis. Similarly, his pieces on the French historians were intended to be contributions towards the development of a general historical theory, just as his reviews of Grote's history were in effect manifestos for democracy, and so on. 'I have on most of the subjects interesting to mankind, opinions to which I attach importance & which I earnestly desire to diffuse.' In pursuing this goal, the mature Mill husbanded his energies with principled care; as a moralist he never missed a chance to instruct, reproach, and exhort.

Such a performance was bound to excite strong feelings of one

[33] Quoted in William Thomas, *The Philosophic Radicals: Nine Studies in Theory and Practice 1817–1841* (Oxford, 1979), 160.

kind or another. As a contemporary comment on his articles about the American Civil War noted, in such writings Mill 'ceases to be a philosopher and becomes the partisan',[34] and appreciation of his role as a controversialist should furnish something of a corrective to caricatures of Mill as the eirenic spokesman for some factitious 'Victorian orthodoxy'. It was because of such writings, above all, that he was regarded in many respectable circles as incorrigibly 'extreme', a zealous root-and-branch man; even many of those who had been enthusiastic admirers of his earlier works in philosophy and political economy found these later writings too 'doctrinaire'.[35] Others, by contrast, regarded them as among his best works.[36] This contrast, and some indication of the strength of feeling that Mill's late work as a public moralist aroused, can be gauged from the juxtaposition of two representative quotations. The first is from a review of *The Subjection of Women*, where the reviewer, irked by Mill's 'assumption of especial enlightenment, of a philosophic vantage-ground from which he is justified in despising the wisdom of mankind from the beginning of things', saw in this the source of his considerable unpopularity: 'His intense arrogance, his incapacity to do justice to the feelings or motives of all from whom he differs, his intolerance of all but his own disciples, and lastly, in natural consequence of these qualities, his want of playfulness in himself and repugnance to it in others, all combine to create something like antipathy.'[37] On the other hand, John Morley, commending Mill's 'moral thoroughness', concluded: 'The too common tendency in us all to moral slovenliness, and a lazy contentment with a little flaccid protest against evil, finds a constant rebuke in his career. . . . The value of this wise and virtuous mixture of boldness with tolerance, of courageous speech with courageous reserve, has been enormous.'[38]

[34] 'J. S. Mill on the American contest', *The Economist*, 20 (8 Feb. 1862), 144.

[35] For examples of this response, see Christopher Harvie, *The Lights of Liberalism: University Liberals and the Challenge of Democracy 1860–1886* (London, 1976), 152–3; cf. John Vincent, *The Formation of the British Liberal Party 1857–1868* (London, 1972 1st pub. 1966), 190. It is a view which pervades Bain's account: see e.g. *John Stuart Mill*, 192. See also the discussion in Ch. 5 below, pp. 176–80.

[36] For John Morley, for example, they represented 'the notable result of this ripest, loftiest, and most inspiring part of his life', and he regarded *The Subjection of Women*, in particular, as 'probably the best illustration of all the best and richest qualities of its author's mind'; John Morley, 'Mr Mill's Autobiography', *Fortnightly Review*, NS 15 (1874), 15, 12.

[37] [Anne Mozley], 'Mr Mill on the subjection of women', *Blackwood's Magazine*, 106 (1869), 320–1.

[38] Morley, 'Death of Mr Mill', 673, 672.

III

Although Mill addressed a seemingly disparate range of political issues in the 1860s and early 1870s, all his most controversial interventions can be seen as expressions of his deep commitment to equality. (Bain, increasingly sceptical of Mill's later political enthusiasms, considered the 'doctrine of the natural equality of men' to be his master's greatest error as a 'scientific thinker'.[39]) Whether the victims of inequality were Negroes, as in his writings about the American Civil War or the Governor Eyre controversy, or women, as in his support for enfranchisement and the removal of other disabilities as well as in his campaigning against the Contagious Diseases Acts, Mill was conscious of confronting the deeply held inegalitarian prejudices of the bulk of the educated classes of his own society. At times, he could seem to address the issue as essentially a question of proper scientific method, making his opponents' belief in natural inequalities seem a corollary of their defective grasp of the nature of induction. He constantly maintained that no reliable inference about what men and, more particularly, women would be like under a quite different set of circumstances could be made on the basis of our knowledge of their behaviour under the circumstances of systematic inequality which, he alleged in a rather brisk characterization of human history, had shaped that behaviour up to the present. His belief in the nearly limitless malleability of human nature provided one crucial ingredient of this claim, though here as elsewhere he was hampered (as he at times acknowledged) by his failure with his pet project of an 'Ethology', the scientific demonstration of the ways in which character is formed by circumstances.[40]

More generally, his position reflected the larger problem of negative evidence, a recurring motif in radical arguments against the existing order of things. That is to say, to the premiss that individuals should be treated equally unless good cause can be

[39] Bain, *John Stuart Mill*, 146.

[40] For his conception of 'Ethology', see *System of Logic*, *CW*, viii. 561–74; for his 'failure' with it, see Bain, *John Stuart Mill*, 78–9. His correspondence reveals that he continued to entertain hopes of returning to the project: e.g. letter to Alexander Bain of 14 Nov. 1859, where he referred to it as 'a subject I have long wished to take up, at least in the form of Essays, but have never yet felt myself sufficiently prepared' (*LL*, *CW*, xv. 645). For an example of his acknowledgement that 'there is hardly any subject which, in proportion to its importance, has been so little studied', see *Subjection of Women*, *CW*, xxi. 277.

shown to do otherwise, Mill wanted to attach the rider that history could not *in principle* furnish the evidence needed to show such cause in the case of traditionally subordinate groups such as 'the lower races', the lower classes, or women. Actually, of course, Mill did wish to appeal to history in one way, namely (as suggested in general terms above), to present it as exhibiting a broad movement towards equality, but he was not, strictly speaking, attempting to have it both ways: the historical and epistemological claims are logically independent of each other. After all, it would be possible to uphold a belief in equality as in some sense 'natural' whilst acknowledging that the march of history seemed to be in the direction of ever greater inequality, though unless buttressed by some ingenious supporting arguments this position might make the initial claim less plausible as well as, and perhaps more consequentially, less inspiriting. In practice, needless to say, Mill combined the two claims to good polemical effect:

> The course of history, and the tendencies of progressive human society, afford not only no presumption in favour of this system of inequality of rights, but a strong one against it; and . . . so far as the whole course of human improvement up to this time, the whole stream of modern tendencies, warrants any inference on the subject, it is, that this relic of the past is discordant with the future, and must necessarily disappear.[41]

He did not, in fact, always press the second, quasi-historicist, claim quite so hard; but he squeezed the first, negative, point very hard indeed, and it is this, above all, that imparted such a strongly destructive flavour to some of the polemical pieces he wrote during this period.

Even during his earlier exchange with Carlyle over 'the Negro Question' referred to above,[42] Mill had presciently concentrated on the prospects for the abolition of slavery in the United States. He always followed American developments very closely, convinced that they would eventually prove decisive for several of the causes he cared most about: the fate of popular government, in particular, seemed to him and many others in England to be bound up with the successes and failures of 'the great democratic experiment' of the United States.[43] (It is even possible that in this respect America was coming to

[41] *Subjection of Women*, *CW*, xxi. 272.

[42] See also the 'Introduction' to *CW*, xxi, pp. xxi–xxii.

[43] For a useful survey of opinion, see D. P. Crook, *American Democracy in English Politics 1815–1850* (Oxford, 1965).

replace France in Mill's thinking, especially once France was saddled with the despotism of Napoleon III, which he so abhorred: in 1849 he could still write: 'The whole problem of modern society however will be worked out, as I have long thought it would, in France & nowhere else,' but by the 1860s he seemed to assign at least equal importance to the United States.[44]) Although Mill shared many of Tocqueville's misgivings about the pressures making for mediocrity and conformity in American society, he did not let these misgivings override his principled optimism about the future of democracy, and he was always alert to the ways in which anti-democratic opinion in England, with *The Times* in the van, tried to exploit the acknowledged weaknesses of American political life and constitutional arrangements to discredit all popular causes at home. The Civil War, therefore, touched several nerves in Mill's moral physiology; not only did it involve the most blatant case of institutionalized inequality in the civilized world and the whole question of popular government's ability to combine freedom with stability; but, always powerfully active in determining Mill's interest in public issues, it provided a thermometer with which to take the moral temperature of English society as a whole.

The question of British attitudes towards the American Civil War is a notoriously complex and disputed one,[45] but it is uncontentious to say that in the early stages of the war a very large majority among the educated classes was hostile to the North, and that within that majority there was an influential body actively sympathetic to the Confederate cause. It was not simply that the upper classes largely sided with what they perceived to be the aristocratic or gentlemanly character of plantation society, nor even that for many in all classes commercial self-interest seemed to dictate a prudent regard for the prosperity and independence of the cotton-exporting states. It was also that the Confederate cause was widely represented as the cause of freedom: that in defending their 'right to secede' in the face of the

[44] Letter of 28 May 1849 to Henry Samuel Chapman, *LL*, *CW*, xiv. 32; cf. *LL*, *CW*, xvi. 1307 and xvii. 1880. See also *Autobiography*, *CW*, i. 266–8.

[45] The standard account was for long Ephraim Douglass Adams, *Great Britain and the American Civil War*, 2 vols. (London, 1925); a strongly revisionist attack on the view that the cotton workers of Lancashire had, against their economic interests, supported the North is provided in the controversial study by Mary Ellison, *Support for Secession: Lancashire and the American Civil War* (Chicago, 1972). There is a judicious synthesis in D. P. Crook, *The North, the South, and the Powers 1861–65* (New York, 1974).

superior force of an essentially alien power, the Southern states were acting analogously to those peoples 'rightly struggling to be free' who had aroused such enthusiasm in Britain in the preceding decade. Jefferson Davis was elevated to stand alongside Kossuth and Garibaldi. The issue was thus not one on which opinion divided (in so far as it very unequally did divide) along party lines: Gladstone and Russell were among those who considered the Federal attempt to 'coerce the South' to be unwarranted, while Radicals were told by some of their spokesmen that 'the first doctrine of Radicalism . . . was the right of a people to self-government'.[46]

Mill, to whom the real issue at stake in the war had from the outset been the continued existence of slavery, considered that much of this sympathy for the South rested on ignorance or, even more culpably, moral insensibility, and 'The contest in America' (1862) was his attempt to educate English opinion on both counts. He expected it, Bain recorded, 'to give great offence, and to be the most hazardous thing for his influence that he had yet done'.[47] Mill made this judgement not simply because he found himself on the side of the minority, and a pretty small one at that; this he had taken to be the more or less constant character of his intellectual life from his earliest Benthamite propaganda onwards. Bain's phrase suggests, rather, that Mill was now the self-conscious possessor of a 'reputation' which he was about to deploy in an outspoken condemnation of the moral myopia of the reputation-making classes. For, 'the tone of the press & of English opinion', as he confided to Thornton, 'has caused me more disgust than anything has done for a long time'; he regarded the 'moral attitude' displayed by 'some of our leading journals' (*The Times* and the *Saturday Review* particularly galled him) as betraying an unavowed partiality for slavery.[48] In some cases, he sneered, this arose from 'the influence, more or less direct, of West Indian opinions and interests', but in others—and here he warms to a favourite theme—it arose

> from inbred Toryism, which, even when compelled by reason to hold opinions favourable to liberty, is always adverse to it in feeling; which likes the spectacle of irresponsible power exercised by one person over others;

[46] Quoted in Ellison, *Support for Secession*, 9.

[47] Bain, *John Stuart Mill*, 119.

[48] Letter to W. T. Thornton of 25 Jan. 1862, where he also places his characteristic two-way bet that his article 'if noticed at all is likely to be much attacked'; *LL*, *CW*, xv. 774.

which has no moral repugnance to the thought of human beings born to the penal servitude for life, to which for the term of a few years we sentence our most hardened criminals, but keeps its indignation to be expended on 'rabid and fanatical abolitionists' across the Atlantic, and on those writers in England who attach a sufficiently serious meaning to their Christian professions, to consider a fight against slavery a fight for God.[49]

Slavery is thus treated by Mill as the extreme form of undemocracy, a kind of Toryism of race to match the 'Toryism of sex' that he saw in women's exclusion from the franchise.[50] The 'warmth of his feelings' on the issue was remarked by friends and opponents alike: he was, Grote recorded, 'violent against the South . . . embracing heartily the extreme Abolitionist views, and thinking about little else in regard to the general question'.[51] It was the outspoken public expression of this passion which, more than anything else, gave Mill that identity as a 'partisan' controversialist which was such a marked feature of his reputation in the last decade of his life.

Mill was adamant that even if secession were the main issue at stake, this would still not automatically entitle the South to the support of those who thought of themselves as ranged on the side of freedom. Brandishing his own radical credentials, he announced: 'I have sympathized more or less ardently with most of the rebellions, successful and unsuccessful, which have taken place in my time', but he emphasized that it was not simply their being rebellions that had determined their moral status: 'those who rebel for the power of oppressing others' were not to be seen as exercising 'as sacred a right as those who do the same thing to resist oppression practised upon themselves'.[52] The nature and aims of Southern society were the decisive test, and in educating English opinion on this matter Mill found his chief ally in the Irish economist John Elliot Cairnes. The younger man had already won his senior's approval with his very

[49] 'The contest in America', *CW*, xxi. 129.

[50] He used this phrase in a reference to the exclusion of women from the suffrage in the otherwise unusually democratic Australian colonies; letter of 8 July 1858 to Henry Samuel Chapman, *LL*, *CW*, xv. 557.

[51] Harriet Grote, *The Personal Life of George Grote* (London, 1873), 264. Recommending Mill's article to Gladstone, the duke of Argyle particularly emphasized how 'the cold-blooded philosopher comes out with much warmth' (quoted in Adelaide Weinberg, *John Elliot Cairnes and the American Civil War: A Study in Anglo-American Relations* (London, 1969), 22). See also *The Economist*'s suggestion that on this issue Mill was carried away 'by the very warmth of his own feelings' ('Mill on the American contest', 171).

[52] 'The contest in America', *CW*, xxi. 137.

Millian statement of the method of classical political economy,[53] and when in the summer of 1861 he sent Mill the manuscript of a course of lectures that he had just delivered on the nature of American slavery, Mill immediately recognized its polemical value and urged its publication.[54] The resulting book, accurately entitled *The Slave Power: Its Character, Career, and Probable Designs: Being an Attempt to Explain the Real Issues Involved in the American Contest*,[55] fully satisfied Mill's expectations, and led to the growth between the two men of what Mill, in a revealing phrase, referred to as 'the agreeable feeling of a brotherhood in arms'.[56]

The chief contentions of Cairnes's book were that the nature of Southern society was determined by its basis in the economy of slavery, that such a system of production needed, under American conditions, continually to expand the territory cultivated by slave labour, and that this inherent dynamic accounted for the expansionist activities of the Southern states which, when the action of the Federal government threatened to curb them, naturally led to war. Secession was not, therefore, the demand of an oppressed people to be left alone: it was the inevitable outcome of an insatiably aggressive policy, which could only be halted by the destruction of slavery itself. Mill was obviously right about the topical resonance of the work, which received considerable critical attention and was republished in a second, enlarged edition in 1863. But it is worth noting that Cairnes himself recorded that his purpose had initially been of 'a purely speculative kind—my object being to show that the course of history is largely determined by the action of economic causes'.[57] It is perhaps surprising that Mill should let Cairnes's historical materialism pass without comment, since he was himself always so concerned to insist that moral and intellectual rather than economic causes are the motor of history, but he presumably felt that this was no time to be parading differences over the finer points of method; brothers-in-arms have more important things to do than criticizing the cut of each other's armour.

The review of Cairnes, the first half of which is a faithful paraphrase of the original in both tone and content, provided Mill

[53] *The Character and Logical Method of Political Economy* (London, 1857). For Mill's favourable view, see letter to Cairnes of 22 Apr. 1858, *LL*, *CW*, xv. 554.

[54] Letter to Cairnes of 18 Aug. 1861, *LL*, *CW*, xv. 738.

[55] For further details, see Weinberg, *Cairnes and the American Civil War*, ch. 2.

[56] Letter to Cairnes of 24 June 1862, *LL*, *CW*, xv, 785.

[57] Cairnes, *Slave Power*, p. vii.

with another opportunity to read a lesson on the debased state of 'public morality' in England, 'this sad aberration of English feeling at this momentous crisis', which he contrasted unfavourably with the right-mindedness of liberal feeling in France.[58] As he recognized, opinion in England was at first very much affected by estimates of the likely outcome of the military struggle—in 1861 and early 1862 many people were not convinced that the North would win—and throughout the war there was hostility to the North on the grounds that, even if it did win, it could not permanently govern the South in a state of subjection. Indeed, the one point on which Mill and Cairnes initially differed was that the latter thought that the best outcome would be an independent South confined, fatally for its slave economy, to the existing slave states, whereas Mill looked for nothing short of complete surrender and re-incorporation in the Union on the North's terms, a view with which Cairnes seems to have come to agree by 1865.[59] It is indicative of Mill's passion on the subject that he immediately fastened on a potentially valuable aspect even of Lincoln's assassination: 'I do not believe the cause will suffer,' he wrote to one correspondent. 'It may even gain, by the indignation excited.'[60] Keeping the indignation-level well topped up in such cases Mill seems to have regarded as one of the routine tasks of the public moralist, and he hoped that one consequence of the feelings aroused by the assassination would be to 'prevent a great deal of weak indulgence to the slaveholding class, whose power it is necessary should be completely and permanently broken at all costs'.[61]

This disposition to fight *à outrance* manifested itself even more strikingly in Mill's contribution to the Governor Eyre controversy, which flared up later in 1865. This was one of those great moral earthquakes of Victorian public life whose fault-lines are so revealing of those subterranean affinities and antipathies of the educated classes which the historian's normal aerial survey of the surface cannot detect. Faced with a native insurrection of uncertain proportions in October 1865, the English Governor of Jamaica had declared martial law, under which justification he apparently

[58] Letter to Cairnes of 25 Nov. 1861, *LL*, *CW*, xv. 750; cf. Cairnes, *Slave Power*, 16.

[59] This point of difference emerges in 'The contest in America', *CW*, xxi. 162–4; see also Weinberg, *Cairnes and the American Civil War*, 42, for Cairnes's later agreement.

[60] Letter of 1 May 1865 to John Plummer, *LL*, *CW*, xvi. 1042.

[61] Letter of 3 May 1865 to William E. Hickson, *LL*, *CW*, xvi. 1044.

condoned several brutal acts of suppression carried out by his subordinates, some of them after the danger was, arguably, past, and including the summary execution of the leader of the native opposition party in the local assembly.[62] Considerable uncertainty at first surrounded many of the facts of the case, but opinion in England immediately divided. On the one side were those who thought that, though the reported brutality was no doubt regrettable, Eyre's unorthodox and vigorous action in a situation of great danger had saved the population, especially the white population, from far worse evils (the Indian Mutiny, after all, was still fresh in the memory). On the other side were those, including Mill, who regarded Eyre's actions as both morally unpardonable and flagrantly illegal, and who thought it their duty to see that he was brought to justice, and the moral stain on the character of English rule thereby removed. The intensity of Mill's commitment to this view is strikingly illustrated by his comment in December 1865, on the next session's business in Parliament: 'There is no part of it all, not even the Reform Bill, more important than the duty of dealing justly with the abominations committed in Jamaica.'[63] He immediately joined the Jamaica Committee, which was founded in the same month to ensure that Eyre and his subordinates were brought to justice, and when its first Chairman, Charles Buxton, thinking it sufficient simply to secure Eyre's dismissal and disgrace without also having him prosecuted for murder, resigned in June 1866, Mill, then in Parliament and sternly resisting other calls on his time even for causes to which he was sympathetic, took over the chairmanship and retained it until the Committee was wound up in May 1869.[64]

The three aims of the Committee were summarized in the progress report which Mill, together with the treasurer and the secretary, issued to members in July, 1868: 'To obtain a judicial inquiry into the conduct of Mr. Eyre and his subordinates; to settle the law in the interest of justice, liberty and humanity; and to arouse public

[62] For an account of the episode which pays considerable attention to Mill's role, see Bernard Semmel, *The Governor Eyre Controversy* (London, 1962); see also Gillian Workman, 'Thomas Carlyle and the Governor Eyre controversy: an account with some new material', *Victorian Studies*, 18 (1974), 77–102.

[63] Letter of 14 Dec. 1865 to William Fraser Rae, *LL*, *CW*, xvi. 1126. For further discussion of Mill's conduct of the case in Parliament, see below, pp. 164–6.

[64] For further indication of the importance Mill attached to making a stand on this issue whether or not the prosecution proceedings were successful, see letter of 23 Feb. 1868 to Lucy Middleton Aspland, *LL*, *CW*, xvi. 1365.

morality against oppression generally, and particularly against the oppression of subject and dependent races.'[65] On the first point they had to acknowledge defeat: despite repeated efforts, which had earned for Mill in particular a reputation as the vindictive persecutor of the unfortunate Eyre, no court had proved willing to put him on trial. The second aim had met with some success as far as the status of martial law within the English legal system was concerned, though whether the inconclusive outcome of the whole affair vindicated the principle of 'government by law', which Mill had always insisted was at stake in the matter, must be open to question. Quite what counted as success on the third point was obviously harder to say. 'A great amount of sound public opinion has been called forth', the statement reported,[66] and for Mill this effect was something of an end in itself, though it is not obvious that the campaign exercised that morally educative influence which he always looked for in such cases. T. H. Huxley, predictably a member of the Jamaica Committee, may have been nearer the mark when he wrote to Charles Kingsley that 'men take sides on this question, not so much by looking at the mere facts of the case, but rather as their deepest political convictions lead them'.[67] Certainly, attitudes towards the working class and democracy at home played a large part in the controversy; Eyre's supporters were not slow to suggest, for example, that the Hyde Park riots of 1866 called for a similarly vigorous use of force by the authorities. Conversely, as far as Mill was concerned, right feeling on the matter transcended more pragmatic party loyalties: when in 1871 the Liberal government decided to honour a previous Tory promise to pay Eyre's legal expenses, Mill, deeply disgusted, announced: 'After this, I shall henceforth wish for a Tory Government.'[68] Such issues of public righteousness provide surer touchstones by which to understand Mill's later career than do any of the conventional political labels. It will always be difficult to say with certainty which of those liberal and reforming measures enacted in the decades after his death he would have approved of, but there can surely be no doubt that had he lived he would have been among the leaders of the agitation against the Bulgarian atrocities in 1876.[69]

65 'Statement of the Jamaica Committee' (1868), *CW*, xxi. 433.

66 Ibid. xxi. 434.

67 Quoted in Semmel, *Governor Eyre*, 122.

68 Letter to Cairnes of 21 Aug. 1871, *LL*, *CW*, xvii. 1828–9.

69 Cf. the observation of R. T. Shannon, in what remains the best study of this

The question of the proper conduct of nations towards each other, particularly the appropriate role for Britain in international affairs, was one which exercised Mill throughout the latter part of his life. Although observations on it can be found in several of his other writings, most notably in *Considerations on Representative Government*, published in 1861, only two essays, both dating from this last phase, were devoted exclusively to it. The first, 'A few words on non-intervention', which appeared in *Fraser's Magazine* in 1859, was occasioned by Palmerston's reported attempt to defeat an international project to build a Suez canal, on the grounds of the harm it might do to England's commercial and strategic position in the East. Mill's particular concern here was with England's moral reputation, and with the harm done to that reputation by statements which seemed to confine English policy to the pursuit of purely selfish aims: the affair, he observed to Bain, 'is damaging the character of England on the Continent more than most people are aware of' (a remark in which his sense of his special intimacy with Continental opinion is again evident).[70] In fact, as he recorded later in the *Autobiography*: 'I took the opportunity of expressing ideas which had long been in my mind (some of them generated by my Indian experience and others by the international questions which then greatly occupied the European public) respecting the true principles of international morality and the legitimate modifications made in it by difference of times and circumstances.'[71] His premiss was that nations, like individuals, 'have duties . . . towards the weal of the human race', and that the whole issue must accordingly be considered 'as a really moral question', a phrase that signals a return to the dominant key in Mill's compositions.[72]

Viewing the question from this higher ground, he showed himself to have little sympathy with a policy of strict and complete 'non-intervention', a policy much canvassed in England in the 1850s and often popularly, if not altogether justifiably, associated with the names of Cobden and Bright. Mill disavowed slavish adherence to this (or any other) maxim in foreign affairs, just as he did to that of *laissez-faire* in domestic policy: the decisive test was rather whether

episode, *Gladstone and the Bulgarian Agitation 1876* (London, 1963), 208: 'Had John Stuart Mill been alive in 1876, he would have been prominent in support of the Bulgarian atrocities agitation.' For further discussion of the role of intellectuals, see Ch. 6 below, pp. 230–2.

[70] Letter to Bain of 14 Nov. 1859, *LL*, *CW*, xv. 645.

[71] *Autobiography*, *CW*, i. 263–4.

[72] 'Non-intervention', *CW*, xxi. 116, 118.

intervention might promote the good of enabling a people with legitimate aspirations to independence to render themselves fit to exercise genuine self-government, a view with special resonance in the period of liberal nationalist uprisings in Europe. The stage of civilization reached by the society in question was a crucial consideration here; as he demonstrated in his better-known works on liberty and representative government, Mill thought a civilized power might have a duty *not* to leave a backward people stagnating in a freedom they could make no profitable use of. Where, on the other hand, a foreign despotism had been enlisted to suppress a genuine popular movement in another country, a liberal power had a duty to intervene, and it is an illustration of the seriousness with which Mill regarded this duty that he even maintained that England should have acted to prevent the Austrian suppression, with Russian aid, of the Hungarian uprising of 1849.[73] One of the things that drew Mill to Gladstone in the 1860s, however much they differed on specific policies, was the latter's professed commitment to determining England's international role by such moral principles.[74]

That Mill's idealism in such matters was at the same time tempered by a kind of realism was suggested by the second of his two pieces on international affairs, the brief article on 'Treaty obligations', published in the *Fortnightly Review* in 1870, which was written in response to a different kind of crisis. On 31 October 1870, Russia declared its intention of repudiating the clause in the Treaty of Paris—the peace forced on Russia by the victorious Anglo-French alliance at the conclusion of the Crimean War in 1856—whereby the Black Sea was to remain neutral waters. This declaration produced an ill-considered cry in England for war against Russia to force her to honour the agreement, during which agitation the principle of the indefinite inviolability of treaty obligations was frequently invoked. Mill regarded the whole agitation as resting on this mistaken notion that treaties forced upon defeated powers ought to be regarded as binding in perpetuity: 'Were they terminable, as they ought to be, those who object to them would have a rational hope of escape in some more moral way than an appeal to the same brute force which imposed them'.[75] But as ever, he was also addressing himself to the

[73] 'Non-intervention', *CW*, xxi. 124.

[74] For Mill's enthusiasm for Gladstone at this point, see Vincent, *Formation of the Liberal Party*, 160–1.

[75] Letter to Morley of 18 Nov. 1870, *CW*, *LL*, xvii. 1778. See also Mill's letters in *The Times*, 19 Nov. 1870: 5; and 24 Nov. 1870: 3.

state of mind—or, more accurately, the state of character—of which such misguided public responses were symptomatic. In both cases, it was 'that laxity of principle which has almost always prevailed in public matters' which he denounced with especial warmth, moved yet again by the conviction that the unrebuked expression of such views was 'injurious to public morality'.[76]

Questions of 'public morality' were also at the heart of the other topic which particularly engaged Mill's polemical energies in these years, the position of women.[77] Despite the importance he attached to the subject—he later remarked that the 'emancipation of women, & cooperative production, are . . . the two great changes that will regenerate society'[78]—Mill did not actually publish anything substantial on it until 1869. In part this was a matter of waiting for a less hostile phase of public opinion. (Mill, surely influenced here by Harriet's uncompromising antagonism to contemporary society, was particularly pessimistic about the state of opinion in England in the 1850s.) As he had explained to the editor of the *Westminster Review* in 1850: 'My opinions on the whole subject are so totally opposed to the reigning notions that it would probably be inexpedient to express all of them.'[79] In 1854 he and Harriet included it among the subjects on which they hoped to leave some record of their thoughts, but it was not until some two years after Harriet's death that Mill wrote the first draft of *The Subjection of Women*, and only nine years later still that he considered the world ready to receive it. It may also have been the case that Mill's failure to make any progress with the Ethology deterred him from attempting a systematic exploration of an issue which, as I have suggested above, was so closely dependent on that project as he conceived it. The extent to which his dispute with Comte over the alleged differences between the sexes turned on what Mill regarded as the questions to be settled by Ethology is revealing here.[80] In complaining to Harriet in 1849 about the prevalence of false assumptions about women's nature ('on which the whole of the present bad constitution of the relation rests'), he had declared: 'I am convinced however that there are only two things which tend at all to shake this nonsensical prejudice: a better

[76] 'Treaty obligations', *CW*, xxi. 343, 345.

[77] For a fuller discussion of this topic, see Collini, 'Introduction', *CW*, xxi, pp. xxix–xxxviii.

[78] Letter of 1 Jan. 1869 to Parke Godwin, *LL*, *CW*, xvii. 1535.

[79] Letter of 19 Mar. 1850 to William Hickson, *LL*, *CW*, xiv. 48.

[80] See *The Earlier Letters of John Stuart Mill 1812–1848* (hereafter *EL*), *CW*, xiii. 604–11, 616–17, 696–8.

psychology & theory of human nature, for the few; & for the many, more & greater proofs by example of what women can do.'[81]

When Mill did decide that the time was ripe to issue a systematic statement of his views, it was a ripeness he had played an important role in bringing on by his activities in Parliament (discussed more fully below). In particular, his presentation in June 1866 of a petition for the extension of the suffrage to women, and his proposal during the debates of May 1867 to amend the Reform Bill then before the House by omitting reference to the gender of householders entitled to the vote, had aroused a great deal of attention, not all of it hostile.[82] That his amendment received the support of over seventy MPs, including John Bright, Mill found 'most encouraging', and in the wake of this triumph the National Society for Women's Suffrage was formed, actively prompted by Mill and Helen Taylor.[83] When *The Subjection of Women* was published, therefore, Mill was unusually optimistic about the progress the cause was likely to make in the immediate future.[84]

That sustainedly provocative book was one of the peaks of Mill's rhetorical achievement, and it has proved rich enough to invite analysis from several different angles.[85] Confining ourselves here to what it reveals of Mill's role as a public moralist, we may remark, above all, its concern with moral education. The forensic centrepiece of the work is its condemnation of existing marriage arrangements: as he pungently put it: 'There remain no legal slaves except the mistress of every house.'[86] He was, of course, arguing for far more

[81] *LL*, *CW*, xiv. 12–13.

[82] For Mill's speech proposing the amendment, see speech of 20 May 1867, *CW*, xxviii. 151–62. The amendment received 73 votes in addition to the support of Mill and other tellers. Mill considered his proposal of this amendment as 'by far the most important, perhaps the only important public service [he] performed in the capacity of a Member of Parliament' (*Autobiography*, *CW*, i. 255).

[83] Letter of 26 May 1867 to Cairnes, *LL*, *CW*, xvi. 1272. See Ann P. Robson, 'The founding of the National Society for Women's Suffrage', *Canadian Journal of History*, 8 (1973), 1–22; and, for women's suffrage organizations in general, see Constance Rover, *Women's Suffrage and Party Politics in Britain, 1866–1914* (London, 1967).

[84] For an example of this optimism, see Mill's letter of 23 June 1869 to Charles Eliot Norton, *LL*, *CW*, xvii. 1618. The optimism was, of course, misplaced in that no women received the vote in national elections until 1918. Consider here Bain's judgement: 'His most sanguine hopes were of a very slow progress in all things; with the sole exception, perhaps, of the equality of women question, on which his feelings went farther than on any other' (*John Stuart Mill*, 132).

[85] See e.g. Susan Moller Okin, *Women in Western Political Thought* (Princeton, NJ, 1979), and Julia Annas, 'Mill and the subjection of women', *Philosophy*, 52 (1977), 179–94.

[86] *Subjection of Women*, *CW*, xxi. 323.

than the removal of the legal disabilities of married women, important though he always considered the law as a means of wider improvement. He was also proposing a different conception of marriage, in which the couple, meeting as equals, are held together by the bonds of affection and mutual respect. But his concern in doing so goes beyond that of improving woman's lot: he constantly treats marriage as 'a school of genuine moral sentiment',[87] demonstrating once again his intense preoccupation with the consequences institutions have on the character and moral habits of those whose lives they structure. 'Any society [in the sense of social contact] which is not improving, is deteriorating, and the more so, the closer and more familiar it is.' This, Mill argued, was why 'young men of the greatest promise generally cease to improve as soon as they marry, and, not improving, inevitably degenerate'. Marriage for a man whose closest daily contact is with someone whom he regards as his inferior, and who herself acts as his inferior, becomes 'a school of wilfulness, over-bearingness, unbounded self-indulgence, and a double-dyed and idealized selfishness'. Mill's argument here could be represented as a localized variant, expressed in the distinctive idiom of the time, of Hegel's famous parable of the need to recognize another's autonomy and worth before that person's response could provide any worthwhile confirmation of one's own identity and value. 'The relation of superiors to dependents is the nursery of these vices of character.'[88]

Mill's critics found his ideal of marriage a little too much like a two-member Mutual Improvement Society. 'To him marriage was a union of two philosophers in the pursuit of truth,' was how Goldwin Smith unkindly but not altogether unfairly put it, adding, 'not only does he scarcely think of children, but sex and its influences seem hardly to be present to his mind.'[89] Certainly his prim dismissal of the role of the 'animal instinct' might well be seen as something of a handicap for anyone wishing to alter the relations between the sexes. Bain, who thought Mill deficient in 'sensuality' ('he made light of the difficulty of controlling the sexual appetite'), presented this criticism in the cautious form of reported speech: 'It was the opinion of many,

[87] Ibid. 293.

[88] Ibid. 335, 289, 288.

[89] Goldwin Smith, 'Female suffrage', *Macmillan's Magazine*, 30 (1874), 140; see also Brian Harrison, *Separate Spheres: The Opposition to Women's Suffrage in Britain* (London, 1978), 62.

that while his estimate of pure sentimental affection was more than enough, his estimate of the sexual passion was too low.'[90] Mill's own professed view was that 'the force of the natural passions' has been 'exaggerated': 'I think it most probable that this particular passion will become with men, as it already is with a large number of women, completely under the control of the reason,' which surprising proposition he sought to buttress with a somewhat feeble appeal to authority: 'I have known eminent medical men, and lawyers of logical mind, of the same opinion.'[91]

Faced with Mill's call for a radical alteration in the nature of marriage as commonly understood, an alteration which women did not by and large seem to be demanding for themselves, contemporary critics were inclined to ask *Cui bono*?[92] But for Mill this was not a matter of sectional interests. It was not just that wives were denied opportunities for self-fulfilment: he saw the existing pattern of marriage as systematically warping the moral sensibilities of men as well, and thus inhibiting the moral growth of society as a whole. 'The moral regeneration of mankind will only really commence, when the most fundamental of the social relations is placed under the rule of equal justice, and when human beings learn to cultivate their strongest sympathy with an equal in rights and in cultivation.'[93] The emphatic, insistent note here—'only', 'really', 'most fundamental', 'strongest', and so on—is a sign of Mill's anxiety that in these matters those who listen do not hear, while 'moral regeneration' (the implication of the peculiarly debased state of the present is the cultural critic's occupational failing) shows what high stakes are being played for. So much did this issue dominate the last years of Mill's life—Helen Taylor showed some of her mother's skill here—that he could announce in 1872: 'The time . . . is, I think now come when, at Parliamentary elections, a Conservative who will vote for women's suffrage should be, in general, preferred to a professed Liberal who will not. . . . [T]he bare fact of supporting Mr Gladstone in office, certainly does not now give a man a claim to

[90] Bain, *John Stuart Mill*, 149, 89–90.

[91] Letter of 2 Feb. 1870 to Lord Amberley, *LL*, *CW*, xvii. 1693.

[92] The most persistent criticism of the feminist position was to be found in the *Saturday Review*, for Mill's hostility to which on this score see, in addition to p. 126 above, Harrison, *Separate Spheres*, and M. M. Bevington, *The Saturday Review 1855–1868* (New York, 1941), 114–18.

[93] *Subjection of Women*, *CW*, xxi. 336.

preference over one who will vote for the most important of all political improvements now under discussion.'[94]

Mill's concern not just with the rights of women but with the moral sensibility exhibited in publicly condoned attitudes towards them came strongly to the fore in the agitation against the Contagious Diseases Acts, the final example of Mill's performance as a public moralist to be discussed here. These Acts, passed between 1864 and 1869, provided for the compulsory medical inspection and, if necessary, treatment of women suspected of being prostitutes in certain specified garrison towns, in an attempt to control the incidence of venereal disease among the troops stationed there. The Acts raised several questions of principle in relation to police powers and the treatment of women, as well as provoking a variety of less rational responses, and in 1869 a public campaign for the repeal of the Acts was launched with Josephine Butler at its head.[95] Mill supported the campaign—'Of course one need scarcely say that to any man who looks upon political institutions & legislation from the point of view of principle the idea of keeping a large army in idleness & vice & then keeping a large army of prostitutes to pander to their vices is too monstrous to admit of a moment's consideration'—though he was anxious lest the peculiarly emotional controversy that it aroused should injure the campaign for the suffrage.[96] The agitation led to the setting up of a Royal Commission on the Acts in 1870; by Easter 1871 it had heard forty-eight witnesses in favour of the maintenance or extension of the Acts and only twelve in favour of their repeal. The National Association for the Repeal of the Contagious Diseases Acts argued that the Commission should hear more witnesses known to favour repeal, and Mill was among those called as a result.[97]

[94] Letter of 5 Nov. 1872 to G. C. Robertson, *LL*, *CW*, xvii. 1917. It should be remembered that Mill was already disillusioned with the Gladstone ministry by this point. For a sharp assessment of Helen Taylor's influence over Mill on this subject, see the editors' 'Introduction', *LL*, *CW*, xiv, pp. xxxvi–xxxvii.

[95] For details of the campaign and the issues it raised, see F. B. Smith, 'Ethics and disease in the later nineteenth century: The Contagious Diseases Acts', *Historical Studies* (Melbourne), 15 (1971), 18–35; and Paul McHugh, *Prostitution and Victorian Social Reform* (London, 1980).

[96] Letter of 18 Jan. 1870 to William T. Malleson, *LL*, *CW*, xvii. 1688. For the anxiety that to 'the mass of the English people as well as to large numbers already well disposed towards some little improvement in women's condition, the union of the C.D.A. agitation with that for the suffrage, condemns the latter utterly, because they look upon it as indelicate and unfeminine', see Mill's letter of 15 Nov. 1871 to Robertson, *LL*, *CW*, xvii. 1854.

[97] McHugh, *Prostitution and Social Reform*, 61.

It is worth observing in passing that Mill was called as a witness despite having no official standing in any of the organizations or professions involved, having no expert knowledge of the subjects at issue, and having, on his own admission, made no special study of the working of the Acts. As with the Westminster candidacy in 1865, his being John Stuart Mill was sufficient recommendation. In fact, he proved to be a model witness as, under hostile and unfair questioning from some members of the Commission, he maintained a calm and lucid hold on the essential questions of principle.[98] The National Association were evidently pleased with his performance, since they had his evidence published in pamphlet form later in the year, thereby in effect adding it to his list of occasional publications for this period.

What is striking about Mill's evidence, particularly when read in conjunction with his discussion of related issues in *On Liberty*, is the extent to which he made the question of the Acts' official endorsement of vice the chief ground of his objection to them. This is not to say that he scouted objections based on the Acts' potential invasion of individual liberty or the inequity of their effectively penalizing women but not men, for he stated both very forcibly. But when the hypothetical case was put to him of women voluntarily submitting to the examination and treatment, he replied: 'I still think it objectionable because I do not think it is part of the business of the Government to provide securities beforehand against the consequences of immoralities of any kind.' Similarly, his primary objection to any system of licensing prostitutes was that licences 'have still more the character of toleration of that kind of vicious indulgence'. And although he would not have been opposed in principle to state provision of hospitals for the treatment of *all* contagious diseases, he insisted that it would be improper to provide treatment for this class of disease alone, as again condoning publicly the sexual activity that led to it. As things stood, he feared that the troops themselves would infer from the very existence of the Acts 'that Parliament does not entertain any serious disapprobation of immoral conduct of that kind', and he concluded his testimony by reiterating that the tendency of such Acts was 'to do moral injury'.[99]

[98] Cf. McHugh, *Prostitution and Social Reform*, 63: 'The most impressive witness of all was John Stuart Mill'.

[99] *The Evidence of John Stuart Mill, taken before the Royal Commission of 1870, on the Administration and Operation of the Contagious Diseases Acts of 1866 and 1869, reprinted verbatim from the Blue Book* (1871), *CW*, xxi. 353, 356, 360, 371.

Furthermore, he placed great weight on the distinction between the provision of assistance for those whose circumstances had left them unable to provide it for themselves (essentially the principle of the Poor Law), and the provision, before the event, of securities against the natural consequences of immoral or imprudent conduct (the principle, as Mill saw it, of the Contagious Diseases Acts). Not only could the latter provision be taken as encouraging or endorsing the behaviour in question, but the crucial unstated premiss of his objection to such provisions was that they interfered with the proper operation of the calculation of consequences upon the formation of the will—hence his overriding anxiety about 'moral injury.' Ultimately, this moral psychology lay at the heart of all Mill's reflections on the shaping of character by institutions, whether the character in question was that of a selfish voter at the polls, or of a feckless peasant on his smallholding, or of a randy young trooper in Aldershot.

IV

In considering Mill's performance as a public moralist during this period, and indeed the whole vexed question of his exemplary status as a public intellectual, special attention has to be devoted to his three years in Parliament. It is an episode which has provoked sharply conflicting assessments in subsequent scholarly commentary, assessments which, as so often, have reproduced divisions first manifested among contemporary observers of Mill's career. Doubts about the wisdom of his candidacy for Parliament in 1865 were in fact voiced from the start:

> Whether it be wise for Mr Mill to enter Parliament; whether the position he will take there will be adequate either to his great abilities or to his paramount reputation; whether the time and strength which he will have to spend within its walls, listening to dreary speakers and grappling with wearisome details, would not be better employed in following out those philosophical principles which he, far beyond any other writer of this age, is fitted to handle; whether in a word the man of speculation and thought will not be somewhat lost and wasted among the men of action and routine—these are questions which may well admit of doubt.[100]

[100] Walter Bagehot, 'Mr Mill's address to the electors of Westminster', *The Economist*, 29 Apr. 1865: 497; repr. in *The Collected Works of Walter Bagehot*, ed. Norman St John Stevas, 15 vols. (London, 1965–86), iii. 541.

Bagehot's collusive tone clearly invited his readers to treat this doubt pretty hospitably, and there were many among Mill's admirers who feared that the philosopher would descend from his proper sphere only to reveal his lack of political nous and his inability to adapt to the rough-and-tumble of Parliamentary politics. In similar though much less sympathetic vein, Mill's detractors sneeringly dismissed his subsequent performance in Parliament as that of a 'lost philosopher' out of his element, and on his death less than five years after his defeat at the election of 1868, the more hostile obituarists almost routinely referred to his Parliamentary career as conclusive evidence of his doctrinaire and 'crotchety' impracticality.[101]

It was not long, however, before a rather different and apparently contrasting charge was laid. Leslie Stephen provided the keynote for this interpretation with his observation that 'in spite of his philosophy, [Mill] appeared to be a thorough party man' once in the Commons (or again, that 'the philosopher was really the follower of the partisan'), and several modern scholars have taken a similar line.[102] The damaging suggestion here was that Mill, either out of a willing acceptance of party discipline or out of an infatuation with an idealized perception of Gladstone, abandoned the standards of open-minded rationality he had long promoted in his writings and became little better than lobby fodder. 'Impartiality never led him to think the Tories had the better case', is how the charge has been most damagingly made; 'the Apostle of Rationalism left the uncertainty of theoretical creeds' to 'proselytize' for Mr Gladstone. What Mill said in Parliament 'could have been said by a much lesser man than Mill', and hence we should see his period as an MP as 'in the nature of an excursion from his serious career as political instructor to the nation'.[103]

[101] For the 'lost philosopher' jibe, see *Pall Mall Gazette*, 28 July 1866: 11; for an example of the obituarists' judgement that he was a 'manifest failure as a statesman', see *Illustrated London News*, 17 May 1873: 456. These assessments were, of course, contested by Mill's supporters; see e.g. Millicent Garrett Fawcett, 'His influence as a practical politician', *Examiner*, 17 May 1873: 514–17.

[102] Leslie Stephen, *The English Utilitarians*, 3 vols. (London, 1900), iii. 66–7; for an influential view by a modern historian, see Vincent, *Formation of the Liberal Party* 194.

[103] Vincent, *Formation of the Liberal Party*, 192, 194, 184. Stephen had also already suggested part of this line of criticism in his obituary article on Mill, complaining that he had descended 'too easily from the judgement-seat into the open arena': 'What is the use of being a great philosopher if, after all, you can add nothing to the ordinary cry of every popular agitator?' *Nation*, 5 June 1873: 382.

On further reflection, it soon becomes evident that these two interpretations are not the opposites they may first appear: they implicitly concur in minimizing Mill's effective agency as an MP, emphasizing his lack of command of the means for making a distinctive impact upon or successful use of the peculiar and highly ritualized institution of which he now found himself a member. Both 'doctrinaire philosopher' and 'party hack' are descriptions which deny even the modest effectiveness Mill claimed for himself in his account of this period in the *Autobiography*. And yet I would suggest that if one considers his activities as an MP in the context of this larger discussion of his role as a public moralist, that episode falls into place as an integral and not discreditable part of 'his serious career as political instructor to the nation'. As in his journalism and other occasional writings, Mill exploited the opportunities provided by the medium of Parliament to press for short-term pragmatic gains while never losing sight of long-term educative goals. In transferring his attentions from writing to direct political participation, Mill still held by the ideal which he had announced for the statesman as long ago as 1833: 'to make no compromise of *opinions*, except by avoiding any ill-timed declaration of them, but to negociate [*sic*] the most advantageous compromises possible in actual *measures*'.[104]

Concentrating on his Parliamentary speeches and associated activities, we may discern three different levels at which Mill operated. The first level was that of the party struggle.[105] Throughout his period in Parliament (he came in some respects to have doubts about this during his period of deep disillusion with Gladstonian Liberalism after 1870), Mill believed that the Liberal Party was far more likely to promote the cause of progress than was the Tory, even when, perhaps especially when, the latter was led by the opportunistic and tactically brilliant Disraeli. Mill had felt, and frequently expressed, a deep disgust at the moral laxness and practical jobbery of decaying Palmerstonian Whiggism. Part of his respect for Gladstone came from seeing him as the one man of principle in Palmerston's cabinet, and in the 1868 election he hoped that a resounding victory for Gladstone 'would proclaim in thunder to the

[104] 'The ministerial manifesto', *Examiner*, 22 Sept. 1833: 593; repr. in *Newspaper Writings*, *CW*, xxiii. 599.

[105] There is a helpful discussion of the place of parties in Mill's political thought, with particular reference to *Considerations on Representative Government* (1861), in Bruce L. Kinzer, 'J. S. Mill and the problem of party', *Journal of British Studies*, 21 (1981), 106–22.

whole world that the Palmerstonian period was at an end'.[106] In the mid-1860s, therefore, his genuine admiration for Gladstone's moral integrity and apparent freedom from the worst prejudices of his class, combined with the hope that any extension of the franchise would make the Liberal Party more firmly the party of the working class, led Mill to give his support at all crucial moments to obtaining a Liberal ministry and keeping it in office.

Thus, when Mill first took up his seat in February 1866 Russell's fragile ministry had enough difficulties of its own, and Mill abstained from compounding them by raising embarrassing issues or proposing damaging amendments. For example, the warm welcome he extended, in his speech of 17 May 1866, to the government's very modest and unambitious Irish Land Bill must at least in part be attributed to this tactical consideration, since the Bill essentially embodied the familiar presumption that the goal of British policy should be to turn Irish cottiers into English farmers, a presumption against which Mill had consistently argued for over two decades.[107] A more obvious example is provided by the way in which he largely supported the Liberal Reform Bill though it fell far short of his ideal. Indeed, his first major speech in the Commons, delivered on 13 April 1866, endorsed the principle of Gladstone's Bill on the grounds that 'I look upon a liberal enfranchisement of the working classes as incomparably the greatest improvement in our representative institutions, which we at present have it in our power to make. (*Hear*)'.[108] The speech was widely reckoned a success: *The Times* exceptionally recorded at the end of it that 'many members, as they passed down the gangway, close to where the honourable member sits, shook hands with him in congratulation for his able address', and Gladstone appreciatively noted in his diary for that day: 'Reform Debate. Mill admirable.'[109] But in June 1866 Gladstone was defeated in the Commons and the Liberal ministry resigned, allowing the Tories led by Disraeli and Lord Derby to form a government. Opposition, as always, allowed a looser rein to those with more radical inclinations than were apparent among the party leadership, and

[106] Speech to the electors of Westminster, 13 Nov. 1868, *CW*, xxviii. 361.

[107] Speech of 17 May 1866, *CW*, xxviii. 75–83. For a discussion of this speech in relation to Mill's earlier writings on the topic, see Bruce L. Kinzer, 'J. S. Mill and Irish land: a re-assessment', *Historical Journal*, 27 (1984), 119–21.

[108] Speech of 13 Apr. 1866, *CW*, xxviii. 58–68, quotation at 68.

[109] *CW*, xxviii. 68; Gladstone's diary entry is cited by Bruce Kinzer in his introduction to this volume, *CW*, xxviii, p. xxx n.

Mill felt able to take several Parliamentary initiatives of his own in the next two sessions.

Similar judgements about the moments appropriate for toeing the party line came into play outside the House as well: Mill may have made some ill-judged epistolary interventions in the election campaign of 1868, but when he did finally and reluctantly make an appearance at the hustings at the close of the campaign, he did not over-complicate his message: 'Liberals of all shades of opinion' needed to be united 'in the grand and paramount objective of keeping out a Tory'.[110] But both in and out of Parliament, Mill was far from acting in slavish subjection to Gladstone. Rather, he gave the party his support on account, as it were, expecting to be reimbursed in the future by their carrying out of more radical reforms than were practical in the present.[111]

This points the way to the second level at which Mill operated. Subject to the constraints imposed by his tactical support for the Liberal Party, he was very active in proposing useful amendments to legislation, introducing measures of his own, and acting as spokesman for the unenfranchised classes in the political nation, notably, of course, women and the organized working class. One way in which Mill continued the Radical tradition of representing the unrepresented was his willingness to be the means of presenting petitions to Parliament, even where he did not agree with the purposes or arguments of the petitioners.[112] Two issues on which Mill played a particularly active part, not only speaking often in the House but taking the lead in the respective Select Committees, were the question of the terms of extradition treaties with other countries, and the question of establishing a single metropolitan authority for the government of London. On the first of these Mill played a small part in inducing the government eventually to bring in an Act which

[110] Speech to the electors of Westminster, 2 Nov. 1868; *CW*, xxviii. 335. From his Avignon retreat, Mill had not only written to pledge his support for the controversially 'godless' Bradlaugh, standing at Northampton against two well-established Liberals, but he had also pressed the candidacy of his friend Edwin Chadwick at Kilmarnock against another sitting Liberal member; see *LL*, *CW*, xvi. 1433, 1453–4.

[111] Cf. Kinzer's judgement that 'the Liberal party was important to Mill for what it could become'; 'Introduction', *CW*, xxviii. p. xxxviii.

[112] The lists of the titles alone of the petitions he presented occupy over twenty pages in the Toronto edition of his speeches (*CW*, xxix. 572–93), 'an index', as the editors remark, 'of his repute nationally as well as locally, and of his exceptionally busy and regular Parliamentary activity' (572).

allowed foreign citizens accused of political crimes the benefit of English legal procedure (rather than, for example, being extradited merely on the basis of a deposition laid in secret before a French magistrate).[113] But the most notable feature of his contributions was once again his insistence that the overriding consideration in such matters should be Britain's moral standing in the eyes of the rest of the world. As in his articles on foreign policy, he wanted to see Britain exercise moral leadership, and feared that the surrender of a bona fide political refugee under the terms proposed 'would cover this country with ignominy'.[114]

The second issue, the proposal to establish a single metropolitan authority for the government of London, furnishes a good example of the way in which Mill could take a practical part in the current legislative business while at the same time also raising questions of principle for the future. It was a topic which engaged Mill's long-standing hostility to privilege and the abuse of power and endowments by closed corporations, the City of London providing some flagrant examples of this. But local government also promised to be a proving-ground in miniature for some of his more recent preoccupations concerning the prospects for democracy, especially on matters such as the possibility of inducing persons of 'superior attainments' to offer themselves for elected office and the likelihood that a system of proportional representation would secure the election of a larger number of such candidates. In addition to his speeches in the House, Mill took a prominent part in the work of the Select Committee on Metropolitan Local Government: he attended twenty-three sessions of the Committee between 9 March and 29 July 1866; he demonstrated great command of the details of the work of the London vestries and boards; and he was clearly responsible for the calling of certain witnesses known to be favourable to the reform of London government.

[113] His reference in the *Autobiography* to his contribution on this issue thus contains, as the editors of the speeches point out (*CW*, xxviii. 114), a considerable exaggeration, since he there refers to helping to 'defeat' the Extradition Bill, whereas the most he seems to have achieved was to insert a clause limiting its duration to one year (*Autobiography and Literary Essays*, ed. John M. Robson and Jack Stillinger (Toronto and London, 1981), *CW*, i. 282–3). But it does seem to have been the case that his and others' objections encouraged the government to set up the Select Committee, whose recommendations led, after Mill had left Parliament, to amendment on the point in question.

[114] For his speeches on this topic on 3, 4, and 6 Aug. 1866, see *CW*, xxviii. 115–18, 119, 120–3 (quotation at 123); for his questioning in the 1868 Select Committee, see *CW*, xxix. 542–71.

The more strategic side of Mill's involvement with this issue is seen in his introduction of 'A Bill for the Better Government of the Metropolis' in 1867, and two similar bills in 1868, not with any hope of their actually being enacted (for which they would have needed government support that he knew would not be forthcoming), but largely so that 'public opinion [might be] called forth to give them a sufficient degree of support' and the issue thereby placed on the political agenda for future sessions. But at this level it was the terms in which the issue was defined that mattered most to Mill, and his speech proposing his Bill in June 1868 has very much the air of a lecture by the author of *Considerations on Representative Government*: 'It is well understood what is the special danger of democratic institutions: it is the absence of skilled administration . . . the great political problem of the future, not only for this country, but for all others, is to obtain the combination of democratic institutions with skilled administration. . . . I am anxious to impress on the House the importance of reviewing our institutions in this particular point of view.'[115] Not surprisingly, *Hansard's* reporter recorded an almost complete absence of the usual encouraging interjections; a lecture does not naturally call forth cries of 'Hear! Hear!', even when delivered in the House of Commons.

A further issue in which his constructive practical involvement was particularly extensive was the reform of corrupt electoral practices. Mill constantly denounced the illegitimate power of money at both Parliamentary and municipal elections, and he spoke on twelve different occasions during the debates on the Corrupt Practices Bill between March and July 1868. In this case his efforts met with little success as far as the final form of the Act was concerned. As he reported to a correspondent the day after his final intervention: 'You will have seen that after many days and nights of hard fighting, all our efforts to improve the Bribery Bill have been defeated.' But Mill was, as always, no less concerned with the indirect consequences of such debates: 'Good however has been done by the discussion, and a foundation laid for future success, as even the Saturday Review acknowledges.'[116]

This points to the third level at which Mill operated, where he used his prominence as an MP to get attention for principles he

[115] See speeches of 21 May and 7 Aug. 1867, and 5 May, 17 June, and 30 June 1868; *CW*, xxviii. 162–5, 230–1, 273–5, 290–5, 300–1 (quotation at 291–2).

[116] Letter of 27 July 1868 to W. D. Christie, *LL*, *CW*, xvi. 1425. For Mill's speeches on the Corrupt Practices Bill see *CW*, xxviii. 262–328.

regarded as important and to engage in further instalments of the larger task of moral education. Writing to a European correspondent in 1867, Mill alluded to this level of his activities: 'You will easily understand that I look upon the House of Commons not as a place where important practical improvements can be effected by anything I can do there, but as an elevated Tribune or Chair from which to preach larger ideas than can at present be realised.'[117] This slightly self-excusing characterization was obviously not the whole truth about Mill's conception of his role, but it certainly catches an important part of his performance; there seems to be no reason to read any self-irony into his choice of the verb 'preach'. The issues upon which Mill spoke in this vein were those where there was little hope of his opinions finding favour among the majority of MPs, still less of having any chance of being embodied in legislation in the near future —issues such as the enfranchisement of women, the adoption of proportional representation, land reform in Ireland, or the prosecution of Governor Eyre.

These issues were in themselves quite heterogeneous, and the extent to which they engaged the attentions of Parliament varied considerably. On both the enfranchisement of women and the introduction of proportional representation, Mill could not hope for any practical gains to be made in the Parliamentary sessions in which he raised them; the majority of Members regarded them, especially the latter, as his personal 'crotchets', and Mill was engaged as much in a symbolic as a pragmatic activity in rehearsing the arguments in their favour. Ireland and Governor Eyre were a different matter, partly because they required a response from Parliament independently of Mill's promotion of them, and partly because in both cases he had, or seemed to have, a definite practical outcome he was seeking to achieve (namely, the introduction of fixed rents and, ultimately, tenure for the Irish cottiers in the one case, and a commitment from the government to prosecute Eyre in the other). Yet with respect to both Ireland and Jamaica it is arguable that, whatever the realistic expectations of success in his specific proposals, Mill's overriding concern was to get certain moral principles declared and acknowledged.

This raises again the question of the 'voice' in which Mill spoke as a public figure, and the kinds of authority he deployed as a public

[117] Letter of 7 Feb. 1867 to Arnold Ruge, *LL*, *CW*, xvi. 1234.

moralist. It is, of course, true that his reputation in 1865, his claim to be heard, rested upon his writings, and there is an occasional reference to these during his public career, above all to his *Principles of Political Economy*. Yet his activities as an MP did not really rest upon a recognized claim to special or technical expertise. Remarking an affinity between Mill and Gladstone, one historian has observed that they both, in their different ways, 'chose to act only indirectly on the basically recalcitrant M.P.s, in all but the final stages bypassing them in favour of an appeal, on the one hand, to whatever was expert, disinterested, scientific, and open-minded in society: on the other hand, by drawing on the support of classes and institutions which still carried little weight in Parliament.'[118] But the affinity may have been closer than this contrast suggests: there is little in Mill's speeches that could really be described as an appeal to what was 'expert' or 'scientific', but considerable evidence of how, like Gladstone, he exercised a moral authority, not least in his constant denunciation of the habitual selfishness and indifference of the possessing classes.

In so far as Mill did claim, explicitly or implicitly, the authority of the specialist, he did so in his speeches on Ireland, where his proposals for recognizing the differences between English and Irish agriculture and, eventually, establishing peasant proprietors, though they ultimately rested upon a view of what was conducive to forming the kind of self-improving character necessary to sustain prosperity, gained some cogency from his standing as a political economist. Even here it is worth noting that his arguments involved not so much an appeal to economic theory as a marshalling of comparative empirical information about landholding in other parts of Europe. Only at one point is he recognizably the author of the classic definition of political economy as a hypothetical science, namely when delivering an extended rebuttal to Robert Lowe's use of political economy conceived as 'a particular set of practical maxims'. But the average county Member was evidently less than enthralled by his intellectually fastidious disquisition on this topic: this is the only point in his Parliamentary speeches where *Hansard* records '(*The honourable member was here interrupted by expressions of impatience from several members*)' followed shortly by '(*Ironical cheers and laughter*)'.[119]

[118] Vincent, *Formation of the Liberal Party*, 185.

[119] Speech of 12 Mar. 1868, *CW*, xxviii. 255–6.

Mill's views on Ireland in the 1860s have been extensively studied elsewhere,[120] and focusing on his Parliamentary speeches does not reveal any distinctive addition to those views. At most, it suggests that Mill was willing to adopt a more conciliatory tone when trying to persuade MPs of the feasibility of his proposals than is usually evident in the uncompromising prose of his pamphlets and articles. But essentially the burden of his message was the same whatever the medium: England faced moral 'disgrace' if it failed to adopt measures sufficiently radical to conciliate the mass of the Irish people. 'When a country has been so long in possession of full power over another, as this country has over Ireland, and still leaves it in the state of feeling which now exists in Ireland, there is a strong presumption that the remedy required must be much stronger and more drastic than any which has yet been applied (*Hear, hear*).'[121] The almost Johnsonian cadence of this is characteristic of those moments when Mill is charging his countrymen with dereliction of a moral duty; the balanced periods and elevated tone were among the rhetorical resources he used to stir ordinary indifference and inattention to confront the full gravity of his charge.

Moral arguments of this kind, as I have argued above, necessarily involve some appeal to values shared by speaker and audience alike, yet that in itself is obviously not sufficient to guarantee persuasiveness. Mill's contributions to the Governor Eyre controversy reveal the nature, and the limits, of his role as a public moralist particularly sharply, for his Jamaica speeches furnish some of the purest examples of this appeal, and yet this was arguably the issue on which Mill most conspicuously failed to make much impression on those he was addressing. The very importance Mill attached to the issue already suggested an idiosyncratic perspective,[122] and it was consistent with this estimation that he considered his speech on the matter in July 1866 to be the best of his Parliamentary speeches.[123] That speech certainly dealt in telling forensic style with the weaknesses in the

[120] See, particularly, E. D. Steele, 'J.S. Mill and the Irish Question: reform and the integrity of the empire 1865–1870', *Historical Journal*, 13 (1970), 419–50; Lynn Zastoupil, 'Moral government: J. S. Mill on Ireland', *Historical Journal*, 26 (1983), 707–17; Kinzer, 'J. S. Mill and Irish land'; and the 'Introduction' by Joseph Hamburger to *Essays on England, Ireland, and the Empire*, ed. John M. Robson (Toronto and London, 1982) (*CW*, vi).

[121] Speech of 12 Mar. 1868, *CW*, xxviii. 248–9.

[122] See the letter of 14 Dec. 1865, cited in text to n. 63 above.

[123] *Autobiography*, *CW*, i. 281–2.

government's case for taking no further legal action against Eyre and his subordinates, and it restated the Jamaica Committee's purpose in highly charged language. The Committee was attempting 'to procure a solemn reassertion of the principle, that whoever takes human life without justification must account for it to the law', and in pursuing this goal, the Committee were doing no less than attempting to discharge a 'great public duty', and so on.[124] No Member of the House (or reader of the speech in the form in which it was printed by the Jamaica Committee) could fail to recognize that for Mill the issue was 'whether we are giving up altogether the principle of government by law, and resigning ourselves to arbitrary power', and hence that what was at stake was a choice between flouting or affirming the most fundamental moral and political values, values the assertion and defence of which was supposed to be the distinctive glory of English political history (Mill was willing to appeal to this Whiggish piety when it suited his purpose).

And yet Mill and the Jamaica Committee failed. Far from succeeeding in having Eyre brought before a legal tribunal, Mill ultimately succeeded only in attracting a great deal of criticism, some of it abusive and extremely hostile, for his apparently vindictive pursuit of the unfortunate Eyre. On the basis of the content of Mill's speeches themselves, one cannot say that he overplayed his hand: he invoked principles whose validity and importance were agreed to be beyond dispute. Yet there must remain the suspicion that in the eyes of his listeners and readers he either over-simplified the case, in failing sufficiently to allow for the demands of prompt action in a threatening emergency of uncertain proportions, or else that he sought unreasonably severe punishment, given that the official report had strongly condemned many of the actions apparently undertaken on the orders of Eyre or his immediate subordinates, and that Eyre had since been removed from his post. Presumably, the view expressed by Sir Frederic Rogers, Permanent Under-Secretary at the Colonial Office, represented a feeling common among the official classes: writing to his chief, Earl Carnarvon, in August 1866 he confessed 'a personal desire that a courageous & honourable man who has done his best under very trying circumstances and with advantages—we none of us [know] how much to the whole Western hemisphere—should be generously dealt with'. Carnarvon's Liberal

[124] Speech of 31 July 1866, *CW*, xxviii. 113.

predecessor, Edward Cardwell, expressed a similar perception of the matter in his comment two months earlier that, following the publication of the official report, only 'extreme men' would attempt to 'raise a Jamaica Debate' when Parliament resumed.[125] Part of the explanation of why Mill pursued this cause with such single-minded, and ultimately self-defeating, commitment may lie not just in his sense of outrage at what Eyre had actually done or allowed to be done, a feeling shared by many who did not support the policy of the Jamaica Committee, but in a visceral aversion to the moral laxness and indifference, especially to the plight of 'subject peoples', of the English public and its political leaders which he regarded as on trial in this matter. In exhorting his audience to live up to the highest standards of their announced ideals, the public moralist always treads a fine line between a discomfiting effectiveness and a dismissable priggishness, and perhaps in this instance Mill tilted that delicate balance too far in the direction of moral rigorism. Leslie Stephen's general comment on Mill's public performances may be pertinent here: 'He did not, I fancy, obtain that kind of personal weight which is sometimes acquired by a man who, though he preaches equally offensive doctrines, is more obviously made of the same flesh and blood as his adversaries.'[126]

Success as a speaker in the House of Commons, as in any assembly that placed such weight upon oral performance, was not, of course, determined solely by the intellectual or even moral content of one's speeches. In the light of the few scraps of evidence we have about Mill's actual delivery, it seems almost certain that he now reads better on the page than he sounded in the debating chamber. His voice was described as being nearer to 'thin' than to 'rich'; he was impatient of even those minor theatrical indulgences necessary properly to command the medium; and his sentences could be long and somewhat baroque in construction, even by what may now seem the ample oratorical conventions of the time. Yet he undoubtedly won the respect of many discerning judges, especially after the success of his Reform Bill speech of 13 April 1866, and although few Members may have been persuaded by him out of their established prejudices, the 'close reasoning' of his speeches was more than once

[125] Both quoted in B. A. Knox, 'The British Government and the Governor Eyre controversy, 1865–1875', *Historical Journal*, 19 (1976), 892, 888.

[126] Stephen, *English Utilitarians*, iii. 65.

singled out for favourable comment. As one experienced judge put it:

> Mr Mill has no oratorical gifts and he knows it. Nor can he be called a rhetorician. He is a close reasoner, and addresses himself directly to our reasoning powers; and though he has great command of language, as all his hearers know, he never condescends to deck out his argument in rhetorical finery to catch applause. His object is to convey his thoughts directly to his hearer's mind, and to do this he uses the clearest medium—not coloured glass, but the best polished plate, because through that objects may be best seen.[127]

Less predictably, Mill's late public speeches show him to have been adept at modifying the pitch and style of his reasoning when addressing larger and more enthusiastically partisan audiences. The nicely turned compliment to the Chair, the opening flourish, the sarcasm at the expense of opponents, the repetition of key phrases or telling facts, the rousing finale—Mill's armoury as a public speaker was well stocked by the end of his life, and the reports indicate scenes of really quite tumultous enthusiasm at some of the large meetings he addressed.

This was surely connected to the fact that once out of Parliament, following his defeat in November 1868, Mill appeared as a yet more 'extreme' radical in his popular speeches on those topics which most stirred him in this last phase, especially non-sectarian education, the enfranchisement of women, and land reform. As his disillusion with the Liberal Party and its leaders increased, as it did very markedly after 1870, he explicitly appealed beyond them to an implied popular constituency in the country at large where, uniquely, right-mindedness could be expected to outweigh the habitual selfishness of the comfortable classes. In this vein he could evidently be an effective platform orator: 'Our Liberal Government is as bad on this subject [land reform] as the Tories (*Hear, hear*)—perhaps even worse. (*Loud cheers.*) The passion of the many is needed to conquer the self-interest of the few. (*Cheers.*)'[128] The land question, which disturbed the sensibilities of the propertied classes so profoundly, particularly lent itself to this more populist style. In the last recorded speech of his life, made at a meeting of the Land Tenure Reform

[127] William White (Door-Keeper of the House of Commons), *The Inner Life of the House of Commons*, 2 vols. (London, 1897), cited in *CW*, xxviii, p. xliii n.

[128] Speech to the Land Tenure Reform Association, 18 Mar. 1873; *CW*, xxix. 428.

Association in March 1873, Mill explicitly allied the LTRA with Joseph Arch's new Agricultural Labourers' Union, looking forward to 'concerted and organized cooperation'.[129] Appropriately, the final words in the report of his last speech were '*(Loud Cheers)*': Mill had become an accomplished public speaker, and this was the 66-year-old philosopher on the stump, threatening to out-Gladstone Gladstone.

These late speeches are also a reminder how little the historical Mill resembled that figment created by twentieth-century textbooks in the history of political thought, the individualist liberal opposed to all 'intervention' by the state. His proposals for land reform alone, particularly for the taxation of the 'unearned increment', give the lie to this stereotype, and he insisted that the days had gone by when any increase in the role of central government meant only an increase in aristocratic jobbery and self-serving. Above all, the *moral* obligation of the state towards its citizens now required increased rather than diminished activity:

> It is my conviction that, if the State employed all the means it possesses of raising the standard of morality, and even, in some respects, of physical well-being, in the community, it would find that it has much more in its power than it is now the fashion to believe; and that Governments in these days are quite as blameable in neglecting the right means of promoting those objects, as in days yet recent they were in pursuing the wrong. The time has passed away when Governments, speaking generally, were actively tyrannical; their favourite sins in the present time are indolence and indifference.[130]

Mill's hostility to 'indolence and indifference' pervaded his performance as a public moralist, and one of the less obvious forms it took, documented in one of these late speeches, was enthusiasm for the idea of a citizen, as opposed to a professional, army. In proposing that 'henceforth our army should be our whole people trained and disciplined', Mill was obviously moved by some of the same considerations that had, up to the end of the eighteenth century, animated the long tradition in favour of a militia, but they were here expressed in distinctive Victorian form. Thus, it was the 'good effects of military training in making [young men] more steady and vigorous for the ordinary pursuits of life' that he particularly insisted

[129] Speech to the Land Tenure Reform Association, 18 Mar. 1873; *CW*, xxix. 430–1.

[130] Speech to a meeting of the London National Society for Women's Suffrage on 26 Mar. 1870; *CW*, xxix. 387.

upon, rather than the eighteenth-century sense of the intimate connections between a militia, liberty, and virtue. Similarly, his objection to a standing army was not the traditional anxiety about the threat it posed to the constitutional government of the country, but firstly the expense, and secondly that in peacetime soldiers kept in barracks 'are idle and something worse', a concern which had obviously been given greater vividness as a result of his participation in the movement for the repeal of the Contagious Diseases Acts in the same year.[131]

As all these examples suggest, Mill had become in the last phase of his career an eminent public figure—recognizable, in demand as a speaker, an ornament (and more) on the councils of several radical and reform organizations. In addition to being Chairman of both the Jamaica Committee and the Land Tenure Reform Association, his final years saw Mill on the Council of the Commons Preservation Society (an organization effectively led by his friend Henry Fawcett), and of the National Association for the Promotion of Social Science, as well as being one of the initiators and most prominent supporters of the National Society for Women's Suffrage. But although his intellectual achievements had been the initial basis of Mill's public standing, his effectiveness as a speaker, both inside Parliament and out, ultimately rested upon a moral rather than a technical authority. Gladstone's recommendation of Mill to the electors of Westminster in 1868 is hardly a disinterested source, but it is notable that in his brief eulogy he made no reference to Mill's 'expertise' or intellectual authority, but spoke rather of the example he had set by his 'forgetfulness of self' and 'absolute devotion to public duty', and emphasized that 'his presence in the House of Commons has materially helped to raise and sustain its moral tone'.[132] Gladstone was no doubt indulgently exaggerating the effect of Mill's contribution, but the terms of the description do surely point fairly accurately to its essential character, and, as we have seen, they could equally be applied to Mill's role in public debate more generally.

[131] Speech to a meeting of the Working Men's Peace Association on the government's Army Bill, 10 Mar. 1871; *CW*, xxix. 411–15.

[132] Gladstone's letter was read out at a meeting of the electors of Westminster, at which Mill spoke, on 24 July 1868; *CW*, xxviii. 329.

5

Manly Fellows
Fawcett, Stephen, and the Liberal Temper

I

'What in Mr Mill is but a yielding to a spirit of irritable injustice, goes on and worsens in some of his disciples, till it becomes a sort of mere blatancy and truculent hardness in Professor Fawcett.'[1] Matthew Arnold may not always have exhibited enough of his own cherished quality of 'disinterestedness' when speaking of the leaders of radical Liberalism, but as we move on to consider some of those who lived under Mill's shadow, this judgement provides a useful, if teasing, starting-point. It is not, it has to be said, immediately obvious what is meant by the phrase 'a sort of mere blatancy and truculent hardness', yet anyone who has read much of Fawcett's writing would be bound, I think, to come to find these words uncannily apt. They are not, needless to say, at all similar to the theoretical labels which historians of political thought conventionally use when referring to those who might be considered in some sense Mill's followers. But an essential part of the argument of the present chapter is that we shall not understand the political attitudes of someone like Henry Fawcett, still less Leslie Stephen, if we confine ourselves to the abstract propositions of Utilitarianism or classical political economy. Rather, we need to attend once more to what may seem the un- or pre-political predispositions and allegiances which animated the otherwise dry bones of their political creed.

I take Stephen's phrase 'manly fellows' as my title since it points to a generally neglected part of the dynamic of the political

[1] Matthew Arnold, *St Paul and Protestantism* (1870), in *The Complete Prose Works of Matthew Arnold*, ed. R. H. Super, 11 vols. (Ann Arbor, Mich., 1960–77), vi. 126 (in later editions Arnold replaced the words 'Professor Fawcett' with 'some of them').

allegiances of Fawcett, Stephen, and several of their contemporaries. As I acknowledge below, 'manliness' could mean more than one thing in Victorian England, and this chapter certainly does not pretend to provide anything like a comprehensive discussion of that variety. Though I mention both 'Christian manliness' and 'muscular Christianity', I am dealing with something less specific than either. As the names of Fawcett and Stephen suggest, the ethos of manliness could take an almost wholly secular form, although this is one of those places where the larger surrounding context of Victorian *religious* belief and sensibility needs to be borne in mind. Perhaps I should also add that, despite what may now appear to be the primary connotation of the term, questions of sexual identity and gender construction are not the direct concern here.

Instead, the focus is on the political temper exhibited by Fawcett, and to some extent by Stephen, and upon the place of that temper in Victorian culture more generally. By background and education, Fawcett was initially somewhat marginal to the world of the well-connected Victorian intellectuals described in Chapter 1 above. But his talents, especially his talent for self-promotion, soon took him to the heart of that world; indeed, he epitomized its opportunities by combining for almost twenty years the roles of Member of Parliament and Professor of Political Economy at Cambridge. Yet at the same time, Fawcett's Liberalism can appear more primitive than that of many of his intellectual contemporaries, and, by the 1870s and 1880s, even more dated, for he was shaped by, and continued to embody, several earlier political and intellectual fashions. Though this may have reduced his interest for subsequent historians of political and economic theory, it makes him a particularly revealing witness to the actual dynamic of individualist Liberalism at its zenith.

II

'There has been no more striking example in our time of how self-reliance and strength of purpose can triumph over adverse fortune than that presented by the career of Henry Fawcett.'[2] Even discounting for memorialist's piety, we are properly reminded by Bryce's words that in dealing with Fawcett we are dealing with a

[2] James Bryce, 'Preface' to Winifred Holt, *A Beacon for the Blind: Being a Life of Henry Fawcett, the Blind Postmaster General* (London, 1915), p. vii.

figure who commanded his contemporaries' attention as much for his exemplary value as for the substance of his achievements. On his death, the tributes, from Gladstone down, all emphasized the 'example' of his life, his possession of qualities 'which all of his fellow countrymen may in their degree emulate and follow', especially, as Sidgwick put it, 'the wonderful success and example of this life . . . which did not draw its force from self-love alone, [but] continually demanded and obtained further force given by consciousness of the power of serving others'.[3] We may do well to follow this lead, for it would be foolish to pretend that as an economist and political theorist Fawcett can be credited with any significant originality, or that as a writer he displayed any qualities more remarkable than vigour and a high tolerance for repetition. (Bryce was perhaps putting a similar point in the more favourable idiom of the day when he wrote in his obituary: 'Mr Fawcett's career is an admirable illustration of the truth that in life—literary and scientific life almost as much as practical life—force of character counts for more than pure intellectual capacity.'[4]) And even his career, remarkable though it was given his blindness, would not in itself have required extensive consideration by historians: after all, Parliamentary politics was his chosen *métier* yet he never attained Cabinet rank. But during his lifetime Fawcett represented a particularly important set of political attitudes with a revealing purity, and I think he provides a rewarding route to a historical understanding of the intellectual and emotional dynamic underlying those attitudes.

First, however, we must acknowledge a special difficulty about the nature of the evidence available for this particular enquiry. We cannot but approach Fawcett through the medium of the *Life* written by his old friend Leslie Stephen.[5] Indeed, one may be forgiven for thinking that it was Fawcett's greatest achievement, or at least stroke of good fortune, as far as posthumous celebrity was concerned, to have obtained the affectionate attention of the acknowledged master among Victorian biographers. Certainly the *Life* enjoyed considerable contemporary success, going into its fifth

[3] Gladstone and Sidgwick are quoted by, respectively, Lawrence Goldman and Christopher Harvie in Lawrence Goldman (ed.), *The Blind Victorian: Henry Fawcett and British Liberalism* (Cambridge, 1989), 36, 187–8.

[4] James Bryce, 'The late Mr Fawcett', *Nation* (NY), 39 (1884), 457.

[5] Leslie Stephen, *Life of Henry Fawcett* (London, 1885); no changes were introduced in subsequent editions. Hereafter cited as *Life*.

edition within a year, thereby firmly establishing its subject's exemplary status. Maitland recorded that it was 'often thought of as the most attractive of [Stephen's] books', and recent historians have treated it as one of the best guides to the economic and political thought of the whole generation of young intellectuals to which Fawcett and Stephen belonged.[6] (Stephen himself was characteristically dissatisfied. As his friend Henry Sidgwick reported in his journal after a conversation with Stephen's wife: 'She tells me that Stephen is depressed because his life of Fawcett has only reached a 4th edition.'[7]) The book effectively falls into two halves—a fact which Stephen himself seems to have recognized[8]—and these judgements must both apply only to the first half, that perceptive, evocative, sympathetic portrait of the young Fawcett, and especially of his circle at Cambridge, which displayed Stephen's special talent for capturing the interplay between temperament and belief. The second half, the somewhat dry narrative of Fawcett's Parliamentary career, is not without interest, but Stephen was, as he acknowledged, too remote from that world to bring it to life with anything like the same sureness of touch, and it does not offer that kind of insider's view of the machinations of high politics contained in the 'Life and Letters' of some of the more eminent politicians of the time.

What may not be so obvious is that through Stephen's biography we are encountering Fawcett at a double remove. To begin with, it is an account of a set of political attitudes which were already coming to be regarded as distinctly old-fashioned. There are frequent reminders in the book that it is being written with the controversies of the 1880s in full swing,[9] and Stephen is constantly having to defend —and where he cannot defend, at least make intelligible—a claim about the essential principles of Liberalism which he knew many of his readers would regard as either archaic or tendentious. In

[6] F. W. Maitland, *The Life and Letters of Leslie Stephen* (London, 1906), 374; Christopher Harvie, *The Lights of Liberalism: University Liberals and the Challenge of Democracy 1860–1886* (London, 1976), 305, where Stephen's chapter on Fawcett's political economy is described as the 'best account of the economic beliefs held by Fawcett's generation'.

[7] Sidgwick Journal, 25 Mar. 1886; Henry Sidgwick MSS, Trinity College, Cambridge, Add. MSS d.70.

[8] Maitland, *Life of Leslie Stephen*, 387–8.

[9] See, e.g. his remarks about Spencer's 'New Toryism', in *Life*, 265, a reference to a series of articles on 'The man versus the state' that Spencer published in 1884, and which caused a considerable controversy about the changing nature of Liberalism.

several areas, notably on the question of the grounds of state intervention, Stephen could do this with conviction because he was presenting a view which, as I shall bring out later, he still shared, and to this extent the book constituted something of an appeal from the old to the new Liberals. But, secondly, we have also to recognize that intellectually and, in some ways, politically Stephen and Fawcett had moved far apart since the days of their Radical comradeship of the 1850s and early 1860s. Partly this involved a growing distaste on Stephen's part for active politics generally, and in particular for what he, like so many others of his type, saw as the disappointment of the reforming hopes of the mid-1860s and the decline into Gladstonian demagoguery. ('My friends have sometimes accused me, indeed, of indifference to politics. I confess that I have never been able to follow the details of party warfare with the interest they excite in some minds; and reasons, needless to indicate, have caused me to stray further and further away from intercourse with the society in which such details excite a predominant—I do not mean to insinuate an excessive—interest.'[10]) It also involved Stephen's increased absorption in literature, scholarship, and family life; it involved an intellectual development which led him to emphasize more strongly than before the power of history and the forces of social change at the expense of mere political 'machinery'; and it involved what might be called an emotional development as a result of which the confident no-nonsense relation to life which they had shared in their twenties, and which stayed with Fawcett to the end, came to Stephen to seem thin and unsatisfying.

Indeed, on reflection one is bound to wonder, as some of Stephen's later friends like Maitland clearly did,[11] how the ironical, sceptical, moody Stephen could ever have been so close to the straightforward, emphatic, insufferably cheerful Fawcett. In part it was the usual story of a friendship made in youth becoming itself the chief bond of attraction between two men who have become very different; the loyalty is now to the friendship as much as to the friend, a nostalgic and slightly contrived celebration of an intimacy that was once spontaneous. But when a later biographer, pondering this puzzle, observed that the two men 'seem to have shared little but their earlier politics and their love of walking',[12] she was pointing,

[10] Leslie Stephen, *Social Rights and Duties*, 2 vols. (London, 1896), i. 45–6.

[11] See Noel Annan, *Leslie Stephen: The Godless Victorian* (London, 1984), 40.

[12] Holt, *A Beacon for the Blind*, 78.

unknowingly, to a cluster of associations which lay at the heart of the affinity between Stephen and Fawcett, associations which pervade Stephen's biography, and which, I want to argue, were a crucial source of the political attitudes of which Fawcett was such an undeviating representative. But first we need to look very briefly at the alleged theoretical basis of those attitudes, and to examine more closely the nature of the political identity they expressed.

As I have already implied, part of Fawcett's interest for the intellectual historian of the period lies in the fact that whatever position he took up he could be relied upon to take it up in its purest and most uncomplicated form. Politically, he stood, proudly conscious of his unswerving rectitude, for a severe form of Individualism, and economically for a dogmatic attachment to the principles of classical political economy, though he considered himself a pragmatist in their application. In so far as Fawcett is credited with any systematic theoretical basis for his political convictions, he is normally described as a Utilitarian.[13] Since my way of stating these received views may hint at revisionist intentions, let me say at once that I am not about to make the improbable suggestion that Fawcett was in fact a proto-Socialist, an unrecognized forerunner of historical economics, or, more unimaginable still, an adept of the mysteries of philosophical Idealism. But in trying to understand Fawcett's political thinking and political identity, and to place it on the map of Victorian public debate, I do want to suggest that we need to operate with slightly more probing categories than those provided by the conveniently prefabricated label 'Utilitarian Liberal'.

We may begin with the question of Utilitarianism. Whatever its importance at the level of systematic moral and political philosophy, I would argue (though the case cannot be substantiated here[14]) that historians have tended to speak in exaggerated terms of its impact on political discourse and political action in mid-nineteenth-century England. Certainly, a number of originally Utilitarian formulae found their way into the language, or, less generously, perhaps just the rhetoric, of political debate; it is also true that some of the views

[13] See, e.g. the discussion in J. C. Wood, *British Economists and the Empire* (London, 1983), 77–93.

[14] For further elaboration of this point, see Stefan Collini, *Liberalism and Sociology: L. T. Hobhouse and Political Argument in England 1880–1914* (Cambridge, 1979), 43–6; and id., 'Political theory and the "science of society" in Victorian Britain', *Historical Journal*, 23 (1980), 218-19.

and policies historically associated with the Philosophic Radicals, though not necessarily derivable from strict Utilitarian theory, continued to command attention long after the demise of their sponsors as an active Parliamentary force. But mid-Victorian political discourse, even among those of reforming inclinations, was effectively constituted by allegiances and arguments drawn from other sources, largely of a more traditionally constitutional, historical, religious, or, above all, moral kind. Certainly it could matter *which* vague formulae a writer chose to flourish, and at this level Fawcett undeniably relied upon broadly Utilitarian considerations. Thus, he explains his purpose in his book, *The Economic Position of the British Labourer*, as being to show 'what arrangements may be adopted so as to bring the greatest happiness to the community in general', and later he emphasizes that no arguments in favour of the greater economic efficiency of enclosures ought to be allowed any weight 'if it could be shown that this augmented wealth has tended not to promote but to diminish the comfort and happiness of the people'.[15] But when such phrases are not part of any systematically deployed theoretical framework, as in Fawcett's writings they are not, they tell us very little about the really operative sources of the ideas to which they are juxtaposed.

What mattered far more was that Fawcett saw himself as, was seen by others as, and to a surprisingly consistent extent was, a disciple of John Stuart Mill. I say 'surprisingly' consistent extent because although historians refer expansively to the impact of Mill's teaching in the mid-century, in many cases this turns out on inspection to involve less than meets the eye. Fawcett's exceptional fidelity may be brought out by distinguishing three categories or stages of discipleship among the alleged teeming Millians. The first, both chronologically and in terms of its incidence, was to be a keen student of Mill's double-decker treatises on logic and political economy.[16] In general terms, basing oneself on Mill's work in these fields might well involve laying claim to a modern, scientific, often secular and 'advanced' identity, a process of self-definition particularly common at the universities in the 1850s and 1860s, but even then it did not

[15] Henry Fawcett, *The Economic Position of the British Labourer* (London, 1865), 7, 63.

[16] For the impact of his *A System of Logic* (1843) see, in particular, Alexander Bain, *John Stuart Mill: A Criticism, with Personal Recollections* (London, 1882), ch. 3; and for his *Principles of Political Economy* (1848) see N. B. de Marchi, 'The success of Mill's *Principles*', *History of Political Economy*, 6 (1974), 119–57.

necessarily entail agreement with all of his later writings. The second stage involved enthusiastic endorsement of Mill the public moralist, applauding his outspoken support for the North in the American Civil War, exulting in the symbolic value of his election to Parliament, admiring (though perhaps with some reservations here) his campaign to have Governor Eyre brought to justice. Again, by no means all the readers of his earlier treatises welcomed Mill's ardent partisanship on these issues, but for many of the radically inclined young intellectuals of the period his public career was an important embodiment of their ideal of the role to be played by 'the man of principle', and his courage and disinterestedness attracted a respect bordering on reverence. The third stage, the real inner sanctum of discipleship, was actually to advocate the same range of political and social measures as Mill. The number of true believers was considerably reduced at this stage, since on many practical matters Mill was thought to be the prisoner of certain theoretical 'crotchets', such as the extension of the co-operative principle, Hare's scheme for proportional representation, the enfranchisement of women, land tenure reform, and so on.[17]

Leslie Stephen himself provides a good example of these modulations of enthusiasm, in that as a young don he swore by the reasoning of Mill's treatises[18] (and as a young don swearing seems to have been his chief form of expression). In the 1860s he admired and shared Mill's moral protests against the selfishness and indifference of the governing classes, though increasingly uneasy with what he saw as the rather priggish dogmatism with which Mill pressed his case (a point to which I shall return later). But he never felt able to endorse the full range of Mill's enthusiasms, and the note of reservation one detects in his references to Mill in the early 1870s has swollen to a full-throated peal of distaste by the time he settled accounts in his study of the English Utilitarians in 1900.[19] Interesting variations on this theme could be played with comparable figures such as Sidgwick, Dicey, Fitzjames Stephen, and Morley, in all of

[17] This was a pronounced feature of the assessments of Mill which followed his death; see the discussion of these below, Ch. 8 s. III. For further examples of those who had reservations about his 'crotchets', see Harvie, *Lights of Liberalism*, chs. 2 and 7.

[18] In addition to the biographies by Maitland and Annan, see Leslie Stephen, *Some Early Impressions* (London, 1924 (repr. from the *National Review* for 1903)), 71 f., on his early admiration for the 'pure, passionless reason' of Mill's treatises.

[19] e.g. Leslie Stephen, 'The value of political machinery', *Fortnightly Review*, 24 (1875), 836–52; id., *The English Utilitarians*, 3 vols. (London, 1900), iii. 63–72.

whose cases account would have to be taken of degrees of reservation or levels of ambivalence that fell some way short of uninhibited discipleship, though Morley came closest.[20] In purely intellectual terms, Sidgwick's was the most interesting case, since much of his mature work can be seen as a prolonged wrestling-match with the ghost of Mill, with Sidgwick constantly apologizing for so briskly pinning his former master to the floor. Even after Sidgwick had outgrown his initial absorption in Mill's system, we get a glimpse of the significance Mill retained for him when he, least hyperbolic of men, suddenly broke off from university gossip in a letter in May 1873: 'I cannot go on—Mill is dead! I wonder if this news will have affected you as it does me.' Several days later, Sidgwick, having recovered enough to write an obituary tribute, resumed his letter with some interesting reflections on Mill's standing:

> There is no doubt that Mill's prestige has been declining lately: partly from the cause to which most people attribute it—the public exhibition of his radicalism: but partly to the natural termination of his philosophical reign—which was of the kind to be naturally early and brief. . . . I should say that from about 1860–65 or thereabouts he ruled England in the region of thought as very few men ever did: I do not expect to see anything like it again.[21]

In terms of more strictly political ideas, it is significant that the authors of the *Essays on Reform*, a group of university men who formed part of Mill's natural constituency and most of whom had earlier enthusiastically embraced the first two stages of discipleship, conducted their analysis of the established political system with scant reference to the categories of Utilitarian philosophy, and endorsed a set of proposals that omitted most of Mill's distinctive constitutional recommendations.[22]

Fawcett, by contrast, was among that much smaller band of

[20] For Sidgwick see Stefan Collini, Donald Winch, and John Burrow, *That Noble Science of Politics: A Study in Nineteenth-Century Intellectual History* (Cambridge, 1983), ch. 9; for Dicey see Richard Cosgrove, *The Rule of Law: Albert Venn Dicey, Victorian Jurist* (London, 1980), ch. 1; for Stephen see K. J. M. Smith, *James Fitzjames Stephen: Portrait of a Victorian Rationalist* (Cambridge, 1988), ch. 7; for Morley see Christopher Kent, *Brains and Numbers: Elitism, Comtism, and Democracy in Mid-Victorian England* (Toronto, 1978), ch. 8.

[21] Letter of 10/15 May 1873 to C. H. Pearson; Pearson MSS Bodleian Library, Oxford, MS Eng. Lett. d.190.

[22] Stephen and Dicey were both among the contributors to this volume, published in 1867; there is a good discussion of the group as a whole in Harvie, *Lights of Liberalism*.

followers who took up *Representative Government* and the *Subjection of Women* as ardently as they had subscribed to the *Logic* and the *Political Economy*, though since Fawcett had nothing like the range or subtlety of mind of his master, we should not be surprised to find the original ideas somewhat simplified in the process of transmission. Jevons's jibe about 'Mill and Water' had some force.[23] Fawcett's enthusiasm for Mill's *Principles of Political Economy*, in particular, was legendary. He announced in his inaugural lecture in 1864 that Mill's 'great book' was 'undoubtedly the most complete and the most perfect treatise that has ever been written on the science'.[24] He knew that book 'as a Puritan knew the Bible' commented Stephen later,[25] and given Stephen's known convictions, neither party was altogether being flattered by being compared, however flippantly, either to a Puritan or to the Author of the Bible. It possibly says something about the limits of all discipleship that even Fawcett could not be an utterly orthodox exponent of the holy book. Not only did he omit or minimize the role of Mill's speculations about the influence of social development on economic arrangements, but he was sceptical of the theory of the unearned increment and the proposed taxation of land-values, he did not share Mill's tenderness for certain forms of Socialism, and, more technically, he adhered to a form of the 'wage-fund' doctrine after Mill had rejected it, and he denied the validity of Mill's 'infant industry' argument for Protection.[26] On the whole, however, it was certainly true, as he himself insisted, that Fawcett's economic writings, the widely used *Manual* above all, were faithful expositions of Mill for a more popular audience.

This was almost as true of Fawcett's political writings as well. He was a persistent advocate of Hare's scheme, and was, with his wife,

[23] R. D. C. Black and R. Könekamp (eds.), *Papers and Correspondence of William Stanley Jevons*, 7 vols. (London, 1972–81), vi. 4.

[24] Henry Fawcett, 'Inaugural lecture on political economy', *Macmillan's Magazine*, 9 (1864), 495–503. See the similarly extravagant praise in the preface to his *Manual of Political Economy* (London, 1863); this work went through six editions in Fawcett's lifetime.

[25] Stephen, *Early Impressions*, 75.

[26] Fawcett's *Manual* contains no real equivalent of Mill's book IV on 'The influence of the progress of society on production and distribution'; for the 'unearned increment' and the taxation of land-values, see *Manual* (6th edn., 1883), 286–7, and *Life*, 165–6; on the wage-fund doctrine see Pedro Schwartz, *The New Political Economy of J. S. Mill* (London, 1972), 91-100, and D. P. O'Brien, *The Classical Economists* (Oxford, 1975), 111–18; for the 'infant industry' argument see Fawcett, *Free Trade and Protection* (London, 1878), 111.

an active campaigner for women's rights.[27] He closely followed Mill's lead in the 1865 Parliament, which confirmed his reputation as a doctrinaire, for, as Stephen observed, 'if the regular party-managers had an instinctive suspicion of Mill as a theorist and a crotchet-monger, they were not likely to be favourable to Mill's most ardent disciple'.[28] Indeed, Mill himself later confided to a correspondent that Fawcett was apt to be 'a little doctrinaire—to see a principle in full force, and not to see the opposing principles by which it must be qualified'.[29] Characteristically, Fawcett was to prove more intransigent and less adaptable even than Mill when faced with the demands of political compromise: thus, Mill conceded that in the short term a reformed Upper Chamber would have to contain a substantial number of hereditary peers, whereas Fawcett would allow no concession to 'the hereditary principle in legislation', and pressed for the immediate 'abolition of all political privileges enjoyed independently of merit'.[30] In other ways, too, he leaned towards a rather more conventional form of Radicalism than his master: he continued, for example, to support the secret ballot despite Mill's well-publicized volte-face on the issue.

In considering what sort of political identity these views expressed in mid-Victorian England, it might seem natural to begin with some notion of Liberalism. But it is worth remembering—and may provide a more useful starting-point for the enquiry—that Fawcett's own preferred label was not 'Liberal' but 'Radical'. This was the identity he claimed, self-consciously invoking a Philosophic Radical pedigree, as a young don in the 1850s; it was how he described himself when trying to enter Parliament in the 1860s; and it was the term by which he and a small group of MPs chose to be classified in

[27] In his last public speech before his death in 1884 he reaffirmed his devotion to Hare's scheme; see Goldman, *Blind Victorian*, 35. The same volume contains a very full discussion of Fawcett's feminism in David Rubinstein, 'Victorian feminists: Henry and Millicent Garrett Fawcett', 71–87.

[28] *Life*, 182; see also Fawcett's early endorsement of Mill's *Considerations on Representative Government*, in 'Mr. Mill's treatise on representative government', *Macmillan's Magazine*, 4 (1861), 97–103.

[29] Letter of 6 Nov. 1871 to G.C. Robertson; *The Later Letters of John Stuart Mill 1849–1873* (hereafter *LL*), *The Collected Works of John Stuart Mill*, ed. John M. Robson, 31 vols. (Toronto and London, 1965–91) (hereafter *CW*), xvii. 1850.

[30] Henry Fawcett, 'The House of Lords', *Fortnightly Review*, NS 10 (1871), reprinted in Henry and Millicent Garrett Fawcett, *Essays and Lectures on Social and Political Subjects* (London, 1872), quotations at 301, 317.

Dod's Parliamentary Companion in the 1870s.[31] 'The most thorough Radical now in the House' was how he was described at the height of Gladstone's first Liberal government.[32] The relationship of the various types of Radicalism to what came to be known as Liberalism was complex and far from static. By the time of Fawcett's death in the mid-1880s, it was common to regard Radicals as naturally forming a subsection of the Liberal Party, though this was recognized as a recent development. A popular history of *The English Radicals* published in the 1890s, for example, traced the origins of Radical principles back to the early years of George III's reign and attributed a continuous existence to a distinctive Radical party from the 1820s to the 1880s, by which point it had become indistinguishable from the Liberal Party itself.[33] It is important to remember that the notion of Liberal*ism* as a set of coherent political principles which found expression not only in the actions of the party formed at Willis's Rooms in 1859 but also in the reforming legislation of the 1830s and 1840s was itself essentially a retrospective creation, with its own polemical point, that only became current in the last three decades of the century. In the more fragmented political world of the 1850s, a world still very much dominated by Whig peers and Tory squires, Fawcett and his associates naturally and unhesitatingly classified themselves as 'Radicals'.

Fawcett's Radicalism was of a distinctively mid-nineteenth-century kind. It was not genuinely continuous with older and more popular notions of rights or of the protection, or restitution, of ancient liberties, nor did it embody any of those residues of the 'Country Party' ideology which lived on into early nineteenth-century Radicalism.[34] It was far more directly descended from the Philosophic Radicalism of the 1830s, though with a stronger emphasis upon self-help and with less sympathy for the centralizing impulse in Benthamism; and it had much in common with the 'Manchester School's' fixation with what Cobden called 'the two

[31] Annan, *Leslie Stephen*, 39–40; *Life*, 189–95 and 203–14; John Vincent, *The Formation of the British Liberal Party 1857–1868* (Harmondsworth, 1972; 1st edn. London, 1966), 65–8; Bryce, 'The late Mr. Fawcett', 457.

[32] Quoted in *Life*, 268.

[33] C. Roylance Kent, *The English Radicals* (London, 1899), esp. 7, 397; see also Leslie Stephen, 'The Good Old Cause', *Nineteenth Century*, 51 (1902), 11–23.

[34] For these forms of Radicalism, see Gareth Stedman Jones, *Languages of Class: Studies in English Working-Class History 1832–1982* (Cambridge, 1983), ch. 3.

plague-spots of aristocracy and landlordism'.[35] Crucially, it meant erecting hostility towards privilege to the status of a principle, and it was itself a mark of the Radical that his politics were explicitly based on principle, as opposed to the despised 'empiricism'—or, at best, the pious traditionalism—of the average county Member. Fawcett's political career was shaped by his consistent antagonism to the aristocratic habits of privilege, patronage, and corruption, an antagonism that always made his relations with the Whigs an uneasy one, and this alone ensured that he would be a fractious member of the Liberal Party of the 1860s and 1870s. His denunciations of 'people who spend a great part of their lives in slaughtering half-tamed pheasants' can hardly have endeared him to many of his Parliamentary colleagues.[36] His relative indifference to religious sentiment further distanced him from large portions of that party; he was exasperated, for example, by what he dismissed as the 'miserable religious squabbles' over the Education Act.[37] His own sense of political identity was evident in his remark of 1871, where he sounds very like the elder Mill forty years earlier: 'Each day it is becoming more clearly proved that there is a far greater difference between Radicals and Whigs than between Whigs and Conservatives.'[38] To such an extent had Fawcett acted on this conviction in criticizing Gladstone's ministry, that by 1872, as Stephen tersely recorded, the Whips 'ceased to send him the usual notices'.[39]

The corollary of Fawcett's principled aversion to privilege was an almost wilfully serene faith in the virtues of free competition. He had a very attenuated notion, at best, of the actual obstacles to the ideal working of the market, and a quite exaggerated sense of the capacity of individuals to control their own lives. As he remarked in opposing further state regulation of the hours of labour, 'if grown-up persons overwork themselves they do it of their own free-will',[40] and he used much the same sort of reasoning whether opposing any restriction on the drink trade or resisting any interference with the old Cambridge system of awarding Fellowships on the basis of success in the Tripos. The ideal of 'a fair field and no favour' elicited a very deep response in Fawcett, to which I shall return. He acknowledged that there

35 Quoted in Kent, *English Radicals*, 388.

36 Henry Fawcett, 'The enclosure of commons', *Fraser's Magazine*, 81 (1870), 191.

37 *Life*, 263.

38 Fawcett, 'House of Lords', in *Essays and Lectures*, 297.

39 *Life*, 275.

40 Fawcett, 'The general aspect of state intervention' (1872), in *Essays and Lectures*, 36.

continued to be real obstacles to the operation of this competitive principle in English life, the chief of which he, in common with Mill—and, for that matter, with Spencer and Green and Radicals of various hues—identified as 'landlordism' and the distorting effect of hereditary landed wealth and power. This analysis provided Individualism with a standing alibi—it meant, as Mill pointed out, that the principle of free competition had yet to be given a fair trial[41]—and it was the nearest Fawcett came to underpinning his politics with anything like an interpretation of history.[42]

At the other end of the scale, he also found the institution of the Poor Law a derogation from the principles of strict Individualism. Like several other Radicals of this type, he considered the principle on which the Poor Law rested to be essentially 'Socialistic': after all, it provided non-contributory benefits to those in need at the community's expense, and thus could not be justified in the same way as the state action involved in maintaining law and order or even sanitation.[43] This being so, the 'less eligibility' test and associated conditions imposed by the 1834 Poor Law seemed, if stringently enforced, to be the best means of limiting the damage such an institution might do, where the damage was seen primarily in terms of the 'moral injury' done to the habits of the class to which those in receipt of doles belonged. It is important to remember that the pre-1834 system of outdoor relief was still fresh in the memory, and also that political economy had provided an interpretation, well established by the time Fawcett was writing, of how that system had nearly brought the country to economic ruin. This interpretation of the effect of the so-called 'Speenhamland system', and the tendentious explanation of the economic troubles of post-Waterloo England which it embodied, formed what might be called one of the crucial 'foundation myths' of Victorian Individualism, just as the coincidence of free trade and prosperity enabled a similar moral to be drawn from a celebratory account of the repeal of the Corn Laws and other pieces of economically liberalizing legislation.

That Fawcett's politics drew heavily on the theorems of classical

41 Mill, *Principles of Political Economy* (1848), *CW*, ii. 207.

42 This, admittedly pretty exiguous, historical account is sketched in the opening chapter of *The Economic Position of the British Labourer*.

43 Fawcett, 'Modern Socialism' (1872), in *Essays and Lectures*, 25. For a more analytical exposition of the 'Socialistic' principle of the Poor Law see Henry Sidgwick, *The Elements of Politics* (London, 1891), 156–9; and the discussion in Collini, *Liberalism and Sociology*, 21, 107–8.

political economy hardly requires emphasis: his credentials as a 'scientific Radical' depended upon this fact. By the 1850s and 1860s this association no longer excited the almost axiomatic working-class hostility of earlier decades, and among the developments that made this, and hence Fawcett's career as representative for popular constituencies, possible was what might be called the 'moralizing of political economy'. It is certainly true that the reproachful contrast between the amoral, 'heartless', and even 'selfish' teachings of political economy and the dictates of humanity and morality never altogether disappeared—presumably something of the sort we shall have always with us—and Fawcett never let pass unchallenged 'the statement so often repeated about political economy being hard-hearted' which 'was about as unreasonable as if they were to say that a proposition in Euclid, or any physical fact, was hard-hearted or selfish'.[44] But in the fifty years after Waterloo there was a subtle change both in the moral tone of political economy itself and in its cultural standing. The morally educative effect of the discipline imposed by economic activity, for instance, bulked larger in the work of Fawcett's generation of economists, and perhaps in the characteristic preoccupations of their readers, than it had in that of, say, Ricardo and his contemporaries. The widely remarked improvement in political economy's reputation after the success of Mill's morally sensitive and socially conciliatory *Principles* also marked a significant expansion of the subject's political acceptability.[45] It is true that we can find a not dissimilar tone in some earlier writers, notably the Evangelical political economists of the 1810s and 1820s, but in the later period this tone is independent of any sectarian beliefs about the operation of the Divine sanction and the rewards of the afterlife.[46] Where the Evangelicals had been primarily concerned about the way economic disasters revealed the workings of Providence, mid-Victorian economists tended to concentrate on the human moral failings manifested in improvidence.

Though some may see only the cloven hoof of that protean

[44] In this case Fawcett was addressing the annual congress of the National Association for the Promotion of Social Science in 1863; quoted in Goldman, *Blind Victorian*, 164.

[45] On this, see de Marchi, 'Success of Mill's *Principles*'.

[46] For Evangelical political economy, see Boyd Hilton, *Corn, Cash and Commerce: The Economic Policies of the Tory Governments 1815–1830* (Oxford, 1977), esp. 'Conclusion'; and above all his *The Age of Atonement: The Influence of Evangelicalism on Social and Economic Thought 1795–1865* (Oxford, 1988).

creature 'bourgeois ideology' in Fawcett's concern with maintaining the 'moral standard' of the labouring class and with the danger of 'moral injury' in indiscriminate charity, there was, as I have argued in general terms above, a consistent and widely shared picture of life as the unremitting exercise of will embodied in these considerations, and these in turn were inextricably interwoven with the fabric of his economic writings.[47] When Fawcett was summarizing his view of the limits of state action, he declared that 'any scheme, however well-intentioned it may be, will indefinitely increase every evil it seeks to alleviate if it lessens individual responsibility by encouraging the people to rely less upon themselves and more upon the state'.[48] It would be hard to disentangle the purely economic arguments in the pages that led up to this declaration from those more general, and arguably more influential, moral assumptions which he shared with the kind of audience his writings were intended to reach. Or again, when Stephen spoke, as he did more than once in his chapter on Fawcett's political economy, of the 'nobler' aspects of the policy of non-intervention, he was using a term—a very important term in the Victorian literature of 'enthusiasm'—which his readers would not have found incongruous in such a context.[49]

III

Here, then, we are approaching that pre- or sub-political level of moral and aesthetic sensibilities which informed the kind of political attitudes Fawcett represented. The topic may be approached indirectly in the first instance, by way of a contrast between two stereotypes. There is a familiar dichotomy in Victorian thought and sensibility between, on the one hand, the temper of rational science, leaning to positivism, receptive to Utilitarianism and political economy, and most commonly issuing in some kind of Liberal or reforming politics; and, on the other hand, the temper of essentially Romantic cultural critique, uneasy with modernity, suspicious of the reductive tendencies of science, hostile to the soulless reasonings of political economy, a temper whose political expression, where not

[47] For these phrases, see *Life*, 154, 161.

[48] Fawcett, *Manual*, 310.

[49] e.g. *Life*, 162, 173; for 'enthusiasm' see Walter Houghton, *The Victorian Frame of Mind 1830–1870* (New Haven, Conn., 1957), 263–304.

straightforwardly Tory, veered, by an intelligible affinity, from a Carlylean authoritarianism to a Ruskinian or Morrisian Socialism.

At first sight, there may seem no great difficulty in knowing on which side of this dichotomy to place the mid-Victorian cult of 'manliness.' This term denoted a widely esteemed Victorian quality, of course, not one that was the exclusive property of any single sect, but in general terms its cultural affinities would seem to have been with the second of my contrasting tempers. Certainly, this would seem to be the case where the epitome of manliness is taken to be (as it so often is) Charles Kingsley, striding across field and ditch, vigorously cursing 'fastidious, maundering, die-away effeminacy'.[50] The list of virtues given in the *OED* definition of manliness indicates well enough its core meaning: 'courageous, independent in spirit, frank, upright.' Its opposite was held to be, in an interesting progression, 'childlike', 'effeminate', 'sentimental'. The pejorative sense of 'sentimental' ('addicted to indulgence in superficial emotion; apt to be swayed by sentiment') is, in fact, a nineteenth-century usage—the eighteenth century had known a more favourable sense—and manliness expressed a deep, possibly in some cases a revealingly pathological, aversion to this trait.

But recent discussions of the diversity of senses of 'manliness' exhibited in Victorian England at least require us to make some preliminary discriminations before proceeding too far with this identification.[51] In particular, one needs to separate from this stereotypically masculine and athletic sense the connotations which made it possible to speak of 'shedding a manly tear' or to write a book, as Thomas Hughes did, called *The Manliness of Christ*. Here, the shaping contrast was less with the 'feminine', and more with the 'bestial', non-human, childlike, or immature. These latter states might involve considerable expenditure of energy and zest for life,

[50] Quoted in Norman Vance, *Sinews of the Spirit: The Ideal of Christian Manliness in Victorian Literature and Religious Thought* (Cambridge, 1985), 38.

[51] Among older works, Houghton, *Victorian Frame of Mind*, ch. 9, contains a brief discussion of the term, and David Newsome, *Godliness and Good Learning: Four Studies on a Victorian Ideal* (London, 1961), esp. ch. 4, was a pioneering account. More recent studies include Vance, *Sinews of the Spirit*, and J. A. Mangan and James Walvin (eds.), *Manliness and Morality: Middle-Class Masculinity in Britain and America, 1800–1940* (Manchester, 1987). Above all, I have particularly profited from the comments on an earlier version of this chapter in Boyd Hilton's 'Manliness, masculinity, and the mid-Victorian temperament', in Goldman, *Blind Victorian*, 60–70, where he very perceptively, and very gently, criticized certain over-simplifications in my earlier treatment of this theme.

but they lacked those elements of self-restraint and devotion to others which were central to that tradition of 'Christian manliness' which was developed out of Coleridge, Thomas Arnold, and F. D. Maurice.[52] This was the manliness which could express itself by turning the other cheek rather than by glorying in a scrap.[53] 'True manliness', wrote Hughes in a sentence which should warn us against too readily bracketing him with Kingsley, 'is as likely to be found in a weak as in a strong body.'[54] 'Self-forgetfulness' figured as the ideal here; self-absorption, self-importance, and simple selfishness characterized the abyss. That, however, is not the emphasis most relevant to the present discussion. In the usage of the wider culture, not always scrupulously attentive to the niceties of Mauricean theology, it was the masculine and athletic emphasis which predominated, and here the governing contrast, though it certainly embraced an antipathy to all forms of self-absorption, was crucially with the allegedly related vices of effeminacy and sentimentalism.

Appropriately, the illustrative quotation appended to the *OED*'s definition of this sense of 'sentimentalism' is Carlyle's inclusive denunciation of 'that rosepink vapour of Sentimentalism, Philanthropy, and Feasts of Morals', and it was Carlyle above all who put into circulation a particular conception of manliness as part of a larger vision of the place of bracing conflict and stoically borne suffering in a power-governed universe. As the reference to 'philanthropy' also suggests, the political bearing of this vision involved a stern antipathy to well-meant schemes of social reform and other expressions of the humanitarian impulse, which he pilloried in his satires on the 'Universal Abolition of Pain Association'. This impatience with the delicate scruples and tender consciences of the liberal humanitarians (led, in this instance, as we have seen, by Mill) found classic expression in the confrontation over the Governor Eyre case, where Carlyle and several others prominently associated with the ethos of manliness, such as

[52] For these sources, see Newsome, *Godliness and Good Learning*, 195–206.

[53] Cf. Owen Chadwick's comment: 'There was manliness and manliness—and Christian manliness was consistent with the virtue of meekness, a grace which some might mistake for effeminacy' (quoted in Newsome, *Godliness and Good Learning*, 209).

[54] Thomas Hughes, *The Manliness of Christ* (London, 1879), 24–5; quoted by Boyd Hilton in Goldman, *Blind Victorian*. I am greatly indebted to Hilton's excellent discussion of this contrast.

Kingsley, lined up to support a man who had bravely done his duty, and they implied that it was not obviously to be regretted that the execution of that duty had involved the spilling of blood and the assertion of a masterful white man's will over a mob of riotous Negroes.[55]

But as we begin to touch upon the political expression of this sense of manliness we must acknowledge complexities of another kind. The eighteenth century had, after all, been familiar with the idea of a 'manly freedom', where this connoted independence, freedom from patronage and servility above all. The Kingsleyean form of manliness certainly retained some continuities with this idea, not least in its disdain for the fashionable fop and the craven place-holder; but it also imported (here directly stimulated by Carlyle) a celebration of uncompromising decisiveness and a related respect for the smack of firm government which entailed a slight but consequential shift away from the Whig ideal of measured and adaptive political judgement. Moreover, the mention of Kingsley should alert us to the fact that we are not so far from Leslie Stephen as my concentration on Carlylean anti-liberalism might at first suggest. For the term 'muscular Christianity', which designated the variant of manliness particularly associated with Kingsley, had in fact been freely applied to the Reverend Leslie Stephen in his days as a long-striding and strong-mouthed athlete and rowing coach; indeed, it is alleged that Stephen ought to be recognized alongside Kingsley as the founder of muscular Christianity.[56] Certainly, at this stage of his life he incarnated the tenets of the creed: 'the duty of patriotism; the moral and physical beauty of athleticism; the salutary effects of Spartan habits and discipline; the cultivation of all that is masculine and the expulsion of all that is effeminate, un-English, and excessively intellectual'.[57] Though Stephen outgrew his always partially assumed identity as a 'rowing rough', the underlying sensibility, and much of the language, of this form of manliness was characteristic of him for the rest of his life. His later assessment of Kingsley did not hold back on criticism, but he still found a good word to say for his expression of 'masculine vigour' and the

[55] See Bernard Semmel, *The Governor Eyre Controversy* (London, 1962).

[56] Annan, *Leslie Stephen*, 29; for a contemporary application of the term to Stephen, see Maitland, *Life of Leslie Stephen*, 77.

[57] This list of the constitutive qualities of 'muscular Christianity' is given in Newsome, *Godliness and Good Learning*, 216.

undeniable fact that he 'hated the namby-pamby'.[58] Similarly, Stephen was being only half ironic when he wrote of himself that 'I am much inclined to measure a man's moral excellence by his love of walking'.[59] He made this remark in speaking of Fawcett, and this recalls the slightly puzzled observation of a subsequent biographer, which I cited above, that 'they seem to have shared little but their earlier politics and their love of walking'. Not only were these, for both Stephen and Fawcett, no insignificant matters to share, but, I now want to suggest, there was a more than contingent connection between them.

If this is so, however, it generates a minor paradox, or at least calls for a modification of my earlier contrast of tempers. For Stephen and Fawcett were not only undeniably Radicals and emphatically of the 'humanitarian' party on such test issues as the American Civil War or the Eyre case; but they were also keen devotees of political economy, sympathetic to Utilitarianism, eager to apply the methods of science. They seem, in other words, to be on the wrong side. This is, of course, partly an illusion created by the starkness of my initial dichotomy and by the too-exclusive association of manliness with the second of my stereotypes. Still, the recognition that in Stephen and Fawcett this sensibility was congruent with, or even partially explanatory of, their politics is in itself a worthwhile modification of the familiar contrast, and may point towards a conclusion of more general interest. For, in so far as Stephen and Fawcett are representative of one important strand in mid-Victorian Liberalism, it may indicate that the temper of that Liberalism had more in common with that of some of its best-known contemporary critics than the later Liberal myth would suggest, or even, perhaps, than it did with that of later Liberalism itself. If the cardinal values of the mid-Victorian Liberal intellectuals turn out to have more to do with stoicism and strenuousness than with liberty or utility, it would then hardly be surprising if those of them who lived on into the rather different moral world of the early twentieth century were to find what then passed for Liberalism pretty alien, despite some much-touted theoretical continuities.

[58] Leslie Stephen, 'Charles Kingsley', *Cornhill Magazine*, 35 (1877), 442.
[59] *Life*, 57.

IV

When we look more closely at Stephen's evocative description of the frame of mind that he and Fawcett and their Cambridge circle shared, we find running through it a constant stylistic contrast between the cluster of terms centred on 'manly' and 'masculine' and that centred on 'sentimental'. There are fashions in these as in other matters, and Fawcett's set affected a stern contempt for 'gushing' or the expression of 'high-flown' feelings. Stephen recognized that they may have cultivated this to excess, but he was unwilling to disown their youthful tastes altogether:

> The kind of stoical severity which was our pet virtue at Cambridge, the intense dislike to any needless revelations of feeling, had certainly its good side. It was at worst an exaggeration of a creditable and masculine instinct. We preferred to mask our impulses under a guise of cynicism rather than to affect more sensibility than we really possessed.

'I for one', he added with appropriate gruffness, 'should be sorry to see the opposite practice come into fashion.'[60] In addition to the obvious contrast between sincerity and affectation, the superiority of 'downright straightforwardness' over either aristocratic hauteur or intellectual finesse also came into play here (interestingly, imported French words are needed to designate the rejected qualities).

One begins to wonder whether Stephen ever met anyone who was not a 'downright, straightforward, manly fellow', so frequent is this description in his recollections. Indeed, in his *Life of Fawcett* alone he uses the terms 'manly' and 'masculine' fifteen times before the narrative reaches 1865 (and my patience ran out). In several instances he is using the term in the expected way to characterize Fawcett, praising his spirit of 'manly independence' or his 'masculine courage'. But on other occasions he is referring to institutions or practices. For example, when explaining Fawcett's defence of the prize Fellowship system at Cambridge against proposals for the 'endowment of research', he commented: 'The "endowment of research" is a pretty phrase, but it may cover much that was condemned by the old narrow but masculine school to which Fawcett belonged.' He amplified the point by describing the danger that 'instead of the old strenuous competition, the students would be encouraged to listen to professors spinning fine phrases and creating

[60] *Life*, 37; a similar account is given in *Some Early Impressions*, 71–6.

sham science to justify the existence of their chairs'.[61] That the competition should be 'strenuous' is clearly the chief positive ingredient in this judgement, and is the clue to why an attitude to educational arrangements might be characterized in these ostensibly incongruous terms. The same responses are at work when Stephen describes the dominant intellectual style of the place as favouring 'a masculine but limited type of understanding', and as providing 'a most strenuous and masculine training'.[62] The range is extended at later points in the book when a particular course of political action is described as the 'plainer or more manly course', when a style of argument is referred to as 'manly and outspoken criticism', and so on.[63] In other words, terms that are literally descriptive of human qualities are constantly being applied to subjects apparently far removed from their literal sense. What is at work here is surely something like what literary critics are identifying when they investigate 'image-clusters'; that is, the repetition signals the presence of a set of responses which are activated by some, possibly only subliminal, association between the human qualities and certain congenial properties of the ideas or policies or whatever that are under discussion. In the strong version of this kind of analysis, the very congeniality of the latter properties may be dependent upon the prior work of association.

In Stephen's case, the contexts in which the contrasting pejorative term 'sentimental' occurs reveals the same patterns of association. For example, when he is seeking to explain the appeal of Mill's work to their circle, it is not strictly the theoretical content of the treatises he cites, but something more like a style of reasoning: the *Logic* and

[61] *Life*, 114–15. And note the positive qualities associated with this: 'A prize openly offered and fairly won has certain definite and intelligible merits.'

[62] Ibid., 90.

[63] Ibid. 172, 291. On this point, at least, I think Boyd Hilton's criticism of the earlier version of this chapter is not altogether justified. He suggests that in the passages I am referring to here '"manly" is always used as a term of unqualified praise whereas "masculinity" is invariably qualified' (Goldman, *Blind Victorian*, 65). But this is not really so: when Stephen speaks of 'a creditable and masculine instinct' (37), or 'a thoroughly masculine nature' (38), or 'the masculine common sense' encouraged by the Cambridge curriculum (96), he is using the term in a positive sense. Hilton's suggestion that there may have been 'more daylight between the two terms' than I had allowed is no doubt right about general usage in the period, but not altogether persuasive about Stephen's usage. When in the space of a few sentences Stephen speaks of Fawcett's preference for 'the plainer or more manly course' and of his 'thoroughly outspoken and masculine temper' (291), the terms, and their positive force, seem very similar.

Political Economy 'possessed the merits which we most admired—good downright hard logic, with a minimum of sentimentalism'. Or again: 'We held . . . that Ruskin, when he attacked Mill, was a sentimentalist, who could neither look facts in the face nor reason coherently.'[64] The suggestion, of course, is that the 'facts' might not be pleasant; all the more reason why the intellectual equivalent of 'funk' has to be severely repudiated. By contrast, political economy gratified this taste for uncluttered reasoning and unsentimental description. Science did not flinch. The same associations are evident in his and Fawcett's political attitudes. Stephen described the 'kindly philanthropists' who advocated the relaxation of the conditions of the Poor Law as 'sentimentalists': they were indulging their immediate feelings of pity or guilt at the expense of 'facing' the facts. Those whose hostility to the concerns of political economy Fawcett anticipates in the introduction to his *Manual* he refers to as 'sentimental moralists', and so on.[65]

The ideal of 'fair competition' excited a similar set of associations for both Stephen and Fawcett. When Stephen wrote of his friend that 'a spontaneous and intense hatred of everything unfair showed itself in all his most active impulses', his mind immediately associated this key value of Individualism with manliness: 'Fairness of this kind is a fine quality, and is common to many virile athletes of Fawcett's stamp.'[66] When Fawcett had attacked primogeniture, a traditional Radical target to be sure, it was its 'unfairness' that particularly roused him: 'Every feeling in our nature is opposed to it.'[67] In fact, the very notion of struggle and effort in itself had an invigorating suggestive power for Fawcett, and his zealous propagation of the gospel of self-help involved projecting an ideal charged with these associations on to the economic activity of the working classes. This is one of the many places where it would be misleading to see the influence of Social Darwinism in such idealizations of struggle by Victorian moralists.[68] The 'struggle' in question was not in

[64] *Some Early Impressions*, 73, 84.

[65] *Life*, 153; Fawcett, *Manual*, 7.

[66] Leslie Stephen, 'Henry Fawcett: in memoriam', *Macmillan's Magazine*, 51 (1884), 131; see *Life*, 180.

[67] Fawcett, *Economic Position of the British Labourer*, 9–11.

[68] See, e.g. J. A. Mangan, 'Social Darwinism and upper-class education in late-Victorian and Edwardian England', in Mangan and Walvin, *Manliness and Morality*, 135–59. It is noticeable that all the imagery of 'struggle' in the sources which Mangan quotes is either athletic ('the game', 'the race', and so on) or else religious.

fact a competition between individuals designed to eliminate the 'unfit', but rather a struggle with oneself and one's weaknesses of character.[69]

The outcome of this struggle was dependent upon what Leslie Stephen elsewhere referred to as 'the old maxim . . . that one virtue lies at the base of all others: call it force, energy, vitality, or manliness, or whatever you please'.[70] Energy thus represented both the prerequisite and the expression of the manly life, and the constant refrain of Fawcett's political recommendations was the need to 'call out the *energy* of all classes'. As Stephen paraphrased Fawcett's non-intervention principle: 'It meant . . . be exceedingly jealous of all restrictions upon the *energies* of any class, especially of the poorest class', and the test of all proposed measures was whether they were 'calculated to stimulate the *energies* of the persons affected'.[71] The association between the 'enervating' effect of dependence and the 'invigorating' impact of self-reliance is a constant feature of Fawcett's writing, as deep an expression of his temperament as Kingsley's refrain about 'healthiness' and 'sickliness' was of his. When Fawcett wrote that the aim should be to 'replace the depressing misery of dependence by the buoyant activity which comes from self-reliance and from the consciousness of the power to earn one's living', he might well have been referring to policies to encourage working-class thrift; in fact he was speaking of the best way to help the blind.[72] After he was blinded, 'there was only one thing, he told his sister, which he dreaded—namely, a loss of energy'.[73]

Clearly, we are once again confronting the centrality of the idea of 'character' from another angle, and there should now be no need to

69 Mangan (*Manliness and Morality*, 143) quotes a representative justification for public schools from 1860, and comments: 'In time such Darwinian arguments became commonplace.' But his own quotation reveals that the source of such arguments lay in the kind of sensibilities being discussed here, for which 'Social Darwinism' only provided one, late, systematization: 'Boys, like nations, can only attain to the genuine stout self-reliance which is true manliness by battling for themselves against their difficulties, and forming their own characters by their own blunders and their own troubles,' and so on.

70 Leslie Stephen, 'Thoughts of an outsider: public schools', *Cornhill Magazine*, 27 (1873), 290.

71 *Life*, 162–3 (my emphases).

72 Speech of 18 Mar. 1884, quoted in *Life*, 171.

73 *Life*, 54–5. For an interesting contemporary discussion of energy as the essential foundation of 'character', see Alexander Bain, *The Study of Character* (London, 1861), esp. ch. 7.

elaborate on this theme. But there is one further point which belongs here, especially given my earlier remarks about the ambivalence with which Mill was regarded even by many of his ostensible disciples. It is arguable that this aspect of their sensibility, though it initially led them to find the style of reasoning of Mill's treatises attractive, was not in fact something they shared with Mill himself, and in Stephen's case it surely contributed to his growing impatience with a figure whose personal qualities were in some respects so far from 'manly.' Looking back on the culture of athleticism which he had so enthusiastically fostered when a young don, Stephen conceded that it was not without its limitations, but even in 1903 he could not resist adding: 'Interest in such pursuits is, at any rate, antagonistic to the intellectual vice of priggishness.'[74] His aversion to priggishness was deep and abiding, and it is clear that he increasingly associated Mill with this quality, though at first he only suggested the identification indirectly. In scorning Hare's scheme in the early 1870s, for example, he referred to Mill's contention that it would lead to the selection of a better class of representatives, and then noted: 'A cynic would say that the scheme would probably result in selecting half a dozen prigs and twice as many slaves of a crotchet.'[75] The 'cynic' was one of Stephen's favourite defensive aliases: his own characteristic snort is plainly audible in this judgement. By the time he wrote his study of Mill for his book on the English Utilitarians, he could make the identification more openly. Brooding on what he saw as a contrast between Mill's own character and the ideal held up in *On Liberty*, he concluded: 'At the bottom of his heart he seems to prefer a prig, a man of rigid formulae, to the vivid and emotional character whose merits he recognises in theory.' Having frequently remarked —he was far from alone in doing this—the prominence in Mill of 'feminine qualities', he could now drive home the negative charge: what, in the end, was wrong with the Saint of Rationalism was that he lacked 'masculine fibre'.[76]

[74] *Some Early Impressions*, 48; Stephen's definition of 'philistine' (another of his assumed identities) was 'a name . . . which a prig bestows on the rest of the species'. For Stephen's enduring hostility to priggishness see Annan, *Leslie Stephen*, 39, 142.

[75] Stephen, 'Value of political machinery', 850.

[76] Stephen, *English Utilitarians*, iii, 70, 72. Unsurprisingly, his brother was of the same opinion; Fitzjames 'subscribed to a traditional ideal of masculinity and considered Mill deficient in it. Mill seemed to him to neglect the grand passions and to be over-intellectual and over-sensitive'; Jean O'Grady, 'Mill and Fitzjames Stephen: personal notes', *Mill News Letter*, 22 (1987), 7–8.

That, at least, was one charge against which he did not have to defend Fawcett. Rather to the contrary, he was aware that the style of his friend's rigorous adherence to his Individualist principles invited the accusation that such hard-headedness was indistinguishable from hard-heartedness, while, on a broader front, Arnold's shaft about 'a sort of mere blatancy and truculent hardness' had clearly been well aimed. In the *Life* Stephen was consequently at pains to bring out Fawcett's warmth and generosity of feeling, and the strength and genuineness of his concern for the welfare of the working classes. Though Stephen could no longer muster the same enthusiasm as Fawcett for the full hand of their early political convictions, he remained resistant to the new Collectivist fashions of the 1880s and 1890s. For him they represented the old sentimentalism in new guise. Even in the 1890s he was still upholding the merits of 'the good old orthodox system of Political Economy', and insisting that

> the essential condition of all social improvement is not that we should have this or that system of regulations, but that the individual should be manly, self-respecting, doing his duty as well as getting his pay, and deeply convinced that nothing will do any permanent good which does not imply the elevation of the individual in his standards of honesty, independence and good conduct.[77]

Modern Radicalism seemed devoid of the old 'masculine' virtues, and 'the contrast is painful to many who recall the ideals of their youth'.[78] Perhaps Stephen was not altogether displeased to have the opportunity offered in writing the life of Fawcett to display those ideals in an attractive light.

And here I return to my starting-point. Fawcett himself embodied the very virtues of character which his political creed had elevated as its ideal and which the measures he supported had always been designed to foster. One of the chief means of diffusing this ideal and rendering it with the vividness necessary to inspire emulation was, of course, the exemplary biography. Such biographies constituted the devotional literature of Individualism. Stephen was expressing what amounted almost to a professional as well as a personal credo when he wrote in the *Life* of his brother Fitzjames: 'The impression made

77 Leslie Stephen, 'The sphere of political economy' and 'Social equality', both in *Social Rights and Duties*, i, quotations at 131–2, 219.

78 Stephen, 'Good Old Cause', 11.

upon his contemporaries by a man of strong and noble character is something which cannot be precisely estimated, but which we often feel to be invaluable. The best justification of biography in general is that it may strengthen and diffuse that impression.'[79] And in the conclusion to the *Life of Fawcett* he made this educative purpose explicit when he referred to 'the living influence still exercised upon the hearts of his contemporaries by a character equally remarkable for masculine independence and generous sympathy', and he concluded with the suitably hortatory flourish: 'My sole aim has been to do something towards enabling my readers to bring that influence to bear upon themselves.'[80]

[79] Stephen, *The Life of Sir James Fitzjames Stephen* (London, 1895), 481.
[80] *Life*, 468.

III

Moral Sciences

6

Their Title to be Heard
Professionalization and its Discontents

I

On 16 November 1872 a meeting was held at the Freemason's Tavern in London to discuss the question of 'University Reform'. In choosing that venue, the organizers deliberately recalled the historic meeting on 10 June 1864 of university reformers and leaders of Nonconformity to press for the repeal of the Test Acts, and thus to open the ancient universities to those who were not members of the Church of England.[1] By 1872 the focus of attention had shifted rather to the internal organization of the universities and its bearing on what were increasingly recognized as their national functions: particularly at issue was the conflict between the traditional collegiate tutorial ideal and the newer schemes to promote 'research'. The publication in 1867 of Mark Pattison's book, *Suggestions on Academical Organization*, and an orchestrated campaign in the *Academy*, a journal founded in 1869 to help promote the cause of 'the endowment of research', had ensured that the question did not lack for public attention.

Henry Sidgwick, then aged 34 and occupying the special post of Praelector in Moral Philosophy at Trinity College, Cambridge, took an active part in this campaign, and it was he who made the opening speech, proposing Pattison as Chairman of the meeting. It is, however, to some remarks he made later in the meeting that we must look for a revealing expression of the complexities of the sense of identity, both individual and collective, involved in this newer ideal of academic life. Considerable enthusiasm had been voiced for

[1] On this campaign, see Lewis Campbell, *The Nationalization of the Old English Universities* (London, 1901).

encouraging research as well as teaching in the natural sciences. Sidgwick could genuinely support this, but went on: 'I think it is also important to point out the extreme need of having a body of mature students who can form a body of experts in other studies and departments of thought, those which more immediately relate to practice.' These, he argued, were enquiries

> which everyone thinks he understands if he has read a handbook upon the subject; I think that these studies deal with subjects upon which confident opinions are expressed every day by half-instructed persons; and opinions, too, which have often had an important effect on practice. Therefore it is of extreme importance that there should always be a body of persons who are able, to a certain extent, to pour the stream of pure science into the somewhat muddy channel of current opinion.[2]

Sidgwick, it is hardly necessary to add, was not a thrilling speaker; it seems unlikely that the gentlemen gathered in the private room of the Freemason's Tavern were brought to their feet by the contagion of his oratory. Even his introduction of an abstraction-leavening metaphor in the last sentence was policed by his usual contingent of 'to a certain extent's and 'somewhat's, seemingly fearful lest the metaphor get out of hand and provoke some riotous and disorderly thinking. Even so, the visual image conjured up by those last phrases can hardly have been quite the thought Sidgwick intended to implant in his hearers' minds, since it suggests a rather discouraging picture; clean water added to dirty invariably produces a complete victory for the latter. But perhaps this infelicity was a symptom of a deeper difficulty in the substance of Sidgwick's plea: he evidently envisaged a 'body of experts' in various 'departments of thought' whose authority 'half-instructed persons' would recognize in matters which 'immediately relate to practice'. Optimism about the growth of the necessary kind of cultural deference seems to be one unmentioned ingredient in this recipe, and confidence about the intimacy of the connection between study and practice might be considered another. Still, whatever their failings as oratory, Sidgwick's remarks exemplified an aspiration, and a concomitant sense of identity, which was to have a profound, if surprisingly complex, impact upon the role of the public moralist in late nineteenth- and early twentieth-century Britain.

[2] The printed minutes of the meeting, headed 'The re-organization of academical study', are in the Sidgwick Papers, Trinity College, Cambridge; Add. MSS c.97.23 (quotation at p. 8).

Indeed, in his own career, Sidgwick increasingly embodied many of the tensions which this new ideal introduced into the lives of late Victorian intellectuals. As a young don in the 1860s, he had been driven to pursue a variety of philosophical and historical studies largely by an always-frustrated urge to allay his inhibiting scepticism in matters of religious belief. During this period he participated actively in that flowering of periodical writing described in Chapter 1 above, writing on a whole range of topics of general cultural interest. But as he moved into middle age, he tended to concentrate his energies (or, as is so commonly the case, discovered retrospectively that he had already been doing so for some time) in two chief activities: pursuing systematic and technical enquiries in moral philosophy, and contributing to the reform and better administration of Cambridge University.[3] On the publication in 1874 of his first major work, *The Methods of Ethics*, he explained to his mother, as authors are defensively prone to do, why his book would of course be neglected: 'I don't expect the "general public" to read much of my book. In fact the point of it rather is that it treats in a technical and precise manner questions which are ordinarily discussed loosely and popularly.' 'Indeed', he warned her, 'it can scarcely be said to belong to *literature*.'[4] His sense that his academic position set him a little apart from the common run of authors was displayed in another way when he wrote to his publisher, Macmillan, objecting to the customary distribution of free copies to distinguished individuals: 'Really I believe that sending to distinguished strangers is, for a man in the position of a university teacher, a needless cheapening of oneself.'[5] Even when he turned to more obviously 'practical' subjects like politics and political economy, he continued to write in the same 'technical and precise manner'. As a consequence of this concentration of his energies, his contributions to the general periodicals fell away sharply after the early 1870s. By 1886 he could report to one correspondent that he was not in a good position to advise about opportunities for making a living by one's pen: 'Perhaps I ought to say that I am personally now less in the way of knowing about

[3] 'His truest monument is . . . the difference between Cambridge as it is now and the Cambridge of forty years ago.' *Pilot*, 15 Sept. 1900; cutting in Sidgwick Papers, Add. MSS c.104.13.

[4] Sidgwick to his mother, 11 July and 28 Dec. 1874; Sidgwick Papers, Add. MSS c.99.177 and 180.

[5] Sidgwick to Alexander Macmillan, 12 Dec. 1874; Macmillan Papers, British Library Add. MSS 55159/6.

literary opportunities than I was 10 years ago, having eschewed all writing except on professional subjects in an academic way.'[6] The stream of pure science was taking an increasingly roundabout course towards the muddy channel of current opinion.

Yet Sidgwick was far from being without connection and influence among the late Victorian political class; as I have remarked elsewhere, 'a man is hardly to be classed as an outsider when one of his brothers-in-law is Archbishop of Canterbury and another well on his way to becoming Prime Minister'.[7] He mixed socially with Cabinet ministers from both parties; he helped to devise schemes for the education of future Indian administrators. And he was recognized as having some standing as a political economist, at one moment being asked to write an article on Socialism 'from the Professor's chair', at another being invited as 'one of those who have studied economic questions' to be a member of the Royal Commission on the Financial Relations between Great Britain and Ireland.[8] But in addressing these wider audiences, he was conscious that his academic status was both a source of authority and an announcement of the limits of the contribution he could be expected to make. More is involved in such a situation than simply tailoring one's literary tactics to the needs of particular occasions. Mill, as we have seen, was conscious of deliberately shifting between registers and levels of abstraction, now pursuing a systematic argument, now engaging in targeted polemic. But he did not do so as one venturing out from his 'proper' sphere, nor as one deploying an authority that was accorded to an office or institution rather than to an individual. Sidgwick, on the other hand, constantly referred to the obligations of his position, and the title 'Professor' became as constitutive a part of his public identity as the name of his diocese is of a bishop's.

The term most commonly employed by historians to characterize

[6] Sidgwick to A. J. Patterson, 26 July 1886; Sidgwick Papers Add. MSS c.98.9. Not, of course, that the discontents endemic to the academic life were unknown to him: on his fiftieth birthday he confided to his journal the desire to leave Cambridge, and 'the desire of literary independence, to be able to speak when I like as a man to men, and not three times a week as a salaried teacher to pupils'; A. and E. M. S[idgwick], *Henry Sidgwick: A Memoir* (London, 1906), 489.

[7] Stefan Collini, Donald Winch, and John Burrow, *That Noble Science of Politics: A Study in Nineteenth-Century Intellectual History* (Cambridge, 1983), 303.

[8] H. J. Paton (editor of the *Contemporary Review*) to Sidgwick, 10 Mar. 1886; Sidgwick Papers, Add. MSS c.95.2; Sidgwick, *Memoir*, 457, 561. Paton's phrase may have been an allusion to the so-called *Kathedersozialisten* who were receiving a lot of attention in Germany at the time.

changes in the social standing and sense of identity of intellectuals of the kind illustrated by Sidgwick is 'professionalization'. For certain purposes, this is undoubtedly an indispensable term, and I have already used it as a convenient shorthand when referring to some of the changes in question. But, as so often with terms that have enjoyed a vigorous life in the social sciences in the late twentieth century, it can bring with it conceptual baggage that makes it a doubtful or even misleading guide when applied to the very different social structures and cultural patterns of earlier periods. More specifically, the use of the category as a general explanation for the changes in intellectual life in late nineteenth- and early twentieth-century Britain not only risks importing inappropriate expectations, but also tends to foreshorten the past and to arrange the changes that did take place in a sequence that can easily be mistaken for a teleology.[9] Undoubtedly 'professionalization' does helpfully describe much of what differentiated intellectual life in 1930 from that of 1850, but the implied assumption about a direct path of development between those two dates may lead us to misperceive what was actually happening in, let us say, 1890. Since the use of the term in the recent literature on this subject may still suggest too uniform and too complete a process, this chapter begins by exploring the diversity of, and limits to, the professionalization of intellectual life in late-nineteenth-century Britain.

It does so, however, not as an exercise in revisionism, useful though that might be as a corrective both to triumphalist accounts of the 'emergence' of the modern university and to critical or nostalgic accounts which appear to find in that development a key to all pathologies. Rather, it is a way of carrying on the discussion of several of the themes discussed in earlier chapters. The relations between reflective political debate and the broader currents of intellectual life remain the central concern, but the focus is now shifted to the impact of the development of academic 'disciplines.' (The special case of the law and its relation to political thought needs to be considered in somewhat different terms as well as in a much

[9] The most ambitious attempt to use the term to explain this and much more in modern British history is Harold Perkin, *The Rise of Professional Society: England since 1880* (London, 1989); for a thought-provoking (though in my view rather over-simple) attempt to characterize changes in intellectual life in these terms, see T. W. Heyck, *The Transformation of Intellectual Life in Victorian England* (London, 1982). These books contain ample reference to the general literature on professionalization; studies of specific disciplines and developments are cited below.

longer perspective, and so is discussed separately in the next chapter.) This was an uneven, ragged process, but it was accompanied by an increased awareness, manifested in a variety of ways, of the existence of authoritative academic opinion, and even where this authority was then challenged, dismissed, or derided, it could not be entirely ignored. As I have already suggested, every social critic lays claim, explicitly or implicitly, to a title to be heard. For many of the leading sages earlier in the nineteenth century this had largely consisted of exhibiting their special intimacy with those great brooding deities of the age such as Science or History or Culture. But as these mighty presences were progressively tamed, stripped of their dignifying capital letters, and reduced to the all-too mundane status of academic studies, the kind of authority which their attendants and acolytes could try to exercise in society at large also changed. These changes inevitably impinged upon the role of the public moralist, though we may leave open for the moment the question of whether this created rival voices, expressing the identity of the 'expert', or whether it furnished an added source of authority for the still recognizable figure of the gentleman of letters. This chapter explores these developments in a deliberately selective way; and in ranging widely across the disciplines, I have inevitably been dependent upon the original research of other, more specialized, scholars whose work I have tried to acknowledge in my footnotes.

At first sight, the whole question of professionalization and academic specialization may seem far removed from the moral preoccupations of 'the culture of altruism' discussed in the preceding chapters. But certain larger continuities need to be borne in mind. To begin with, such developments never take place in a cultural vacuum: the interests guiding them and the categories informing them were necessarily continuous with, if also modifications of, those in the culture more generally. Then, it is worth remembering that the matrix out of which the relevant disciplines developed was, broadly speaking, that of the 'moral sciences', a traditional category which still embraced both descriptive and prescriptive ambitions. The enquiry into 'the moral nature of man' could be understood not just as a consideration of human qualities and behaviour in their distinctively spiritual or non-physical aspect (by contrast to the enquiries classed as the 'natural sciences'); it allowed or even encouraged the hope of arriving at a rational or empirical foundation for the ethical ideal. Moreover, the very activity of scientific enquiry was endowed with positive ethical properties, drawn from the prevailing evaluative scheme: its proponents emphasized the 'disinterested' nature of scientific investigation, its 'selfless' purpose, its inculcation of 'patience' and 'steadiness', ultimately its value in developing 'character'.[10] And finally, one must not lose sight of the way in which an ideal of 'service', drawing in associations of 'altruism' and 'trust', permeated the characterization of the social position of the professional scholar or thinker. In so far as this ideal (with its implied dichotomy between disinterested service and self-interested gain) was generally acknowledged, the academically-based writer could appear to be in a stronger position as a moral critic by virtue of not being dependent on the market.[11] The gain of a certain sort of limited moral authority, therefore, needs to be offset against the undoubted loss of relevance and purchase which was, as ever, the price of greater detachment, just as the assertion of specially trained expertise inevitably brought with it charges of unworldly remoteness and lack of practical judgement. There was, one might say, returning to Sidgwick's phrase, more than one route by which 'the stream of pure science' might flow into 'the muddy channel of current opinion', while it is one of the several defects of the metaphor that it may encourage us to overlook the flow of the current in the reverse direction.

II

Any account of the alleged professionalization of intellectual life in this period must begin with the universities. Beyond question, universities played a far more important role in national life in 1900 than they had in 1850. Although this was not only a consequence of numerical expansion, the bare facts of that expansion tell their own story. At the beginning of this period, the number of students was tiny and almost entirely confined to Oxford and Cambridge. In 1860, out of a total of 3,300 undergraduates in England (the situation in

10 For a discussion of this characterization of science in late 19th-century American intellectual life, see the essay by David Hollinger in Thomas L. Haskell (ed.), *The Authority of Experts* (Bloomington, Ind., 1984). A very similar set of associations was also present in French discussions: see Christophe Charle, 'Intellectuels et élites 1880–1900' (Thèse d'état, Paris I, 1986), 575.

11 Some helpful remarks on this topic are made in passing in Thomas L. Haskell, 'Professionalism vs. capitalism: R. H. Tawney, Emile Durkheim, and C. S. Peirce on the problem of self-interest', in Haskell, *Authority of Experts*.

Scotland had long been different, of course), 2,500 were at Oxbridge; by 1900, following the establishment of the civic universities, the overall total had grown to some 17,000, of whom 6,000 were at Oxbridge; by 1930 (following a very significant expansion of London University, in particular), the total number had grown to approximately 37,000 of whom 10,000 were at Oxbridge.[12] The number of career 'academics' is harder to determine. The term could hardly be applied to the majority of the Fellows of Oxbridge colleges at the beginning of this period; the Royal Commissions of the 1850s attempted to create the rudiments of an academic career, though the Financial Commission of 1871 reported that of the 345 Fellows in receipt of some form of income from the Oxford colleges, only 98 were directly involved in teaching.[13] Even by 1900 there was no uniform career structure for those who might be primarily regarded as 'university teachers'.[14] But the least misleading estimate would be that by the end of the century there were some 800 'academics' at Oxford and Cambridge, and a further 700 at London and the civic universities.[15] An important related development, especially as far as the growth of a sense of corporate professional identity was concerned, was the de-clericalization of Oxford and Cambridge: at Oxford in 1845, 325 out of the estimated 470 Fellows of colleges were in holy orders, but thereafter—and especially, of course, after the relaxation of the celibacy restrictions in the late 1860s and 1870s—the number of clerics diminished far faster than the total number of dons expanded: by 1895 only 61 Fellows were in orders.[16]

[12] K. Jarausch (ed.), *The Transformation of Higher Learning 1860–1930: Expansion, Diversification, Social Opening, and Professionalization in England, Germany, Russia, and the United States* (Chicago, 1983), 13, 45 (Jarausch frequently refers to 'Britain', but it is clear these figures relate only to England). Matriculation figures are not an entirely reliable guide to total numbers of students; Stone calculates that there were already some 2,500 students in residence at Oxbridge in the early 1850s, and that the number had increased considerably by 1860; Lawrence Stone, 'The size and composition of the Oxford student body', in Stone (ed.), *The University in Society*, 2 vols. (Princeton, NJ, 1975).

[13] A. J. Engel, *From Clergyman to Don: The Rise of the Academic Profession in Nineteenth-Century Oxford* (Oxford, 1983), 92–6.

[14] Arthur Engel calculates that in 1814 only 9% of the Fellows of Oxford colleges were engaged in 'educational work': by 1900 the figure had risen to 58%, though this indicates that the category still allowed room for other priorities and identities; Engel, *Clergyman to Don*, 3–4.

[15] A. H. Halsey and M. Trow, *The British Academics* (London, 1971), 139.

[16] Harry Hanham, 'Cambridge history', *History of Education Quarterly*, 15 (1975), 344; by 1939 the number of clerical Fellows, according to Hanham's classification, had fallen to 30.

At the same time, the range of subjects taught in the universities increased even more dramatically. Before 1850, only Classics and Mathematics were recognized as routes to Honours at Oxbridge, and although the two London colleges supported a wider syllabus, the small numbers involved, and the somewhat marginal status of the institutions themselves, meant that these courses were of little broader significance.[17] But in the second half of the century, Oxford and Cambridge established courses in a range of the natural and the moral sciences, including History, Law, Oriental Studies, Modern Languages, English, and Anthropology. The new civic institutions, which largely took shape in the 1870s and 1880s even though they sometimes only acquired full university status later, initially offered several more vocational and commercial subjects, but it is arguable that by 1930 the academic ethos and hierarchy of disciplines familiar at Oxbridge had come to dominate the provincial universities as well.[18] (The fact that the majority of chairs in these universities were filled by Oxbridge products obviously encouraged this process.[19]) The London School of Economics might seem the most obvious exception to this pattern, yet even here what began as a kind of business school-cum-advanced institute for applied social research came in time to be largely devoted to the conventional pattern of undergraduate education. For a long time, the small numbers of teachers involved in these institutions and the diversity of their circumstances were not conducive to the development of a sense of corporate professional identity: 'university teachers' only formed their first professional association in 1919, and did not make their appearance as a census category until 1921.[20]

[17] This may be least true of the teaching of English, which was an extremely popular subject at London, with several notable professors; see D. J. Palmer, *The Rise of English Studies: An Account of the Study of English Language and Literature from its Origins to the Making of the Oxford English School* (Oxford, 1965).

[18] This is certainly the conclusion suggested by R. A. Lowe's survey, 'The expansion of higher education in England', in Jarausch, *Transformation of Higher Learning*, 37–56, though he perhaps understates the initial diversity; see the essay by Sheldon Rothblatt in the same volume, 'The diversification of higher education in England'.

[19] See the figures cited in Roy Lowe, 'Structural change in English higher education', in Detlef K. Muller, Fritz Ringer, and Brian Simon (eds.), *The Rise of the Modern Educational System: Structural Change and Social Reproduction 1870–1920* (Cambridge, 1987), 162–78.

[20] See Harold Perkin, *Key Profession: The History of the Association of University Teachers* (London, 1969), ch. 1. This sense of identity can only have been reinforced by the fact that the University Grants Committee and the Committee of Vice-Chancellors and Principals were also both set up in 1919; Perkin, *Key Profession*, 35.

Marked though these changes were in quantitative and institutional terms, they hardly signified the wholesale professionalization of intellectual life that some historians have since ascribed to them. The ideals and aspirations of the gentleman-don continued to shape and limit these changes in subtle ways. The question of status and the protection of the college Fellow's independence remained governing preoccupations.[21] Furthermore, the 'research-ideal' itself enjoyed only a very partial victory at Oxford and Cambridge in this period.[22] The tutorial relation with the young, which involved, of course, more than merely teaching them, commanded possibly greater rather than diminished standing by the end of the century.[23] At both Oxford and Cambridge, the teaching Fellows found various ways to ignore, rebuff, or limit the influence of the professors who were to be the vanguard of the new research-orientated university.[24] At Oxford, in particular, associations of college tutors remained the locus of real power, with lasting consequences. And the informing ideal of the tutorial role was continuous with the public-school ethos of character-formation and moral guidance rather than with any purely academic notion of specialist instruction. (Even new subjects, therefore, had to justify their claims partly in terms of this ideal, as in Alfred Marshall's rehearsal of the case for the establishment of an Economics Tripos at Cambridge, where he spoke of 'that training of personal character, which is offered by life at Oxford and Cambridge. . . . On the river and in the football field the student learns to bear and forbear, to obey and to command.'[25]) Consequently, this cultural role took priority over a disciplinary label as the prime

[21] In the middle of the century, as Engel observes, 'a critical aspect of the Fellowship's status-value was that it was legally a type of property and not a salary'; much of the resistance to the reforms of the second half of the century came from an unwillingness to surrender this status; Engel, *Clergyman to Don*, 65.

[22] Cf. Rosemary Jann's comment, speaking of history: 'The triumph of the research ideal was in many ways more apparent than real; especially at the ancient universities, the enduring vitality of liberal education provided a medium in which traditional assumptions about history's practical and moral importance continued to thrive'; *The Art and Science of Victorian History* (Columbus, Ohio, 1985), 224.

[23] Hanham concludes that changes in the second half of the century actually strengthened the dominance of the college tutors, with their conviction that 'the determining factor in life was moral training'; Hanham, 'Cambridge history', 347.

[24] This is fully documented in Engel, *Clergyman to Don*, and in Sheldon Rothblatt, *The Revolution of the Dons: Cambridge and Society in Victorian England* (London, 1968).

[25] Alfred Marshall, *A Plea for the Creation of a Curriculum in Economics and Associated Branches of Political Science* (Cambridge, n.d. [1903]), quoted in Collini, Winch, and Burrow, *That Noble Science of Politics*, 335.

constituent of the identity of many late nineteenth-century 'academics': one was a 'tutor' first, a Fellow of a particular college, and a 'philosopher' or 'historian' second. A devious form of snobbery was at work here, too: as an Oxbridge tutor one could have continuing contact with those who came from higher social backgrounds or who enjoyed greater subsequent worldly success than was common among the professional class. Living through one's pupils could mean several things, but it included having access to—having, indeed, a share in shaping—the most influential members of the governing class in ways which one's own obscure scholarly contributions could never themselves have justified.

None the less, these traditional concerns were forced into new shapes by the pressure of the changes affecting the late nineteenth-century university, and it is certainly true that having a licensed standing in the pursuit of a particular field of knowledge became central to the identity of all of those who can be classed as academics. To have 'five hundred a year and a field of one's own' conferred a kind of independence. And even although there continued in the early twentieth century to be a certain amount of traffic between universities and the adjacent political, legal, and literary worlds for particularly talented, ambitious, or well-connected individuals, the notion of a purely academic career, with its own internal criteria for achievement and advancement, was now clearly established as the dominant pattern. Moreover, in considering the impact of the various attempts to reform the universities in this period, one must not only attend to the actual institutional outcomes: even if the research-ideal enjoyed strictly limited victories at this level, the unignorable presence of the standards and aspirations it expressed subtly altered the identities even of those who most scornfully or defiantly repudiated it. This, and the associated redefinition of the role of universities in national life, also introduced a new inhibition about the propriety of academic intervention in partisan political controversy (to which I shall return below). Thus, although the expansion and enhanced status of the universities in the last few decades of the nineteenth century certainly altered the public role of intellectuals in various ways, these changes did not all tell in one direction.

If the multiple functions and not entirely coherent values fostered within universities betray the tensions as much as the triumphs of professionalization, one might hope to obtain a more clear-cut picture of change from the establishment towards the end of the century of specialized professional associations for the promotion of particular disciplines. But even if the general import of these developments is unmistakable, here too their immediate bearing on the relation of intellectuals to public debate could be more complicated. There had, of course, long been groups and associations who assembled to discuss common intellectual interests; the Political Economy Club, in particular, which was founded in 1821, allowed economists, politicians, and businessmen to engage in both theoretical and policy debate. But two later institutions suggest, in their markedly different ways, the highly integrated world of mid-Victorian intellectual and political life, and may serve as symbolic benchmarks against which to measure later changes. The first was the National Association for the Promotion of Social Science, founded in 1857, which provided a forum for all 'those engaged in all the various efforts now happily begun for the improvement of the people'.[26] As this suggests, the NAPSS busied itself with social reform, directing its discussions towards the improvement of legislation. It divided itself into five 'departments': legal reform, penal policy, education, public health, and 'social economy'. Although leading politicians and intellectuals participated from time to time in its annual congresses—both Gladstone and Mill addressed at least three such meetings—the bulk of members were drawn from those professions most actively engaged with practical social problems—doctors, coroners, charity organizers, and the like.[27] In other words, NAPSS did not represent an attempt to cultivate a particular intellectual activity, and its discussions betrayed little sense of anxiety about stepping outside one's proper sphere or, apart from frequent wrangles over the practical teachings of political economy, even any acknowledgement of the existence of putatively authoritative academic disciplines. As contemporary descriptions implied, the model for its activities was rather Parliamentary than academic,[28] and its success was measured by the particular pieces of

[26] From the account of the founding of the Association as given in *Transactions of the National Association for the Promotion of Social Science for 1857* (London, 1858), p. xxi.

[27] See the useful general discussion in Lawrence Goldman, 'A peculiarity of the English? The Social Science Association and the absence of sociology in nineteenth-century Britain', *Past and Present*, 114 (1987), 132–71.

[28] It was frequently described as a 'supplementary Parliament' or 'Parliament out of session'; quoted in Lawrence Goldman, 'Henry Fawcett and the Social Science Association', in Goldman (ed.), *The Blind Victorian: Henry Fawcett and British Liberalism* (Cambridge, 1989), 149.

legislation it helped to promote. The Association met for the last time in 1886; thereafter, the kinds of issues it had discussed were increasingly divided among more specialized bodies. By that date, the discussions which led to the founding of what became the Royal Economic Society had already begun.[29]

At first sight, there could hardly be a sharper contrast than that between the NAPSS and the other mid-Victorian institution which forms something of a symbolic contrast to later developments, namely the Metaphysical Society. Where the NAPSS was public and inclusive, the Metaphysical Society was private and selective; where the former devoted its energies to securing concrete legislative changes on practical matters, the latter cultivated the most abstract level of philosophical discussion. The Metaphysical Society was founded in 1869, largely on the initiative of James Knowles, then editor of the *Contemporary Review* and from 1877 founder and editor of the *Nineteenth Century*.[30] Its purpose was to bring together for frank discussion the leading representatives of all varieties of religion and unbelief, and 'to collect, arrange, and diffuse Knowledge (whether objective or subjective) of mental and moral phenomena'.[31] In the course of its twelve-year existence it recruited many of the luminaries of Victorian culture, though several of the most obvious big names, such as Mill, Spencer, and Arnold, escaped its net. Among its sixty-two members, one finds the familiar names of Bagehot, Harrison, Morley, Ruskin, Seeley, Sidgwick, and both Stephens (as well as Balfour and Gladstone among politicians, Huxley and Tyndall among scientists, Froude, Hutton, and Knowles among editors, and so on). Though its meetings were private, it may be said to have exercised considerable cultural authority indirectly, not least because no fewer than nine of its members were editors of one or more of the widely read periodicals.[32]

[29] See below, pp. 214–16.

[30] See above, Ch. 1, pp. 54–5.

[31] Quoted from the minutes of the founding meeting in Apr. 1869, in Alan Willard Brown, *The Metaphysical Society: Victorian Minds in Crisis 1869–1880* (New York, 1947), 26; see 310–12 for the list of members of the society.

[32] H. Alford edited the *Contemporary* until succeeded by James Knowles in 1870; R. H. Hutton co-edited the *Spectator*; W. G. Ward edited the *Dublin Review*; Bagehot moved from editing the *National Review* to *The Economist*; J. A. Froude edited *Fraser's Magazine*; George Grove edited *Macmillan's*; Leslie Stephen edited the *Cornhill*; John Morley edited the *Fortnightly*. The total could be increased if one included G. Croom Robertson who edited *Mind*, the first (founded in 1876) of the more specialized scholarly journals. 'The Metaphysical Society thus became a focal point for the dissemination of ideas and the cultivation of a tone, a manner, and a temper destined to put its mark upon the whole subsequent history of English journalism'; Brown, *Metaphysical Society*, 170.

But the Metaphysical Society was never more than a forum: it did not attempt to promote any specialized studies, and when, for a variety of reasons, some of its leading members ceased to attend, it had no purely professional or practical purposes to fall back upon to sustain its existence.

Moreover, the range of issues which it addressed was increasingly coming to be annexed by more specialized enquirers; both the older, psychology-based forms of empiricism and the newly fashionable Idealism were developing more technical vocabularies, encouraging philosophers to address other philosophers rather than a wider public. Indeed, Alexander Bain had donated the money needed to found *Mind*, the first 'professional' philosophical journal, in 1876 partly because the great periodicals of general culture no longer seemed to be publishing very much serious philosophy.[33] Two small details indicate the direction of the changes. When its remaining members wound up the Metaphysical Society in 1880, they resolved that its accumulated funds should be paid over to the proprietors of *Mind*.[34] And in the final year of the Society's meetings, a new society was set up in London 'for the systematic study of philosophy'. In fact, the subsequent proceedings of the Aristotelian Society, as the new body was called, continued to include a miscellaneous range of topics, so much so that by 1891 the organizing committee was complaining that not enough attention had been given to 'philosophy proper', though that complaint itself indicates a heightened sense of vocation. But once again there is a sense in which 'specialization' preceded 'professionalization': Shadworth Hodgson, founder and (for fourteen years) first President of the Aristotelian Society, held no academic post but published numerous works of philosophy, and in practice the chief common denominator, apart from their interest in philosophy, among the gentlemen from different professions who attended the early meetings was that they lived in London.[35] None the less, after 1880 the kinds of discussions which had sustained the Metaphysical Society were, one could say, now divided, symbolically, between the pages of the *Nineteenth Century* on the one hand and of *Mind* and the *Proceedings of the Aristotelian Society* on the other.

Where the NAPSS and the Metaphysical Society represented two faces of the world of the mid-Victorian intellectual, from the 1880s

[33] See the details as given in Brown, *Metaphysical Society*, 197 f.

[34] Ibid. 341.

[35] On Hodgson, see ibid. 248–51.

onwards gatherings with a putatively disciplinary focus increasingly became the typical institutional form. Their distinguishing mark was the acknowledgement of impersonal and often international scholarly or scientific standards within one particular field of enquiry which imposed their own imperatives and which relegated the practical utility, if any, of their enquiries to a subordinate status. Such scholarly associations frequently took the initiative in founding new journals in which this goal of specialized and self-consciously 'disinterested' enquiry could be prosecuted without regard to the vagaries of the market. Merely to cite the dates of the founding of the better known of these journals sufficiently indicates the pattern. *Mind*, as we have seen, led the way in 1876; the *Law Quarterly Review* followed in 1884, the *English Historical Review* in 1886, the *Proceedings of the Aristotelian Society* in 1887, the *Classical Review* in 1887, the *Economic Journal* in 1891, and so on. The establishment of such specialized publications usually reflected (perhaps it always does) what one might call 'supply push' rather than 'demand pull': the dynamic came from those who wished to write in a more specialized idiom at least as much as from those who wished to have more such material to read. The impact of the expansion of the universities is already evident here. Furthermore, the affiliation to a scholarly society often lay behind the financial viability of the new journal, whether by means of direct subsidy or simply by providing a near-captive market. And, of course, such journals presupposed the existence of a sufficiently numerous group who had reasons for wishing to contribute other than direct financial reward; in none of the above-mentioned cases were the early contributors exclusively university teachers, but increasingly this form of publication came to reflect the career advancement of those who received an academic salary.

Yet although these journals and professional associations were in some sense 'specialized' in the range of topics they dealt with, they were not in any simple way 'professional', still less exclusively academic. The foundation of such associations could, needless to say, serve many purposes, social and practical as well as intellectual. There were usually no very demanding requirements for membership, and they functioned as something of a cross between a club and a special interest pressure-group rather than as a professional testing and licensing body. Moreover, in most cases, they continued to include questions of 'practical' application within their remit, albeit accompanied by increasing agitation over the propriety of publicly pronouncing on such matters.

Economics (as political economy was increasingly coming to be called in this period) provided the most obvious example of the difficulties of combining practical application with scientific detachment, and these tensions came to the surface in the discussions leading to the founding of the British Economic Association (subsequently the Royal Economic Society) in 1890. One crucial issue needing to be resolved was whether such an association should be open to all, cranks and dabblers included, or whether there should be some qualification for membership or other test of professional competence (with the attendant risk of imposing a constricting doctrinal orthodoxy). The unsatisfactory nature of the 'open' constitution of Section F of the British Association for the Advancement of Science, the chief previous forum for economic discussion, was increasingly remarked. 'It seems to me impossible to make the discussions very valuable', reflected Sidgwick in 1886. 'The time must necessarily be limited; and there are certain familiar bores who turn up at every meeting and limit still further the fruitful minutes.'[36] The accumulation of such discontents in the course of the 1880s became, it seems, the prime stimulus to the founding of a separate association.[37] 'The absolute necessity of some qualification' was urged by several proponents of the new body; otherwise 'everything would be a wrangle about "first principles"'.[38] Marshall, the single most influential figure in these developments, insisted upon an 'absolutely catholic basis', though some of his characteristic equivocation, or slyness, is evident in his rider that the association should 'include every school of economists which was doing genuine work'.[39] Given the paucity of full-time academic economists at this time, the result was a very heterogeneous body indeed. This

[36] Journal entry 13 Sept. 1886; Sidgwick, *Memoir*, 456.

[37] See Donald Winch, 'A century of economics', in John D. Hey and Donald Winch (eds.), *A Century of Economics* (Oxford, 1990), 7–8. As early as 1887, H. S. Foxwell could explain to an American audience that the projected new society would 'aim at the advancement of theory, at the consolidation of economic opinion, at the encouragement of economic research, and at the criticism and direction of industrial and financial policy'; quoted in Alon Kadish and R. D. Freeman, 'Foundation and early years', ibid. 24.

[38] E. C. K. Gonner, quoted by Kadish and Freeman in Hey and Winch, *A Century of Economics*, 28.

[39] Quoted in A. W. Coats, 'The role of authority in the development of British economics', *Journal of Law and Economics*, 7 (1964), 97.

reflected the situation of economics more generally: even at the turn of the century, as one historian has noted, 'the conventional nineteenth-century "practical" businessman or city financier type of economist still predominated, and the views of such ex-Chancellors of the Exchequer as Viscount Goschen and Hicks-Beach, leading statisticians like Robert Giffen and Charles Booth, and, behind the scenes, permanent officials of the Treasury and the Board of Trade, usually carried more weight than academic opinion'.[40]

It was partly in order to redress this balance that the idea of founding a specialized journal appealed to many academic economists. As H. S. Foxwell remarked, welcoming the establishment of such publications in France and the United States, 'They will tend both to strengthen and to exhibit the substantial agreement which exists between trained economists, and thus enormously to increase the legitimate influence of the study on practical affairs.'[41] His casual reference to 'trained' economists and their 'legitimate' influence expressed one, primarily academic, conception of the matter, but he thereby glossed over what were to be extremely contentious issues. In fact, there were deep divisions within the ranks of economists about the very scope and nature of their subject, divisions which were neatly symbolized in 1891 by the inauguration within a few months of each other of two rival journals: the *Economic Journal*, the main though not the sole informing inspiration of which came from Marshall's attempt to marry neo-classical theory to a systematic study of economic facts, and the *Economic Review*, founded in Oxford largely under the auspices of the Christian Social Union and of German-influenced historical economists. (One indication of the lack of a purely academic base for these ventures, as well as perhaps of a greater financial shrewdness among economists than other types of scholar, is the fact that, like its less specialized predecessors, the *Economic Journal* continued to pay its contributors.[42]) In his initial proposal for a new journal, Marshall had spoken of the need to have somewhere to publish work which was 'too technical for the ordinary magazines', indicating the growing estrangement between specialized scholars and the general periodicals. But as it turned out, what a

40 A. W. Coats, 'Political economy and the Tariff Reform campaign of 1903', *Journal of Law and Economics*, 11 (1968), 185.

41 Quoted by Kadish and Freeman in Hey and Winch, *A Century of Economics*, 26.

42 Contributors were paid 10*s*. per page for articles and 5*s*. per page for reviews and other contributions; Edgworth received £100 as editor (Hey and Winch, *A Century of Economics*, 35).

later generation would class as, at best, 'applied' topics predominated in both these journals, and a recent account of the 'professionalization' of economics concludes that at this period the newly established organizations and publications were 'wide open to people with little training or knowledge. If one imagines hospital orderlies writing in *The Lancet* or village churchwardens addressing the Synod, that hardly conveys an exaggerated picture of the *Economic Journal* in its early days, or the economic section of the British Association for the Advancement of Science throughout the Marshall era.'[43]

The complexities and ambiguities of the partial professionalization of the disciplines in this period were particularly evident in the case of history. At first sight, this is a subject whose development may appear to fit the familiar model of professionalization very readily. The great narrative historians of the middle of the century such as Macaulay or Froude had not only addressed a wide general readership; their interpretations of the national past had helped to provide that audience with a sense of identity and hence with some guidance about future developments.[44] But in the later part of the century it might seem that this manner of writing history was challenged and eventually displaced by more 'scientific', archive-based research; the scale of the history written became more minute, the standards of evidence more exacting, the withdrawal from public debate more marked. Figures such as Stubbs or Maitland or Tout came to be venerated by later generations of guild members for their mastery of the demanding technical expertise of the craft. The new research historians began to found their own associations and journals; the subject was securely established in the universities; the 'professional', in short, appeared to displace the 'amateur'. But in fact, the more closely recent scholars have investigated both the intellectual and the institutional history, the more the inadequacies of this oft-told story have become apparent.[45]

[43] John Maloney, *Marshall, Orthodoxy, and the Professionalisation of Economics* (Cambridge, 1985), 2. For this reason, Maloney eschews an institutional focus for his account, and concentrates instead on trying 'to trace the rise of a self-conscious sense of profession among economists', the chief source of which he finds in the ultimate dominance of 'the neo-classical paradigm' (3, 235).

[44] See John W. Burrow, *A Liberal Descent: Victorian Historians and the English Past* (Cambridge, 1981).

[45] The 'professionalization' of history and the development of historiography in the late nineteenth century has been particularly well served by recent scholarship. I can only indicate one or two of the relevant conclusions of this literature here: for further

To begin with, the extended slanging-match, at its most vehement in the 1870s and 1880s, between those who stigmatized each other as 'merely literary' or 'narrowly fact-grubbing' cannot be taken entirely at face value. Both groups (in a fuller account one would need to demonstrate that there was in fact no single, clear-cut division) were laying claim to a certain kind of cultural authority; the two labels indicated two different ways of failing to command the interest and respect of the educated public. The self-described 'scientific' historians, that is to say, were adopting a different strategy for exercising this authority, a strategy adapted to an age increasingly responsive to the ideal of scientific expertise and the ethic of professionalism. Exaggerating the scholarly failings of their predecessors did not necessarily indicate a withdrawal from the public eye: 'Attacks on "literary" amateurs were a publicistic way of aggrandizing the historian's position. . . . Since it was the specialty that provided the academic person with his self-assurance and his success, it was in his interest both to advance his subject and to enlarge its general importance.'[46] The idiom became in some sense cooler, the route to public influence perhaps more indirect; but the leading historians at the end of the century remained convinced of the national, and particularly political, significance of their subject and of the education it could provide to the governors and administrators of the next generation.[47] Their polemics should thus

details see particularly: P. B. M. Blaas, *Continuity and Anachronism: Parliamentary and Constitutional Development in Whig Historiography and the Anti-Whig Reaction between 1890 and 1930* (The Hague, 1978); Deborah Wormell, *Sir John Seeley and the Uses of History* (Cambridge, 1980); Burrow, *A Liberal Descent*; Doris Goldstein, 'The organizational development of the British historical profession 1884–1921', *Bulletin of the Institute of Historical Research*, 55 (1982), 180–93, and id., 'The professionalisation of history in Britain in the late nineteenth and early 20th centuries', *History of Historiography*, 3 (1983), 3–26; Jann, *Art and Science of Victorian History*; Philippa Levine, *The Amateur and the Professional: Antiquarians, Historians, and Archaeologists in Victorian England 1838–1886* (Cambridge, 1986); Peter R. H. Slee, *Learning and a Liberal Education: The Study of Modern History in the Universities of Oxford, Cambridge, and Manchester 1800–1914* (Manchester, 1986); Alon Kadish, 'Scholarly exclusiveness and the founding of the *English Historical Review*', *Historical Research*, 61 (1988), 183–98; J. W. Burrow, 'Victorian historians and the Royal Historical Society', *Transactions of the Royal Historical Society*, 5th ser., 39 (1989), 125–40.

46 Jann, *Art and Science of Victorian History*, 223–4, 185.

47 This conviction received a kind of public endorsement from the subject's evident success in attracting students: 'In the first quarter of the [20th] century, nearly one third of the undergraduates at Oxford were reading for the History School; as many as two hundred took the Historical Tripos [at Cambridge] each year in the late twenties and early thirties'; Jann, *Art and Science of Victorian History*, 229.

partly be seen as an attempt to protect that public standing: lacking any elaborate body of theory or even a particularly technical vocabulary, professional historians found it difficult to preserve the virtuous reputation of their discipline against the contamination of that motley body of romancers, enthusiasts, and hacks who continued to publish works of a broadly historical character.

The early years of the Royal Historical Society furnished a revealing institutional expression of these complexities. From its founding in 1868, it attracted a notably miscellaneous group of scholars, antiquarians, genealogists, and self-styled seers, and the early volumes of its *Transactions* seem to have been more a form of collective vanity-publishing than of concerted scholarly enquiry.[48] The 1880s saw something of a take-over of the Society by the new breed of academic historian, and one might be tempted to assimilate this to the familiar story of 'professionalization' outlined above. Yet this hardly constituted the displacement of public figures addressing a wide audience by footnote-governed pedants. In fact, it might be nearer the mark to see the change as representing a move in the reverse direction: the obscure antiquarians and eccentric scholars who were to some extent displaced hardly belonged in the same category as the great names of Victorian narrative history, while the group of academic infiltrators ultimately included figures such as Acton and Seeley who were not exactly unknown scholars working in monkish seclusion. As John Burrow properly reminds us, 'just as there were different sorts of "amateur", so there were different professionalisms'.[49]

Despite their greater presence in the Society, the academics of the 1880s clearly felt that its *Proceedings* were an inadequate vehicle for their scholarly work, and the idea of a 'strictly scientific' historical journal, mooted on several occasions in the 1860s and 1870s, was revived in earnest.[50] The chief proponents of such a journal had previously been that group of Oxford-linked friends centred around Stubbs, Freeman, and J. R. Green, who were anxious to

[48] See Burrow, 'Victorian historians', esp. 130–5, though the terms of this description are mine not his; the rest of this paragraph draws directly upon Burrow's excellent discussion.

[49] Burrow, 'Victorian historians', 138. Burrow also observes that recent work has 'made us aware that the process of the professionalization of history in this country and the associated claims for it as a "science" exhibit complexities which defy simple characterization' (138).

[50] For details of the earlier discussions, see Kadish, 'Foundation of the *EHR*', 183–8.

establish an 'English School' of critical history. The preferred form of such a project proved to be 'a small and purely scientific publication, counting on a small circulation supported by a list of subscribers, and written without payment'.[51] The familiar anxieties about protecting the scientific reputation of the subject against the damage done by more popular writers were at work in these proposals. Freeman, for example, complained that 'everybody thinks himself qualified to write history, to criticize history, and . . . there is no security that the competent scholar will win the public ear rather than the empty pretender'.[52] (Note that it was still the 'public ear' that he wished the 'competent scholar' to gain.) A further difficulty concerned the increasingly delicate question of overt political partisanship. Indeed, at one point, the Syndics of Cambridge University Press, always a cautious body, decided against publishing some such journal partly because 'history was connected with politics, and the Press ought to be neutral in politics'. It could countenance the idea of printing documents or bibliographies, but 'essays were dangerous'.[53]

When plans for the new historical journal finally took definite shape in 1885, the question had to be faced of whether they should try to keep the 'empty pretenders' out of its pages, the question, as Green had put it at the time of the first discussions, of 'what to do with the Stanleys and Kingsleys.'[54] Clearly, several of the founding group (in which Acton, Bryce, Creighton, and Ward were now active) baulked at the possibility of a contribution from the despised Froude, but after some heart-searching they concluded they had no option but to 'be entirely catholic'.[55] The 'Prefatory note' in the first issue of the review (drafted by Bryce) struggled with these conflicting considerations: it advised that articles should be accessible to 'an educated man not specially conversant with history', but at the same time it sternly announced that 'no allurements of style will secure insertion for a popular *réchauffé* of facts already known or

[51] Green to Alexander Macmillan 15 June 1876, in *Letters of John Richard Green*, ed. Leslie Stephen (London, 1901), 436; quoted in Kadish, 'Foundation of the *EHR*', 185. Green feared that attempts to address 'the general reader' would produce a journal 'hardly distinguishable from a very superior number of the *Edinburgh*'.

[52] E. A. Freeman, 'On the study of history', *Fortnightly Review*, NS 29 (1881), 325; also quoted in Kadish, 'Foundation of the *EHR*', 195–6.

[53] Quoted in Kadish, 'Foundation of the *EHR*', 190.

[54] Letter of 28 Jan. 1867 to E. A. Freeman, in *Letters of J. R. Green*, 173; quoted in Burrow, 'Victorian historians', 133–4.

[55] Kadish, 'Foundation of the *EHR*', 196–8.

ideas already suggested'. It also endorsed what was now coming to be the orthodox academic position concerning the light the review's contents might cast upon practical issues: 'We shall not hesitate to let that light be reflected from our pages', it declared, 'whenever we can be sure that it is dry light free from any tinge of partisanship.'[56]

This unsteadiness about the proper scope and purpose of scholarly associations devoted to a single discipline was part of a broader preoccupation in the last couple of decades of the century with the question of the accreditation or 'licensing' of those who should be recognized as speaking with authority on a given subject. This remained, of course, a far more vexed question in the moral sciences than in the natural sciences where there was in practice increasing agreement about the need to follow certain approved courses of study if one was to be recognized as a competent scientist.[57] An indication of the sensitivities engaged by this apparently abstract and impersonal issue is provided by those several celebrated cases from this period in which the work of an 'amateur' was publicly exposed by a scholar purporting to represent the latest standards of accredited scholarship.[58] In such cases, the acceptance of the term 'amateur' already conceded more than half the case: an amateur is defined *against* a standard. But the standard was not fixed; it was alluded to, and shifted, to meet polemical need, and those who used the term in this dismissive way to disparage the work of their predecessors and rivals were vulnerable to similar scorn from the next generation of yet more specialized scholars. Nor should we assume that those who took the high line always conformed to the career pattern of the professional academic. Among historians there was no severer critic of the lax standards and lack of archival research of his 'literary' predecessors than William Stubbs, and it is presumably for this reason that he has been taken to epitomize the 'professionalization' of intellectual life in this period.[59] But his actual career suggests some of the ways in which the overlapping of the

[56] 'Prefatory note', *English Historical Review*, 1 (1886), 1–6.

[57] For a provocative suggestion that the much-discussed 'conflict between religion and science' in the mid-Victorian period should be seen as an episode in the history of professionalization, leading to the withdrawal of claims of authority by the Church, see Frank Miller Turner, 'The Victorian conflict between science and religion: a professional dimension', *Isis*, 69 (1978), 356–76.

[58] Though not particularly celebrated, Sidgwick's criticism of Benjamin Kidd, which I discuss at s. v below, belongs in this category.

[59] See Heyck, *Transformation of Intellectual Life*, ch. 5.

various traditional hierarchies within the educated class set certain limits to that process: Stubbs was a private scholar holding a country living for 16 years before being appointed to the Regius Chair at Oxford in 1866, and he effectively abandoned historical research after resigning his chair in 1884 to accept ecclesiastical preferment as bishop of Chester (hardly a course one could imagine being followed by, let us say, Seignobos or Droysen). He was succeeded at Oxford by his friend E. A. Freeman, private scholar and country squire who up to that point had sported no official title other than 'JP'. And Freeman provides a particularly piquant example of how the exacting specialist of one generation is belaboured as a loose generalist by the next: his attacks on Froude in the 1860s and 1870s had been a byword for pedantic ferocity, but he was himself to become the target for one of the more celebrated scholarly demolitions of the 1890s when the medievalist J. H. Round savaged the mistakes in his account of the Norman Conquest. 'We have weighed [Freeman's work] in that balance in which he weighed the work of others, and we have found it wanting.'[60]

That same example, however, could be taken to illustrate a different aspect of the significance of these exchanges, namely that such attacks were in danger of backfiring precisely because the severity of their scholarly standards, and the ungentlemanly manner of applying them, could seem excessive to the non-specialist audience before whom such gladiatorial combats were still played out (Round's assault on Freeman had initially been launched in the pages of the *Quarterly Review*). One of the most notorious of such public squabbles was that which followed John Churton Collins's attack on Edmund Gosse in 1886. Although neither of these men play any further part in this book, save for a brief re-appearance in Chapter 9 below, the episode is worth briefly attending to for illustrative purposes. Gosse, minor poet and general journeyman of letters, had been appointed to the Clark Lectureship in English Literature at Trinity College, Cambridge, in 1884. The Clark Lectureship was not a regular teaching post; it required the delivery of twenty lectures a year on English Literature, not then part of the Cambridge syllabus. Leslie Stephen had been appointed its first holder in 1883—'I shall have to go to Cambridge three times a week

[60] J. H. Round, 'Professor Freeman', *Quarterly Review*, 175 (1892), 37. See also J. H. Round, *Feudal England: Historical Studies on the XIth and XIIth Centuries* (London, 1895), preface.

to talk twaddle about Addison and Pope to a number of young ladies from Girton and a few idle undergraduates and the youthful prince'—but resigned after one year and was succeeded by Gosse.[61] In 1885 Cambridge University Press published Gosse's first set of lectures in a volume entitled *From Shakespeare to Pope: An Enquiry into the Causes and Phenomena of the Rise of Classical Poetry in England*. Collins, a more thorough scholar and a fierce reviewer who made his living as an Extension lecturer, had for some time been energetically campaigning to have the subject of English Literature recognized by the universities, particularly Oxford. As he put it in a collection of polemical pieces, the failings of the books under review demonstrated that 'until the Universities provide adequately for the proper study of English Literature . . . there will be small hope of its finding competent critics and interpreters'.[62] The appearance of Gosse's error-stuffed volume provided him with an ideal opportunity: he could combine an attack on the slipshod scholarship of one who enjoyed so much more social and academic recognition than himself (envy and resentment may have played more than their usual part) with a pointed reiteration of his general case about the intellectual anarchy that resulted from the universities not fostering the proper scholarly standards. It is important to note that had Gosse's lectures been delivered at an institution of lesser academic prestige than Trinity College, Cambridge, or the ensuing book published by a less authoritative house than Cambridge University Press, Collins would not, on his own account, have felt that public demolition was called for.[63] As his prose gasps in the middle of itemizing Gosse's staggering number of errors: 'And this is a University lecturer.'[64]

But although the attack damaged Gosse's reputation somewhat, and certainly wounded him, it would seem that in the eyes of several of those of whose opinion we have some record it was Collins who came off worse, being dismissed as a fanatical pedant, a disappointed candidate for academic appointments, and, typically, an unmannerly blackguard. For example, Rider Haggard wrote to Gosse in

[61] F. W. Maitland, *The Life and Letters of Leslie Stephen* (London, 1906), 380.

[62] For Collins's campaign, see his *The Study of English Literature: A Plea for its Recognition and Organization at the Universities* (London, 1891); and for examples of his ferocity as a reviewer, see his *Ephemera Critica: or Plain Truths about Current Literature* (London, 1901), quotation at 76.

[63] See the remarks quoted in Ann Thwaite, *Edmund Gosse: A Literary Landscape* (Oxford, 1985; 1st edn. 1984), 281.

[64] Quoted ibid. 282.

sympathy, saying he did not himself know much about eighteenth-century literature, but 'I do know what conduct one gentleman has a right to expect from another'.[65] In assessing the place of this controversy in late Victorian sensitivities about the role of academic authority, we need to remember, first, that Collins's article appeared in the *Quarterly Review*, and, secondly, that it generated considerable discussion in the pages of equally non-specialist publications such as *The Times* and the *Pall Mall Gazette*. Though specialization was certainly making its inroads into the shared culture of the Victorian educated class, it still had some way to go, and the ambivalence towards excessive scholarly zeal manifested on this occasion may have reflected a deeper unease about the price to be paid for allowing the specialists to divide the kingdom of culture among themselves.

Finally, two developments of different kinds indirectly point to the increased self-consciousness at the end of the century about the standing and role of the academic specialist. The first may be found in a small shift of linguistic usage. The pejorative sense of the adjective 'academic'—'not leading to a decision; unpractical; theoretical, formal, or conventional'—first makes its appearance in the mid-1880s, particularly, it seems, in *The Times*'s rather dismissive characterization of certain debates in Parliament.[66] This usage soon caught on, as in Foxwell's observation, during the discussions in the late 1880s leading to the founding of the British Economic Association, that though in Ricardo's day the political economists 'were perhaps too immersed in current business and politics', now 'the theorist was apt to become academic in the bad sense of that word'.[67] J. A. Hobson was trading upon this sense when he, brandishing his sense of exclusion from the ranks of recognized economists like an aggressive beggar with a war wound, polemicized against 'the academic spirit' in intellectual life (and sometimes 'the "academic" spirit', the quotation marks signifying a sense neither entirely novel nor entirely established). Its negative application was constantly surfacing in such phrases as his reference to 'a few less

[65] Quoted ibid. 288.

[66] The first example of this sense given in the *OED* has this provenance (*The Times*, 31 Mar. 1886), while the second (from 1888) suggests this was widely recognized: 'She thought his question "academic"—the term she used to see applied in the *Times* to certain speeches in Parliament.'

[67] Quoted in Coats, 'The role of authority', 98.

academic and more liberal-minded members' of the universities.[68] The appearance of this usage suggests, brutally enough, some of the costs which accompanied the redefined authority of the intellectual expertise located in universities.

The other revealing symptom was a heightened sensitivity to the question of preserving the public 'neutrality' of the academic as the quid pro quo for his freedom to pursue his research without external political direction. This partly reflected the way in which staff at the new civic universities were vulnerable to such pressure, since initially it was local businessmen or corporations who paid the piper.[69] Interest in the topic was also stimulated by the far more elaborate and consequential debates about *Lehrfreiheit* and 'ethical neutrality' in late nineteenth-century Germany, which was still regarded as setting the pace in most aspects of the higher learning. But it was surely also the case that attentiveness to the topic in England indicated an increased sense of a distinctive academic role with its own privileges and responsibilities. 'Disinterestedness' implied that one's judgement deserved a special respect which could be eroded or forfeited if it descended too readily from its pedestal.[70] We are still far from the position of those modern 'policy sciences' which ostensibly limit their public role to that of furnishing, in response to external request, the findings of research that bear upon a given issue. None the less, even the slightly increased concern with the propriety of engaging in political debate which I am referring to indicates, in the terms I have used before, the pressure to invoke a different authority, the need to speak in a different voice.

III

We may approach the issue of the changing 'voices' available to the public moralist from another direction by returning to the question

[68] J. A. Hobson, 'The academic spirit in education', *Contemporary Review*, 63 (1893), 245, 247. Hobson's article was chiefly a plea for a more democratic system of higher education in England, and in his view this would entail its being a less specialized one: 'The academic view of knowledge', he alleged, 'is the worst result of excessive specialism' (243).

[69] For examples of this, see Stuart Wallace, *War and the Image of Germany: British Academics 1914–1918* (Edinburgh, 1988), 10–11; the attempted prohibition in some cases was against lecturers associating themselves 'at all openly with any political party'.

[70] Cf. Heyck's observation, which also supports the argument of Ch. 2 above, that 'the much-used term "disinterested" meant to them "not-for-self-interest" as well as non-partisan'; *Transformation of Intellectual Life*, 226.

of an audience and the means of addressing it. One of the least remarked consequences of the expansion of universities was the higher proportion of intellectual energy which was thereby devoted to the task of addressing the young. This need not, of course, be to the exclusion of addressing any other audience. Indeed, it is a more commonly noted aspect of the growth of scholarly professionalism that scholars now write for the small community of other competent scholars, their peers, and this process was clearly at work in this period. But having a student audience constantly in mind both provided one kind of role and arguably affected the tone and scope of the resulting published work.

One simple way to indicate the practical dimensions of this change would be to juxtapose to the list I offered earlier[71] of those subsequently renowned works of political thought which began life as essays in the general periodicals, a no less impressive list of works which began life as lectures (quite a few of which were, with that piety which academic life seems to encourage, assembled and published posthumously). Both T. H. Green's *Lectures on the Principles of Political Obligation* and his *Prolegomena to Ethics* began as professorial lectures at Oxford; the latter he had himself almost prepared for publication before his early death in 1882, but the former were assembled by Nettleship and first published in the second volume of Green's *Works* in 1886. Only in 1895 were they published in the separate book form in which they subsequently became familiar. Sidgwick illustrates a slightly different aspect of this trend, since he essentially used his lectures as a means of writing the first drafts of his books, nearly all of which began in this way. But after his death in 1900 three further volumes appeared made up of more or less unrevised lectures, among them *The Development of European Polity* (1903) which openly declared in its preface: 'The book here offered to the public consists of lectures delivered in the University of Cambridge to students of history and of moral sciences.'[72] Seeley's influential *The Expansion of England* (1883) had the same provenance, and his widely used *Introduction to Political Science* (1896) was in fact an amalgam of two sets of lecture notes prepared for the press by Sidgwick after Seeley's death in 1895. Similarly, the first edition of Dicey's canonical work on the constitution bore the bald title *Lectures Introductory to the Study of the*

[71] See above, Ch. 1, 51–2.

[72] Henry Sidgwick, *The Development of European Polity* (London, 1903), p.v.

Law of the Constitution, and was presented as the first fruits of his tenure of the Vinerian Chair at Oxford.[73] Dicey's other well-known work, on law and public opinion, illustrates another form which enjoyed a new prominence in this period in the wake of the enhanced status of universities, the invited or endowed lectures: *Lectures on the Relation between Law and Public Opinion in England in the Nineteenth Century* (1905) were first delivered at Harvard, just as Maitland's widely ramifying *Township and Borough* (1898) was first given as the Ford lectures at Oxford.

Needless to say, the lecture and the periodical essay could coexist as sources of books, sometimes of the same book, and a figure like Maine who appeared in my first list with *Popular Government* could also be included here with works like his *Lectures on the Early History of Institutions* (1875). Yet the trend towards 'professor's books' is clear. The frank presentation of a volume as 'lectures' can, of course, serve many functions, including exculpating the author from any obligation to a profounder or more searching treatment. But it may also be that at this period it signalled a special claim to authority. The appearance of such volumes certainly confirmed the centrality of the universities to the national culture: the publication of the lectures expanded their audience, allowing other members of the educated class to eavesdrop on performances that were now recognized as significant and likely to be influential.

Making one's role as a teacher central to one's identity, which was far from being the inevitable consequence of holding an academic post, then as now, could involve adopting a different tone and argumentative horizon from those who spoke primarily from the periodical page rather than the lectern. One may feel that in Sidgwick's case the tendency towards precise definition, carefully balanced qualification, and cautious judgement was over-determined, but he himself certainly recognized these aims as part of his pedagogic role, and they were obviously virtues that dovetailed particularly well with the task of educating the next generation for public service.[74] A sense of the requirements and burdens of his position is implicit in his gentle reproof to Mill's *Utilitarianism*: 'But this seems to be a mere looseness of phraseology, venial in a treatise aiming at a popular style.'[75] His own style has been aptly described as

[73] See the discussion of Dicey in Ch. 7 s. VI.

[74] This aspect of Sidgwick's role is discussed more fully in Collini, Winch, and Burrow, *That Noble Science of Politics*, essay IX.

[75] Henry Sidgwick, *The Methods of Ethics* (London, 1907; 1st edn. 1874), 93.

'offering few bribes to those who require them'.[76] T. H. Green occupied at Oxford a comparable position to Sidgwick's at Cambridge, as both men recognized, and there is still less temptation to describe Green's prose as spare and direct. But in his case the convolution had an anguished quality which surely owed something to his awareness that he was wrenching the language into unfamiliar shapes in his effort to give shared moral intuitions a more adequate philosophical basis. Green was also somewhat more disaffected from the prevailing cultural ideals of educated society than many of the figures discussed here, and at times he could seem to be so censorious of the moral laxness of the present that he invested all his hopes in stirring the conscience of the next generation, and even of their successors. But Green did not go all the way down this road; he was personally very active, for example, in contemporary politics and reform organizations, and his case is thus helpful in establishing the limits to academic withdrawal in this period. After all, persuading oneself that one's role is the shaping of future generations can be a beguilingly easy identity, absolving one from direct engagement with the present or from any assessable measure of success or failure. This can combine—as it did very markedly among late-nineteenth-century German academics—with a comprehensive political and cultural pessimism to produce a particularly lofty, mandarin form of social criticism which is content to await its vindication from posterity. In England in this period the only partially professionalized academic class remained more comfortably integrated with the prevailing political and cultural ideals, particularly with their underlying moral optimism.

Another convenient device for highlighting some of the shifts in self-definition that accompanied and in turn helped to promote such changes in forum and audience is provided by contrasting the *œuvre* of two figures subsequently regarded as major political theorists, one from the beginning of this period and one from the end. The careers of John Stuart Mill and Bernard Bosanquet could be contrasted in many ways, and choosing them for comparison in these terms should not be taken to imply any judgement about the comparability of their intellectual achievements. None the less, both command an assured place in the history of political thought, and there was at least a superficial symmetry in their positions as leading

[76] Oliver Elton, *A Survey of English Literature 1830–1880*, 2 vols. (London, 1920), i. 85; 'it is full of doublings back, qualified qualifications, and densely-crowded sentences'.

representatives of the second generation of Utilitarianism and Idealism respectively. Moreover, they make a convenient comparison for my purpose, since Mill's writing life, discussed more fully in Chapter 4 above, spanned the half-century from the early 1820s to the early 1870s, while Bosanquet's stretched over the half-century from the early 1870s to the early 1920s.

Their careers were, of course, different in ways which reflect individual peculiarities as well as larger social changes. Bosanquet's formation was emblematic of the changes in the composition of the intellectual élite mentioned in Chapter 1: he was educated at Harrow, he read Greats at Balliol, and in 1870 he became a Fellow and Tutor in Classics at University College, Oxford. But he thereafter departed from what was becoming the standard pattern of an academic career by resigning his Fellowship in 1881, moving to London to devote himself to practical social work while continuing to write philosophy as a private scholar. He briefly re-engaged with the standard academic pattern by becoming Professor of Moral Philosophy at St Andrews from 1903 to 1908, but while there was no doubt of his standing as a professional philosopher, he lived the greater part of his adult life as a private scholar and active public figure.[77] The contrasts with Mill's career, therefore, need to be characterized rather carefully.

One way to identify a difference which had more than personal significance is to consider their output of occasional writings. The most obvious difference is that Mill wrote more than 430 pieces for daily or weekly newspapers, whereas Bosanquet only contributed a handful of such articles and letters to the press.[78] But a subtler difference appears in comparing their more extended articles, the kind of source likely to be cited by subsequent historians of political thought. Mill wrote approximately 150 such pieces. We have already seen how he, particularly in the later phases of his life, would choose particular journals for particular purposes, but they all belonged to the class of the non-specialist periodicals of general culture. Thus, in the period after 1840—that is, the period after the close of his propagandistic career as a Philosophic Radical and the ending of his

[77] For details of Bosanquet's career, see Helen Bosanquet, *Bernard Bosanquet* (London, 1924).

[78] See John Stuart Mill, *Newspaper Writings*, 4 vols., *The Collected Works of John Stuart Hill*, ed. John M. Robson, 31 vols. (Toronto and London, 1965–91) (hereafter *CW*), xxii–xxv; for Bosanquet see Peter P. Nicholson, 'Bibliography of the writings of Bernard Bosanquet (1848–1923)', *Idealistic Studies*, 8 (1978), 261–80.

special connection with the *London and Westminster Review*—he published twelve articles in the *Edinburgh Review*, ten in the *Fortnightly Review*, seven in *Fraser's Magazine*, seven in the new *Westminster Review*, and so on.[79] He wrote in these journals even, as we have seen, when dealing with somewhat technical or abstruse subjects, such as Aristotle's metaphysics or Austin's jurisprudence. The 'voice' of these articles is certainly that of someone very much better informed than his readers, and at times—as, for example, on political economy—he wrote as an acknowledged expert. But there remained an implied community of interest in these subjects between an author who claimed no professional title or institutional accreditation to speak on them, and his readers who in reading that periodical may have indicated a certain political or literary preference, but who did not thereby declare themselves to be already identified with a particular professional enquiry.

An examination of Bosanquet's minor writings indicates a revealing change. His bibliography lists 110 articles, of which only four were published in the periodicals of general culture. Seventy-nine of them appeared in the specialist journals of philosophy which were only founded during his writing life (above all in *Mind* and the *Proceedings of the Aristotelian Society*). Moreover, a further seventy-four items are listed as 'reviews', a sign of the times since earlier in the century there had on the whole been no hard-and-fast distinction between the 'essay-like review' and the 'review-like essay' (to use Bagehot's terms[80]). Nearly all of Bosanquet's reviews were of other works in philosophy, with a sprinkling of books in the general area of political theory and 'social problems' (especially those contributed to the deliberately more eclectic *International Journal of Ethics*, founded in 1891). The one other significant group of articles is made up of those published in the *Charity Organization Review*, an interesting indication both of the distribution of Bosanquet's energies and of the cultural possibilities available for making a distinctive contribution. This was not a discipline-based, still less an

[79] I take the figures from J. M. Robson, 'The rhetoric of J. S. Mill's periodical articles', *Victorian Periodicals Newsletter*, 10 (1977), 122–9.

[80] Walter Bagehot, 'The first Edinburgh Reviewers' (1855), repr. in *The Collected Works of Walter Bagehot*, ed. Norman St John Stevas, 15 vols. (London, 1965–86), i. 312. See the further discussion of the relation of the 'review' and the 'essay' in Walter Houghton, 'Periodical literature and the articulate classes', in Joanne Shattock and Michael Wolff (eds.), *The Victorian Periodical Press: Samplings and Soundings* (Leicester, 1982), 3–27.

academic, journal, but one devoted to a particular area of practical interest, and Bosanquet wrote rather self-consciously as the COS's philosopher—not as an expert with a 'technique' to apply, but rather as one who bore a cultural and to some extent institutional validation beyond that of merely being interested in the issues.[81]

Thus, the contrast between Mill and Bosanquet in these respects both illustrates a change and at the same time indicates the limited nature of that change. New forms of publication grew up, and this did signal an alteration in the means by which the intellectual entered the public arena. Furthermore, Bosanquet was conscious of coming to the discussion of practical social and political questions equipped with a training and a vocabulary not possessed by most of his audience. Yet he was neither a career academic nor a reclusive and purely technical philosopher. Indeed, those historians who have exaggerated the contrast between men of letters addressing a common audience and academics addressing a specialized audience might be reminded of the ways in which a writer can have more than one identity and can learn to address more than one audience. Moreover, the terms of analysis have to be fine-grained enough to capture *degrees* of self-consciousness about an allegedly professional identity, rather than suggesting the simple presence or lack of it.

IV

These themes may be approached from a different angle by considering the sense of identity displayed by intellectuals on the occasion of their participation in some of the great divisive episodes in the public life of the period, like the Bulgarian agitation in 1876 or the opposition to the Boer War twenty-five years later. These tended to be occasions when what I have been calling 'the primacy of morality' was very clearly exhibited and was expressed in a correspondingly exalted register. Such episodes should perhaps be discriminated from another class of public controversy in which emotions could certainly run high and divisions cut deep, but where the complex constitutional or economic issues involved called for discussion in a somewhat different voice, including that of the 'expert.' The Home Rule crisis in 1886 or the Tariff Reform

[81] For examples of Bosanquet's role, though they are not discussed in these terms, see Andrew Vincent and Raymond Plant, *Philosophy, Politics, and Citizenship: The Life and Thought of the British Idealists* (Oxford, 1984).

controversy in the first few years of the twentieth century could be placed in this category. But on both sorts of occasion, the part played by scholars and academics indicates some of the complexities of their sense of identity during this period.

Intellectuals played a prominent part in the agitation against the 'Bulgarian atrocities' in 1876, though they were proportionately less significant than in the comparable Governor Eyre agitation simply because in 1876 their efforts were part of a much wider and more popular movement, one eventually dominated by Gladstone himself. The agitation provided the occasion for a great public display of righteousness, and the utterances of the 'agitators' (as those who supported the Conference on the Eastern Question were known) were laced with references to the 'conflict between right and wrong', the 'moral shame' of supporting the Turks, and so on.[82] But in the present context it is worth remarking that the intellectuals did not on the whole participate in this movement as representatives of a particular profession or discipline; such weight as they added to the cause came from their general standing as 'leading minds', not as possessors of a relevant expertise.[83] This general characterization needs to be partially modified in the case of the historians, where figures like Freeman and Bryce did lay claim to a special knowledge of the history of the region, and the large number of their fellow-historians whom they induced to declare their sympathy for the cause enabled Gladstone to boast that the agitation was supported by the 'gentlemen who represent the historical school of England'.[84] But neither the speaker nor the wording of this remark exactly suggests the peak of professional self-consciousness, and such authority as the historians were accorded was effectively shared by the others on that impressively large list of intellectuals who in one way or other declared their support, a list which included, but was far from confined to, the names of Acton, Browning, Bryce, Carlyle, Darwin, Fawcett, Freeman, Froude, J. R. Green, T. H. Green, Lecky,

[82] For the prevalence of this language, see Richard Shannon, *Gladstone and the Bulgarian Agitation 1876* (London, 1963), esp. ch. 6 on 'The High Victorian intelligentsia'.

[83] John Morley confessed he was impressed 'to see Mind in such force' on the side of the agitation (Shannon, *Bulgarian Agitation*, 216).

[84] Quoted ibid. 221. Referring to the speech by Gladstone in which this phrase occurred, J. R. Green remarked: 'It was certainly well worth remarking that every conspicuous historian in England goes with Gladstone in this matter'; *Letters of J. R. Green*, 466.

Thorold Rogers, Ruskin, Sidgwick, Goldwin Smith, Spencer, Leslie Stephen, Stubbs, and Trollope.[85] The inadequacy (or as some saw it, sheer wickedness) of the policy of the Tory government in this matter invited the strictures of the liberal moralist more straightforwardly than did many of the details of domestic policy, and this easily took priority over any assertion of professional expertise or academic standing.

Twenty-five years later the majority of educated opinion seems rather to have supported government policy in South Africa, or at least not to have been conspicuously present in the ranks of opponents of the war.[86] The two episodes raised rather different issues, of course, and public hostility to the 'Pro-Boers' was far greater and more widespread than anything seen on the earlier occasion. But it may also have been true that many of the most distinguished members of the educated class in this generation were beginning to lose some of that sense of themselves as public figures, directly and influentially engaged in national affairs, that had been taken for granted by the 'leading minds' of the earlier generation. At the same time, those academics who did speak out, such as the Oxford Classicist Gilbert Murray, did not invoke their academic standing, but worked through general organizations like the South Africa Conciliation Committee or even the Liberal Party.[87]

The felt demands of patriotism were certainly no less exigent in 1914. Again, a few *ad hoc* committees were hastily convened to protest against British involvement, with intellectuals like Murray, Lowes Dickinson, Hobson, and Wallas taking a prominent part, while John Morley, the by now venerable guardian of the Gladstonian shrine, took the opportunity to resign from the Cabinet. But again the academics did not attempt to deploy the authority of their position as such to make their collective presence felt. On the day Germany declared war on Russia (1 August), *The Times* carried a tiny news item headed 'Scholars' protest against war with Germany',

[85] I have extracted these names from Shannon, *Bulgarian Agitation*, *passim*. A much smaller list could be compiled of those who were critical or had significant reservations about the agitation, and in the nature of the case the evidence here is less clear-cut; but the list could arguably include Arnold, Bagehot, Harrison, Jowett, Morley, Seeley, Fitzjames Stephen, Tennyson.

[86] Stephen Koss (ed.), *The Pro-Boers: The Anatomy of an Anti-War Movement* (Chicago, 1973), p. xxxiv; see also John W. Auld, 'The Liberal pro-Boers', *Journal of British Studies*, 14 (1975), 78–99.

[87] Koss, *Pro-Boers*, p. xxxv.

reporting a letter from 'a number of University professors and others' appealing for 'the support of English scholars' in objecting to war with Germany. The nine signatories were miscellaneous, mostly professors of theology or heads of Nonconformist colleges; there was no indication that they represented any larger body.[88] The question of the need for scholars to attempt to preserve a certain distance from the public expressions of bellicose nationalism was raised in an acute form by the publication of the notorious 'Manifesto of the intellectuals of Germany' (known as 'the ninety-three', after the number of signatories) in October 1914, which 'became a byword for the subordination of German scholarship to the dictates of state policy'.[89] Needless to say, there were some no less blatant examples of jingoistic propagandizing by individual British scholars in the course of the war, but the discussion of the German scholars' manifesto indicated that there was now a deep sense that academics had a collective responsibility *not* to let their special standing be compromised by their political activity. This sense was clearly evident in the terms of the reproach subsequently issued by the President of the British Academy (Sir Frederick Kenyon) in 1920:

> It was nothing that these ninety-three persons should, as individuals, believe that their country was right, or should accept as gospel the statement of the case put before them by their unscrupulous politicians, but that, speaking as scholars (*and their scholarship was their only title to be heard at all*), they should make emphatic affirmation of the truth of statements which they had not investigated and on which they were not in a position to pass judgement, was a gross crime against scholarship.[90]

The question of the intellectuals' 'title to be heard', and the corresponding delicacy of speaking out from an academic position, also arose with some of those great opinion-dividing issues of domestic politics, especially where a special disciplinary expertise was thought to be relevant. The Home Rule debates of 1886, for example, acknowledged the special authority of constitutional lawyers and legal historians; both Bryce and Dicey had their scholarly work cited in Parliament in support of the Home Rule and

[88] 'Scholars' protest against war with Germany', *The Times*, 1 Aug. 1914: 6; see the discussion in Wallace, *War and the Image of Germany*, 24–5.

[89] Wallace, *War and the Image of Germany*, 33.

[90] Frederick G. Kenyon, *The British Academy: The First Fifty Years* (London, 1952), 22 (my emphasis).

Unionist positions respectively.[91] Liberal academics proved to be overwhelmingly Unionist, but it is indicative that their best-known collective statement of their allegiance—a letter reported in *The Times* declaring their support for Lord Hartington—employed no more restrictive self-description than 'resident graduates'; the signatories included several who were not academics in career terms, and none appeared as spokesman for a discipline. As *The Times* put it in an accompanying leader-article, they were expressing 'the general sentiment of the educated portion of the community'.[92]

The occasion which raised in acutest form the question of the part that specialist academic expertise should play in public debate was the intervention of teachers of economics in the Tariff Reform debate in 1903. On 15 August of that year, *The Times* published a letter which suggested that Chamberlain's Tariff Reform proposals were in various respects contrary to the basic findings of 'economic science.' The fourteen signatories had attempted to establish their title to be heard on the matter by giving their institutional affiliation as university teachers of economics; for this reason, their letter was subsequently referred to, slightly inaccurately, as 'the manifesto of the fourteen professors.' (It seems probable that this term was in part an ironic echo of the 'manifeste des intellectuels' of 1898 which was thereafter so frequently referred to in all discussions of the Dreyfus Affair.) But this use of their academic authority in what could easily be seen as a partisan manner provoked criticism. There were demands from some correspondents that a body of 'impartial' experts was required to pronounce on the economic merits of Tariff Reform, while others denounced the inevitable bias and, still more, impracticality of all academic opinion.[93] And there were the familiar sneers at the pretensions of economics to be a science in the first place. But much of the discussion turned upon the legitimacy of academics attempting to exercise their authority in this way at all. H. S. Foxwell, doubly out of tune with the signatories given his

[91] 'The Law Faculty of the University', observed the *Oxford Magazine*, 'was never so much before the country or, we believe, so genuinely useful as it is now.' Quoted in Christopher Harvie, 'Ideology and Home Rule: James Bryce, A.V. Dicey, and Ireland, 1880–1887', *English Historical Review*, 91 (1976), 298; Harvie concludes that as a consequence of the Home Rule debates 'the study of constitutional law was perceptibly enhanced' (314).

[92] 'Lord Hartington and the universities', *The Times*, 27 June 1887.

[93] Coats ('Political economy and the Tariff Reform campaign', 210) observes that such unflattering views of academics preponderated.

sympathies for historical economics as well as for Tariff Reform, objected that 'the vital issues involved are more political than scientific, [and] I do not think that economists have any right to attempt to prejudge these issues by a pronouncement which assumes scientific authority, though nearly every sentence is obviously and necessarily political'.[94] Others objected to having 'the pistol of authority' held at their heads, while Haldane expressed a more encompassing scepticism: 'In these days when everybody has studied everything, it is of no avail to quote the economists from Adam Smith to Professor Marshall.'[95] What distinguished this from controversies involving political economy throughout the first three quarters of the nineteenth century was not the suggestion that the oracles of economic science could be divided, misleading, or impractical, but rather the sense that university teachers now had an obligation to preserve their impartiality. There was certainly a feeling afterwards that the episode had discredited the standing of the professors, yet against this one has to set the evidence of politicians' continuing sensitivity to the influence of academic experts in the remark made by Andrew Bonar Law, future leader of the Conservative Party, in a letter to W. J. Ashley, the leading protectionist academic economist: 'There is one point, however, which, if you agree with me as to its importance, I wish you would bring to the notice of Mr Chamberlain. There is nothing, I think, which so tells against us than the idea that *scientific* authority is against us.'[96]

In all these and similar cases, one slight but revealing indication of a sense of possessing a particular standing in the eyes of the relevant public is the form in which an author chose to describe his own position or credentials on the title-pages of his books or when writing letters to the press. In the middle of the century it was not uncommon to describe oneself simply as an MA of one of the ancient universities or even 'Lately Fellow of' a particular college. But these affiliations were not primarily claims to specialist authority; they were an indication, rather, that the author had enjoyed a certain level of education, essentially the general liberal education appropriate to

[94] H. S. Foxwell, letter to *The Times*, 20 Aug. 1903; I have previously cited this letter, for another purpose, in Collini, Winch, and Burrow, *That Noble Science of Politics*, 275.

[95] Both quotations from Coats, 'Political economy and the Tariff Reform campaign', 214.

[96] The letter, which is undated, is quoted ibid. 220 (emphasis in original).

a gentleman, and perhaps that he had moderately distinguished himself in it. They indicated social standing rather than intellectual expertise, whereas the signatories to the 'manifesto of the fourteen professors' were obviously displaying their credentials in this latter sense.

In practice, where the topic or problem at issue seemed to involve to the layman a baffling opacity, then the expert had to be conceded a certain authority.[97] The tone characteristically employed by the mid-Victorian moralist had rested upon an intellectual as well as a social confidence. The matters at hand were accessible to reflective common sense, and in so far as he spoke with an authority beyond that simply of his social standing, it most frequently derived from practical acquaintance with actual social and political problems, not mastery of a discipline, still less of a theory. (A partial exception always has to be made for the political economist, though even here the general description largely applies.) Increasingly, however, the claim to exclusive or officially licensed possession of a body of theory, which could bring order to the disorientating complexity of intractable social or economic phenomena, was accorded a particular, if sometimes grudging, respect, especially where these phenomena came to seem less transparent, less immediately and concretely knowable, more in need of having their hidden forces illuminated. This was the case, for obvious reasons, in relation to the greatly intensified preoccupation with the problem of poverty from the 1880s onwards.

Of course, the term 'layman' that I used a moment ago, though less dismissive than 'amateur', is also defined against a recognized standard of expertise. Though there may have been little agreement in the late nineteenth century about how far the circle of expertise had extended in social affairs, there was certainly an increasing sense that the terms of debate were being altered. In grumbling to his friend Lord Lytton in 1879 that 'this is not the age for public life; it is emphatically the age for special knowledge and study',[98] Fitzjames Stephen may have been indulging his growing taste for apocalyptic exaggeration, but he was also registering a change that was to become very marked in the following decades.

[97] See the introduction to Haskell, *Authority of Experts*.

[98] Letter of 1 Oct. 1879 to Lord Lytton, quoted in John Roach, 'Universities and the national intelligentsia', *Victorian Studies*, 3 (1959), 147.

V

Professions, like clubs, are about excluding people. It is important to remember that the degree of professionalization and academic specialization which did take place, however partially and unevenly, from the 1880s onwards did so in an intellectual world that was now dominated by that restructured 'educated class' whose formation in the mid-Victorian years was discussed in Chapter 1. The form taken, therefore, by the nascent disciplines and their associated professional organizations embodied many of the intellectual habits, social prejudices, and practical preoccupations of this stratum of society. One consequence of this was that, in a manner that has become increasingly familiar in the twentieth century, the more marginal or unrecognized types of intellectual activity tended to be cultivated by those who felt themselves to be excluded from the shared background and assumptions of this class, and this naturally issued in marked differences of tone and literary strategy. Yet 'outsider' is an over-dramatic term which simplifies a complex reality. We get a better feel for the delicate dialectic between 'orthodoxy' and 'heresy', and the consequent shaping of a different style of public voice, by exploring the experience of particular individuals. No one career better illustrates the complex interweaving of these themes than that of Benjamin Kidd.

In 1893 Kidd was a 35-year-old Lower Division clerk to the Inland Revenue Board. Like thousands of other Mr Pooters created by the late nineteenth-century growth of clerical employment, he commuted to central London from a rented surburban villa where he maintained his family on the respectable though constraining salary of £231 per annum.[99] Like who knows how many of his black-coated brethren, he nursed large literary and scientific ambitions. He was, typically, an avid naturalist, a scientific autodidact, and just a little bit of a crank. Like those thousands of lesser Darwins who were inspired by the great man's modest methods, he compiled lovingly detailed botanical and zoological descriptions and engaged in homely experiments. His first published literary efforts were popular nature essays, with such coy titles as 'Concerning the cuckoo' or 'The frog and his relations'.

[99] D. P. Crook, *Benjamin Kidd: Portrait of a Social Darwinist* (Cambridge, 1984), 83. My account of Kidd's career is heavily indebted to Crook's very detailed study.

It was as exercises in applied Darwinism that these essays laid claim to the title of science. This was, of course, one of the favourite intellectual pastimes of the day: the facts could always be established by sufficiently diligent observation, and the ultimate explanation for their existence was given in advance by the theory of natural selection. The ingenuity lay in displaying in plausible detail how a particular and at first sight irrelevant characteristic might have been developed in the struggle for survival, an enquiry classically carried on in the back bedrooms of late Victorian suburban semis, just as the game which it had dislodged—of explaining, in the style of natural theology, how these details exhibited the resourceful benevolence of the Creator—had classically been carried on in the studies of country rectories. Kidd, however, was not content with humbly helping to affix one or two pieces in the enormous jigsaw of nature; he always sought after the 'secret key' to the cosmos, the principle or theory which would unlock the deeper coherence and meaning of both the natural and the social world.[100] He was a variant on the contemporaneous Jekyll and Hyde theme: Pooter by day, Casaubon by night.

In this way he threaded together his own eclectic synthesis of several of the intellectual fashions of the age. He was, for example, an enthusiastic early follower of the German biologist August Weismann, whose theory of the successful transmission of the 'germ plasm' as the regulatory goal of natural selection was intended to banish all vestiges of the Lamarckian doctrine of the inheritance of acquired characteristics. Then, like Kropotkin and others in the 1890s, Kidd denied that this evolutionary mechanism favoured the selfish individual member of the species, at least where the higher species were concerned: evidence of 'altruism' and co-operation among animals was by this date much in vogue,[101] and Kidd clearly adapted these findings to argue that, despite the progressive role of competition in general, the survival value of group solidarity increased as one ascended the evolutionary scale. The fatally dangerous defect of pre-Darwinian social theory, he maintained, was its tendency to exalt individual rationality or selfishness—it was part of the polemical strength, though ultimately a fundamental weakness, of his theory that he equated the two—at the expense of long-

[100] Crook, *Benjamin Kidd*, 5.

[101] See the sources cited in Stefan Collini, *Liberalism and Sociology: L. T. Hobhouse and Political Argument in England 1880–1914* (Cambridge, 1979), ch. 6.

term group interests.[102] But, fortunately for human progress, especially in its modern European embodiment, such individualism had generally been overborne by a much stronger force which reinforced solidarity and provided a non-rational sanction for the evolutionarily necessary altruism, namely religion. The moral imperative to give priority to the welfare of others turned out to have impeccable scientific credentials; Kidd's theory, that is to say, played yet another variation on the theme of altruism versus selfishness discussed in Chapter 2 above. All this, and much more besides, was spelled out, with an impressively wide range of not very closely investigated historical examples, in a hefty manuscript which Kidd finally completed in the summer of 1893.

He then took the shrewd step of showing this product of his leisure hours to his chief at the Inland Revenue, Alfred Milner, soon to achieve fame as an imperial proconsul. With Milner's help it was submitted to two publishers: Longman rejected it, on the basis of unfavourable readers' reports, as unlikely to prove a paying proposition; Macmillan accepted it, cautiously agreeing to print 1,500 copies and to give the author half of any profits that might accrue after all costs had been covered. The book, simply titled *Social Evolution*, was published early in 1894: it was an immediate best-seller, and Kidd's life was transformed. In the first eighteen months he netted the enormous sum of £2,400, ten times his annual salary. In four years the book sold a remarkable 200,000 copies (though the then common problem with pirated editions in the United States meant that the author was denied his full royalties).[103]

Kidd soon gave up his Civil Service job, living the last twenty years of his life (he died in 1916) on the royalties from his books, the dividends on the lucrative investments he made with them, and the income from the journalism and other freelance commissions which his early success thereafter sent his way. He became something of a public figure, whose views on the social and intellectual developments of the day were solicited by editors alert to the value of an opinionated scientific sage, and whose authority was cited on both sides of the Atlantic on subjects as diverse as the proper form of imperial trusteeship or the nature of sociology. In fact—and this is again typical of that class of quirky pseudo-scientific social prophets

102 Benjamin Kidd, *Social Evolution* (London, 1894), ch. II 'Conditions of human progress'.

103 Crook, *Benjamin Kidd*, 52, 128.

who capture public attention with one inspired theoretical hybrid—Kidd was never able to repeat the success of *Social Evolution*, and the period leading up to the First World War saw a steady decline in his reputation. Ironically, he became increasingly alarmed at the possible political consequences of the 'Social Darwinism' he was popularly identified with, diagnosing it, in a late middle-aged mood of cultural nostalgia, as part of a wider revolt against the moral standards of nineteenth-century civilization. When his last book, *The Science of Power*, was posthumously published in 1918, it briefly caught the attention of an audience primed to feel concerned about the way 'irrationalist' ideas had led Europe to Armageddon, and his reputation enjoyed a short Indian summer. Thereafter, his name fell into oblivion, surfacing occasionally in the footnotes of the more conscientious historians of sociology or of Social Darwinism.

However much or little intrinsic interest Kidd's ideas may now have for social theorists, his *career* is particularly instructive for the historian of English intellectual life. To begin with, Kidd's background and education set him apart from the world of the well-connected, well-educated Victorian intellectuals described in Chapter 1 above. The son of an Irish policeman, Kidd followed the strenuous lower middle-class route of self-improvement by studying for exams while working as a commercial clerk: in 1877, aged 18, he passed the entrance examinations for the Lower Division of the Civil Service. As we have seen, he cultivated his scientific and literary ambitions, and it is an indication of the partial accessibility of the higher reaches of metropolitan culture that in 1886 he managed to get an article published in the then immensely prestigious *Nineteenth Century*.[104] On the whole, however, before the success of *Social Evolution* launched him into the public eye, the only cultural authority he could draw upon derived from his claims as a naturalist. A small but revealing indication of his position is given by the fact that before 1894 no journal editor seems to have thought it worth soliciting his pronouncements by sending him books for review.

If one were to look for roughly analogous figures in the first half of the nineteenth century, one would expect to find them among the provincial rather than the metropolitan élites of the time, among Radicals rather than Whigs, among Dissenters rather than Angli-

[104] Benjamin Kidd, 'The Civil Service as a profession', *Nineteenth Century*, 20 (1886), 491–502. This, as his biographer observes, was 'quite a coup for an unknown writer'; Crook, *Benjamin Kidd*, 24.

cans. But these were no longer the structuring polarities in the late nineteenth century; in particular, a less significant part was now played by an autonomous provincial intellectual and political culture. At the same time, the establishment of cultural authority in the expanded universities had altered the conditions for making a mark in any of the recognized 'fields', and this in turn affected the reception of an ambitious, idiosyncratic, or otherwise unclassifiable work by an 'unlicensed' individual. In the first half of the century, the universities scarcely impinged on the independent social theorist except as representatives of *religious* orthodoxy, and even slightly later figures like Spencer or Buckle (Kidd's most obvious predecessors) had worked out their synthetic and self-consciously scientific interpretations of history without constantly looking over their shoulders at the response from academics. Kidd's works, by contrast, were reviewed in such recently established professional journals as the *English Historical Review* and *Mind*, and his anticipations of their judgements as much as the judgements themselves shaped his identity and characteristic tone of voice in oblique but important ways. He felt he needed to pitch his appeal explicitly to the non-specialist, at the same time preening himself on his modernity and freedom from a (prejudged) academic narrowness and obscurantism. It mattered to him to see himself not as a popularizer but as an independent thinker, and if there was defensiveness as well as dismissiveness in his characterization of that authority of which he was independent, that was because it represented, among other things, officially validated standards of exact scholarship which he could not measure up to and only half did not want to. The two faces of his touchiness were neatly conjoined in a letter in 1902 to J. S. MacKenzie, Professor of Philosophy at Cardiff and editor of the *International Journal of Ethics*. Kidd complained that his second book, *The Principles of Western Civilization*, had been slighted by critics because it was so far ahead of its time: 'I am looking to the younger thinkers to justify me in the end', he declared defiantly, but he could not resist adding: 'I hope you will give me a good review in the journal of ethics.'[105]

However, it would be far too simple—and would, indeed, be to succumb to a favourite piece of 'outsider' mythology—to think of Kidd as ostracized by some exclusive 'establishment'. Consider, for

105 Kidd to J. S. MacKenzie, 20 Feb. 1902; quoted in Crook, *Benjamin Kidd*, 163.

example, the ways in which the periodicals of general culture were open to him, not a negligible matter given their status and readership. Even before his *annus mirabilis* he had managed to place articles in the *Nineteenth Century* (as we have seen) and the *Cornhill Magazine* among others, and after it his pieces appeared in *The Times* and other leading morning papers, in the *Pall Mall Gazette* and the *Westminster Gazette*, in the *National Review* and the *Fortnightly Review*, and so on. Such opportunities were also financially important in enabling him to sustain his independent position. Even his early popular scientific articles brought payments of up to £15, the equivalent of almost a month's salary for him at the time, and once he had made his name he could command much higher rates: for a series of very short articles in the *Daily Graphic* in 1904 on 'Colonial Preference and Free Trade', for example, he received £200.[106]

Or, again, consider his political contacts. His success brought him membership of those cross-party dining-clubs that sprang up around the turn of the century, where he rubbed shoulders with politicians, professors, and other public figures; he corresponded with Joseph Chamberlain and advised him about the presentation of his tariff policies; and, a different but revealing kind of contact, he felt able to ask for Milner's help in 1908, having recently renewed contact with his former chief at the dinners of the Compatriots Club, in getting two of his sons nominated to posts in the Bank of England. Kidd, a critic both of *laissez-faire* and of Socialism, was naturally drawn to the kind of politician who frequented these unorthodox gatherings; among them, his credentials as a man of science were not scrutinized too closely, and his meta-historical speculations found a favourable resonance among those on the look-out for justifications for the dangerously fascinating activity of mould-breaking. Too prickly to be a willing camp-follower, he none the less responded to the grandeur of Chamberlain's aims and the flattery of his attention, and was correspondingly exasperated at the triumph of what he regarded as the atavistic tribalism which produced the Liberal landslide of 1906. This characterization gains added plausibility when we discover that during the previous Parliament Kidd had been sounded out as a candidate for two constituencies—once by the Liberals and once by the Tories.[107]

Even the universities could not be said to have neglected him

[106] Crook, *Benjamin Kidd*, 229.   [107] Ibid. 240.

altogether: Cambridge asked his advice during one of its periodic ruminations on the advisability of acknowledging the existence of sociology, and Oxford invited him to deliver the prestigious Herbert Spencer lecture in 1908. Kidd's career may even seem to illustrate some old truths about the absorptive capacities of the English educated classes—he might have remained more excluded in Germany in this period, for example—and about the plurality of worlds that may be obscured by a too hasty ascription of homogeneity. Kidd, it has to be said, was a willing recruit: the scientifically self-educated son of poorly educated parents bought for his own sons the most traditional of classical educations at Tonbridge, after which the clever one went to Cambridge and the other two into the City. That outcome is only too familiar in modern English social history, but we should not forget the successful career that led up to it. Kidd was neither a hack nor a don; he made his living as a man of ideas.

In so far as Kidd claimed the title of a particular intellectual discipline, it was that of 'sociologist'. Indeed, we have to remember that he was hailed, particularly in the United States, as a master-theorist of the new subject. 'In the chronology of that science', declared an American reviewer of *Social Evolution*, '1894 will hereafter be known as the Year One, and Mr Kidd's book as Volume One in its bibliography.'[108] His name almost invariably stood alongside those of the home team, Ward, Giddings, and Small, in the reading-lists of the new departments of sociology then being established in the rapidly expanding American universities.[109] Admittedly, his reputation as a sociologist never quite touched these heights in Britain, where the subject had no academic recognition at this point, but it was still considerable. He managed to persuade the editor of the *Encyclopaedia Britannica* that the Ninth Edition of 1902 should carry an entry on 'Sociology', hitherto absent, and that he should be commissioned to write it. Kidd was not the clearest writer who ever spilled ink—not always a handicap for an author with a vague and portentous message—but there was no mistaking the importance he attached to sociology, whatever it was: 'It is the meaning of the social process which is constructing the human mind. This is the most

[108] A 'New York reviewer', quoted in 'One of the notable books of the age-end', *Review of Reviews*, 11 (15 May 1895), 473.

[109] Small was later to speak dismissively of Kidd's standing as a sociologist; see Collini, *Liberalism and Sociology*, 189 n.

pregnant idea in Western thought at the present time, and it places sociology in its true place as the sovereign of all the sciences.'[110] Not all of his contemporaries, by any means, were persuaded by this sort of thing; but a wide audience was excited by the vistas opened up by the second sentence, and was willing for a while to regard Kidd as the king-maker behind the new sovereign.

Faced with what he perceived as the conventionally educated class's monopoly on those subjects which enjoyed recognized academic standing, and professing to disdain the pedantry and practical aridity of such studies, Kidd sought an alternative source of cultural authority, which the identity of a 'sociologist' briefly promised to provide. 'Each of the departments of knowledge which has dealt with man in society has regarded him almost exclusively from its own standpoint. . . . The time has come . . . for a more radical method.'[111] This identity also justified pontificating at a gratifyingly grandiose level of abstraction. Kidd clearly obtained a certain *frisson* from dwelling on the universality and irresistibility of the great biological forces underlying human history; he was gratified to find that nature, too, was intolerant of uncertainty. Notoriously, part of the wider appeal of such mono-causal theories of history lies in the reassurance they offer that there is a pattern in the carpet, that the forces at work are few and simple, that 'complexity' is a dodge invented by pedants to hide their fear of commitment. Kidd's ideas, like his style, were adapted to addressing a wider audience than the favoured circles to which his 'orthodox' critics belonged.

The vogue for sociology in the 1890s and 1900s temporarily provided Kidd with a convenient label and an exploitable role. The title was, following Comte and Spencer, freely bestowed on attempts at a synthetic interpretation of the whole of the human history, and in Britain at this time it was mandatory for such accounts to display their cognizance of the biological foundations of human social development.[112] Kidd, unlike such potential rivals as Hobhouse and Geddes, was not interested in sociology as a putative 'discipline': he did not concern himself with the finer points of methodology, and it is not surprising that he founded no school and inspired no disciples.

[110] Benjamin Kidd, *The Two Principal Laws of Sociology* (Pamphlet in two parts) (London, 1907 and 1908), part II, p. 15.

[111] Kidd, *Social Evolution*, 28.

[112] See Collini, *Liberalism and Sociology*, 187–208.

This view of his relation to the enterprise is perhaps borne out by the fact that it was Kidd who rejected sociology before sociology rejected him. He had been a founder-member of the Sociological Society, started in London in 1903, and played an active part in its early proceedings, but he did not really belong to any of the rival groups within the Society who were struggling to have their own theoretical preferences recognized as constitutive of the new discipline, and eventually he drifted away. In 1908, in attacking the flourishing craze of Eugenics, he could still call for an anti-individualist 'sociology' as the antidote (by which he meant his own theory of the biological role of 'social efficiency'), but in his last few years he abandoned the term, no longer finding that it suggested an appropriate identity for his civilization-saving thoughts, and by 1914 he was openly scornful of current claims for its scientific status.[113] But although his had always been a highly idiosyncratic vision of how history could be made to yield up its inmost secrets, he had not been straining at the limits of the contemporary usage in presenting his synthesis as 'sociology'.

Certainly, the task of such academic critics of sociology as Henry Sidgwick was made easier by the fact that Kidd's work was so widely taken as exemplifying the state of the art.[114] It was hardly surprising that Sidgwick, pukka representative of the universities' sense of their own dignity, should deal rather dismissively with Kidd, best-selling popularizer who was asset-stripping the failing enterprise of sociology. Kidd had characterized the range and fertility of his own approach by contrasting it to that of 'the professional historian', and it is revealing of the contrasting forms of intellectual authority displayed on this occasion that Sidgwick should have begun his criticism by instancing some of Kidd's more egregious mistakes in *ancient* history.[115] But to Kidd this was precisely an example of that 'criticism of adventitious details' to which his book had been subjected by those 'in universities and centres of learning', who had thereby avoided acknowledging the real value of his far-reaching contribution to human thought. (There was no excess of modest inhibition in his own estimation of that contribution: 'the whole

[113] Crook, *Benjamin Kidd*, 270.

[114] Sidgwick's criticisms are discussed more fully in Collini, *Liberalism and Sociology*, 193–6.

[115] Henry Sidgwick, 'Political prophecy and sociology' (1894), repr. in *Miscellaneous Essays and Addresses* (London, 1904), 216–34.

drama of human history' turned upon the 'natural law of human evolution hitherto unenunciated' which he had discovered, with the result that 'there cannot be a single department of science concerned with man in society which will stand quite where it did'.[116]) But then, in his view, apart from a few other creative souls who 'stand more or less aloof from the main body of professional thought, we have really in England at the present day no school of thought producing men fitted to deal with the science of human society as a whole'. The disdain was clearly mutual.

The autodidact with a message for mankind can be a tiresome antagonist: unshakeably convinced that he had something original and important to say, Kidd resented advice, neglect, disagreement, and criticism in equal measure. Reviewing the *Memoir* of Sidgwick twelve years later, Kidd implied that there was a narrowness to the professor's views which derived from 'the nature of the highly artificial and protected life which Sidgwick lived so long at Cambridge'. He had disdained to reply to the 'hostile' review, feeling the divergence in their positions to be too great. But it had clearly hurt enough for him still to wish to pull rank on the cloistered scholar in the only way open to him: 'The subsequent history of *Social Evolution* in translation, including its recent translation into Chinese, is perhaps a better reply to that article than any I could have given at the time.'[117]

More generally, Kidd attempted to turn to advantage the *odium academicum* of which he liked to see himself as the victim. In responding to the critics of *Social Evolution* (though he did not actually deign to reply to any of the criticisms), he maintained that its thesis

> could not, in the nature of things, receive any criticism on its merits at the present time, and that its reception from the professional exponents of knowledge must necessarily be hostile. . . . What has really happened is that the book has been received with favour by that large outside world in which the social instincts are strong and deep, and which had recognized in it an echo of its own experience and a justification of much which it has always felt and known to be true despite authoritative statements to the contrary from recognized leaders of thought.

[116] Benjamin Kidd, 'Social evolution', *Nineteenth Century*, 37 (1895), 227.

[117] Benjamin Kidd, review of *Henry Sidgwick: A Memoir*, *Outlook*, 14 Apr. 1906: 519–21.

Kidd's literary manner was of a piece with this conception of his audience: it was repetitive, insistent, dogmatic. He was prone to bully his readers with claims that his arguments followed from each other with 'the cogency of mathematical demonstration'. His prose has none of the openness and indirectness that can flourish where author and reader are assumed to be on a reasonably intimate and equal footing. Perhaps inevitably, he fell back on the most hackneyed piece of 'outsider's' self-justification: his book was not really addressed to 'exponents of the older schools of thought'. It was addressed to 'the rising generation' of scientific enquirers; it was addressed to the future.[118]

VI

There would be a certain Proustian satisfaction in being able to conclude this discussion with an account of the establishment of the very discipline out of the shadow of which this book itself has had to escape, namely 'the history of political theory', but that would require too detailed an account of syllabuses and committees to be appropriate here (and I have already touched on some aspects of this story elsewhere).[119] Suffice it to say that the remorseless molecular process of self-division which we call specialization did begin to turn 'political thought' into simply one discipline alongside other primarily academic enterprises, though that change was certainly not completed during this period, if indeed it ever could be. But even the beginnings of this development were bound to have an impact upon the ways in which intellectuals contributed to political debate, and upon their audience's perception of the standing and relevance of those contributions. I remarked above that despite T. H. Green's reputation as something of a prophet to the earnest Oxford young during his lifetime, at the time of his death in 1882 he had published no substantial work of political thought. Invocation of his principles in the political debates of the 1880s relied largely on oral tradition and on the work of his pupils, a situation only partly altered by the eventual appearance of his *Lectures on the Principles of Political*

[118] Kidd, 'Social evolution', 231, 239, 240.

[119] Collini, Winch, and Burrow, *That Noble Science of Politics*, essay XI and epilogue. See also Julia Stapleton, 'Academic political thought and the development of political studies in Britain 1900–1950' (unpublished D.Phil. Dissertation, University of Sussex, 1985).

Obligation in the hardly popular form of Nettleship's three-volume edition of Green's philosophical works. But, revealingly, it was not really his purchase upon current political debate that led to his work being made available in a more accessible form. Explaining in 1895 why the lectures were now being reprinted as a separate book, Bosanquet reported that 'the course of lectures in question has long been known to teachers as a most valuable text-book for students of political theory' (and again, that it had been suggested as a result of 'discussing the selection of a text-book for a projected course of instruction on political theory').[120] The very existence of such students and such courses changed the way the works set for them were regarded. It was during these years that a variety of works, addressing very disparate historical preoccupations and written at quite different levels of abstraction, were retrospectively recruited to the canon of the history of political thought. Mill on liberty or Green on political obligation or Maine on popular government were treated as taking up the ghostly baton handed on by Locke and Bentham and others.[121] (Mill's posthumous conscription is discussed at greater length in Chapter 8 below.) And this, in turn, meant that a new identity was created, that of the scholar who, though not necessarily an original political thinker himself, claimed a certain expertise on the basis of his professional acquaintance with works in 'the history of political thought'.

This topic reminds us once again of the limits of considering only one national tradition, since this was in part an international development manifesting itself in various but recognizably similar forms in several countries. The attempt to follow the German lead in teaching 'politics' in the second half of the nineteenth century was, of course, directly geared to the felt need to provide the appropriate training for a future administrative and governing class, whether in the form offered by Boutmy and his École Libre des Sciences Politiques in Paris, by Burgess and his teaching of 'Government' at Columbia, or by Seeley and his courses in 'Political Science' in Cambridge. A central place in this enterprise was occupied by what was usually referred to as 'the theory of the state', a subject on which Aristotle and Hobbes were understood to be no less relevant

[120] T. H. Green, *Lectures on the Principles of Political Obligation* (London, 1895), p.v.

[121] See e.g. W. Graham, *English Political Philosophy from Hobbes to Maine* (London, 1899); cf. below, Ch. 8, 330.

authorities than, say, Bluntschli or Sidgwick. At the same time, the immense impact of German historical scholarship was, as I have already remarked, still being felt across a range of intellectual activities outside Germany, especially those activities which wished to lay claim to an academic title as 'science.' One of the more obvious ways in which this impinged on the nascent study of politics was in the so-called Comparative Method, with its tracing of the lines of descent, notably from Aryan roots, of modern political forms.[122] This was frequently married without noticeable friction to an emphasis which it would be too narrow to describe simply as Hegelian, but which was an integral part of that Idealism which pervaded German historical thinking and thus left its mark elsewhere, namely the belief that the skeleton of world-history in its centrally political dimension could be traced in the most reflective forms of the political consciousness of each epoch. These strands coalesced in a fresh interest in charting the phases of the history of political thought, an interest one can see developing in that series of works which begins with Gierke and Bluntschli in Germany from the 1860s onwards, with Janet in France from the 1870s, with Pollock and later Figgis and the Carlyles in England from the 1880s and 1890s, and with Dunning and others in the United States from the 1890s and 1900s.

The pedagogic form eventually taken by this development was the formation of a canon of classic texts. Initially, this was little more than a selection from the established names in the history of moral philosophy, but in practice the canon of great political theorists as it was built up in the late nineteenth and early twentieth centuries was influenced by very different concerns, most notably by the judgements of political historians about which writers had been influential in affecting the course of actual political developments. Figures such as Machiavelli or Rousseau who were not part of the more venerable moral philosophy canon owed their prominence to this kind of judgement (which was often mistaken, of course, or at least very disputable), and the more the study of political history was expected to yield an inductive science of politics, the greater the say the political historians had in deciding who was a significant political theorist. But while the enthusiasms which dictate the inclusion of particular texts in all selections of this kind inevitably pass out of

122 See Collini, Winch, and Burrow, *That Noble Science of Politics*, essay VII.

fashion, the canon thus established remains, a brooding cultural presence with which some sort of treaty has to be made by anyone wishing to enter its territory.

Naturally, this did not mean that contributions to contemporary political argument were henceforth to be restricted to works which were candidates for a place in the syllabus of 'political thought'; the interaction between the polemical and the reflective remained more varied and unpredictable than that. But the very existence of a recognized academic 'field' which trenched so closely upon the central questions of political life was significant in itself. Looking back from 1915 at the previous half-century or so, Ernest Barker noted that 'political philosophy not only advances of itself . . . it also advances through the contribution of other studies'. Elaborating the point, he laid down that 'to discover the immanent political philosophy of the last sixty years we have thus not only to study the works they have produced in philosophy proper; we have also to consider the contributions of method, of data, of outlook, from biology and political economy, from law and history, from psychology and anthropology'. Barker was one of T. H. Green's intellectual stepchildren, and at this stage of his career he construed 'political philosophy' in markedly Idealist terms as 'in itself . . . essentially an ethical study, which regards the state as a moral society, and inquires into the ways by which it seeks to attain its ultimate moral aim'.[123] But in speaking of the constitutive role of 'other studies', and in organizing his little book largely in terms of their separate contributions, he was faithfully reflecting the developments discussed in this chapter. Not only did this implicitly acknowledge the academic standing which these studies were coming to have, but his reference to them as '*other* studies' casually assigned political theory to this company on a more or less equal footing. And once political theory could thus be classified not just as part of 'the somewhat muddy channel of current opinion' but also as part of 'the stream of pure science', we have witnessed a slight but ultimately significant change in the larger relations between political thought and intellectual life.

[123] Ernest Barker, *Political Thought in England 1848–1914* (London, 1947; 1st edn. 1915, under the title *Political Thought in England from Herbert Spencer to the Present*), 5. There was some unsteadiness in his use of terms, since he pretty much treated 'political philosophy', 'social philosophy', and 'political theory' as synonyms, giving the latter pride of place in the book's ringing conclusion (224).

7

An Exclusively Professional Subject
The Jurist as Public Moralist

I

'The connection between law and political science', lamented Ernest Barker in 1934, 'is far closer on the Continent than it is in England. With us, the subjects have generally tended towards a divorce; and there has been little study of political science in terms of law.' His elaboration of this contrast was suggestive. 'Few of our lawyers', he continued, 'have turned their attention to the fundamental questions of politics. . . . On the whole our law has been a close and empirical preserve of the legal profession; and our political science has proceeded not from lawyers or professors of law, but from politicians with a philosophic gift or philosophers with a practical interest.' This, he fairly conceded, had had its merits as well as its drawbacks, and 'the English system of political science, so far as we can speak of such a thing, has combined an instinct for actual fact with some sense of the moral foundations on which the action of states, like all human action, must necessarily rest'. The strong presence of classical humanism in the English universities, he further speculated, had reinforced 'a native sense of the moral foundations of politics.' But whatever its merits, this tradition stood in sharp contrast to the situation on the Continent where 'political education and political speculation have generally gone along the lines of law. . . . To study modern French political theory is to study the lawyers. To study modern German political theory is equally to study the lawyers.' The same could not be said of England, however, and perhaps as a result 'our English political science has hitherto had no great method'.[1]

[1] Otto Gierke, *Natural Law and the Theory of Society 1500–1800*, trans. with

To the historian of intellectual life in nineteenth-century England, Barker's lament is bound at first to appear puzzling, even wilfully wrong-headed. As Barker half acknowledges in the course of the same paragraph, an impressively long list of names could be assembled of lawyers and legal scholars who had played a major part in the political thought of the period: the names of Austin, Maine, Stephen, Dicey, Bryce, and Maitland make the point forcefully enough. Indeed, so impressive is that roll-call that one begins to wonder whether Barker's dictum should not be reversed, and the *peculiarly* jurisprudential quality of much Victorian political thought emphasized instead. In fact, when one returns to Barker's little volume on *Political Thought in England 1848–1914*, cited at the end of the previous chapter, it is rather the prominence of legal thought that catches the eye. Of the three chapters (out of seven) not devoted to either Idealism or Evolutionism, one is simply entitled 'The lawyers', and deals above all with Maine, and secondarily with Stephen, Dicey, and Maitland.[2] And yet a closer look at this chapter complicates the issue because, until he arrives at the congenial proto-Pluralism of Maitland's work, Barker does not in fact demonstrate that the contribution of the other writers he mentions rests on a distinctively *jurisprudential* basis at all. Rather, he discusses their work in terms of categories drawn from the intellectual fashions dominant in the culture more generally. For example, he treats Maine as the exemplar of 'the historical method', and makes that sound almost indistinguishable from biologically based evolutionism; he concentrates on both Maine's and Stephen's critique of democracy; and he emphasizes Dicey's account of the supersession of Individualism by Collectivism. In this sense, the chapter seems rather to support than to contradict his later assertion about the lack of a jurisprudentially grounded political thought in England during this period.

Barker's complaint (for such it surely was) that 'our law has been a close and empirical preserve of the legal profession' had been a favourite theme with the figure who had done most in this period to

intro. by Ernest Barker, 2 vols. (Cambridge, 1934), i. p. xix; (this volume was a translation of selections from the fourth volume of Gierke's *Das deutsche Genossenschaftsrecht*). By 'political science' Barker meant to embrace the activity that would today be referred to as 'political theory'.

[2] Ernest Barker, *Political Thought in England 1848–1914* (London, 1947; 1st edn. 1915), ch. VI.

attempt to alter that situation, namely Sir Henry Maine. He, too, had made the point in the form of a contrast with the position in the rest of Europe: 'We in Great Britain and Ireland are altogether singular in our tacit conviction that law belongs as much to the class of exclusively professional subjects as the practice of anatomy.' In Maine's view, this was largely the result of the growth of the common law, a body of 'customary law' inaccessible to any but the practising lawyer, which meant that 'we, accordingly, have turned our laws over to experts'. The remedy he had long proposed for this ailment was the formulation and dissemination of 'aptly-framed general propositions' about this body of law, or in other words the cultivation of jurisprudence.[3] But the health and centrality of this enquiry depended in turn, as he had argued in one of his earliest essays, upon 'the proportion of the national intellect' devoted to it, and here the contrast he had drawn had been not with contemporary Europe, but with ancient Rome. There, jurisprudence had for some centuries occupied the best minds, issuing in the great practical and intellectual achievement that was Roman Law. But in England, the best talents had been preoccupied with other matters—'Art, Literature, Science, and Politics claim their share of the national intellect'—with the result that 'the practice of jurisprudence is confined within the circle of a profession'.[4]

Both writers had axes to grind, of course: Barker was, in the passage cited, trying to call attention to the merits of Gierke's deeply juristic work, and one certainly has to make allowances for Maine's almost habitual tendentiousness—he was at the time propagandizing for the cause of legal education, as well as being perennially anxious to have his own intellectual authority recognized more widely. None the less, these passages raise a question—or, rather, several questions—which the intellectual historian needs to consider. What is the significance of the fact (if it is a fact) that contributions from lawyers and jurisprudents seem to figure more prominently in Victorian political thought than in that of adjacent periods? Was the outcome the development of a more distinctively juristic political theory? Why did the whole issue of the place of legal thought in the

[3] H. S. Maine, *Village Communities in the East and West* (London, 1889; 1st edn. 1871), 59–60.

[4] H. S. Maine, 'Roman Law and legal education', 1st publ. in *Cambridge Essays, contributed by Members of the University* (London, 1856); repr. in *Village Communities*. Maine was sufficiently attached to this passage also to reproduce it in H. S. Maine, *Ancient Law* (London, 10th edn., 1884; 1st edn., 1861), 360–2.

wider culture appear particularly problematic in this period? This chapter does not attempt to provide a direct answer to these questions; rather, it surveys, necessarily somewhat schematically, the work of the main figures involved, treating them in the framework of the themes addressed in this book as a whole. The particular pertinence of three of these themes may be worth noting at the outset.

First, any discussion of the range of idioms within which political argument was conducted, and particularly one concerned with how these idioms derived from or were mutations of other established intellectual traditions (or, in so far as these took academic form, 'disciplines'), needs to consider the case of law. The historian of early modern political thought, after all, takes for granted that even in Britain natural jurisprudence formed the chief matrix of the subject up till at least the late eighteenth century. On the face of it, only political economy could seem to rival jurisprudence as an established 'moral science' by the middle of the nineteenth century, and, more broadly, no other form of enquiry rested upon as entrenched and powerful a basis as that provided by the social and intellectual position of the law. If one considers how the shifting configuration of established forms of thought issued in what became known as the social sciences, the law again promises to be central and inescapable. At least, so it seems when the topic is seen in a comparative perspective: one only has to consider, for example, the centrality of the *Facultés de Droit* in the French university system and the ways in which various branches of economic and political study have grown up within that institutional framework.[5] Or, to take a different kind of example from another national tradition, one might ponder the implications of the fact that someone like Max Weber should have begun his studies of ancient economic life within the larger context provided by a training in the Civil Law tradition, and that he then went on to hold successive appointments in Law, Economics, and Sociology. Such configurations may not necessarily be superior in themselves (and may anyway depend upon one's legal system having much deeper continuities with Roman Law), but reference to them helps remind us that the local pattern may have

[5] Cf. Stefan Collini, '"Discipline history" and "intellectual history": reflections on the historiography of the social sciences in Britain and France', *Revue de synthèse*, 109 (1988), 387–99.

had significant indirect consequences for other aspects of English intellectual life.

Secondly, any discussion of the 'voices' available to the public moralist in this period, and especially of the impact of academic professionalization upon the register and persuasiveness of those voices, needs to be able to accommodate the particular kind of authority laid claim to by the writer who draws upon a legal or jurisprudential idiom. There was a kind of expertise to be acknowledged here, especially with the emergence of the law professor as a public figure, and yet it would be misleading to see such writers as occupying the role of 'outside experts' called in to give specialist, technical advice. They need, rather, as I argued in general terms in the first chapter of this book, to be seen as members of the intellectual wing of an extended governing class, whose political pronouncements carried a distinctive jurisprudential inflection.

Thirdly, any account of the relation between political thought and the wider intellectual life of the period which emphasizes, as mine has done in previous chapters, the determining role of moral sensibilities and only half-articulated assumptions about human character seems to encounter its most difficult challenge in discussing the contribution of the lawyers. Yet here too, I shall argue, the 'primacy of morality' found expression in a pattern of ethical categories and judgements that coloured their political thinking at least as much as did their peculiarly juristic concerns. More generally, these writers need to be seen less as working within a separate or autonomous 'discipline', and more as voices in a public debate, sharing the common preoccupations of the educated class of their generation, from celebration of England's peculiarly fortunate history to anxiety about the extension of democracy.

This chapter will not, therefore, explore the actual content of particular jurisprudential views, still less developments in the law and legal reasoning as such. It will look instead at the place of jurisprudence in the wider cultural conversation of the period, and the ways in which it provided, or failed to provide, a distinctive identity for several of the most notable contributors to Victorian political thought. An important part of the supporting argument about the institutional context will be the suggestion that developments in legal education, especially within the newly revived universities, were initially the precondition for the greater public prominence of legal theorists; but that, ultimately, the logic of those developments was to intensify professional specialization, which rendered jurisprudence increasingly marginal to the activities of the political theorist and the practising lawyer alike. The leading parts in the story will be played by Maine, Fitzjames Stephen, and Dicey. But first, as with so many topics in this book, we have to begin with John Stuart Mill.

II

Had the young John Stuart Mill not entered the service of the East India Company in 1823, he might have had a very distinguished legal career. His father at first intended him for the Bar,[6] that great avenue of advancement for ambitious and politically inclined young men, and although his extreme radical views would perhaps have made him an unlikely candidate for the Bench, it is not hard to imagine the brilliant, analytical, outspoken young barrister commanding the intricacies of the English law as well as cutting a considerable figure in public life. But this reflection only reminds us how surprisingly slight was Mill's actual involvement with the law in his mature years. He had, after all, been brought up in a milieu suffused with legal categories and with a sense of the importance of the law; the whole fabric of Bentham's theory, to take the central intellectual component in that milieu, had grown out of a concern with legal reform and was primarily constituted by the project of a science of legislation, imparting an emphasis that endured into early Philosophic Radical thought. Moreover, the young Mill's most extensive literary work was the editing of the five volumes of Bentham's *Rationale of Judicial Evidence*, and not only did this work contain 'the most elaborate exposure of the vices and defects of English law, as it then was', but in preparation for its editing Mill read 'the most authoritative treatises on the English Law of Evidence, and commented on a few of the objectionable points of English rules, which had escaped Bentham's notice'.[7]

Certainly, several of Mill's later writings on politics, at both the topical and systematic levels, were concerned in a general sense with

[6] *Autobiography* (1873), *The Collected Works of John Stuart Mill*, ed. John M. Robson, 31 vols. (Toronto and London, 1965–91) (hereafter *CW*), i.

[7] Ibid. i. 119, 117. See also Mill's preface to Jeremy Bentham, *Rationale of Judicial Evidence* (1827), *CW*, xxxi. 5–10.

questions of legislation, and even at the height of his preoccupation with the power of sociological and moral forces he retained the conviction that the law was the most important instrument a government could exercise directly for influencing both the actions and the character of its citizens. But this is obviously still some distance either from a sustained concentration on jurisprudential issues, or even from the working-out of a political and social theory pervaded by legal categories. There is no need to exaggerate this perception into a paradox: the trajectory of Mill's actual intellectual development sufficiently accounts for his not having followed either of these courses. Still, even if we merely remark the fact that jurisprudence found no place in his map of the moral sciences in book VI of the *Logic*, or that, in striking contrast to his wide-ranging work in several branches of philosophy, logic, politics, and political economy, he made no original contribution to legal thought, we thereby register how comparatively slight was the residue from his early exposure to the law.

At a less elevated level, a large part of the political activity of the circle of young Radicals that formed around Bentham and James Mill in the 1820s had been addressed to legal issues.[8] Naturally, any proposals for change grounded in Benthamite political theory were likely to treat the law as the chief means by which self-interested individuals could be prompted to contribute to the general happiness. But such Radical critics went further, identifying the existing state of English law as an elaborate protective screen to disguise the oppressive reality of aristocratic privilege. To this political antagonism towards the law-making class was added an intellectual impatience with the sheer muddle of English law at the beginning of the nineteenth century. This had been the spur which, half a century earlier, had stirred Bentham to pursue what became his lifelong project, and the hope of bringing some order to the bewildering maze of English legal practice continued to animate the analytical jurisprudence of his successors. Radical critics complained that in many cases there existed no definitive statement of the law, that the latitude allowed judicial interpretation was practically limitless. The young Mill had traced the extraordinary variations in the existing libel laws to this source: 'it is an evil inseparable from a system of

[8] See *Autobiography*, *CW*, i. 91, for some remarks on their criticism of 'that most peccant part of English institutions and their administration'.

common law'.[9] His later support for measures for the limited codification of English law had its roots in this distrust, at once political and intellectual, of a legal system that was, in the dismissively pejorative sense of the term, merely 'empirical'.[10] But the early propagandistic pieces in which he voiced such criticisms could in no sense be called 'jurisprudential', and it is perhaps surprising that, in his long writing career, Mill only once addressed issues to which that term could properly be applied. This, however, was in his substantial review-essay 'Austin on jurisprudence', first published in 1863, and for what it says about Mill, about Austin, and about the place of jurisprudence in mid-Victorian culture, that essay, and the relationship it betokened, requires somewhat fuller analysis.

Very shortly after Austin's death in 1859, his work was to have classic status thrust upon it, partly as a result of his wife's editorial labours, partly because he was taken as an exemplar of the deductive method in the historical school's attacks on that approach, and above all because the developments in legal education created a demand for a systematic textbook of jurisprudence (a role for which Austin's clogged and digressive work might not seem to be naturally fitted).[11] But although this larger fame was only to come to him posthumously, he had already played a significant part in Mill's intellectual development. Moreover, his career, though chiefly expressive of the complexities of his own troubled character, also has its interest as evidence of the position of the systematic jurisprudent before the mid-century expansion of legal education.

Called to the Bar in 1818, at the age of 28, after having abandoned a military career, Austin conducted a somewhat desultory practice in Lincoln's Inn for seven years, in the first of several unsatisfactory attempts to find a suitable setting for his talents. He became a close associate of Bentham during this period, but, though a convinced Utilitarian, he maintained a characteristic distance from the extreme political radicalism of the circle gathered around the sage of Queen Square. He was none the less held in high esteem by those few who knew him well, and when James Mill thought of preparing his eldest

[9] John Stuart Mill, 'Law of libel and liberty of the press' (1825), *CW*, xxi. 20.

[10] See e.g. his brief notice 'Smith on law reform' (1841), *CW*, xxi. 84.

[11] For discussion of Austin's work and its subsequent reputation, see W. L. Morison, *John Austin* (London, 1982), and Wilfrid E. Rumble, *The Thought of John Austin: Jurisprudence, Colonial Reform and the British Constitution* (London, 1985).

son for the Bar, it was natural to send him to be coached by Austin, under whose supervision the young Mill read Roman Law and the works of Blackstone and Bentham in 1821 and 1822.[12] Mill's most sustained exposure to Austin's own legal thought came after the latter was appointed to the Chair of Jurisprudence at the newly founded University College, London. Having first spent two years in Bonn to prepare himself, Austin began lecturing in the autumn of 1828, and continued, with some intermissions, until the spring of 1833. After a promising start, the lectures quickly dwindled in popularity, but Mill remained one of the faithful to the end: in his correspondence in 1832 and 1833 he recorded that Austin was lecturing to 'a very small but really select class', only six or seven students 'but those of a *kind* he likes' (his audience included several others who were to attain distinction, including G. C. Lewis, John Romilly, and Charles Buller).[13] Austin clearly had all the qualities that make for a really unsuccessful lecturer—he was painstakingly thorough, unrelievedly dry, remorselessly analytical. In contrast to, say, Maine or Dicey, he did not attempt to present his special study as bearing directly upon the absorbing cultural and political issues of the day, nor did he deploy any of the seductive arts of the reviewer and essayist. 'He never had the slightest idea of rendering his subject popular or easy', his formidable wife Sarah later recalled with loyal respect, but also, perhaps, with a hint of exasperation (her own energies were of a more practical and direct kind).[14] As Leslie Stephen coolly observed: 'Austin thought it a duty to be as dry as Bentham, and discharged that duty scrupulously.'[15]

When his introductory lectures were published in 1832, under the title *The Province of Jurisprudence Determined*, these same qualities were much in evidence. 'It must be admitted that the reception given to his book at first was not encouraging', his wife reported, and the major reviews ignored it.[16] But 'some eulogistic articles appeared in journals of less general currency', the chief of these being a brief

[12] Mill, *Autobiography*, *CW*, i. 67; *The Earlier Letters of John Stuart Mill 1812–1848* (hereafter *EL*), *CW*, xii. 13.

[13] Mill, *EL*, *CW*, xii. 51, 107, 134, 141.

[14] Sarah Austin, 'Preface', to John Austin, *Lectures on Jurisprudence*, 3 vols. (London, 1863), i, p. xxxii. For the confusing publishing history of Austin's *Lectures*, as a result of which this edition is sometimes referred to as the '2nd edition', see John M. Robson, 'Textual introduction', *CW*, xxi, p. lxv.

[15] Leslie Stephen, *The English Utilitarians*, 3 vols. (London, 1900), iii. 318.

[16] Austin, *Lectures*, p. xv.

notice by Mill in the short-lived *Tait's Edinburgh Magazine*, which, its author confided to Carlyle, 'was chiefly intended as a recommendation of that work',[17] a species of puffery relatively common in the early nineteenth-century world of anonymous 'reviews'. Most of the points made in this review, and even some of the phrasing, recur in the larger essay thirty years later, though it is noticeable how Mill, in his high Carlylean phase, recruits Austin to his own campaign against the debased tastes of an increasingly democratic culture ('When every unit is individually weak, it is only multitude that tells. Who wonders that the newspapers should carry all before them?', and so on).[18]

Austin never shared the ardent democratic enthusiasms of James Mill and his immediate circle. As Sarah Austin recalled of her husband's relations with Bentham: 'My husband used vainly to represent to him that the ignorance and wrong-headedness of the people were fully as dangerous to good government as the "sinister interests" of the governing classes. Upon this point they were always at issue.'[19] There is some reason to think that his reservations about such matters, especially his ideas about the proper authority of the more enlightened elements in society, played an important part in fostering the young Mill's reaction against his inherited creed.[20] In the later 1830s and 1840s, however, Austin's apprehensive political sensibilities led him to develop an increasingly conservative line of thought, opposing all further constitutional reform, in which Mill was unwilling to follow him. This difference of view reached its peak in a strong disagreement over the French Revolution of 1848 (Mill was a warm advocate of the popular cause), and some real or imagined slights by Sarah Austin to Harriet Taylor over her relations with Mill brought about a complete estrangement between the two couples, marked by that unyielding bitterness which characterized all Harriet's social antagonisms.[21] Despite these differences, Mill

[17] Letter to Carlyle, 17 Sept. 1832, *EL*, *CW*, xii. 117.

[18] John Stuart Mill, 'Austin's Lectures on Jurisprudence' (1832), *CW*, xxi. 53–4.

[19] Sarah Austin to Guizot, 18 Dec. 1861, quoted in Janet Ross, *Three Generations of Englishwomen*, 2 vols. (London, 1888), ii. 114.

[20] See esp. the excellent discussion by Richard Friedman, 'An introduction to Mill's theory of authority', in J. B. Schneewind (ed.), *Mill: A Collection of Critical Essays* (New York, 1968), 379–425.

[21] Letter to Sarah Austin, n.d. (?Mar. 1848), *EL*, *CW*, xiii. 734). On John Austin's death, Mill could at first bring himself to write only a stiff, brief note to the Austins' granddaughter, later checking with Helen Taylor to ensure that any further communication with Sarah Austin was consistent with what her mother would have

always retained his regard for Austin's intellect and character, and when in 1863 Sarah Austin published her edition of her husband's full lecture notes under the title of *Lectures on Jurisprudence*, Mill took the opportunity publicly to pay his respects to his former tutor and, in passing, to display his own familiarity with the subject. Mill himself could now command a much larger audience than when he had sought to recommend Austin's *Province* thirty years earlier, having the spacious pages of the *Edinburgh Review* open to him for such a purpose.[22] But it was also true that the topic was becoming almost fashionable: the appearance of Maine's *Ancient Law* and the second edition of Austin's *Province* in the same year had helped stir attention in the reviews, which were themselves expanding and hungry for subjects.[23]

Bain, always relieved when the later Mill followed his analytical rather than his polemical inclinations, ranked the essay on Austin as 'among the best of his minor compositions', adding, 'it does not seem to contain much originality, but it is a logical treat.'[24] Mill would no doubt have acknowledged the justice of both parts of this judgement. He had himself described Austin's project as an enquiry into 'the logic of law', and his review made clear that he extended full and sympathetic approval to this project (indeed, Mill hardly expressed any substantive criticisms of Austin at all, beyond suggesting a mild corrective to his definition of a 'right').[25] Later commentators have not always found it so easy to characterize the nature of the project of analytical jurisprudence as practised by Austin and endorsed by Mill. The chief difficulty seems to lie in determining what relation the apparently a priori analysis of the essence of law has to the variety of actual historical legal systems,

wished (*LL*, *CW*, xv, 658, 671). Under Harriet's influence, Mill penned a very harsh portrait of Sarah Austin in the early draft of the *Autobiography*, which he later omitted from the published version (*Autobiography*, *CW*, i. 186).

[22] See Ch. 4 above, pp. 125–7, for Mill's choice of periodical depending upon his subject-matter.

[23] See, e.g. [James Fitzjames Stephen], 'English jurisprudence', *Edinburgh Review*, 114 (1861), 456–86; [T. E. Cliffe Leslie], 'Modern phases of jurisprudence in England', *Westminster Review*, NS 26 (1864), 261–76.

[24] Alexander Bain, *John Stuart Mill: A Criticism, with Personal Recollections* (London, 1882), 124.

[25] John Stuart Mill, 'Austin on jurisprudence' (1863), *CW*, xxi. 178–81. For a discussion of the similarities in method between Austin's jurisprudence and that recommended by Mill in his *Logic* for the moral sciences generally, see Morison, *Austin*, 55–60.

especially when Austin's subject-matter is defined, as it is by Mill at one point, as 'positive law—the legal institutions which exist, or have existed, among mankind, considered as actual facts'.[26] The way both Austin and Mill seem to contrast the philosophy of law with the history of law only makes the difficulty more acute: as Mill puts it in a revealing phrase, existing bodies of law 'having grown by mere aggregation', they are subject to 'no authoritative arrangement but the chronological one', and therefore do not furnish the student with any general principles of classification. The task of the philosopher of law is thus that of 'stripping off what belongs to the accidental or historical peculiarities' of any given system in order to identify the 'universal' elements.[27] The echoes in this last phrase of the ancient philosophical ambition to distinguish essences from accidents recalls one of Austin's few self-revealing remarks: 'I was born out of time and place. I ought to have been a schoolman of the twelfth century—or a German professor.'[28] Part of the poignancy of Austin's career comes from the fact that he was by nature a professor, but that he lived in a society which had not yet conceived a need for the academic treatment of his subject.

The primary task of jurisprudence as Austin conceived it was essentially classificatory: it involved 'clearing up and defining the notions which the human mind is compelled to form, and the distinctions which it is necessitated to make, by the mere existence of a body of law of any kind'. It is true that to this statement Mill appended the potentially relativizing rider, 'or of a body of law taking cognizance of the concerns of a civilized and complicated state of society';[29] but in practice neither he nor Austin allowed this consideration to limit the effectively universalist ambitions of analytical jurisprudence. In fact, rather than creating a system of classification of his own *ab ovo*, Austin took that displayed in Roman Law (albeit Roman Law as systematized and abstracted by the Pandectists) as his basis, a decision that Mill warmly defended: 'The legal system which has been moulded into the shape it possesses by the greatest number of exact and logical minds, will necessarily be

[26] 'Austin on jurisprudence', *CW*, xxi. 169. Both Austin and Mill considered that the same terms could be applied to the project of classical political economy, of which Austin gave an admiring account; Austin, *Province*, lecture 3.

[27] 'Austin on jurisprudence', *CW*, xxi. 171, 173.

[28] Quoted in Austin, *Lectures*, i, p. xviii.

[29] 'Austin on jurisprudence', *CW*, xxi. 168–9.

the best adapted for the purpose; for, though the elements sought exist in all systems, this is the one in which the greatest number of them are likely to have been brought out into distinct expression, and the fewest to remain latent.'[30] Though the goal is recognizably Benthamite, the route may seem curiously roundabout: English readers of the 1860s, the great majority of whom would not have been lawyers, are being urged to think about the nature of law in terms of a set of principles developed in the 1820s out of Austin's encounter with the German Pandectist rationalization of the legal system of the Roman Empire. Of course, the hostility to the common law which Austin and Mill shared came into play here: 'Turning from the study of the English, to the study of the Roman Law,' Austin declared, 'you escape from the empire of chaos and darkness, to a world which seems by comparison, the region of order and light.'[31] It is noticeable how by far the longest extract from Austin's work Mill permits himself to reproduce is that wherein Austin demolishes the common arguments against codification. The argument is conducted in general terms, but there is no doubting the local moral Mill intended his contemporaries to draw from it.

This underlying preoccupation with reform also explains why Mill can so unequivocally commend the work of Maine, who similarly extolled the educative value of Roman Law, but who otherwise defined his own historical enquiries in explicit repudiation of Austin's analytical method and who called into doubt some of the latter's most fundamental contentions, such as the very definitions of law and sovereignty.[32] None the less, Mill had been among the earliest admirers of *Ancient Law*, and his reference to it in the 1862 edition of his *Principles of Political Economy* as a 'profound work' set the tone for all his future citations, of which there were several in the next decade, culminating in a glowing review in 1871 of Maine's second book, *Village Communities*.[33] In 'Austin on jurisprudence' he treats Maine's work as complementary to Austin's without really drawing attention to the differences of approach and sensibility that informed them. But the terms of the commendation reveal that the focus of

[30] Ibid. xxi. 172–3.

[31] Austin, *Lectures*, i, p. xciv.

[32] See *Ancient Law*, 7–8; his criticisms of Austin were to be set out most explicitly in *Lectures on the Early History of Institutions* (London, 7th edn., 1897; 1st edn. 1875), ch. 12. For Maine's work, see the references cited in n. 53 below.

[33] John Stuart Mill, *Principles of Political Economy* (1848), *CW*, ii. 219; John Stuart Mill, 'Maine on village communities', *Fortnightly Review*, NS 9 (1871), 543–56.

Mill's attention is ultimately political. 'The historical value' of such studies as Maine's, he announces,

> is the smallest part of their utility. They teach us the highly practical lesson, that institutions which, with more or less of modification, still exist, originated in ideas now universally exploded; and conversely, that ideas and modes of thought which have not lost their hold even on our own time, are often the artificial, and in some sort accidental product of laws and institutions which exist no longer, and of which no one would now approve the revival.[34]

Similarly, his use of *Ancient Law* in his *Principles* is to buttress his claim that existing property arrangements cannot be taken as natural or unalterable; Maine's book is cited to demonstrate that no 'presumption in favour of existing ideas on this subject is to be derived from their antiquity'. The sentiment itself was present in the first edition of 1848; the reference to *Ancient Law* was simply appended in 1862.[35] As so often, the heat of Mill's enthusiasms is sufficient to melt the awkwardly hard edges of the authors whom he discusses: in his account, Maine and Austin stand side by side as contributors to 'the improvement of law'.

'Austin on jurisprudence' offers one of the best examples of Mill's use of an extended essay in one of the great reviews to instruct the relevant section of the reading public on abstract subjects. The value of Austin's rigorous analysis, he asserts, transcended its contribution to the special science of jurisprudence: it functioned 'as a training school for the higher class of intellects', and Mill's own essay was intended as a small instalment of this training. It proceeded on the assumption that the readers of the *Edinburgh Review*—a class which even the critics of that journal could not by this date suggest was confined to Scotch lawyers—would be willing as part of their general self-culture to apply themselves to such subjects as the classification of public and private wrongs in the *Corpus Juris*. Mill's prose betrays none of that defensiveness of the teacher who needs to justify his subject; on the contrary, the voice expresses confidence in an advanced community of interest: 'We would particularly direct attention to the treatment of *Dominium* or Property, in its various senses, with the contrasted conception of *servitus* or easement.'[36] How

[34] 'Austin on jurisprudence', CW, xxi. 170.
[35] *Principles*, *CW*, ii. 218–19.
[36] 'Austin on jurisprudence', *CW*, xxi. 167, 198.

far his audience in fact met these expectations it is impossible to say; certainly Mill's later correspondence suggests there were always some readers who received, and sometimes challenged, instruction at the appropriate level.

But it is Mill's own untroubled self-assurance as he moves across the details of yet another field of knowledge which is most remarkable. To have been able to give such a clear and forceful précis of the agonizingly involuted contents of Austin's three volumes, and to have been able to take issue with him on disputed points as an equal, is some indication that Mill's early immersion in the law was not, after all, without its effect.[37] Yet, though he declared Austin's subject to deserve the attention 'not merely of a particular profession, but of all liberal and cultivated minds', he never explored elsewhere its place among the moral sciences. He did allude to what he referred to as 'Jurisprudence' in setting out his impractically ambitious prospectus for a university education in his *Inaugural Address*, but once again the terms of the commendation are determinedly pragmatic and do not seem to distinguish anything strictly jurisprudential from the larger concerns of the 'art of politics': its subject-matter, he announced somewhat blandly, is 'not only the chief part of the business of government, but the vital concern of every citizen', and its 'improvement affords a wide scope for the energies of any duly prepared mind, ambitious of contributing towards the better condition of the human race'.[38]

III

The fact that Mill's extended discussion of Austin's work only came after the latter's death was entirely appropriate, for Austin enjoyed a far more popular and vigorous existence posthumously than he ever had during his lifetime.[39] This, as I have already hinted, was due in large measure to the expansion in legal education that took place in

[37] Interestingly, Mill's essay remained required reading for several generations of jurisprudence students, and even a century later the leading scholarly authority on Austin could still rank it as one of 'the best comprehensive accounts' of its subject (H. L. A. Hart, 'Introduction', to John Austin, *The Province of Jurisprudence Determined* (London, 1954), p. xx).

[38] John Stuart Mill, *Inaugural Address Delivered to the University of St Andrews* (1867), *CW*, xxi. 245.

[39] As Fitzjames Stephen rightly observed of Austin's work: 'Till the late reforms in legal education created a demand for it, its value was known only to a few studious persons' ('English jurisprudence', 475).

the middle of the century, and it is necessary briefly to take the measure of that expansion before looking in more detail at the work of later figures, since it provided the institutional, and to some extent the intellectual, context for their writing.

It would hardly be an exaggeration to say that from the seventeenth to the mid-nineteenth century there had been no legal education as such in England: the craft was essentially acquired by apprenticeship, a process only very loosely overseen by the Inns of Court. However, the reforming spirit of the 1830s and 1840s could not easily rest content with this situation, especially since the lack of organized legal education was taken to be an important source of the lack of system, principle, and clarity in the practice of the law itself; Dickens's satires on the obstructive archaism of the legal profession expressed a criticism that was voiced in more sober terms by many others. Addressing this perceived need, the House of Commons set up a Select Committee on Legal Education in 1846, which summarized the present position in no uncertain terms: 'No Legal Education worthy of the name, of a public nature, is at this moment to be had in either England or Ireland.'[40] One fruit of the reforms subsequently proposed was the founding in 1852 of the Council for Legal Education, which established several Readerships at the Inns of Court, one of which (as we saw in Chapter 1) was held by Maine, where he gave in the course of the 1850s the lectures that became *Ancient Law*. The Inns thereafter attempted some modest regulation of the profession and its qualifications, though the speed of such change should not be exaggerated: examinations, for example, were not made compulsory until 1872. But of more significance for the place of jurisprudence in the wider culture were the moves to establish legal education as part of the syllabus at the newly revived universities.

Until the 1840s, law teaching at Oxford and Cambridge consisted of little more than some desultory lecturing on Civil Law and similar topics by largely non-resident professors. (The foundation of the Vinerian and Downing Chairs in English Law at, respectively, Oxford and Cambridge seems not to have led to any very regular teaching of the subject up to this date.) However, with the extension

[40] *Report from the Select Committee on Legal Education*, 25 Aug. 1846, Conclusions, 1. For discussion of the Bar's resistance to the reform of legal education, see Raymond Cocks, *The Foundations of the Modern Bar* (London, 1983), and Peter Stein, *Legal Evolution: The Story of an Idea* (Cambridge, 1980).

of the syllabus that accompanied the expansion and new sense of purpose in the universities in the middle of the century, law was among the first subjects to benefit, especially at Oxford. Not that the establishment there in 1850 of a joint 'Law and Modern History' School should be seen as signifying the arrival of professional education: law was very much the junior partner, and the School was conceived rather as a general introduction to modern politics and history.[41] The creation of a separate Honours School in 'Jurisprudence' in 1872 resulted as much from a desire for divorce on the part of the historians as from increasing pressure for a better preparation for legal practice, and the syllabus of the school, much shaped by Maine and Bryce who had taken up chairs at Oxford in respectively 1869 and 1870, still aimed to provide a liberal education, with general jurisprudence and Roman Law preponderating.[42] In 1884 changes in the syllabus (partly prompted by Dicey, who had become Vinerian Professor of English Law in 1882) introduced a greater concentration on English law, and a similar narrowing of focus was to take place at Cambridge, where Law had also briefly shared a Tripos with History.[43] Gradually, the content of the syllabus became more attuned to the needs of the future practitioner, a pressure increased by the fact that in 1877 would-be solicitors were exempted from the Preliminary Examination of the Law Society, and then further in 1895 from the Intermediate Examination, if they had obtained a law degree at specified universities, and similar exemptions from examinations for the Bar followed.

The whole process created a fresh market for legal works, one of the first consequences of which was that Austin had examinational greatness forced on him. Sarah Austin registered the change in her late husband's reputation immediately. 'I must tell you', she wrote to Guizot in 1863,

> that his book is daily rising into fame and authority to a degree which I never hoped to live to witness, and which he never would have believed. It is become an examination book at both Oxford and Cambridge, and I am

[41] For this account, and what follows, see F. H. Lawson, *The Oxford Law School 1850–1965* (Oxford, 1968), chs. I–III.

[42] For the role of Maine and Bryce, see George Feaver, *From Status to Contract: Sir Henry Maine 1822–1888* (London, 1969), 112–17.

[43] Lawson, *Oxford Law School*, 59, 66. For the relation of law to history and the various forms of 'political science' taught at Cambridge, see Stefan Collini, Donald Winch, and John Burrow, *That Noble Science of Politics: A Study in Nineteenth-Century Intellectual History* (Cambridge, 1983), essay XI.

assured by barristers that there is a perfect enthusiasm about it among *young* lawyers—men among whom it was unknown till since [*sic*] I published the second edition.[44]

In subsequent decades, his *Province* retained this classic status, though students probably *read* the jurisprudence textbooks that more recognizably addressed their needs, such as Sir William Markby's *Elements of Law* (1871) and especially the very widely used *Elements of Jurisprudence* by T. E. Holland, first published in 1880.[45] Though broadly Austinian in approach, these self-consciously 'professional' works represented a narrowing of the scope of his large, if imperfectly realized, ambition to see law as one among the moral sciences.[46] And this shift was representative of the larger changes set in train by the institutionalization of legal education: the more it succeeded in establishing itself as a desirable form of professional preparation, the more it tended to lose its 'liberal' character.

Two snippets may illustrate the reality of legal education under such conditions. As Corpus Professor at Oxford, Maine displayed some of the riches of his mind in lectures on 'Ancient systems of law'; the result was that the ever-pragmatic undergraduates stayed away in large numbers, and he complained that in order to get any sort of audience he had to descend to lecturing on 'elementary Austinism'.[47] A yet more dispiriting picture is suggested by a remark in a work on Maine's ideas expressly written for students preparing for the Council on Legal Education's exams in the 1890s, only a few years after his death: its author complained that in Maine's books 'there is a great deal of writing that is absolutely useless to the student for examination purposes, and page after page has to be waded through in search of a theory'.[48]

[44] Quoted in Ross, *Three Generations*, ii. 138. Thereafter, Austin's work came to be 'the staple of jurisprudence in all our system of legal education'; E. C. Clark, *Practical Jurisprudence: A Comment on Austin* (Cambridge, 1883).

[45] See Morison, *Austin*, ch. 5, 'The scholarly reception of Austin'; and esp. R. A. Cosgrove, 'The reception of analytical jurisprudence: the Victorian debate on the separation of law and morality 1860–1900', *Durham University Journal*, 74 (1981), 47–56.

[46] Cf. the comment of W. L. Morison on analytical jurisprudence in the second half of the 19th century: it 'was turning inward upon law and losing the vital and continuing inspiration for it which came from the determination to understand legal phenomena on the basis of a general philosophy of the world in general [*sic*] and the fields of the social sciences within it' (Morison, *Austin*, 151).

[47] Letter to Bryce, 25 Nov. 1875; quoted in Lawson, *Oxford Law School*, 49.

[48] M. Evans, *Theories and Criticism of Sir Henry Maine* (London, 1896), cited in R. C. J. Cocks, *Sir Henry Maine: A Study in Victorian Jurisprudence* (Cambridge, 1988), 187.

However, for all the disappointment of hopes and narrowing of ambitions that may eventually have been involved in the daily compromises of the classroom, the expansion of legal education not only helped stimulate a demand for systematic legal texts, but it also created a new public role for several of the writers of such books, that of the law professor. The academic teacher of law inevitably found himself in a somewhat different position from other teachers: he needed simultaneously to justify law's place in a liberal education to a sceptical university and to justify the usefulness of academic study to a sceptical profession.[49] However, in relation to the wider world, the role at once legitimated a claim to expertise, the basis of one's special authority as a commentator on current politics, whilst at the same time drawing attention to one's distance from (or above) that debate. Thus, for the jurist in this period, there was the same tension that is discernible in the leading figures in several other increasingly specialized fields; the desire to shape public discussion could pull in a different direction from the desire to contribute to the progress of one's 'discipline'. We must be careful, however, not to impose too modern a notion of the divide between the professional and the academic on the careers of Victorian jurists; Maine, for example, as we have seen, appears to have been more concerned with the doings of the India Council than with the duties of his chair, and many of the most substantial contributions to the movement to provide digests and principled accounts of various hitherto unsystematized branches of law in the 1870s and 1880s came from figures such as Fitzjames Stephen, who held no academic post.[50] Yet even that common framework of engagement with public affairs was itself taking a different form towards the end of the century. The *Law Quarterly Review*, for instance, was not in its early days the most narrowly technical of publications, but its very foundation in 1884, largely the work of the Oxford legal professors, was another example of the fragmentation of the shared culture of the mid-Victorian periodicals.[51] In considering how these developments

[49] On the persistence of the Bar's traditional hostility to systematic education and anything which smacked of 'theory', and its corresponding attachment to practical experience and good judgement, see Cocks, *Modern Bar*, esp. chs. 2 and 5.

[50] He did hold the post of Professor of Criminal Law at the Inns of Court from 1875 until he became a judge in 1879; Leslie Stephen, *The Life of Sir James Fitzjames Stephen* (London, 1895), 377–8.

[51] The founding meeting was held, appropriately, in All Souls; Markby, Anson, Holland, and Pollock seem to have taken the lead, with support from Dicey and Bryce (Lawson, *Oxford Law School*, 73).

affected the relations between law and political thought, we need to look more closely at the three figures whose work was at the heart of that relation—Henry Maine, Fitzjames Stephen, and A. V. Dicey.

All three belonged (Maine more by achievement than by birth) to that well-connected intellectual-cum-political stratum which, as I discussed in Chapter 1, staffed the overlapping worlds of law, administration, and the higher reaches of education and journalism. The more specific similarities in their careers are worth rehearsing again. Both Maine and Stephen had been 'Apostles' at Cambridge, both qualified as barristers, both were among the first generation of contributors to the *Saturday Review*. They succeeded each other in the 1860s as Legal Member of the Viceroy's Council in India, and both, Maine especially, retained a considerable voice in the government of India thereafter. Both became alarmed at the dangers of the extension of the franchise at home, and they wrote two of the classic works of anti-democratic political polemic, Stephen's *Liberty, Equality, Fraternity* (1873) and Maine's *Popular Government* (1885). Maine had, of course, largely made his name on the basis of *Ancient Law* (1861), which was followed by a succession of lesser studies on the early history of law; he taught for several years at the Inns of Court, and managed at various points in his career to occupy three different chairs in law at the universities, ending up as Master of Trinity Hall. Stephen's achievements were less concentrated: he published *A General View of the Criminal Law of England* in 1863, and his *magnum opus*, *A History of the Criminal Law of England*, in three volumes in 1883. But he was above all a controversialist, writing extraordinary quantities of journalism. Unlike Maine, he continued to practise as a barrister, and finally became a somewhat controversial High Court judge.

Dicey's life followed a broadly similar pattern, allowing for the different inflection given by the facts of his being somewhat younger and Oxford-educated. He, too, combined the Bar with political journalism in the 1860s and 1870s, and, as we saw above, he relied on his earnings from the latter to support his never very successful legal practice. But following his appointment to the Vinerian Chair at Oxford in 1882, his career and his public standing rested more exclusively upon his academic credentials than was true of either Maine or Stephen (this was not, it should be said, his own preferred choice: he would far rather have had a political or legal career, and always retained, perhaps as a result, a marked deference towards judges). The publication of *The Law of the Constitution* in 1885 made his reputation (within the year, Gladstone cited it in the Commons as a recognized authority[52]), and thereafter his long life was more or less equally divided between writing (and revising) legal textbooks and vigorously polemicizing against Home Rule. His political allegiances followed the familiar path from the ardent enthusiasm of the typical 'university liberal' of the 1850s, through disillusionment with the demagoguery of Gladstonian Liberalism in the 1880s, extended, in his case, to black Tory hostility to the 'new Liberalism' of the years before 1914. In the case of all three men, the law was the basis of a professional identity which partially distinguished them from other members of the political and intellectual worlds in which they moved; but it was, as we shall see, an identity which could be cultivated and articulated in subtly different ways.

IV

One could hardly now say that Maine's work was suffering from scholarly neglect,[53] so I shall not consider his individual works in detail, despite his being in many ways the most interesting mind among the figures considered in this chapter. Instead, I shall confine myself to three related questions about his role. The first concerns the way in which his work, considered as a contribution to political thought, rests less upon a distinctively jurisprudential basis, and more on the kinds of moral and social assumptions discussed in earlier chapters, especially on the notion of 'character'. (This is not to gainsay the large, sometimes improbably large, part played by legal evidence in his account of social development.) The second takes up the theme of 'voice' and its implied relation with an audience. And the third question, here touched on only very briefly indeed, concerns the proper historical characterization of Maine's particular form of conservatism and the need to distinguish it from those varieties which have perhaps become more familiar. One

[52] See Ch. 6 above, 233–4.

[53] See in particular John Burrow, *Evolution and Society: A Study in Victorian Social Theory* (Cambridge, 1966); Feaver, *Status to Contract*; N. Pilling, 'The Conservatism of Sir Henry Maine', *Political Studies*, 18 (1970), 107–20; K. E. Bock, 'Comparison of histories: the contribution of Henry Maine', *Comparative Studies in Society and History*, 16 (1974), 232–62; Stein, *Legal Evolution*, Collini, Winch, and Burrow, *That Noble Science of Politics*, essay VII; Cocks, *Maine*; Alan Diamond (ed.), *Sir Henry Maine: A Centennial Re-assessment* (Cambridge, forthcoming).

consequence of concentrating on these themes is to give unusual salience to *Popular Government*, the work of Maine's to which recent scholarship has paid least attention.

In the century since his death, Maine has probably attracted greatest interest for his ideas on social development. But to treat him as a 'theorist of progress' can be misleading in several ways, not least if that term is assumed to suggest a benign and optimistic view of the direction one's own society is taking. One elementary precaution is to remember that all accounts of progress involve, at least implicitly, some characterization of stagnation, retrogression, and decline; and, perhaps a slightly less obvious point, theories of progress are one very effective form of social or cultural criticism in that they are attempts to endow with some kind of scientific or moral authority the discrimination of those current social and cultural developments that are welcome from those that are not. A special piquancy attends the politically pessimistic varieties of this kind of criticism, where the future figures more as a source of alarm than of hope, and where the last 'healthy' stage of cultural growth tends to coincide with that of the critic's own youth.

This general point acquires added force if one accepts, as the best recent work seems to do, that, for all his immense contemporary reputation as an analyst of 'the progressive nations of mankind', Maine could not really *explain* progress, or at least that he did not have any general *theory* of progress based on a single motor force.[54] Rather, he offered a selective analysis of the part legal developments had played in the course of the singular (in every sense of the word) development of those West European and European-influenced societies which merited the label 'progressive'. Certainly, he assigned an important role to the adaptiveness and flexibility with which various legal systems had responded to social change. But what accounted for the fundamental difference between the stationary and progressive societies remained, as he put it in a characteristic phrase, 'one of the secrets which enquiry has yet to penetrate', and again when identifying the forces which had generally arrested 'the progress of the greater part of mankind', he could only suggest that there were one or two races 'exempted by a marvellous fate' from some of these calamities.[55]

[54] See esp. John Burrow, 'Maine and mid-Victorian ideas of progress', in Diamond, *Sir Henry Maine*.

[55] Maine, *Ancient Law*, 23, 77–8.

Even if we do not choose to conduct our analysis in terms derived from very recent literary theory, we cannot help but observe how the logical or structural gaps in Maine's argument are in fact filled in by his invocation of certain values whose presence is signalled more by his characteristic choice of adjectives than by explicit acknowledgement. John Burrow has brought out very well how the advance of the progressive societies as expressed in their legal arrangements appears in Maine's account as both an intellectual and a moral achievement,[56] and one could underline this by pointing to the way in which Maine's characterization of the distinctive merits of advanced societies rests upon what Durkheim was later to call 'the non-contractual elements in contract'.[57] Viewed thus, Maine's discussion of the assumptions expressed in modern legal arrangements about contract (essentially in England) turns out to be littered with references to the advance in 'good faith and trust in our fellows', 'scrupulous honesty', the respect accorded to 'the mere unilateral reposal of confidence', and so on.[58]

At this point Maine has no elaborate explanation to offer for this fact of moral progress: he does not, for example, try to explain the occurrence of these qualities by presenting them as in some way functionally superior or advantageous, as various social evolutionary theorists did, nor does he regard them as the working-out of an essentially teleological conception of human nature, slowly overcoming external impediments, as some more philosophical Victorian social theorists did. There is a suggestion of the familiar thought that the pattern of social development can be understood in terms of the life-cycle of the individual, but he does not elaborate this. In practice, I would suggest, the dynamic of his account rests upon an unacknowledged circularity: he takes for granted the superiority of certain qualities of character, and then finds them at work in those developments he regards as progressive. Indeed, even the intellectual achievements which are so crucial to his story are tinged with these *moral* qualities also—they are very much a matter of restraint, steadiness, prudence, and so on.

The connections between this cluster of values and the politics of

[56] Burrow, 'Maine and mid-Victorian ideas of progress'.

[57] See Steven Lukes, *Emile Durkheim: His Life and Work, a Historical and Critical Study* (London, 1973), 276.

[58] These terms all appear in the space of little over a page; Maine, *Ancient Law*, 306–7.

Individualism have been explored in more general terms in earlier chapters, but the relationship in Maine's case is, as one might expect, subtle and indirect. For example, it is to this level of moral sensibility that we must turn to resolve a minor paradox in the argument of *Popular Government*. The natural state of the populace, Maine never tired of insisting, is that of changelessness, sunk in the immobility of habit and custom. In this respect the majority of the population of a modern state continues to exhibit the behaviour that has characterized most historical societies: innovation and progress, in the rare cases where they have occurred, have been the work of enlightened minorities, minorities which, as Maine became more politically pessimistic and more explicitly polemical, he was increasingly willing to allow to be identified with natural aristocracies. But the chief reason why the advent of popular government is such a source of alarm to Maine is not, of course, the prospect of its torpor; he is not, as for example Mill was, haunted by the fear that the imposition of a levelling mediocrity would produce a kind of Chinese stationariness, though there had been hints of such a view in *Ancient Law*. It is, rather, a democracy's excessive *activity*, especially legislative activity, which Maine finds so alarming. Thus, popular government threatens, oddly, to be both inert and over-active at the same time.

But once again I think we can make some sense of this, and see what really determines the contours of Maine's anxieties, if we recognize that this portrait of democracy is a transposition of those qualities, seen as defects of character, which Maine and so many of his contemporaries took to typify the behaviour of the savage, the child, and the mass of the working class. In the absence of those qualities of vigour, independence, and adaptiveness which distinguish strong characters, the mass of the population remains largely passive and governed by habit and custom; but then, when subject to the temptation of excitement and self-indulgence, they lack the qualities of self-restraint and maturity needed to resist. On such occasions, the qualities of 'the multitude' (Maine had a particular weakness for such political haughtiness) prove to be 'haste, irreflection, sudden impulse, and caprice'.[59] Only a few have the

[59] [H. S. Maine], 'Democracy and dissolution', *Pall Mall Gazette*, 9 Feb. 1874; quoted, and attributed, in William N. Coxall, '"The use and misuse of internal evidence in authorship attributions": some further thoughts', *Victorian Periodicals Review*, 20 (1987), 96. Based on an analysis of internal evidence alone, Coxall attributed 186 of the leading articles in the *PMG* in the 1870s to Maine.

strength of character not to give in to what he called 'the craving for political excitement which is growing on us every day';[60] the disdain and the dramatization embodied in 'craving' is very expressive.

Something similar can be said about the language used in Maine's discussion of the role of political generalizations in stirring a democracy to ill-advised action. To begin with, his description of the activity of framing general propositions nicely displays the way such intellectual activities rest on or express ethical qualities: Maine typically emphasizes the difficulty and complexity of doing so judiciously, and contrasts this with 'the modern facility of generalisation'—one can hear the tut-tutting already in 'facility'—which is obtained by 'a curious precipitation and carelessness' in selecting one's facts. Once framed, these generalizations produce 'a loose acquiescence in a vague proposition', and this 'levity of assent'—the headmasterly ticking-off is very pronounced now—is 'one of the most enervating of national habits of mind'. A dreadful example of its operation was not far to seek: 'It has seriously enfeebled the French intellect.' Throughout, the contrast is with 'legislation founded on scientific opinion', but familiar moral qualities turn out to be crucial here, too, since this 'requires tension of mind to understand it and self-denial to submit to it'. Although he naturally refers to constitutional forms at various points in *Popular Government*, especially in the chapter on the American constitution, it is to these qualities of individual character that his analysis constantly returns: 'Here then is the great question about democratic legislation, when carried to more than a moderate length. How will it affect human motives?'[61] We need to recognize, in other words, that the lacunae in Maine's argument reveal that the real dynamic of his position is an untheorized commitment to certain qualities of 'character', in the sense of the term (discussed in Chapter 3 above) that was at once descriptive and normative. This no doubt enhanced the persuasiveness of his work for his Victorian readers, but it dilutes the sense in which his can be said to be a distinctively jurisprudential contribution to political thought.

Persuasiveness is not, in some ways, the most obvious characteristic of Maine's style (to turn to the second of my three questions); other scholars have noted, for instance, his characteristic 'hauteur'

[60] H. S. Maine, *Popular Government* (London, 1885), 151.

[61] Ibid. 106–8, 97, 50.

and 'tone of dismissive confidence'.[62] Maine very clearly cultivated his standing as an exceptionally well-informed and far-seeing commentator, something which contributes an uninviting finality to so many of his pronouncements. 'Whenever men with a grain of statesmanship have set themselves to frame constitutions for countries intended to be democratically governed, they have invariably . . .'; 'at the present moment there is not a single civilised commonwealth that does not furnish some reason for doubting . . .' and so on.[63] But beyond this, his prose invokes for itself not just the authority of historical and legal learning, but also a kind of moral authority, the authority of one who unflinchingly faces up to the demands of complexity, however unpalatable (with the strong suggestion that they nearly always will be unpalatable). Just as there was a rhetoric of sincerity among Victorian unbelievers, so there is in Maine a kind of rhetoric of sobriety and realism, which has the effect of casting opposing views as self-indulgent or weakly deluded. It is not as pronounced in Maine as it is in the figure who most naturally asks to be compared in this as in many other respects, namely Fitzjames Stephen, who took more of the exhibitionist's delight in showing off the virility of his mind. But something of this note of grim satisfaction is audible even in that widely cited passage from one of Maine's addresses to the University of Calcutta, where he insists that 'all truth, of whatever character, must conform to the same conditions, so that if indeed history be true, it must teach that which every other science teaches, continuous sequence, inflexible order, and eternal law'.[64] There is surely a tangible *frisson* in this famous cadence that comes from associating oneself with this awesome impersonal force, as well as an element of self-congratulation for managing to contemplate it without flinching. Again, the language is an extension of that used to describe a certain ideal of character.

Much of Maine's later writing consisted of deploying both his assiduously cultivated identity as a disinterested legal historian, and his habitual tone of grim realism in the face of almost overwhelming complexity, to provide a kind of scientific legitimation for the

[62] Burrow, 'Maine and mid-Victorian ideas of Progress', and Cocks, 'Maine and boredom', both in Diamond, *Sir Henry Maine*.

[63] 'Democracy and dissolution'; [H. S. Maine], 'Liberalism and democracy', *Pall Mall Gazette*, 18 Apr. 1874; both quoted in Coxall, 'Internal evidence', 97, 98.

[64] H. S. Maine, 'Address to the University of Calcutta', repr. in *Village Communities*, quotation at 265–6.

prejudices of the governing class. It is important to bear in mind this intended audience when assessing Maine's role. The essays that make up *Popular Government* first appeared, after all, in the pages of the *Quarterly Review*, and during these years Maine was writing a fair amount of political journalism for the *St James's Gazette*, founded in 1880 as a Tory counterpart to the newly Liberal *Pall Mall Gazette*, and assessed by Lord Cranbrook in 1882 in these terms: 'The paper is addressed to the cultured and critical, who probably do not take it, but read it at their Clubs, and are a class whose tastes and feelings are Conservative.'[65] This was Maine's natural audience by the 1880s, and he clearly had its pulse: *Popular Government* sold out in three weeks.[66] When he died, the *Spectator* observed in an interesting phrase that his great talent was for 'convincing qualified minds'. An alert sensitivity to the workings, and limits, of minds given to electing themselves to this idealized Athenaeum is certainly evident in his later writings, expressing itself in a tone of collusive, head-shaking dismay at the follies of uninstructed mankind. The obverse of this identity was given by the obituary in the *Saturday Review*, indulging for once in understatement, when it recorded that 'he was not a man of wide popular sympathies', and the point was put more bluntly by the *St James's Gazette* itself which called him simply 'a pronounced and uncompromising Anti-Radical'.[67] Although Maine was adept at catching a tone of weary disinterestedness in his more extended works, this sense of his intimacy with a limited audience should help remind us of the almost blatantly ideological cast of much of his writing.

This leads on to my third point, which is to try to bring into focus Maine's relation to more familiar forms of conservative political thought (this also proves to be a further way of approaching his relation with his audience). In the 1930s Benjamin Lippincott called Maine 'the first and last "scientific conservative" in English political thought'.[68] Obviously, the term echoes the usage of the period when connecting political analysis to larger patterns of historical and legal development could still try to lay claim to the prestige of science, but viewed from further away the label may even call into question the

65 Quoted in Stephen Koss, *The Rise and Fall of the Political Press*, 2 vols. (London, 1981, 1984), i. 231.

66 Feaver, *Status to Contract*, 245.

67 All quoted in M. E. Grant Duff, *Sir Henry Maine: A Brief Memoir* (London, 1892), 75, 82.

68 Benjamin Lippincott, *Victorian Critics of Democracy* (Minneapolis, 1938), 169.

accuracy of calling Maine a 'conservative' at all. On some understandings of conservatism, after all, especially that retrospectively created tradition of English conservatism whose genealogy is alleged to run from Hooker to Oakeshott,[69] the phrase 'scientific conservative' is almost an oxymoron. Certainly, we would search Maine's work in vain for some of the supposed hallmarks of 'conservative' political thought—there is no elevating of tradition over analysis, no preference for the implicit over the explicit, little respect for the irrational or marked sympathy for religion, and so on. He remained too much the legalistic administrator and too responsive to the claims of system and rationality for that. To take just a minor example, when in *Ancient Law* he was insisting that feudalism was quite distinct from and more durable than genuinely archaic communities, primarily on account of the legacy of Roman Law, he observed that 'express rules are less destructible than instinctive habits',[70] a remark which hardly strikes a Burkean or Oakeshottian note, and there are many more such examples. He was unremittingly hostile to facile a priori reasoning, but not to reasoning as such; he retained an admiration for Bentham, for example, arguing, with that measured tendentiousness so characteristic of his late style, that 'there is no political writer whose strongest and most fundamental opinions are so directly at variance with the Radical ideas of the moment'.[71] If anything, Maine rather disdained that vulgar irrationality and unreflectiveness in which some kinds of 'conservative' have claimed to detect a hidden wisdom.

Moreover, not only was his account of progress strikingly intellectualist, depending heavily as it did on the role of new ideas, but so was his diagnosis of the current danger of decline: he attributed a quite absurd causal power to the ideas of Rousseau. But in thus shifting the emphasis away from exploring the laudable role of intellectual innovation and towards decrying the pernicious consequences of theoretical fashion, the later Maine was led to express a somewhat more favourable view of the role both of habit and of the value of fixed constitutional forms, two forces which had appeared in *Ancient Law* chiefly as obstacles to progress. There was now a different resonance to his passing, but revealing, reference in

[69] See e.g. Anthony Quinton, *The Politics of Imperfection: The Religious and Secular Traditions of Conservative Thought in England from Hooker to Oakeshott* (London, 1978).

[70] *Ancient Law*, 365–6.

[71] *Popular Government*, 84.

Popular Government to the way in which human nature, 'when left to itself', is not intrinsically disposed to pursue change;[72] there is a suggestion of untoward or 'outside' interference at work here, perhaps the doing of a tightly knit group of politically motivated men. John Morley was surely right, in his review of the later book, to call attention both to Maine's 'tendency to impute an unreal influence to writers and books altogether', and to his tendency to attach 'an altogether excessive and unscientific importance to form', neither of them supposed to be characteristic of what we have come to regard as conservative political thinking. It is always fun, of course, to see the radical berating the conservative for exaggerating the power of abstract political theory, but Morley had a deeper point to press in referring to the absence in Maine's work on democracy of what he called 'anything like a philosophy of society as a whole' or any 'reference to particular social conditions'.[73]

Maine's range of interests, it may be relevant to observe at this point (it was something his contemporaries remarked), was always pretty narrowly political and administrative; for one who had speculated so imaginatively about the early development of society, he seemed curiously uninterested in many of the social changes taking place around him. Like many disillusioned intellectuals, Maine saw the circumstances prevailing in his youth as the last period of sanity, and more specifically this meant that relatively short period after the initial flush of Whig and Peelite reforms in the 1830s and 1840s but before the slide into democracy and demagoguery initiated by the Reform Act of 1867.[74] It is interesting that Grant Duff mentions 'Peelite' as being Maine's earliest political identity;[75] he never really had that period of eager Liberal enthusiasm which so many of his type did, including, for example, Henry Sidgwick with whom he otherwise has much in common, especially the fact of being a terrible political hypochondriac.

His criticisms of democracy belong to a very specific period, too.

72 Ibid. 143.

73 John Morley, 'Maine on popular government' (1886), in *Studies in Literature* (London, 1890), 118, 149. See the further discussion in Collini, Winch, and Burrow, *That Noble Science of Politics*, 234–5.

74 Compare the remark of Dicey's biographer: 'The world of 1854–67 remained ever after for Dicey the zenith of the English political system, and nostalgia for that era was the primary motif of his later politics' (Richard Cosgrove, *The Rule of Law: Albert Venn Dicey, Victorian Jurist* (London, 1980), 30).

75 Grant Duff, *Maine*, 11.

There is in his work, for example, no reference to 'mass culture' as such: he is writing before fears about the proliferation of popular media and the 'Americanization' of 'lowbrow' culture gave their distinctive flavour to the cultural pessimism familiar among English literary intellectuals in the early decades of the twentieth century. Yet nor did he altogether share the much earlier Whig anxiety about maintaining the proper balance of 'interests' in society, a preoccupation that made many in the generation before him come to seem 'conservative' in the decades immediately after 1832. Nor again, I would suggest, does he really belong among those forms of religious or anti-rationalist or merely nostalgic political thought which have been factitiously erected into 'the conservative tradition.' He belongs, rather, with that type prominent in if not strictly peculiar to this period, such as Dicey and Fitzjames Stephen, and to some extent Sidgwick—rationalists with strongly Individualist social and economic beliefs, tinged with a darker hue by their increasingly anti-democratic sensibilities. It was a political identity which surely coloured his account of progress just as it clearly shaped his prognosis of decline. 'Convincing qualified minds' certainly required the display of intellectual authority, and Maine's legal scholarship helped furnish him with this; but even more it required the cultivation of a reputation for judiciousness, and ultimately this is only successfully managed by a writer who shares the prejudices of his readership, but who has mastered a way of seeming to give them restrained, almost impersonal, expression.

V

As I suggested at the beginning of the first chapter, one could hardly choose a better exemplar than Fitzjames Stephen of the ways in which the overlapping worlds of politics, law, administration, and education encouraged the cultivation of a certain sort of public voice. Stephen wrote as one who expected to be heard: his aggressive style was part bravado, to be sure, but it also expressed a confidence that rested upon shared experience and common reference as well as upon an acknowledged claim to authority. In this respect, it is suggestive that he could without strain appear as a central figure in several of the other chapters in this book, particularly those dealing with such themes as 'character', 'manliness', and 'hard-headed' Liberalism's complex Oedipal relation to Mill. It is hardly surprising, therefore, that although he cannot be neglected in any account of Victorian legal thought, he ultimately proves a better illustration of the way in which the work of the jurist expressed a widely shared set of moral and political values than he does of any claim about the distinctively jurisprudential idiom of political thought in this period.[76]

Stephen is a figure whom it is easy to underestimate or caricature. He can seem like the lager-lout among Victorian reviewers: several of his contemporaries (and, in fairness to him it should be added, his seniors—he never lacked for courage) could display the bruises left from a working-over by 'the Gruffian'. The contributors to the *Saturday Review* in its first decade (1855–65) were mostly young men with their way to make: the tackling was what would now be called 'uncompromising', there was a good deal of barging, and anything which suggested cant or sentimentalism (for example, the complete works of Dickens) would have its legs cut from under it very sharply. Stephen was one of nature's 'Saturday Revilers', his relish for the role well caught by his half-jocular comment on Matthew Arnold's genial and amused response to such rough handling: 'There is no pleasure in hitting a man who will not hit you back again.'[77]

But that remark hints at a level of self-awareness and even perhaps of self-parody which ought to complicate our picture, and in writing to his intimates, Stephen revealed himself as a more knowing and more perceptive as well as more endearing and more playful figure than his public booming might suggest. (He also recognized that there was something compulsive about his voluminous journalism—'If I were in solitary confinement, I should have to scratch newspaper articles on the wall with a nail'—and his brother observed that 'it gave him the same pleasure other men derive from dramdrinking'.[78]) However, it is that public world of political debate and higher journalism that concerns us here, a world where Stephen spoke in the common language of the moralist far more than in the

[76] Stephen, too, has received considerable recent scholarly attention: the two fullest accounts are James A. Colaiaco, *James Fitzjames Stephen and the Crisis of Victorian Thought* (London, 1983), and above all K. J. M. Smith, *James Fitzjames Stephen: Portrait of a Victorian Rationalist* (Cambridge, 1988). An early discussion, which has still not been entirely superseded, was John Roach, 'Liberalism and the Victorian intelligentsia', *Cambridge Historical Journal*, 13 (1957), 58–81.

[77] [J. F. Stephen], 'Mr Matthew Arnold amongst the Philistines', *Saturday Review*, 19 (1865), 235; quoted in Colaiaco, *Stephen*, 20.

[78] Stephen, *Fitzjames Stephen*, 241.

professional idiom of the jurist. In fact, the very high register in which he pitched his pronouncements on the social role of the law proves to be a further mutation of those moral sensibilities which, as we have already seen, found expression in an increasingly conservative Liberalism among those members of the educated class who came to maturity in the 1850s and 1860s.

One of the minor contrasts between intellectual attitudes in the earlier and later parts of the nineteenth century is the development of a far more respectful and even admiring regard for the law, especially English law. In the earlier period, as I remarked above in discussing Mill's Philosophic Radical polemics, the complaint was constantly heard, especially of course from radical critics, whether of a Benthamite or Dickensian colour, that the archaic confusion and obstructiveness of English legal procedure was a cloak for corruption and sinister interests. By the end of the century, this form of criticism had become comparatively rare. Similarly, unfavourable comparisons with the clarity and intellectual grasp of Roman Law increasingly yielded to more even-handed appraisals of the respective merits of the two systems, and even, when flushed with imperial pride, to earnest meditations on Roman and English law as two of the great achievements of world history.[79] The actual reform of large areas of English law in the middle of the century, of course, was the crucial precondition for the development of this more positive attitude, but an important part was also played by the legal writers of the 1870s and 1880s who did so much to produce digests of various branches of the law and to exhibit the fundamental principles governing even the disorderly mass of English case-law.[80]

In his rhapsodies on the beauty of this body of accumulated legal reasoning, Stephen gave particularly forceful expression to the belief that legislators are the unacknowledged poets of the world. But Stephen, in many ways an unrepentant Benthamite, was far from being an uncritical admirer of English law, and in fact the development of his own attitudes partly mirrored the larger change. In his early *Saturday Review* days he could inveigh against the

[79] Among many examples of this, see James Bryce, 'The extension of Roman and English law throughout the world', in his *Studies in History and Jurisprudence*, 2 vols. (Oxford, 1901), i. 85–144.

[80] On digests, see Smith, *Stephen*, 53, 78, 84; on the forms of legal literature more generally, see A. W. B. Simpson, 'The rise and fall of the legal treatise: legal principles and the forms of legal literature', *University of Chicago Law Review*, 48 (1981), 632–79.

obscurities of legal procedure in best Circumlocution Office vein, comparing the unpredictability and obscurity of legal procedure to 'a huge heap of building materials', the safe traversing of which was largely determined by chance: 'By signal good luck you may avoid holes, and pick your way in safety over the heterogeneous mass; but if you are not very careful of your steps some treacherous clause will give way, and you may disappear into all sorts of pitfalls and caverns—you may fall from statute to statute, all touching, but none meeting your case—till your descent is arrested by some antiquated monument of medieval legislation or by the unfathomable mysteries of the common law.'[81] After his return from India in 1872 no subject absorbed so much of even his prodigious energies as the attempt to codify various departments of English law. These efforts (including at one point an attempt, in the face of official rebuffs, to produce codification 'by private enterprise') met with no practical success at all; he found himself in the company of several other distinguished jurists in that graveyard. These labours alone indicate—and there is no want of other evidence—how far Stephen was from sharing the Burkean suspicion of system, still less the affection felt by many of his fellow barristers for the hallowed anomalies of legal practice. It is no wonder he was in his element codifying Indian law during his period as Legal Member, undistracted by other cares and relatively unimpeded by political parleying or professional prejudice.

But India is a reminder of just how positive a part Stephen came to think, came to *feel*, that the law had played in the great drama of modern English history. Already in the 1860s the patriotic and imperial dimensions of his engagement with the law were evident:

> There is every reason to believe that by patient and systematic study the law of England might be made a system as complete and not less influential than that of Rome. When we consider the prodigious effects which Roman law produced upon the whole history of modern Europe, and when we bear in mind the fact that the law of England will in another century be the law of immense populations in North America and in the Indian Empire, the importance of making it as good as it can be made cannot be overrated.[82]

The experience of India only heightened this tone. The extraordinary spectacle of a whole subcontinent and its 200 million

[81] [J. F. Stephen], 'Law reform', *Saturday Review*, 1 (1856), 252; quoted in Smith, *Stephen*, 76.

[82] J. F. Stephen, *A General View of the Criminal Law of England* (London, 1890; 1st edn. 1863), 336; quoted in Colaiaco, *Stephen*, 95.

inhabitants being justly and efficiently governed by 'a handful of unsympathetic foreigners' ('I am far from thinking that if they were more sympathetic they would be more efficient') testified to the presence of the virtues Stephen most cherished—'the masterful will, the stout heart, the active brain, the calm nerves, and the strong body'.[83] But above all he saw English law as the distillation of English virtues: 'Our law is, in fact, the sum and substance of what we have to teach' in India; it is 'the gospel of the English'. Moreover, it was a gospel which was none the worse, in his eyes, for the fact that 'it is a compulsory gospel which admits of no dissent and no disobedience'.[84] For Stephen this was no mere metaphor: 'The establishment of a system of law which regulates the most important part of the daily life of the people, constitutes in itself a moral conquest more striking, more durable, and far more solid, than the physical conquest which renders it possible. It exercises an influence over the minds of the people in many ways comparable to that of a new religion.'[85]

This sense of the high, quasi-religious, function of the law informed Stephen's reflection on its role back in England also. This was most evidently and naturally the case when speaking of the criminal law, an area of the law to which he, of course, devoted far more attention than did any of the other figures discussed in this chapter. Without ever ceasing to lament its lack of clear arrangement and its need for codification, he could eulogize the English criminal law as 'generous, humane, and high-minded . . . a great practical school of truth, morality, and compassion . . . eminently favourable to individuals'.[86] His emphasis on the moral significance of the criminal law ('the organ of the moral indignation of mankind') expressed some very deep features of his own temperament. It stirred him in part because it possessed just those qualities which 'sentimental' politics lacked: it was impartial, severe, exact. There is a discernible *frisson* in his constant emphasis on the retributive element in legal penalties, which is more obvious still in his stern endorsement of the elemental satisfaction the public derived from

[83] J. F. Stephen, 'Manchester on India', *The Times*, 4 Jan. 1878: 3; quoted in Colaiaco, *Stephen*, 114.

[84] J. F. Stephen, *A History of the Criminal Law of England*, 3 vols. (London, 1883), iii. 169; quoted in Smith, *Stephen*, 134.

[85] J. F. Stephen, 'Legislation under Mayo', in William Hunter, *Life of the Earl of Mayo*, 2 vols. (London, 1875), ii. 168–9; quoted in Colaiaco, *Stephen*, 118.

[86] Stephen, *General View*, 232–3; quoted in Smith, *Stephen*, 73.

seeing a criminal severely punished ('Murderers are hung with the approbation of all reasonable men'). His dark view of the passions was summed up succinctly in one of his best-known epigrams: 'The criminal law stands to the passion of revenge in much the same relation as marriage to the sexual appetite.'[87] He relished reminding his more squeamish readers of just what was involved in the system of penal sanctions on which their own security rested: as he said in the preface to his *General View*, the book was intended to give a clear account of 'an important part of our institutions, of which surely none can have a greater moral significance, or be more closely connected with broad principles of morality and politics, than those by which men rightfully, deliberately, and in cold blood, kill, enslave, and otherwise torment their fellow-creatures'.[88] Moreover, he believed that with the decline of religious belief, the role of the law as the chief expression of, and sanction for, morality was greatly increased:

> In such circumstances it seems to be specially necessary for those who do care for morality to make its one unquestionable, indisputable sanction as clear, and strong, and emphatic, as words and acts can make it. A man may disbelieve in God, heaven, and hell, he may care little for mankind or society, or for the nation to which he belongs,—let him at least be plainly told what are the acts which will stamp him with infamy, hold him up to public execration, and bring him to the gallows, the gaol, or the lash.[89]

As these quotations suggest, although Stephen could be critical of some of the forms of what he identified as moralism in contemporary attitudes, he essentially took the truths of 'morality' to be unproblematic. He seemed as little inclined as, say, Dr Johnson to relativize those truths, despite occasional, un-Johnsonian, references to 'stages' of historical development. Similarly, it was no part of his purpose to subject the values expressed in the English legal system to fundamental criticism: he could regard individual judicial decisions as mistaken and particular pieces of legislation as unwise, but his role was not that of the social critic who arraigns his society's official beliefs before some supposedly higher moral tribunal. He was concerned, rather, to get the moral significance and social role of law (existing law, essentially) better recognized, and above all he shared

87 Stephen, *General View*, 99; quoted in Colaiaco, *Stephen*, 83, 81.

88 Stephen, *General View*, pp. v–vi; quoted in Colaiaco, *Stephen*, 75.

89 Stephen, *History of the Criminal Law*, iii. 366–7; quoted in Colaiaco, *Stephen*, 210.

the preoccupation—discussed in Chapter 2 above—with finding ways of getting people to live up to the requirements of established morality rather than actually contesting those requirements, save only that he focused more on the use of sanctions when errant humanity strayed too far, and less upon ways of nurturing 'enduring motives to noble action' in the first place.

Although Stephen may have contributed to the development of a more positive attitude towards the law, and although his own temperament clearly found something deeply congenial in the exactness of legal reasoning and the severity of the administration of justice, it is doubtful whether he led many readers to conceive of the great questions of morals and politics in more jurisprudential terms. His persuasiveness as a controversialist, such as it was, rested far more on the uncompromising vigour with which he expressed widely shared moral convictions than on the deployment of his authority as a jurist.[90] *Liberty, Equality, Fraternity*, to take his most significant contribution to the political thought of the period, did not rely upon a distinctively legal idiom any more than *On Liberty* had. The arguments at issue between Mill and Stephen did not require or receive any distinctively jurisprudential formulation: notoriously, they disagreed over where the legal limits to liberty should be set, but essentially they differed in their estimates of human nature and about the need to enforce the religious foundation of morals, rather than in any understanding of the nature of law as such.

Referring to the political writings of both Maine and Stephen, John Morley observed that when the 'scientific lawyer is doubled with the Indian bureaucrat, we are pretty sure . . . that in such a tribunal it will go hard with democracy'.[91] No doubt there is something to the assumption that the mental habits of the lawyer, 'scientific' or otherwise, are not naturally conducive to democratic and reforming enthusiasm, but in Stephen's case neither the tone nor the content of his political writings seems to owe that much to his legal training. Rather, certain deeply individualistic moral convictions seem to have priority, and to have found expression in his reverence for the law in much the same terms as similar

[90] Cf. Barker's observation that *Liberty, Equality, Fraternity* 'is a frank and die-hard statement of the ideas dominant among the educated and governing classes of English society' (Barker, *Political Thought in England*, 150).

[91] John Morley, *Oracles on Man and Government* (London, 1921), 62–3; quoted in Smith, *Stephen*, 196.

sensibilities in some of his contemporaries were gratified by the ostensibly stern and impersonal reasoning of political economy. There was what might be called an Individualist political aesthetic here which Stephen shared. In his earliest, and largely favourable, response to *On Liberty*, he had insisted that self-control and discipline were 'the greatest of all agents in ennobling and developing the character',[92] and hence that Mill's denunciation of the maiming effects of Calvinism was misplaced. Ultimately, it was as a medium for expressing and encouraging these human qualities that Stephen dwelt upon the social significance of the law, and not—to take up the terms of Barker's observation once more—as providing the basis for any systematic kind of *allgemeine Staatslehre*.

VI

As we saw in Section IV above, Maine's intellectual authority, which was so widely felt in the 1870s, only partly rested on his standing as a lawyer: to a much greater extent it derived from the fertility of his historical enquiries, his speculations about types of *society*, and his adroit deployment of his experience of India. In some ways, he found a far more responsive audience for his ideas among proto-anthropologists and future Indian administrators than he did among judges and barristers. Moreover, notwithstanding his celebrated dicta about the modernity of societies based upon contract, it could not be said that he furnished his lay readers with any distinctively *legal* understanding of the nature of the English polity. It is here that Dicey, in other ways so much Maine's inferior in originality and subtlety of mind, pulled off a remarkable coup: his *The Law of the Constitution*, first published in 1885, managed to make the ordinary operations of the common law central to the characterization of the distinctive identity of the English nation. In so doing, he achieved the improbable fusion of the Whig interpretation of English history, the Austinian analysis of law, and the Individualist conception of the state, the whole amalgam presented as the dispassionate conclusion of academic legal science.

This, of course, is hardly the picture of Dicey's significance which emerges from modern legal textbooks, where the question of the accuracy and particularly the continuing relevance of his analysis of

92 [J. F. Stephen], 'Mr Mill on political liberty', *Saturday Review*, 7 (1859), 214.

constitutional law has been the focus of subsequent commentary. In these terms, Dicey's own book has been a striking illustration of the peculiar form of longevity enjoyed by certain classic law texts, treated as they are to the literary equivalent of face-lifts and organ transplants. This process began for *The Law of the Constitution* when Dicey produced eight editions in his own lifetime, the last (1915) with a substantial new introduction surveying changes since 1900. This edition was then reprinted seven times before, in 1939, E. C. S. Wade brought out a fresh edition, which in turn was reprinted six times. The work continued to be such a staple of constitutional law teaching that in 1959 Wade produced a new edition, in which his own introduction outlining the ways in which Dicey's account needed to be brought up to date now ran to over 190 pages, and this edition went through several reprintings, and so on. Dicey's framework, therefore, has exercised enormous influence over several generations of budding lawyers, but the very fact of this continuous use has produced a smooth-surfaced entity known as 'Dicey' whose relation to the historical figure writing in the 1880s has dropped from view. In what follows, I make no pretence of offering a full reconstruction of the historical identity of Dicey's work, still less an adequate assessment of its legal significance: my aim is the more limited one of rereading this particular book in the light of the themes of this chapter.

The most intriguing thing about *The Law of the Constitution* thus considered is how it functioned simultaneously as a legal textbook in search of academic recognition,[93] and as a contribution to a much wider tradition of concern with the distinctiveness of England's historical development. On the surface, the book presents itself as an analytical account of one portion of English law which the student needs to master. Its very title proclaims, after all, that it is an introduction to the 'study' of the constitution, and its author acknowledges several times that it derives from lectures given as Vinerian Professor at Oxford (indeed, as I mentioned in Chapter 6 above, the title of the first edition was, baldly, *Lectures Introductory to the Study of the Law of the Constitution*[94]). Furthermore, Dicey is

[93] An issue which much preoccupied Dicey; see in particular his *Can English Law Be Taught at the Universities? An Inaugural Lecture* (London, 1883).

[94] The revised title first appears in the 3rd edition of 1889. Quotations are taken from the last edition to appear in Dicey's lifetime, the 8th edition of 1915. Apart from converting the original lectures into somewhat differently arranged chapters and

noticeably emphatic in insisting that the book confines itself to expounding one portion of the actually existing law of England, explicitly distancing himself not only from other, historical or political, ways of considering the English constitution, but also from law professors responsible for neighbouring domains. But this apparently modest limitation of the book's purpose in fact disguises a very considerable act of intellectual imperialism.

The most immediate way to begin to recapture some of the larger significance which Dicey's work would have had for his original lay readers is to note that he begins with quotations from Burke and Hallam. He does so, it is true, in order to insist that 'the present generation must of necessity look on the constitution in a spirit different from the sentiments either of 1791 or of 1818', and more especially to insist that the 'duty of a professor' is 'neither to attack nor to defend the constitution, but simply to explain its laws'.[95] (One of the many indications that we are here in the late rather than the early nineteenth century is the way that what was once the most passionately disputed issue in current politics could now be claimed as the province of an academic 'subject'.) Nevertheless, the fact that he does begin in this way indicates that he recognizes that many of his readers will see the book as an intervention in a discussion hitherto largely conducted in the terms he is repudiating: a law professor in the late twentieth century would not, it seems safe to say, feel the need to distinguish his contribution in this way. Dicey presents this attempt simply to establish a clear account of the actually existing *law* of the constitution as something of a novelty in discussion of the subject, the first fruits of the recently established academic legal science.

He distinguishes this enquiry from that of the two groups who have previously contributed most to understanding the English constitution, namely the historians and the 'political theorists'. He lavishes praise on both, but firmly limits the value of their contributions. He takes, as one of the most popular and influential examples of the first of these genres, *The Growth of the English Constitution* by his old Oxford friend and (before the Home Rule split) Liberal ally, E. A Freeman. He cites, surely a little

entirely reorganizing the presentation of the comparison with French *droit administratif* (and adding a series of appendices dealing with technical points), the later editions reproduce the text of the 1st edition with only a few minor modifications.

[95] Dicey, *Law of the Constitution*, 3, 3–4.

mischievously, the topic-headings from Freeman's first two chapters, commending the erudition they represent, and then observes: 'But in regard to English law and the law of the constitution, the *Landesgemeinden* of Uri, the witness of Homer, the earldormen, the constitution of the Witenagemót, and a lot more of fascinating matter are mere antiquarianism.' By contrast, 'the function of the trained lawyer . . . is to know and be able to state what are the principles of law which actually and at present day exist in England'. The slightly prissy or self-important stress on 'trained lawyer' and the reference to 'principles' (as opposed to the mass of cases and statutes themselves) were both small signs of Dicey's campaign to justify the role of systematic legal study. He similarly discriminates the contribution of the 'political theorists' (Bagehot and Hearn are his examples), again valuable in its own way but not 'what as lawyers we are in search of'.[96]

Even within the company of academic lawyers, he distances his own field from that of his immediate neighbours. He mockingly proposed that if, as is sometimes suggested, there is no such thing as constitutional *law* strictly speaking, but only an assemblage of law-like customs and conventions, then the subject should be transferred

> either to my friend the Corpus Professor of Jurisprudence, because it is his vocation to deal with the oddities or outlying portions of legal science, or to my friend the Chichele Professor of International Law, because he being a teacher of law which is not law, and being accustomed to expound those rules of public ethics which are miscalled international law, will find himself at home in expounding political ethics which, on the hypothesis under consideration, are miscalled constitutional law.

In the time-honoured fashion of the sardonic lecturer, the mannered politeness of this only makes its dismissiveness more patent: Dicey was in effect pandering to the prejudices of the practising lawyer in thus confining the sense of law, positivistically, to 'rules enforced by the courts'. Dicey had Austinian sympathies, which may be dimly visible here, but he regarded even Austin as too caught up in 'the metaphysics of law'. For his own project he claimed a more limited but locally more persuasive authority: 'The true law of the constitution is in short to be gathered from the sources whence we collect the law of England in respect to any other topic.'[97] There is surely a hint of professional pride in thus being able to eschew all

[96] Dicey, *Law of the Constitution*, 14, 20. [97] Ibid. 22, 33.

those kinds of speculation which would have no standing among hard-headed judges and barristers. But, at the same time, Dicey was not in fact willing to forgo the opportunity to deploy his authority to comment on matters which lay far beyond this ostensibly modest definition of competence. Though presented as an austere legal textbook, *The Law of the Constitution* constantly exceeds or escapes this limited identity: it is implicitly historical, political, comparative, celebratory.

The three chief explicit claims of the book are well known—indeed, thay have become so familiar as no longer to be regarded as the claims of any one author in particular. Dicey proposed that the distinguishing characteristics of the English constitution were the sovereignty of Parliament, the rule of law, and the ultimate dependence of the conventions of the constitution upon the law of the constitution. These claims have attracted an enormous body of legal comment in the past hundred years that need not detain us here.[98] If, however, one places the book in the context of English political thought of the period, the second claim in particular, about 'the rule of law', assumes a further significance beyond the confines of legal commentary.

Under the heading 'the rule of law', Dicey embraced three 'distinct though kindred conceptions'. The first was that 'no man is punishable or can be lawfully made to suffer in body or goods except for a distinct breach of law established in the ordinary legal manner before the ordinary Courts of the land. In this sense the rule of law is contrasted with every system of government based on the exercise by persons in authority of wide, arbitrary, or discretionary powers of constraint.' The second was 'not only that with us no man is above the law, but (what is a different thing) that here every man, whatever be his rank or condition, is subject to the ordinary law of the realm and amenable to the jurisdiction of the ordinary tribunals'. And the third was that

> the general principles of the constitution (as for example the right to personal liberty, or the right of public meeting) are with us the result of judicial decisions determining the rights of private persons in particular cases brought before the Courts; whereas under many foreign constitutions

[98] Much of this literature is summarized in Cosgrove, *Rule of Law*. Two contributions of particular interest, however, are Ivor Jennings, 'In praise of Dicey', *Public Administration*, 13 (1935), 123–34, and F. H. Lawson, 'Dicey revisited', *Political Studies*, 7 (1959), 109–26, 207–21.

the security (such as it is) given to the rights of individuals results, or appears to result, from the general principles of the constitution.[99]

The continuity between these three statements is at least as much a matter of tone as of substance. A certain dry satisfaction is present in the insistence on the regular, everyday nature of the English situation, the situation 'with us' as he cosily, inclusively, puts it; the words 'ordinary' and 'particular' which occur so often carry a distinctly positive force. This stylistic point also brings out how each conception is in fact defined in opposition to some contrasting set of arrangements, stated or implied, in which exceptional or 'extra-ordinary' categories have a prominent role. But there is an interesting difference between the alternative with which the third conception is contrasted and those implied by the first two. In both of the first two cases the contrast is with a system in which the incidence or application of the law is in some way not uniform, where, that is to say, certain individuals, whether as agents or as victims, can find themselves in an exceptional position, not subject to or protected by the law like everyone else. But the third sense is contrasted with all those systems where individual freedoms are enshrined in some statement of principle having constitutional status: here the actual incidence of the law may be uniform and without defined exceptions, but the rights of individuals are treated as deductions from a general statement of principle rather than as the outcome of a series of piecemeal decisions. Furthermore, Dicey emphasizes that English liberties are the product of the legal remedies operating between private individuals, or between individuals and public authorities, and not part of a separate system of public law.

Focusing on the implied contrasts in this way suggests that Dicey's three senses of the 'rule of law' interestingly run together two different aspects of the traditional celebration of England's exceptional political development. The contrasts in the first two senses restate the classic eighteenth-century view (notably expressed by Voltaire, for example) of England as the land where, uniquely in modern Europe, arbitrary arrest and despotic power were unknown. But the contrast implied in the third conception suggests a more distinctively nineteenth-century, and especially post-Revolutionary, view. It is in fact a version of Burke's famous elaboration of the

[99] *Law of the Constitution*, 183–4, 189, 191.

contrast between empty declarations of principle—Dicey's 'security (such as it is)'—and an achieved heritage of particular liberties.[100]

In the course of the book, Dicey recurs frequently to the ways in which several European states have attempted to reproduce the supposed merits of the English constitution, Belgium providing a particularly quotable example. But the logic of his argument as it emerges in this analysis is that in fact other countries *cannot* reproduce this most distinctive merit of English institutions: the only way in which, starting from the present and working with their existing legal systems, they can attempt to establish a similar set of liberties is by incorporating the supposed principles in a document having constitutional status, whereas the crucial distinctiveness of English arrangements precisely lies in the way that the protection of liberty does *not* derive from the special authority of such a document, but from 'the ordinary workings of the courts'. In several places Dicey addresses what he takes to be a common unreflective assumption among his readers to the effect that the various aspects of the rule of law must surely be something shared by all civilized countries, and hence not distinctive of England. But not only does he want to insist that, as far as his first two senses of 'the rule of law' are concerned, their operation *has* historically been unique and is still in fact not common; he also argues in effect that England is bound to remain beyond imitation with respect to the third sense. Only the United States can compare—'The rule of law is as marked a feature of the United States as of England'[101]—but that owes nothing to any declaration of rights, and derives very precisely from their having inherited a body of law in which the same liberties are effectively protected. In so far as Dicey has been placed in any historical tradition by subsequent commentators, he has, not without reason, been regarded as a disciple of Bentham and Austin; but it ought by now to be clear that he was at the same time far from immune to that 'diffused Burkeanism' that was such a feature of English political thought in the nineteenth century. In this respect, if not in others, Ivor Jennings was right when in 1935 he roundly declared: 'Dicey was a Whig'.[102]

100 For the suggestion that Burke's position itself had involved a celebration of the Common Law tradition, see J. G. A. Pocock, 'Burke and the Ancient Constitution: a problem in the history of ideas', in his *Politics, Language, and Time* (London, 1971).

101 *Law of the Constitution*, 196.

102 Jennings, 'In praise of Dicey', 123. On 'diffused Burkeanism' see Collini, Winch, and Burrow, *That Noble Science of Politics*, 19–20.

That being said, it becomes necessary to establish what, if anything, was distinctive about Dicey's handling of the well-worn theme of England's peculiarly fortunate history. The short answer is that he restated that theme in the coolly professional idiom of the 'trained lawyer'. He did not dilate on the supposed qualities of national character, such as 'the Englishman's love of liberty' or 'taste for independence and self-reliance'; the wildest rhetorical flight of this type he was willing to allow himself was a reference to 'the legal habits of Englishmen'.[103] Nor did he show any great tenderness for the preference for local or voluntary action against central or state power which several Whig historians had noted: he recognized, and did not obviously regret, that the common law owed its early growth to the centralizing tendencies of Norman monarchs. Nor, finally, did he wax eloquent—it is not a term which Dicey's prose invites—about the sagacity of successive generations of distinguished statesmen, the heroes of the story of English liberty in the older, Macaulayesque vein; for Dicey, English institutions were hardly to be seen as a deliberate achievement, but rather as the residue secreted by a long series of legal judgements about particular, complicated cases.

The kind of 'scientific Whiggism' which this represented comes out particularly clearly in his chapter on 'The right to freedom of discussion'. England's proud record of tolerance on this matter was commonly regarded as the jewel in the crown of English liberty. Dicey took some pleasure in showing that there was no such 'right' in England; the terms 'freedom of discussion' and 'liberty of the press' were unknown to the law. What *had* been true was that the expression of opinion, whether in print or orally, had long been subject to the ordinary laws of libel and slander. These laws had not themselves been 'specially favourable to free speech or to free writing', but in contrast to those countries in which these activities had been subject to the rulings of special tribunals, the very fact of the regular application of the ordinary laws of the land had itself provided a degree of protection unknown elsewhere. In France, 'the general reverence for the authority of the state' tolerated the existence of all kinds of special tribunals; 'The control exercised in different forms by the executive over literature has, therefore, in the main fully harmonised with the other institutions of France.' That this had not been true of English history for several centuries was

[103] *Law of the Constitution*, 263.

not, Dicey repeatedly insisted, due to any greater love of tolerance for its own sake in England. None the less, the attempts by Tudor and Stuart monarchs to extend the Royal Prerogative or exercise discretionary power through extra-legal bodies like Star Chamber had been resisted precisely because Englishmen had by then grown used to living under 'the rule of law'. 'Hundreds of Englishmen who hated toleration and cared little for freedom of speech, entertained a keen jealousy of arbitrary power, and a fixed determination to be ruled in accordance with the law of the land.'[104]

One consequence of this deliberately deflating account of English constitutional achievement was that the heroes of Dicey's story, in so far as it had any, prove to be the lawyers, and above all the judges. Since his central claim was that the law of the constitution is nothing other than the ordinary law of the land as it has developed though a series of specific judgements (though statute had played some part, it too was ultimately dependent on judicial interpretation), he is able to assert at several points that 'our constitution . . . is a judge-made constitution'.[105] Moreover, given that the celebrated historic fights about the English constitution were, in Dicey's view, fundamentally fights about upholding or setting aside the law of the land, they necessarily revolved around the question of the independence of the Bench. His account, in this vein, of the great constitutional struggles of the seventeenth century concentrated upon this question, and he re-worked the standard Whig view to insist that 'the Parliamentary leaders . . . saw, more or less distinctly, that the independence of the Bench was the sole security for the maintenance of the common law', and that Coke 'in battling for the rights of judges was asserting the rights of the nation'. Furthermore, Dicey was at pains to insist that judges were still the chief upholders of English liberties: they 'are in truth, though not in name, invested with the means of hampering or supervising the whole administrative action of the government and of at once putting a veto upon any proceeding not authorised by the letter of the law'. Dicey's prose became uncharacteristically heated in speaking of the 'reverence' for the Bench which he alleged had consequently grown up in England (not a view necessarily shared by all his countrymen in 1885, still less

[104] Ibid. 243, 261, 263.
[105] Ibid. 192; cf 217: 'the law of the English constitution is judge-made law', and similar expressions elsewhere.

by the time of the eighth edition in 1915); 'They, rather than the government, represent the august dignity of the State.'[106]

The tone here is about as far as it could be from that of the Philosophic Radical denunciations of judges as the deliberately obscurantist guardians of vested interests. Dicey's book implicitly encouraged a far more favourable view of the role of the contemporary legal profession, something which no doubt contributed to its success as a textbook in the increasingly professionalized world of legal education. But the book also addressed, again implicitly, a more historical and more subtle denigration of the role of lawyers than had been found in either the Benthamite or the more popular Dickensian criticisms. In the more recent versions of the Whig interpretation of English history, notably those by Stubbs and Freeman, lawyers had been represented in a very unfavourable light. In these accounts, the schematizing tendency of the legal mind—its taste for what Stubbs stigmatized as 'theoretic principles'—constantly jeopardized the delicate growth of English institutions by attempting to impose the strait-jacket of legal formulae.[107]

Dicey's account seems at times almost designed to rebut this aspersion on the 'un-English' tendencies of the legal mind. In discussing Habeas Corpus, for example, he contended that it was not in fact some ringing declaration of the right to individual liberty and hence an exception to his general argument, but rather it consisted of the provision, through the ordinary judicial process, of a remedy for an assigned wrong (that is, unlawful arrest). In this respect it was exemplary of the general tendency of English law: 'The whole history of the writ of *Habeas Corpus* illustrates the predominant attention paid under the English constitution to "remedies", that is to modes of procedure by which to secure respect for a legal right, and by which to turn a merely nominal into an effective or real right.' It was 'the great merit' of 'this lawyer-like mode of dealing with a fundamental right', in marked contrast to airy declarations of principle in the Continental manner, that it concentrated upon securing effective enforcement of the right for the individual. In generalizing the implication of this example, Dicey was implicitly

[106] *Law of the Constitution*, 224, 218, 389.

[107] On this, and Stubbs's and Freeman's hostility to lawyers more generally, see John W. Burrow, *A Liberal Descent: Victorian Historians and the English Past* (Cambridge, 1981), 133–5.

controverting the characterization of lawyers offered by Stubbs and Freeman: the Habeas Corpus Acts 'are intended, as is generally the case with legislation which proceeds under the influence of lawyers, simply to meet actual and experienced difficulties'.[108] It would be hard to find any more favourable terms under which to recommend a group of men to an audience drawn largely from the late Victorian governing class.

It will be evident that much of what I am presenting as the polemical significance of Dicey's book rests on teasing out the tone and intended force of his writing rather than upon a straightforward summary of his explicit argument, and this can always arouse suspicions of over-interpretation. But my reading of *The Law of the Constitution* can be buttressed by references to Dicey's minor writings, which indicate, among other things, that his preoccupation with the centrality of the law to England's distinctiveness was of long standing. A particularly revealing source in this regard is his review of the first volume of Stubbs's *Constitutional History of England*, which appeared in the New York *Nation* in 1875. Dicey was duly admiring of the work: he clearly found Stubbs's remorseless accumulation of detail and attentiveness to unintended consequences congenial, and in both men the discipline of mid-Victorian scholarship provided a medium for expressing a temperamental disdain for popular enthusiasm. At the same time, Dicey's desire to construe the book in terms of his own preoccupations was constantly tugging at the respectful prose of his review. Stubbs had almost wilfully eschewed speculation or even generalization, but, suggested Dicey, *after* reading his great work one was far better placed than ever before to answer the question (not actually asked by Stubbs, at least in so many words), 'what is the real character and the true merit of that constitution?' Dicey's answer, now clearly standing on Stubbs's shoulders rather than summarizing him, distanced itself from popular notions about the special excellence of the English constitution resting in the way it had from earliest times represented 'the people', or any of the other shibboleths of what may be called 'vulgar Liberalism.' Instead, Dicey proposed that in its form the English constitution, like so many medieval institutions, was a tissue of 'fictions', while in substance its defining quality had been 'the rule of law.' He recognized the paradox that this foundation of English

[108] *Law of the Constitution*, 216–17.

liberties owed most to the centralizing tendencies of the early Norman kings, but none the less his conclusion was that 'the essential peculiarity of English political development' was to be found in the fact that 'through a fortunate combination of circumstances, the rule of law was established in England at a time when it was unknown in every other great country of Europe'.[109]

Interestingly, Dicey did not, in 1875, attempt to present this view as anything other than an interpretation of English *history*; he did not, in other words, claim to be offering any kind of authoritative digest of the *law* at this point, though the continuity with the implicit argument of his later book is patent. Moreover, one does not have to venture very far in Dicey's other occasional writings to be struck by the way in which he came to generalize this interpretation more broadly still. Long before he even gave the lectures that became *The Law of the Constitution*, he was already insisting that 'English modes of thought and feeling have been profoundly affected by the habits and associations produced by the English law' and, more ambitiously still, that 'English law is the most original creation of the English genius'.[110] Dicey was in general highly sceptical of the value of historical research, but late in his life he came to praise Maitland's work with all the generosity of one who sees his own pet convictions authoritatively supported: Maitland's great achievement, he suggested in 1910, had been to show that the growth of the law was 'the essential characteristic of the history of England. . . . [Maitland] established once and forever that English law lies at the basis of English politics, and at the centre of the development of the English constitution.' And by this date he could allow the patriotic pride which had always underlain this view to receive extravagant expression: 'English law', he declared expansively, 'is the most original creation of the English intellect and will be the most lasting monument of England's greatness.'[111]

Of course, in the context of the dominant end-of-the-century debate about Individualism versus Collectivism, Dicey's characterization of English law involved an obliquely partisan dimension. As

[109] A. V. Dicey, 'Stubbs's *Constitutional History of England*', *Nation*, 20 (4 Mar. 1875), 152–4.

[110] A. V. Dicey, 'Digby on the history of English law', *Nation*, 21 (9 Dec. 1875), 373–4.

[111] A. V. Dicey, 'Professor Maitland', *Nation*, 91 (29 Sept. 1910), 293. This article was, ostensibly, a review of H. A. L. Fisher's *Frederick [*sic*] William Maitland: A Biographical Sketch* (Cambridge, 1910).

he construed it, the rule of law offered a protection of individual freedom against 'interference' by the government: 'Individual freedom is thereby more thoroughly protected in England against oppression by the government than in any other European country.'[112] A similarly 'negative' conception of liberty was implied in his worries about the scope of the state's power in a system of *droit administratif*. As his later work on *Law and Opinion* made plain, he believed that the pressures of democracy were diverting English law away from its 'naturally' Individualist path. Like Maine and others anxious to limit the sovereignty of Parliament under a democratic franchise, he developed a new respect for the obstructive powers of the United States constitution and its Supreme Court interpreters, and a fresh interest in the virtues of devices such as the referendum, both striking departures from English constitutional practice.[113] But perhaps the greatest oddity of his later position is that, having so thoroughly identified an Individualist conception of the state with the English legal tradition, he ends up treating Bentham, of all people, as exemplifying the adaptive wisdom of the common law.[114]

In one sense, Dicey may seem to be the most striking counter-example to Ernest Barker's reflection, cited at the beginning of this chapter, about the absence of fruitful interplay between law and political thought in England. After all, he, more than any other writer in the period except possibly Maitland (who never reached such a wide audience), made the law central to the English people's conception of their own identity and presented it as the concrete embodiment of the dominant political convictions of his class. Yet in another sense Dicey *does* illustrate Barker's point: neither *The Law of the Constitution* nor *Law and Public Opinion* can really be said to represent a contribution to the 'study of political science in terms of law', in part because Dicey's determinedly local focus precluded any aspiration to develop general conceptions. Dicey's work was not even jurisprudential in the Austinian sense, or rather the narrow

112 *Law of the Constitution*, 389.

113 On the former, see Hugh Tulloch, 'Changing British attitudes towards the United States in the 1880s', *Historical Journal*, 20 (1977), 825–40; on the latter see, in addition to Cosgrove, *Rule of Law*, Hugh Tulloch, 'A. V. Dicey and the Irish Question 1870–1922', *Irish Jurist*, 15 (1980), 137–65.

114 A similar point is made, from a somewhat different point of view, by Cocks: 'It is extraordinary that the assailant of Blackstone should end by being used to sustain just those traditions of which Blackstone would surely have approved' (*Modern Bar*, 205).

sense in which Austin's project had been construed after his death; he made no attempt to define the nature of constitutional law as such, or to deal with 'the oddities or the outlying portions of legal science' which he had, only half-teasingly, proposed as the scope of the Oxford Chair of Jurisprudence. Rather than calling up Savigny, Gierke, and *allgemeine Staatslehre*, Dicey's footnotes take the reader into the quill-pen-and-high-stool world of 'Powell v. Apollo Candle Co' and '9 & 10 Will. III. c. 35, as altered by 53 Geo. III. c. 160'.

And yet, to tilt the assessment back in the original direction once more, Dicey very successfully installed the language and preoccupations of the legal profession at the heart of a widely shared understanding of English politics and English history.[115] In these terms, his work had a more direct persuasiveness than Maine's had done, a fact reflected in a marked difference of style or tone between the two writers. Dicey's prose was far less epigrammatic and stylish than Maine's; his strength was rather in clarity of arrangement and thoroughness of analysis, showing the recurrence across a large body of cases of a few simple principles. Much of the excitement of Maine's work derived from the sense that his daring speculations were based upon the most recent findings of international scholarship, whereas Dicey's analysis rested, almost defiantly, upon evidence taken from texts long familiar to the working lawyer. Both authors laid claim to a kind of scientific authority, above partisan sentiment and vulgar prejudice, but in at least one respect the implied relation to the reader was different. Maine cultivated a kind of literary gravity that, as I remarked above, easily slipped into a weary hauteur, expressing disdain for the incorrigible folly of the uninstructed. Dicey's characteristic tone was more directly pedagogic, firmly leading the reader to construct the approved order out of apparent chaos. At one level, this suggests that Maine was addressing his peers, who were few, and Dicey his pupils, who were many, and there is some truth in that way of stating the contrast. But it also meant that Dicey flattered the prejudices of a wider readership than Maine did, despite his more austerely academic literary identity. This was above all true of his Whiggish pride in England's unique good fortune and his continuing confidence in the common

[115] On Dicey's success, particularly in reaching a non-professional audience, see Cosgrove, *Rule of Law*, ch. IV, esp. 69.

law as the guarantee of individual freedom. As a result, though Maine enjoyed a European reputation as a scholar, it was Dicey who left more of a mark on English political language in the three decades before 1914.

VII

Both Maine and Dicey had devoted a considerable part of their energies to justifying, establishing, and improving legal education, yet from this distance one has to conclude that organized legal education was a very mixed blessing for the larger purposes both men entertained of broadening the intellectual culture of lawyers and placing law nearer the centre of Victorian public life. Certainly, the establishment of the university study of law did, as we have seen, encourage the writing of legal texts and create the role of the legal professor as a figure of some public standing. But at the same time, and far more consequentially, it set in train a process which was increasingly responsive to the practical requirements of just that profession whose members Maine and Dicey had hoped it would liberalize. The beginnings of this process have been described above, and by the 1890s its outcome was distressingly apparent to those who had hoped to foster a greater jurisprudential awareness in lawyers and laymen alike. Bryce's valedictory lecture upon his retirement from the Chair of Civil Law at Oxford in 1893 amounted to an acknowledgement of defeat on this score:

> We have accomplished less than we hoped in raising up a band of young lawyers who would maintain, even in the midst of London practice, an interest in legal history and juristic speculation. The number of persons in England who care for either subject is undeniably small, probably smaller, in proportion to the size and influence of the profession, than in any other civilised country; and it increases so slowly as to seem to discredit the efforts of the Universities.[116]

The result, as observed by Vinogradoff, Maine's most faithful disciple, was that 'liberal and professional education are indissolubly connected on the continent; they are separated in England'.[117]

Furthermore, the two 'subjects' Bryce mentioned were themselves

116 James Bryce, 'Valedictory lecture', in *Studies in History and Jurisprudence*, ii. 518.

117 Paul Vinogradoff, 'The teaching of Sir Henry Maine' (1904), *The Collected Papers of Paul Vinogradoff*, 2 vols. (Oxford, 1928), i. 279.

becoming more specialized and less closely related to each other. 'Juristic speculation' became increasingly confined to a rather positivistically conceived form of 'analytical jurisprudence.' The activity carried on under this head by the end of the century tended to exclude reflection upon such matters as the nature of the law as a social institution or its relation to other intellectual traditions or the role of the legal profession, and to concentrate instead upon providing a systematic account of the principles implicit in existing law considered as an autonomous body of rules.[118] This conception of the activity thus encouraged even academic lawyers to distance 'the science of law' from the larger concerns of social and political theory. Viewed from within this framework, even Austin himself could be regarded as deplorably speculative: Pollock complained that Austin's

> philosophy of positive law is encumbered and entangled with trappings of moral philosophy which have no business there. It would not be too much to say that Professor Holland's *Elements of Jurisprudence* is the first work of pure scientific jurisprudence which has appeared in England—that is, of the general science of law distinctly separated from the ethical part of politics.[119]

This austere conception was given canonical expression in the introduction to Pollock and Maitland:

> It has been usual for writers commencing the exposition of any particular system of law to undertake, to a greater or lesser extent, philosophical discussion of the nature of laws in general, and definitions of the most general terms of jurisprudence. We purposefully refrain from any such undertaking. The philosophical analysis and definition of law belongs, in our judgement, neither to the historical nor to the dogmatic science of law, but to the theoretical part of politics. . . . The matter of legal science is not an ideal result of ethical or political analysis; it is the actual result of the facts of human nature and history.[120]

As this last quotation hints, Bryce's other 'subject'—legal history—was also taking an increasingly specialized form. Maitland himself

[118] This case is argued, with a very full range of supporting citations, in David Sugarman, 'Legal theory, the Common-Law mind, and the making of the textbook tradition', in William Twining (ed.), *Legal Theory and Common Law* (Oxford, 1986), 26–61. See also Cocks, *Maine*, chs. VI and VII. Both authors remark that analytical jurisprudence became increasingly deferential towards the assumptions and etiquette of the profession, especially as exemplified by judges.

[119] Frederick Pollock, 'The history of the science of politics', *Fortnightly Review*, 32 (1882), 391.

[120] Frederick Pollock and F. W. Maitland, *The History of English Law before the Time of Edward I*, 2 vols. (Cambridge, 1895), i, p. xxiii.

occupies the major role here, of course, but any attempt briefly to characterize his contribution to this process risks culpable over-simplification. There is ample evidence that he was no friend to jurisprudence in either its Austinian or its Mainian incarnation. His scorn for the former was almost boundless ('J.A. = O' was its pithiest formulation[121]), and although he treated Maine with more respect, he resisted his expansive conception of historical jurisprudence. In 1896 he roundly declared, 'I have not for many years past believed in what calls itself historical jurisprudence.'[122] Maitland may have accentuated the social and linguistic gulf between medieval and modern England in order to counter the practising lawyer's professional need to construe earlier legal documents in the light of subsequent interpretation: 'What is really required of the practising lawyer is not . . . a knowledge of medieval law as it was in the Middle Ages, but rather a knowledge of medieval law as interpreted by modern courts to suit modern facts.'[123] The need to distance his own researches from this Common Law tradition arguably encouraged Maitland to cultivate his scholarly detachment; sheer intellectual fastidiousness played its part, too. But the outcome was a body of work which addressed the concerns of other medieval historians far more directly than it did those of other jurists.

But it would be far too simple to see Maitland as denying legal history any bearing on larger social and political issues. There was, of course, a kind of *sotto voce* commentary on contemporary affairs even in Maitland's apparently chaste scholarship, but it was, so to say, encoded or at one remove. Maine had cowed many of his first readers with the authority of his abstruse learning, yet his writings seem accessible, expansive, and polemical when set beside the mass of historical detail and arcane technicality in which Maitland delighted. For the most part, Maitland's writings are not those of a 'public moralist', and his professional 'voice' did not easily lend itself

121 Letter to Pollock, 4 Dec. 1899; *The Letters of Frederic William Maitland*, ed. C. H. S. Fifoot (Cambridge, 1965), 204; for similar sentiments see 39, 208, 222. Maitland perhaps exaggerated the extent to which current legal and political theory derived from Austin: see his references to 'our popular English *staatslehre*' in his introduction to Otto von Gierke, *Political Theories of the Middle Age*, trans. with intro. by F. W. Maitland (Cambridge, 1900), p. xi.

122 Maitland to Dicey, n.d.(?Autumn 1896), Dicey Papers, Glasgow University Library, Gen. MSS 508 (14). I am grateful to the manuscript librarian for furnishing me with a copy of this letter.

123 F. W. Maitland, 'Why the history of English law is not Written', in *The Collected Papers of Frederic William Maitland*, ed. H. A. L. Fisher, 3 vols. (Cambridge, 1911), ii. 483.

to direct participation in political debate; to that extent he does represent a further stage of academic specialization. Revealingly, his impact on the political controversies of the early twentieth century largely depended upon the work of intermediaries, figures such as Figgis, Laski, or Barker.

Those names are a reminder that there is one late episode in the relations between legal and political thought which, though it falls outside the limits of this chapter, needs to be mentioned, namely Pluralism. Without entering upon a discussion of the episode here, it may be worth observing that for all the application of Pluralist ideas to major contemporary issues like the position of trade unions or the status of churches, the writings in which those ideas were developed bore a decidedly academic stamp when compared to the works discussed earlier in this chapter. It is noticeable that the direct political significance of Maitland's writings about the history of corporations was largely a retrospective matter; when they were published they did not cause the stir among non-specialist readers which, say, Maine's books had done (in part, of course, because the constitution of the audience itself had changed). English political argument in the Edwardian period never really adopted the idiom of Pluralism; only in the form of the partially Pluralist, and not particularly juristic, writings of G. D. H. Cole and, even more remotely, the Webbs after the war did this strand of thinking seem to impinge directly on political debate.[124]

By that point, as I suggested in the opening chapter of this book, the several élites in English society were becoming more specialized and less convergent. This emerging contrast should remind us that Maine, Stephen, and Dicey were emphatically members of a *governing* class, albeit in its most intellectual guise, and discussion of the principles that should guide legislation formed part of a continuous conversation which took place now in their clubs, now in their private correspondence, now in articles in the newspapers and periodicals, now on the India Council or one of the other administrative and legal Boards or Commissions to which they were

[124] There is a substantial secondary literature on Pluralism which, perhaps inevitably, tends to accord it a greater political relevance than I have done here; for a useful introduction, see David Nicholls, *The Pluralist State* (London, 1975), and Rodney Barker, *Political Ideas in Modern Britain* (London, 1978). For an interpretation which, concentrating on the *content* of Maitland's thought, suggests a considerable continuity with earlier Whig political thinking, see J. W. Burrow, *Whigs and Liberals: Continuity and Change in English Political Thought* (Oxford, 1988), ch. 6.

from time to time appointed. To this extent, their concerns were not academic, in either sense of the word: jurisprudence was an ancillary branch of a notional science of politics which itself was above all a school of statesmanship. Some of the items which constantly recurred on the agenda of politics in this period gave these concerns a particular salience; imperial matters, for example, especially India, conferred a kind of relevance on both the comparative jurist and the writer of codes and digests, while, as I remarked earlier, the constitutional implications of successive policies towards Ireland gave a public role to such 'experts' as Dicey and Bryce. Moreover, successive extensions of the franchise conferred a kind of topicality upon the otherwise somewhat abstruse legal arrangements that might check popular sovereignty: Maine's analysis of the working of the American constitution or Dicey's of the operation of the referendum capitalized on this. More broadly, the extent to which all these figures shared what I have called the moral aesthetic of Individualism has to be recognized, a set of values which found a more than purely contingent expression in their better-known teachings about contract and the rule of law. As a result, the kinds of moral values explored in earlier chapters of this book did not function as the basis for a critique of the parochial or otherwise defective qualities of the English legal system; rather they provided the idiom in which its virtues could be celebrated.

But in relation to practising lawyers, the figures discussed here were exceptional, even aberrant. Modern scholars have emphasized the strongly inward-looking nature of the nineteenth-century legal profession, with its deep attachment to its own traditions and mores, and its comparative insulation from, or only belated response to, the political and intellectual currents that disturbed the wider society.[125] To have attempted to address such issues in a systematic way was already to have set oneself at some distance from that profession. The obituary of Fitzjames Stephen in the *Law Times* in 1894 classified him as 'a legislator, a jurist, a controversialist, rather than a lawyer', and when the obituarist in the *Law Journal* observed that he

[125] See esp. Cocks, *Modern Bar*, ch. VIII; cf. Daniel Duman, 'Pathway to professionalism: the English Bar in the eighteenth and nineteenth centuries', *Journal of Social History* (1980), 615–28. The way in which judges and barristers remained attached to strict ideas of *laissez-faire* long after they had become unfashionable among the wider educated population is emphasized by P. S. Atiyah, *The Rise and Fall of Freedom of Contract* (Oxford, 1979).

had been 'a philosopher among lawyers and a lawyer among philosophers', the description was, at the very least, two-edged, and no compliment in the eyes of the majority of the barristers and solicitors who read that professional publication.[126] Subsequent developments, moreover, hardly made it more likely that the law would prove a fruitful seedbed of either social theory or social criticism in Britain in the first part of the twentieth century.

In the preface to the republished version of his controversial 1958 Maccabaean Lecture on 'The enforcement of morals', Lord Devlin observed, with the air of one acknowledging the force of received wisdom: 'A man who has passed his life in the practice of the law is not as a rule well equipped to discourse on questions of jurisprudence', and then added, perhaps ruefully recalling the sharp criticism his lecture had elicited from the legal philosophers, 'and I was certainly no exception to that rule'.[127] Those who disagreed with his potentially illiberal thesis about the law's duty to enforce morality, especially in this instance sexual morality, may well have felt that his lecture bore out the truth of the received commonplace. But, taking a wider view, we may now wonder about the remark's casual assumption of an unbridgeable gulf between legal practice and thinking about the law, and this may lead us to reflect upon the historical oddity of the situation that it takes for granted.

Obviously, one can hardly expect practising lawyers, in any system, to devote a large part of their time to issues of general jurisprudence. But the peculiar historical development of the legal profession in England, reinforced but not entirely determined by the profoundly empirical character of the Common Law tradition, has possibly created a wider division than is to be found elsewhere between, on the one hand, the intellectual habits and preoccupations of lawyers, judges, and even teachers of law, and, on the other, the forms of attention given by the wider culture to jurisprudential issues in the broadest sense. The development of legal education in the late nineteenth century, which promised at first to help bridge this gulf, came eventually to drive a deeper wedge between the legal and the wider intellectual worlds. This outcome was not altogether peculiar to the development of legal education, of course: something similar could be said about several other 'subjects' which grew out of

[126] *Law Times*, 96 (1894), 455, quoted in Cocks, *Modern Bar*, 227; *Law Journal*, 29 (1894), 169, quoted in Smith, *Stephen*, 249.

[127] Patrick Devlin, *The Enforcement of Morals* (Oxford, 1965), p. v.

the shared culture represented by those conversations in the mid-Victorian periodicals. But the special position of law and the structure of the legal profession gave a distinctive twist to the story. Arguably the Common Law tradition, always suspicious of 'theorizing' as alien or at best irrelevant, had never been particularly responsive to the likes even of Maine and Dicey, and the subsequent development of legal education entrenched rather than undermined these attitudes. Questions of jurisprudence soon came to occupy a relatively minor place in the legal syllabus, a decorative extra often thought suitable for those without the talents for practice. Seen in this way, the figures discussed in this chapter represented the moment when the first generation of academic lawyers, writing on broadly jurisprudential matters, could aspire to address lawyer and layman alike. As the habits of the profession reasserted themselves, abetted rather than hindered by the direction taken by educational specialization and other social changes, this moment passed. Thus, the observation with which this chapter began finds its final, and only mildly paradoxical, confirmation in the fact that these writers have come to occupy a more prominent place in Victorian intellectual history, and especially the history of political and social thought, than they have in the history of English law.

IV

English Genealogies

8

From Dangerous Partisan to National Possession
John Stuart Mill in English Culture 1873–1933

I

In a fine passage in his essay on Malthus, Keynes celebrates, with a nicely judged sense of pride in his own intellectual ancestry, what he calls 'the English tradition of humane science'. It is a tradition, he suggests, which has been marked

> by an extraordinary continuity of *feeling*, if I may so express it, from the eighteenth century to the present time—the tradition which is suggested by the names of Locke, Hume, Adam Smith, Paley, Bentham, Darwin, and Mill, a tradition marked by a love of truth and a most noble lucidity, by a prosaic sanity free from sentiment or metaphysic, and by an immense disinterestedness and public spirit. There is continuity in these writings, not only of feeling but of actual matter. It is in this company that Malthus belongs.[1]

Both the roll of honour and the terms of the characterization would repay extended scrutiny: the omission of figures like Bacon, Hobbes, and Burke (as 'English' as Hume or Smith), the elevation of Paley, the inclusion of Darwin but not Newton, the concentration on certain human qualities or dispositions of mind rather than on, say, empiricism, individualism, or similar matters of method or doctrine —in these and other ways the passage ought perhaps to be regarded as idiosyncratic rather than typical, the work of an unusually cultivated Cambridge-educated economist, written at a particular

[1] J. M. Keynes, *Essays in Biography* (London, 1933), 120.

moment in his own career and at a particular juncture of his nation's intellectual history. But in whatever other ways one might be tempted to analyse the mixture of polemic and piety in this passage, the inclusion of John Stuart Mill in the list would seem one of its least contentious features. Indeed, the qualities enumerated in the second half of the passage seem to apply with less qualification to Mill than to almost any of the others—'disinterestedness' is not what immediately strikes one in Locke's writings nor 'prosaic sanity' in Bentham's. But by the time Keynes's essay was published (1933), both the inclusion and the characterization of Mill would have passed without comment.

This had not always been the case. 'To class him with Locke, Bentham, Adam Smith or Malthus is preposterous.' The gruff, dismissive tone is not the least noticeable difference here, and the claim being dismissed clearly bore some similarity to Keynes's later encomium, though we sense that it must at this point have been a more controversial assertion, unable to present itself with quite the same air of judicious distillation. The author of this curt response was Abraham Hayward, man of letters, one-time barrister, and, notoriously, accomplished hatchet-man on behalf of the Tory interest in the pages of *The Times* and the *Quarterly Review*. The occasion of the controversy was his obituary of Mill in *The Times* on 10 May 1873. That obituary had been so sneeringly hostile to Mill that Stopford Brooke, a liberal cleric of unconventional views (and, arguably, unchristian beliefs), denounced it on the following Sunday from the pulpit of St James's, York St. In response, Hayward printed and, privately but extensively, circulated a letter (from which the above sentence is taken), reaffirming his low estimation of the lasting value of Mill's achievement. Hayward's letter further attempted to blacken Mill's character by giving a rather lurid account of the episode early in Mill's life when he was detained by the police for allegedly distributing literature advocating contraception, and by insinuating that he had had an adulterous relationship with Harriet Taylor.[2]

This then provoked further controversy and the publication of at least two pamphlets defending Mill's reputation, the affair leading to the ultimate social convulsion in which one member of the

[2] The unsigned obituary (widely known even at the time to be by Hayward) appeared in *The Times*, 10 May 1873: 5. Stopford Brooke's protest was made on the 11th, and Hayward's letter was dated 12 May.

Athenaeum 'cut' another member at the whist table. One of the people to whom Hayward had sent a copy of his letter was a fellow-member of the Athenaeum, W. D. Christie, who was a long-standing admirer of Mill. Christie objected to its insinuations, an acrimonious exchange of letters ensued in which Christie declared that Hayward's behaviour 'compel[s] me to decline all further acquaintance and private intercourse with you'. This was followed by an episode in the Club's whist-room the exact nature of which it may now be beyond the power of historical scholarship to determine, after which, on 24 May, Hayward circulated a further printed statement, in the course of which he declared that Christie's behaviour constituted 'a deliberate outrage on the proprieties of cultivated life'. Some regret having been evinced by both parties that the once-conventional manner of settling disputes of honour was no longer available, and Christie having failed to obtain satisfaction in the form of any retraction by Hayward or indication of who the recipients of his original letter had been, he then published a 'Reply', to which he appended the correspondence with Hayward.[3] The exchanges were fully reported in several other publications, and many years later they were even alluded to in the account of Hayward given in the *Dictionary of National Biography*. Hayward, who had been one of Mill's Tory antagonists in the London Debating Society some forty-five years earlier, seems to have wished to stir the prejudices of polite society against according Mill any mark of public recognition. The issue was already a somewhat delicate one given Mill's reputation as an outspoken Radical: Lord Derby, for example, was reported in *The Times* as saying that he will 'with pleasure join in any mark of respect to the late Mr Mill which does not take such a form as to imply on the part of the contributors or promoters an agreement in Mr Mill's political opinions'.[4] Hayward had some success, in that as a result of his 'revelations' about Mill's propagandizing for birth control Gladstone felt compelled to withdraw his support for the proposed memorial tribute.[5] Several contemporary comments on the episode took exception to Hayward's

[3] W. D. Christie, *John Stuart Mill and Mr Abraham Hayward Q.C.: A Reply about Mill to a Letter to the Rev. Stopford Brooke, Privately Circulated and Actually Published* (London, 1873).

[4] *The Times*, 14 May 1873: 9.

[5] The episode is summarized in John Morley, *The Life of William Ewart Gladstone*, 3 vols. (London, 1903), ii. 543–4.

tone, even where they could not endorse Mill's inclusion in the company in which Brooke had placed him.[6]

Hayward's remark, therefore, has in some ways even less claim to be considered representative than has Keynes's. But it and the response it evoked do indicate not only that Mill's standing was a matter of partisan dispute at the time of his death, but also that establishing his standing in relation to a certain tradition or pantheon of English thought already formed an important dimension of such disputes. The contrast between the remarks of Keynes and of Hayward can serve as a suggestive pointer to the issues involved in a consideration of the development of Mill's reputation and his place in English culture in the sixty years that separate them. In what follows, I am not intending to offer anything like a comprehensive survey of interpretations of Mill's works in the late nineteenth and early twentieth centuries, still less a study of his purported 'influence' during that period. Rather, I am concerned with one of the minor ways in which a society tries to establish and negotiate its own identity; with, that is, an episode in the intellectual history of 'Englishness' as much as an episode in English intellectual history. Such a concern takes for granted (rather than gleefully seizing an opportunity to 'unmask' ideological distortion) that the development of a major writer's posthumous reputation reveals at least as much about the cultural needs he is recruited to serve as it does about the progress of scholarly discovery or reinterpretation.

A full survey of the mutations of Mill's reputation in these years would fill several large volumes by itself. Here, I shall be highly selective, and simply sketch a few of the principal steps on the path to his canonization as a *political* thinker; I shall largely ignore his posthumous career as logician, economist, and moral philosopher. By the end of this period (one marked, as we have seen, by a great expansion of higher education), Mill had acquired the curious status of a 'set text'—more than simply an author, less than fully an authority. At the same time, he moved from being regarded as 'a violent and even acrimonious partisan', stigmatized by his opponents as 'un-English', to occupying a secure place in the intellectual pedigree of Englishness, property of all parties and of none.[7]

[6] e.g. *Athenaeum*, 17 May 1873: 662. Cf. Sidgwick's comment in a letter to C. H. Pearson, 15 May 1873: 'We do not like any notice which has appeared. *The Times* is thought to be in execrable taste.' Pearson MSS, Bodleian Library, Oxford, MS Eng. Lett. d.190.

[7] The quoted phrase comes from 'Mr Mill as a politician' [possibly by Fitzjames Stephen?], *Saturday Review*, 22 (1866), 167–9; the judgement was occasioned by

Such conclusions as I come to will scarcely surprise those students of Mill's writings who are also familiar with the history of this later period (though such amphibious creatures are perhaps not all that numerous), but I hope that even a preliminary sketch of this kind may prove suggestive to those who are interested in the way in which English culture, at a particular stage of reflective self-consciousness, constructed part of its own genealogy. For, among the ways in which the intellectual life of a sophisticated society is conducted, a special complexity attends the treatment of those earlier figures whom participants in that life choose to regard as in some sense their predecessors. The very identity of a culture is partly constituted by the construction of such traditions (or, more narrowly, genealogies), by the identification (or, more imperiously, appropriation) of precursors, and by the ensuing conflicts, both substantive and symbolic, that arise from the reprinting, re-editing, rereading, and reinterpreting of past writers. We are perhaps most familiar with this process in the case of those groups or regions trying to establish a cultural pedigree distinct from that which they have inherited from the dominant culture, and often in these cases the elaboration of a distinctive literary or intellectual tradition has an explicitly political and adversarial purpose. Such constructions are certainly a familiar part of the cultural nationalism of formerly colonial societies. Perhaps less attention has been given to the ways in which the *ascendant* cultural traditions in a long-established society continually reconstitute themselves through this process. English historians, in particular, have tended to treat nationalism as something that happened to other people, and although there has in recent years been an increased preoccupation with the 'peculiarities' of the development of English society and the allegedly distinctive characteristics of its intellectual life, relatively little attention has been paid to the ways in which certain received notions about that life and its pedigree were themselves historically established and extended (I return to this topic in Chapter 9 below).

The late nineteenth century was arguably a crucial period for the development of such notions, exemplified in projects to assemble the nation's cultural inheritance, such as the *New English Dictionary*, the *Dictionary of National Biography*, and the 'English Men of Letters'

Mill's support for the activities of the Reform League during and immediately after the 'Hyde Park riots' earlier in the year. For similar descriptions at the time of his death, including the charge of 'un-Englishness', see below, s. III.

series and its many imitators.[8] A particularly important feature of this development was a greatly increased preoccupation with the ways in which the national character had expressed itself in what was coming to be seen as a uniquely rich cultural and intellectual tradition. A nice, and in some ways surprising, example of this self-consciousness working on established notions came in T. H. Huxley's proposal in 1878 for an 'English Men of Science' series to parallel the recently launched 'English Men of Letters':

> Among the many peculiarities of the national character, one of the most singular is a certain pride in the assumed incapacity of the English mind for abstract or speculative enquiries. Nevertheless it may be safely affirmed that no modern nation can show a more remarkable muster-roll of great names in philosophy and in physical science; nor point to more important contributions towards the foundations of the scientific conception of Nature than those made by Englishmen.[9]

These preoccupations did not involve a radical discontinuity with the essentially Whig account of the distinctiveness of England's political history and political genius which had particularly flourished in the middle of the century, though as that history became less actively connected to the lived political experience of the society from the 1870s onwards, there was perhaps more room for explorations of the characteristics of recent English history which were less closely tied to constitutional and political issues. This should in turn be seen as part of what might be called 'the nationalization of English culture' during this period. When in 1901 Lewis Campbell used this term in the title of his book *On the Nationalization of the Old English Universities*, he referred not to the possibility of taking Oxford and Cambridge into public ownership, but rather to those changes in recent decades that had led them to be seen as 'national' rather than 'sectional' institutions (Campbell was primarily concerned with the shedding of their exclusively Anglican character and their subsequent incorporation of the Nonconform-

[8] The particular importance of this period has recently been asserted in Robert Colls and Philip Dodd (eds.), *Englishness: Politics and Culture 1880–1920* (London, 1986). For further discussion of both the *NED* (later the *OED*) and the 'English Men of Letters', see below, Ch. 9 s. II.

[9] Huxley's draft proposal, which does not seem to have led to the establishment of such a series, is reproduced in S. Nowell-Smith, *Letters to Macmillan* (London, 1967), 166–7.

ists).[10] Something similar might be said about the development of the culture of the educated classes as a whole during this period, and a historical dimension was given to the attendant process of charting the distinctive *intellectual* achievements of the English people by the construction of those narratives of the history of English thought which developed into a minor genre during this period.

II

In considering the development of Mill's posthumous reputation as part of this larger process, it may be worth distinguishing, briefly and schematically, four stages through which an author and the uses made of him may pass in relation to subsequent politics and political thought.

The first is that in which his pronouncements and the positions he took in his lifetime can still be considered an active part of current political debate on substantive issues, where it still makes sense to talk of other figures 'disagreeing' with or 'rejecting' his views, where the issues are still continuous with those he addressed. Mill continued to have some currency in this way in the 1870s, when Radicals like Dilke, Morley (above all as editor of the *Fortnightly*), to a lesser extent Chamberlain and, in a rather different vein, Fawcett, were regarded as his disciples, continuing his campaigns on certain issues, notably land reform and the emancipation of women. This kind of afterlife is naturally short, given the changing agenda of politics, and I shall say no more about it.[11]

The second stage is that in which later writers and, to a lesser extent, politicians still regard themselves, or are regarded by others, as applying his principles (or, conversely, as thinking it still a worthwhile contribution to current political debate to controvert them). In some areas of social and economic policy, and, less

[10] Lewis Campbell, *On the Nationalization of the Old Universities* (London, 1901). The wider significance of this development is touched on in T. W. Heyck, *The Transformation of Intellectual Life in Victorian England* (London, 1982), esp. chs. 6 and 8.

[11] There is no full study of Mill's political position in the last years of his life, and his relation to the politics of the 1870s has only been touched on in passing. E. M. Everett, *The Party of Humanity: 'The Fortnightly Review' and its Contributors, 1865–1874* (Chapel Hill, London, 1939), contains some useful material, and there is a good discussion of the relation between Mill's activities on behalf of the Land Tenure Reform Association and later progressive thought in Willard Wolfe, *From Radicalism to Socialism: Men and Ideas in the Formation of Fabian Socialist Doctrines 1881–1889* (New Haven, Conn., 1975).

distinctly, on certain constitutional questions, Mill certainly retained this status for two decades or so after his death, and arguably up until 1914.

In the third stage, in practice not always easy to distinguish from the second, the author has become an authority, or, more nebulously, a symbol or part of a tradition which it can still seem useful, in general cultural terms and perhaps at certain moments in more immediate political terms, to invoke and align oneself with (or, conversely, distance oneself from). Mill's reputation may have entered this phase towards the end of the century, above all in the construction of genealogies of Liberalism, and in some quarters, especially where libertarian values are involved, it may be said that he has never altogether lost this standing.

The fourth stage, which often overlaps with the third and even occasionally with the second, is that in which the figure in question ostensibly has no current political resonance, but is recognized as having acquired some kind of classic status or to have become an object of purely scholarly enquiry. Like the previous three stages, this is essentially an analytical construct, not a concrete category, since *some* political assumptions or even motives can usually be detected behind even the most disinterested scholarly enquiry, but it is surely helpful to distinguish this stage from the previous one, if only analytically. The motives leading a modern scholar to undertake an intellectual biography of, say, William Paley may include a certain kind of conservative nostalgia, but that is a far cry from thinking it appropriate or politically effective to stud one's declarations of belief with references to the imperishable value of his ideas. It is always difficult to say quite when this stage begins. In Mill's case, the low point of attention to his work seems to have been reached by the 1930s, after which an initially slow growth of scholarly interest led to the industrial quantities of work on him produced since the late 1950s. However, the fact that the initial revival of interest in the late 1940s and early 1950s was presided over by Friedrich Hayek, as well as the fact that books ostensibly devoted to criticizing his work can still furnish occasions for choleric Tory spluttering, should prevent us from facilely assuming that becoming the object of detailed scholarly enquiry is incompatible with an enduring political resonance.[12]

[12] See the introduction to the 2nd edition of Maurice Cowling, *Mill and Liberalism* (Cambridge, 1989; 1st edn. 1963); cf. n. 67 below.

Probably the reputation of most prominent political writers passes through the first two of these stages, though the second may in many cases be very short-lived. What is particularly interesting to the student of constructions of national intellectual traditions is the point at which the writer in question makes the transition to stage three, where in effect it becomes in everyone's interest, no matter what their political allegiance, to attempt to appropriate him, or at least to establish where they stand in relation to him. For it is surely far more common for a reputation to fade away almost entirely shortly after the author's death, and then, following a long period of neglect, to get taken up in the fourth of the modes distinguished above. In these terms, Mill belongs to that very small group of political writers whose reputation enters the third stage relatively quickly, while retaining the animating and dividing power of the second stage for so long. There could have been little rhetorical effectiveness or implied reflection on the transitoriness of fame in asking in 1903, as Crane Brinton did of Herbert Spencer thirty years after his death, 'Who now reads Mill?'[13] But to understand *how* he was read, both then and thirty years further on when his reputation was approaching its nadir, we need to begin by returning to the competing assessments offered by Hayward and others at the time of Mill's death.

III

Obituaries can be a curiously hybrid form of writing. Their very existence indicates some sort of recognition of stature, and the conventions require that the tone be at least respectful if it cannot be pious. But they are also polemical: their selectivity and emphases constitute a kind of persuasive definition of the value of the subject's achievements. This mixture was interestingly evident in the obituaries that followed Mill's death in May 1873. Those who deplored his politics praised his philosophy, while those who dissented from his ideas lauded his character. The reservations, even when mildly expressed (as they mostly were), are revealing of the sharply divergent responses he evoked.

[13] Cf. Crane Brinton, *English Political Thought in the Nineteenth Century* (London, 1933), 226. The question 'Who now reads Spencer?' was given wider currency than it might otherwise have achieved as a result of being taken as the text by Talcott Parsons for his account of positivist social theory in *The Structure of Social Action* (New York, 1937).

What is particularly interesting for my purposes is the way in which several of the obituarists expressed their criticisms by describing the aspects of Mill's writing or character of which they disapproved as 'un-English'. The *Saturday Review*, for example, an old enemy, was predictably disparaging, rehearsing the familiar charges that he was too doctrinaire—'on certain subjects an obstinate fanatic'—and it twisted the knife by comparing him to the great bogeymen of English political wisdom, the *philosophes* who were held to have inspired the French Revolution.[14] Hayward's *Times* obituary similarly classified as un-English Mill's 'doctrines of dangerous tendency and doubtful soundness' ('we need hardly add', added Hayward with a characteristic sneer, 'that many of his opinions on society and government have been generally and justly condemned').[15] The *Illustrated London News* echoed the term which expresses greatest distrust in English public life, finding him not quite 'sound': 'His judgement was probably misdirected upon several important questions; it was certainly at variance with the soundest and best-informed English minds.'[16] And even among those who did not wish to exclude Mill from the national intellectual communion in this way, there was still considerable unease about the relation between his theoretical writings and his practical activities, and frequent expressions of regret at his having joined the party battle at all. There were several references to 'his manifest failure as a statesman' ('The opinions of a recluse on practical matters are rarely to be trusted', grumbled the *Saturday*), though the terms of criticism differed, as we saw in Chapter 4 above, between those who argued that 'he descended too easily from the judgement-seat into the arena', and those who felt he remained too much a 'man of the study', too much of a 'recluse'.[17]

Both those who were expressing a Tory hostility to his 'partisanship' and those Liberal disciples who were disappointed at the 'sentimentalism' of some of his later crotchets (about women, Socialism, and land) could concur in finding the austere (and politically 'safe') reasoning of the *Logic* his most easily admired achievement. More generally, the *Logic* and the *Political Economy* were regarded as the foundation of his reputation as a thinker; *On*

[14] [Anon.], 'Mr Mill', *Saturday Review*, 35 (1873), 638–9.
[15] *The Times*, 10 May 1873: 5.
[16] [Anon.], 'John Stuart Mill', *Illustrated London News*, 17 May 1873: 456.
[17] See the references cited in Ch. 4 above, pp. 155–6.

Liberty was frequently mentioned, but had not yet acquired its subsequent pre-eminence among his works. There was some particularly discriminating comment upon his special talents from the cooler pens of Bagehot and Sidgwick: the former remarked that 'the great merit of Mr Mill. . . was the merit of intellectual combination', while the latter nicely classed him as 'the best philosophical writer—if not the best philosopher—England has produced since Hume' (Sidgwick was, of course, merely employing the standard usage of the day in referring to Hume as an 'English' philosopher).[18]

Following this flurry of obituary tributes, a second chance for overall assessment was provided by the publication later in the year of the *Autobiography*. Again, there were several attempts to discredit or marginalize Mill by representing him as outside or at odds with the mainstream of English intellectual and political life. Henry Reeve, editor of the *Edinburgh Review* and spokesman for bronto-saurial Whiggism, took up almost forty pages of his journal with a relentlessly uncharitable assessment of Mill's life, especially his relation with Mrs Taylor, developing along the way an extended comparison with Rousseau, another theorist of doubtful morals and dangerous political fanaticism, a figure who occupied a special place in the Whig demonology and its cautionary tales about the doctrinaire politics which had brought such disasters to France.[19] In the Tory *Quarterly*, Palgrave suggested that the 'coterie' (perhaps a case of a foreign word for a foreign thing) around Bentham and James Mill by which the younger Mill had been so largely shaped was outside the main English tradition.[20] Indeed, the pretext of reviewing the *Autobiography* allowed Mill's critics to express their hostility more freely than had been possible within the constraints of an obituary. The book's revelations about the relationship between Mill and Harriet Taylor only provided further evidence with which to blacken his character. Hayward pursued his vendetta in a long piece in *Fraser's Magazine*, concentrating on Mill's 'unconscious

[18] Walter Bagehot, 'The late Mr Mill', *The Economist*, 17 May 1873: 588–9 (it was here that Bagehot made his often-quoted observation that Mill's position within political economy was 'monarchical'); Henry Sidgwick, 'John Stuart Mill', *Academy*, 15 May 1873: 193.

[19] [Henry Reeve], 'Autobiography of John Stuart Mill', *Edinburgh Review*, 139 (1874), 91–129.

[20] [Francis Turner Palgrave], 'John Stuart Mill's *Autobiography*', *Quarterly Review*, 136 (1874), 150–79.

egotism'.[21] The *Saturday Review* found what it was looking for in the *Autobiography*—the portrait of an aloof, humourless, condescending figure, given to the 'supercilious condemnation' of the bulk of the human race—while *The Times* reiterated the charge, for charge it certainly was, that Mill had been un-English, an 'outsider' who had been in 'no immediate practical relation' to England, and so had tried, as a radical, to destroy what he had never really understood.[22]

Other reviewers, of course, presented a far more sympathetic and flattering account of Mill, in some cases explicitly taking issue with the hostile portraits mentioned above. For example, Thomas Hare, in the course of a long and very appreciative article in, predictably, the *Westminster*, was at pains to contest the 'misrepresentations' (and 'the tone of complacent triumph') in the dismissive piece in *Fraser's*, while the author of a very admiring essay in *St Paul's Magazine* took issue with the *Saturday*'s caricature of Mill's coldness and sense of superiority.[23] R. H. Hutton, so often a shrewd judge of contemporary literary figures, devoted a pair of articles in the *Spectator* to examining the man who emerged from the pages of the *Autobiography*, and although Hutton was incapable of descending to the slurs of some of the more remorselessly partisan attacks, he did find Mill's life characterized by 'a monotonous joylessness'. In a subsequent number of the *Spectator* one correspondent attempted to take up arms on Mill's behalf, though it is interesting to see that his chief argument was that 'the life of one who lives and strives in opposition to the ideas of his age. . . will scarcely be expected to be a very bright and cheerful one'.[24] And so it went on.

The chief interest of all this, of course, is precisely that it *did* go on, that at the time of his death Mill could still arouse such strong emotions and provoke such contrary assessments, and moreover that much of the discussion should have been focused on the question of

[21] [Abraham Hayward], 'John Stuart Mill', *Fraser's Magazine*, NS 8 (1873), 663–81.

[22] [Anon.], 'Autobiography of John Stuart Mill', *Saturday Review*, 1 Nov. 1873: 570–1; [?William Ellis], 'The *Autobiography* of John Stuart Mill', *The Times*, 4 Nov. and 10 Nov. 1873.

[23] Thomas Hare, 'John Stuart Mill', *Westminster Review*, NS 45 (1874), 122–59, quotation at 157; 'Henry Holbeach' [pseudonym for W. B. Rands], 'Mr Mill's Autobiography and Mr Fitzjames Stephen on "Liberty"', *St Paul's Magazine*, 13 (1873), 686–701.

[24] R. H. Hutton, 'Mr John Stuart Mill's *Autobiography*' and 'Mr J. S. Mill's philosophy as tested in his life', *Spectator*, 46 (1873), 1337–9 and 1370–2; 'A', 'Mr Mill and his critics', *Spectator*, 46 (1873), 1435.

whether Mill had been such a 'doctrinaire' (again the foreign word for the foreign thing) that he should be placed quite outside the English tradition (singular, as such evocations always are) of 'sound' practicality in political matters. As we have already seen, the question of a public memorial to Mill had to be delicately handled. Gladstone's withdrawal of support may chiefly have revealed, yet again, the eccentric scrupulosities of the GOM's conscience, but a more representative example of the controversy still surrounding Mill's name may be found in the Cobden Club's decision only two months before Mill's death to strike the name of the most celebrated living economist from their list of committee members on the grounds that by his support for the Land Tenure Reform Association he had 'so publicly identified himself with principles radically opposed to those' of the Club.[25]

IV

In considering the subsequent development of Mill's reputation as a political thinker and the essentially external question of how he was seen and placed—the forms taken by the creative response of those who could have been said to have been animated, irritated, or otherwise influenced by him is another matter—our starting-point has to be the dominance of political debate in the generation or so after Mill's death by the issue of Individualism versus Collectivism. This not only concentrated attention on the question of the relation between the individual and the state, but, of great consequence for the placing of Mill, it shaped the interpretation given to the previous fifty years of English history. In essence, the pressures of the debate hardened the contours and extended the acceptability of a narrative of the history of recent English political thought which saw the half-century from the 1820s to the 1870s as marked by a hostility to state action, a hostility whose intellectual sources were to be found in Benthamism and political economy. But towards the end of this period, so the story ran, the deficiencies of this Individualist position became increasingly apparent, leading to the Collectivism of the last

[25] For details of Gladstone's decision, see Morley, *Life of Gladstone*, ii. 543–4; the Cobden Club's decision is briefly discussed in Clive Dewey, 'The rehabilitation of the peasant proprietor in nineteenth-century economic thought', *History of Political Economy*, 6 (1974), 17–47; the letter by Sir Louis Mallet from which the above phrase is taken is quoted on p. 38.

decades of the century, and, importantly, to the elaboration of a new intellectual basis for such policies, whether couched in evolutionary, Idealist, Socialist, or other terms.

There is, I take it, no need to expose once more the inadequacies and distortions of this account, and its bearings upon the evolution of Mill's reputation as a political writer are fairly obvious. For, in the 1870s, before this debate and the attendant interpretation of recent history had fully imposed itself, Mill's legacy was largely divided between what might be called the 'hard-nosed' and the 'soft-hearted' wings of intellectual Liberalism, with Fitzjames Stephen the most obvious and vocal representative of the former and John Morley of the latter. As this suggests, the fault-line ran between those who thought that Mill was at his most admirable when closest to old-fashioned Utilitarian orthodoxy, and those who were more sympathetic to the high moral tone and 'advanced' radical views of his later years (a division which, interestingly, was not a bad indication of likely political allegiance after 1886, the 'hard-nosed' school nearly all becoming Liberal Unionists). But in the 1880s and 1890s Mill was increasingly treated as an 'old-fashioned' Liberal, and *On Liberty*, his protest against the intolerance and bigotry of some of the most active forces in Victorian public life and public opinion, was retrospectively conscripted to be the canonical statement of the Individualist doctrine of the state. The essay provided a convenient target since the Individualist conclusions imputed to it seemed to rest on what could easily be shown to be, especially in the light of later evolutionary or Idealist notions, very disputable premisses about the absoluteness of the distinction between individual and society, and so Mill's name figured most prominently in late nineteenth-century political argument as a kind of shorthand for the now-discredited premisses of Individualism which belonged to an earlier period.[26]

Obviously, not all the references in these decades to Mill as a political theorist were quite this selective, although the other dimensions of his thought which were cited at this level of discussion

[26] I shall refrain from extensive citation here, but the central point can most easily be illustrated by looking at the use made of Mill in some of the most prominent contributions to this debate, such as F. C. Montague, *The Limits of Individual Liberty: An Essay* (London, 1885); D. G. Ritchie, *The Principles of State Interference* (London, 1891); W. S. McKechnie, *The State and the Individual: An Introduction to Political Science with Special Reference to Socialistic and Individualistic Theories* (Glasgow, 1896).

tended to be those which most directly bore on the same issue, such his discussion of 'unearned increment', private property in land, and Socialism. In this context, *Considerations on Representative Government* naturally figured less prominently, even though constitutional questions were hardly minor features of the politics of the 1880s. Even during the last decade of Mill's lifetime, the book had enjoyed a rather mixed reputation, and few of his obituarists singled it out for special praise (Hare was, forgivably, a notable exception). Several of his otherwise enthusiastic admirers expressed guarded or sceptical judgements, especially towards its idiosyncratic endorsement of proportional representation, plural voting, and the open ballot. Moreover, its Tocquevillian and indeed Whiggish tendencies fitted awkwardly with the stereotype of a Utilitarian Individualist earnestly struggling to adapt his inherited creed to accommodate the promptings of the mid-Victorian social conscience.[27]

In the last two decades of the century, therefore, Mill was identified as a political thinker overwhelmingly with the 'Individualism' of *On Liberty*, and as the last major representative of the Utilitarian school of political radicalism. There were potentially considerable tensions in this portrait, of course, given the very *un*-Utilitarian strain of much of the argument of *On Liberty*, and the complexities involved (or suppressed) in so briskly identifying Utilitarianism with both radicalism and Individualism. In other words, by the end of the century there was a widely shared sense that Individualism had been the dominant approach of the previous couple of generations (though this was in fact a construction prompted by the contemporary debate); criticisms of it from the standpoint of fashionable intellectual developments like evolutionism and Idealism identified Utilitarianism as its essential intellectual foundation; Utilitarianism was the acknowledged creed of the Philosophic Radicals (who were taken to include the political economists); and thus the central movement of English political thought in the half-century between Waterloo and Mill's death was held to have been that of Utilitarianism. The extent to which the Philosophic Radicals had been a relatively marginal sect even in their heyday was thereby disguised, and the sustained vitality to at least the 1860s of older modes of

[27] These features of the book are discussed in Stefan Collini, Donald Winch, and John Burrow, *That Noble Science of Politics: A Study in Nineteenth-Century Intellectual History* (Cambridge, 1983), 148–56; see also J. W. Burrow, *Whigs and Liberals: Continuity and Change in English Political Thought* (Oxford, 1988), esp. ch. 5.

political argument, especially those which were either Whiggish or Evangelical in inspiration, tended to be obscured.[28] But by 1900 this had become the dominant interpretation of recent English political and intellectual history. We may therefore pause here, a generation after Mill's death, at roughly the mid-point of our story, to look in a little more detail at some of the most seminal expositions of this view.

Two works, in particular, both summarized and gave influential expression to this account of recent history in ways which were to shape historiographic assumptions for several generations thereafter, Dicey's *Law and Public Opinion in the Nineteenth Century* and Stephen's *The English Utilitarians*, both originally composed at roughly the same time.[29] As I suggested above,[30] Dicey was a representative example of that kind of 'Old Liberal' who had enthusiastically imbibed Mill's logic and political economy as a student in the 1850s, but who had by the 1880s become disenchanted with what he saw as the legacy of the democratic and egalitarian enthusiasms of Mill's later years. 'At Oxford we swallowed Mill, rather undigested: he was our chief intellectual food until 1860', he declared in a lecture on Mill in 1900, and in 1905 he reflected: 'As a young man I owed more to him than to any other English writer.'[31] In seeking to understand the fate that had overtaken the ideals of his youth, Dicey divided the century into three phases: that of 'old Toryism' up to 1830, that of 'Benthamism or Individualism' up to 1870, and that of 'Collectivism' thereafter. Mill, or at least the Mill of *On Liberty*, he took to represent the uncorrupted Individualism of the second phase: in 1859 'John Mill, the hereditary representative of Benthamism, published . . . that treatise *On Liberty*, which appeared, to thousands of admiring

[28] For a similar conclusion, focused more specifically on the neglect of continuities with 18th-century Whig political thought, see Burrow, *Whigs and Liberals*, ch. 1; for the impact of Evangelicalism on social and political thinking in this period see the work of Boyd Hilton, esp. *The Age of Atonement* (Oxford, 1988). The essential marginality of the Philosophic Radicals to the mainstream of English political life in the 1820s and 1830s emerges very clearly from William Thomas, *The Philosophic Radicals: Nine Studies in Theory and Practice 1817–1841* (Oxford, 1979).

[29] Dicey's book was first given as lectures at Harvard in 1898; see Richard Cosgrove, *The Rule of Law: Albert Venn Dicey, Victorian Jurist* (London, 1980), 171. Stephen had intermittently been working on his book—'the Utilitarian bog'—since at least 1891; see F. W. Maitland, *The Life and Letters of Leslie Stephen* (London, 1906), 403, 432.

[30] See Ch. 5, pp. 77–8.

[31] Both quotations from Cosgrove, *Rule of Law*, 12–13.

disciples, to provide the final and conclusive demonstration of the absolute truth of individualism, and to establish on firm ground the doctrine that the protection of freedom was the one great object of wise law and sound policy'.[32] Dicey's analysis of the century's political development did more to shape subsequent perceptions of that development than did any other single work, and by placing the equation of Mill with Benthamism and of Benthamism with Individualism in this larger explanatory framework he helped to fix the received understanding of Mill's significance as a political thinker for many years to came. Barker, for example, was representative in this as in much else in treating Mill as 'the prophet of an empty liberty and an abstract individual'.[33]

Leslie Stephen's *The English Utilitarians*, which was to be hardly less influential in shaping the understanding of Mill's place in nineteenth-century intellectual history more generally, similarly emphasized his Individualist and Utilitarian credentials. As in Dicey's case, Stephen was to some extent attempting to make sense of his own earlier intellectual development: he had, as we have seen, been one of the Liberal young Turks and something of a Utilitarian zealot at Cambridge in the 1850s and early 1860s, but had then seen the light of more historical, evolutionary, and organicist modes of thought, as well as temperamentally growing away from the simplicities of the Radical creed of this period. Stephen's relation to the story he had to tell was thus more complex than Dicey's: though disgruntled with new-fangled Collectivism, Stephen was critical of the atomism he found at the root of the Utilitarian theory. Moreover, he distanced himself from his subjects in various ways—indeed, his very presentation of the Utilitarians as a 'sect' conveyed this. More specifically, Stephen's distaste for Mill's character comes through very clearly, despite his heroically fair-minded summaries of Mill's main theoretical achievements. Again, it is interesting to see that Stephen, who revelled in (indeed almost parodied) his own gruff Englishness, depicted some of Mill's defects in terms of his remoteness from typically 'English' qualities: 'Mill might have been a wiser man had he been able to drop his dignity, indulge in a few amusements, and interpret a little more generously the British

[32] A. V. Dicey, *Law and Public Opinion in the Nineteenth Century* (London, 1905), 183.

[33] Ernest Barker, *Political Thought in England 1848–1914* (London, 1947; 1st edn. 1915), 4.

contempt for high-flown sentiment.'[34] Stephen had already given the essence of his interpretation wider currency through the authoritative pages of the *DNB*, where he wrote the entry on Mill himself (some phrasing from which recurs in his book, which was being written at much the same time). Again, Mill was firmly identified with a political position now on the wane: 'The general disparagement of so-called "individualism" has led for the time to a lower estimate of Mill's services to liberal principles.'[35] In general, the effect of Stephen's account, both in its tracing of continuities through from Bentham and his philosophical predecessors and in his constant criticism of Mill for failing to have been a late nineteenth-century social evolutionist, was to make Mill (as Mill himself had made his father) the last representative of eighteenth-century thought. On this view, the English eighteenth century, in philosophy and political theory at least, ran from Locke to the supersession of Utilitarianism by the Historical and Idealist 'schools' in the 1860s and 1870s.[36]

The end of the nineteenth century saw several other important reassessments of Mill, one of the most interesting of which was by Frederic Harrison in a long essay first published in the *Nineteenth Century* in 1896.[37] Harrison, one of the leading English Positivists, was no uncritical admirer of Mill: 'So far from his being my master, he has attacked my own master with unsparing, and I hold unjust, criticism in an important volume.' None the less, he had great respect for Mill, with whom he had been moderately well acquainted in the late 1860s and early 1870s, and now, at the age of 65, he wished to explain to 'the younger generation wherein lay the influence over us elders of Mill's character and mind some thirty years ago.' For the premiss of Harrison's essay was that Mill's reputation had declined considerably in the last generation. His explanation dwelt on larger changes in intellectual fashion: 'It is

[34] Leslie Stephen, *The English Utilitarians*, 3 vols. (London, 1900), iii. 45, 65–71.

[35] *DNB*, vol. xxxvii (London, 1894), 399.

[36] This is very much the way Stephen's book was read by an Idealist like Pringle-Pattison, who emphasized the persistence of 'eighteenth-century atomism' and its defects in Mill's thought for all the 'incongruous patches' he tried to weave into it. A. S. Pringle-Pattison, 'The Philosophical Radicals', *Quarterly Review* (1901), repr. in his *The Philosophical Radicals and Other Essays* (Edinburgh, 1907), esp. 31.

[37] Frederic Harrison, 'John Stuart Mill', *Nineteenth Century*, 40 (1896), 487–508; repr. in Harrison's *Tennyson, Ruskin, Mill, and Other Literary Estimates* (London, 1899). For an exhaustive account of Harrison's career, including his relation to Mill, see Martha S. Vogeler, *Frederic Harrison: The Vocations of a Positivist* (Oxford, 1984); the essay on Mill is mentioned at 309.

rather the school than the man which has lost vogue.' His characterization of that school has a special interest:

> It must always be borne in mind that Mill essentially belonged to a school, that he was peculiarly the product of a very marked order of English thinkers. . . . Coleridge, Carlyle, Ruskin, can hardly be said to have been either the sons or the founders of any school of thought. John Mill was a singularly systematic product of a singularly systematic school of philosophers. . . . Locke, Hume, Adam Smith, Bentham, Malthus, James Mill, Austin, Grote, Bowring, Roebuck, the philosophic Radicals of the first Reform era, maintained a real filiation of central ideas which reached their complete general systematisation in the earlier writings of John Stuart Mill.

By this date, there was, of course, nothing eccentric about placing Mill in this company; indeed, it was becoming almost the standard way of assigning him his historical place. Harrison's list is perhaps unusual in so blandly asserting a continuity between the great names of philosophical empiricism and the lesser luminaries of radical Benthamite politics: modern scholarship's account of Hume's social and political thought would hardly allow Roebuck to be treated as a natural successor, even leaving aside the more obvious disparity of stature. More interestingly, by contrasting Coleridge, Carlyle, and Ruskin with what he has identified as the central tradition of English thought, Harrison in effect treats them as slightly marginal figures, at odds with the essential qualities of the English mind as well as somewhat tangential to subsequent developments in Victorian culture. This partly arises from arranging the past in terms of 'schools' and treating philosophy as the chief manifestation of 'thought', a tendency not unique to Harrison, of course. Considering the question without these blinkers, one would have to recognize that Coleridge, for example, was a far more 'central' figure in the 1820s and 1830s than was James Mill, and that Carlyle hardly exercised a lesser influence over some aspects of Victorian literary and intellectual life than did John Stuart Mill. But in the passage as a whole, Harrison is conscious that he is merely summarizing, and perhaps amplifying, a view of recent English intellectual history already familiar and perhaps even largely uncontentious among his readers.[38]

[38] Harrison, 'John Stuart Mill', 487–90. Not everything about Harrison's assessment was uncontroversial, of course; in reply, the *Westminster* carried a spirited defence of thinking in terms of individuals: Horace Seal, 'The individual always the unit', *Westminster Review*, 147 (1897), 5–10.

Scarcely more contentious was Harrison's critical assessment of the weaknesses of *On Liberty*, the single work with which, he acknowledged, Mill's name was now most closely identified. Of its influence on his own generation he has no doubt, and, like many later commentators, he extends this influence to legislation: 'It undoubtedly contributed to the practical programmes of Liberals and Radicals for the generation that saw its birth; and the statute book bears many traces of its influence over the sphere and duties of government.' But that influence, he contended, 'is now at its lowest point. . . . [A] good deal of it is condemned as contrary to all the movements and aspirations of the newer schools of social reform.' The movement of thought has left Mill's 'absolute individualism' behind: 'At bottom, the book on *Liberty* is an attempt to ascertain what are the "rights" of the individual against the State. We know that this is like asking what are the "rights" of the stomach against the body.' The untroubled certainty of that 'we know' in part expresses the dogmatism of the Positivist controversialist who never missed an opportunity to press the Comtean case; but in part it reflected Harrison's assurance that the refrain, even if not mostly sung to a strictly Positivist tune, had become much more familiar to his audience over the past decade or so. The polarities of that phase of political debate had increasingly imposed themselves upon the interpretation of the recent past, and Mill's essay was firmly classed as a statement of 'militant Individualism.' Harrison could conclude by assigning Mill 'a permanent place in English thought', where he would 'stand as the most important name in English philosophy between Bentham and Spencer', but he would 'never regain [his] original vogue'.[39]

A similar sense that Mill was now primarily of historical interest and to be seen as part of a tradition of English political thought is evident in other accounts written at much the same time. Surveying 'English Political Philosophy from Hobbes to Maine', W. Graham recorded the opinion that little was now to be learned from Mill's works, 'influential in their day, and formerly much read at the Universities, but from which the life has already in large measure departed'.[40] In the same year, but in more celebratory vein,

[39] Harrison, 'John Stuart Mill', 490, 492, 494, 499, 508.

[40] W. Graham, *English Political Philosophy from Hobbes to Maine* (London, 1899), quotation at 345. Graham's selection is of some interest in itself: Hobbes, Locke, Burke, Bentham, Mill, Maine. Maine's inclusion in what has otherwise become a very

C. Roylance Kent placed Mill in a tradition of 'Radicalism' which stretched back to the days of Wilkes and could claim to have constituted a party since the 1820s. In one way, this was to reaffirm Mill's partisan credentials, though of course the suggestion, propounded in a rather different idiom in the late eighteenth and early nineteenth century and not altogether scouted by Kent, that Radicalism represented the inheritance of the free-born Englishman reasserting itself against various alien or aristocratic impositions, allowed its history to lay claim to a more than merely sectional significance.[41] At a quite different level, the moral theory of Utilitarianism, too, was losing its sectarian associations. When Ernest Albee published his *History of English Utilitarianism* in 1902, he dealt with it as a tradition of moral philosophy running from Cumberland, Shaftesbury, and Hutcheson up to Sidgwick: the 'practical movement' associated with it earlier in the nineteenth century was, he reported, outdated.[42]

V

Needless to say, this flurry of turn-of-the-century stocktaking did not prevent Mill's name being frequently cited in Edwardian political debate. He, or more usually a highly selective account of his 'views', was appropriated by various groups in this period (though as with all such appropriations there had to be sufficient initial plausibility in the proposed filiation to make the tactic worthwhile: there would have been little to be gained, for example, by claiming that had he lived longer James Mill would have been a luminary of the Oxford Movement). There was more than enough in his later writings to make it worth devoting a sympathetic Fabian Tract to him in 1913, and to make not obviously absurd the claim that 'had he lived another ten years he would almost certainly have been

standard canon reflects his immense authority in the late 19th century. Smith, one possible candidate for inclusion, was probably too firmly identified as an economist by this date; Green, another contender, was perhaps regarded as merely reproducing a foreign theory.

[41] C. Roylance Kent, *The English Radicals* (London, 1899), esp. 7; cf. Ch. 5 above, p. 181.

[42] Ernest Albee, *A History of English Utilitarianism* (London, 1902), esp. chs. on Mill, 191–267. For evidence of the continuing sectarian associations of Utilitarianism in the last years of Mill's life, see J. B. Schneewind, 'Concerning some criticisms of Mill's *Utilitarianism*', in John M. Robson and Michael Laine (eds.), *James and John Stuart Mill: Papers of the Centenary Conference* (Toronto, 1976), 35–9.

amongst the founders of the Fabian Society'.[43] More frequently, he was recruited as a New Liberal *avant la lettre*, though understandably *On Liberty* was most enthusiastically deployed when it seemed that the progressive movement of social reform threatened to produce 'illiberal' consequences, while his remarks in the *Autobiography* or the *Political Economy* about his growing sympathy for Socialism were given prominence when some new extension of Collectivism seemed in need of Liberal legitimation.[44]

But for the most part Mill had by now moved to that third stage of reputation where his name acted symbolically to conjure up certain associations rather than to denote any very precise principles or policies. One small indication of this was the very *lack* of excitement that attended the publication in 1907 of an article by Mill entitled 'On social freedom', the manuscript of which had been found among Mill's papers after Helen Taylor's death. This ought to have occasioned considerable interest and surprise, since the essay's argument propounded a notion of freedom which was radically at odds with that of *On Liberty*, an argument whose 'social' interpretation of liberty lent itself far more naturally to supporting the kind of welfare policies then struggling to establish their Liberal pedigree than had Mill's original work. But the essay seems to have received no comment in the political periodicals. It elicited a short, puzzled note by the philosopher Carveth Read in *Mind*, in the course of which he briefly wondered whether it could really have been by Mill at all. This, as we now know, was a shrewd doubt, but Read did not develop it, and thereafter no one seems to have challenged the authenticity of the essay, but nor, more surprisingly, did anyone feel the need to attempt to reconcile its apparent argument with Mill's better-known conclusions.[45]

[43] Julius West, *John Stuart Mill*, Fabian Tract 168 (London, 1913), 21. Subsequent research has in fact suggested that the Mill of the 'unearned increment' and the Land Tenure Reform Association played a significant part in the intellectual formation of several of the early Fabians: see the discussion in my 'Liberalism and the legacy of Mill', *Historical Journal*, 20 (1977), 237–54. Mill had, of course, frequently been claimed for the cause of Socialism; see e.g. the introduction to a selection of his writings by the American Socialist W. D. P. Bliss, *Socialism by John Stuart Mill* (New York, 1891).

[44] Hobhouse's writings in this period provide numerous examples of thus appealing to different facets of Mill; for a particularly striking example of 'returning' to Mill by way of a reappraisal of the merits of Liberalism in the face of the 'reaction' encouraged by imperialism and associated modes of thought, see L. T. Hobhouse, *Democracy and Reaction* (London, 1904), 223–6.

[45] 'On social freedom' was first published in *Oxford and Cambridge Review*, 1 (1907), 57–83; Carveth Read, 'A posthumous chapter by J. S. Mill', *Mind*, NS 17

It is noticeable how, as successive publications or anniversaries provided the occasion for yet further general reassessments of Mill during this period, the judgements became more and more generous. The centenary of his birth in 1906 predictably elicited some pious tributes, not least from the still reverential John Morley.[46] The publication of H. S. R. Elliot's edition of his letters in 1910 attracted attention partly because there had never been the usual volume of 'Life and Letters' for Mill (nor indeed was there to be any adequate biography of him until Packe's *Life* in 1954—the volumes by Bain and Courtney did not pretend to be full biographies). Various inhibitions and obstacles may have played their part here, but it is possible that others were deterred by the thought that John Morley would at some point produce a magisterial study. This is certainly the implication of Harrison's remark in 1896: 'It is much to be wished that John Morley would now give us that estimate of Mill which in 1873 he said would one day have to be made, and that Life which we have so long awaited.'[47] (There is also the evidence of Sidgwick's journal-entry for 9 August 1885: 'Dined in Hall and met Colvin. . . . He tells me that Morley's *J. S. Mill* is nearly ready. I think that I must take the opportunity of its appearance to write my promised article for the *Contemporary* on J.S.M.'[48] Not prompting Sidgwick to write such an article is one of the heavier charges pending against Morley for not writing the book.)

Revealingly, the appearance of Mill's letters at this date provoked far fewer attempts to damn his views by sneering at his character or his relation with Harriet Taylor than their publication in the 1870s would have done. Not that all was sweetness and light: the author of the review-article in *Blackwood's* could still roll out the old abusive caricature—'not a man but a mass of potted inhumanity', 'an ambulant library', and so on—and warn its readers that 'it is from Mill's erroneous opinions . . . that the infamous policy of the English Radicals proceeds'.[49] But even the *Quarterly* could by this date carry a

(1908), 72–8. The essay, still ascribed to Mill, was repr. with intro. by Dorothy Fosdick (New York, 1941). The attribution was decisively challenged by J. C. Rees in the appendix to his *Mill and his Early Critics* (Leicester, 1956), now repr. in John C. Rees, *John Stuart Mill's 'On Liberty'*, ed. G. L. Williams (Oxford, 1985). The identity of its author still remains uncertain.

[46] [John Morley], 'John Stuart Mill: an anniversary', *Times Literary Supplement*, 18 May 1906: 173–5 (repr. in *Critical Miscellanies, Fourth Series* (London, 1908)).

[47] 'John Stuart Mill', 487–8.

[48] A. and E. M. S[idgwick], *Henry Sidgwick: A Memoir* (London, 1906), 420.

[49] [Anon.], 'Musings without method', *Blackwood's*, 187 (1910), 881–92, quotation at 887.

very judicious assessment (by Wilfrid Ward, son of W. G. Ward who had been one of the most trenchant critics of Mill's empiricism), which emphasized how he had been superseded by subsequent intellectual developments, notably Spencerian evolutionism and philosophical Idealism. Indeed, this venerable organ of old Toryism could even allow—mindful, perhaps, in this year which saw two elections over the 'People's Budget', of Mill's strictures on the tendency of a democracy to abuse its powers—that there was now a need to listen to 'the wisdom of many of his political utterances'.[50] As if by way of a reciprocally non-partisan gesture, some of the Liberal journals seemed willing to relinquish their exclusive claim on Mill's name. Hobhouse, for example, contributed a very appreciative review to the *Nation*, claiming that what 'gives him a permanent value, which will survive all expositions of philosophical deficiencies, is not so much the work he did as the temper in which it was done', above all his openness and fair-mindedness.[51] By the time of the fiftieth anniversary of Mill's death in 1923, this tone had become even more common.

A different way in which to monitor the progress of Mill's reputation as a political thinker during these years is to consider the pattern of the reprinting of his major political writings. At the time of his death, almost all his works were in print, often in recently revised or reissued editions. It is perhaps one sign that an author can no longer quite 'speak for himself' to a later generation when he is deemed to need the services of an editor or to require a historical introduction. When W. L Courtney wrote an introduction for a reprint of *On Liberty* in 1901, his presentation was evidently shaped by a sense of Mill's place in the debate between Individualism and Collectivism. Mill's insistence on the rights of the individual against society he treated as a legacy from eighteenth-century thinking, 'an absurd and exploded theory', which failed to recognize 'the intimate communion with his fellows' in which man lives in society. But he

[50] Wilfrid Ward, 'John Stuart Mill', *Quarterly Review*, 213 (1910), 264–92, quotation at 291.

[51] L. T. Hobhouse, 'John Stuart Mill', *Nation*, 14 May 1910: 246–7. This did not, of course, prevent Hobhouse from very firmly assigning Mill to the Liberal pantheon at almost exactly the same time, giving him the crucial role of spanning 'the interval between the old and the new Liberalism', while offering the interesting judgement that Mill, like Gladstone, 'was also a moral force, and the most persistent influence of his books is more an effect of character than of intellect'; L. T. Hobhouse, *Liberalism* (London, 1911), 107.

saw a danger that the Collectivist doctrine could be taken to extremes, and then *On Liberty* would show 'its eternal importance'.[52] Similarly, when the young A. D. Lindsay wrote his introduction to the reprinting of *On Liberty*, *Utilitarianism*, and *Representative Government* in the Everyman volume in 1910 (which probably remained until recently the most widely used edition of Mill's writings), he, too, saw Mill's work in terms of the polarities established by the Individualist/Collectivist debate. Manifesting both his philosophical Idealism and his sympathy with Socialism, Lindsay berated Mill for thinking 'so constantly in terms of individuals', and insisted, in familiar vein, that 'no account of liberty can be satisfactory which does not see the individual as he actually exists, a member of society in relation to other members'. But at the same time Lindsay was eager to establish that support for state intervention in some areas was quite compatible with libertarianism in others, and his whole introduction suggests that he recognized that Mill was too valuable an authority to be relinquished entirely to the Individualist side of the debate (his status as a 'national' intellectual possession above party was reinforced by Lindsay's comparison of him with Locke, 'his great predecessor').[53] From a rather different starting-point, Millicent Garrett Fawcett, in her 1912 World's Classics edition of *On Liberty*, *Representative Government*, and *The Subjection of Women*, also wished to recruit Mill for controversial purposes. She conceded that for many he was now 'but a name, a symbol, and nothing more', but urged that he was still relevant to 'questions of practical politics'. The nature of his relevance was revealed when she, true to her pedigree, insisted, against a recent newspaper article asserting the contrary, that Mill would have supported the Suffragist movement, one of the most bitterly divisive issues in current politics.[54]

[52] John Stuart Mill, *On Liberty*, ed. W. L. Courtney (London, 1901), pp. xxiii–xxiv, xxv. Courtney had expressed similar reservations about the Individualistic basis of *On Liberty* in his earlier biographical study: *Life of John Stuart Mill* (London, 1889), 127–9.

[53] John Stuart Mill, *On Liberty, Utilitarianism, Considerations on Representative Government*, ed. A. D. Lindsay (London, 1910), pp. xxi, xxiii, x. For Lindsay's own political allegiances at this period, see Drusilla Scott, *A. D. Lindsay: A Biography* (Oxford, 1971), and esp. Julia Stapleton, 'Academic political thought and the development of political studies in Britain 1900–1950' (unpublished D.Phil. Dissertation, University of Sussex, 1985), ch. 5.

[54] John Stuart Mill, *On Liberty, Considerations on Representative Government, The Subjection of Women*, ed. M. G. Fawcett (London, 1912), p. v, vi, xiii. By removing

However, when twelve years later Harold Laski wrote his introduction to a World's Classics edition of the *Autobiography*, he treated Mill very much as belonging to 'the intellectual history of the nineteenth century' rather than as still actively addressing contemporary political debate. Laski's tone was immensely respectful (a further sign of Mill's classic status: the young Laski did not deal gently with those contemporary theorists he found wanting), but much of the literary energy of his introduction was devoted to explaining away what now seemed like Mill's shortcomings as the result of changed historical circumstances: 'We should, perhaps, state Mill's problem differently . . . ', 'We, doubtless, should state Mill's problem in different terms . . . ', and so on, where the 'perhaps' and the 'doubtless' express Laski's slight embarrassment at being found in the company of a writer whose assumptions now seemed so patently outdated. With the air of one apologizing for an old friend's evident aberrations, Laski reached, not altogether successfully, for some larger reflection on transitoriness: 'The corroding hand of time lays its fingers more surely on political writing than upon any other kind.' And pressing on in the same funeral-in-the-Abbey register, Laski concluded by escorting Mill to the pedestal reserved for him: 'There are men in the record of English thought, like Hobbes and Hume, whose work has been more universal; there have been men also, like Bentham, whose immediate influence has been more profound. But there are few who have better illuminated the tradition of their age, and whose contribution was more honourable or more nearly stainless.'[55]

By the 1920s the changing face of British politics as well as the vagaries of intellectual fashion and the mere passage of time combined to place Mill in the company of historical exhibits from a previous era. The moral assumptions and vocabulary that Mill had in large measure shared with his contemporary audience and their immediate successors were starting to lose their purchase in the

the issue from the political agenda, the enfranchisement of women in 1918 diminished the immediate political purchase of what had hitherto remained one of Mill's most controversial works.

[55] John Stuart Mill, *Autobiography*, ed. H. J. Laski (Oxford, 1924), pp. ix, xix, xx. Laski had hit a similar note in a brief article he wrote to mark the fiftieth anniversary of Mill's death, where he emphasized Mill's historical role in the transition from *laissez-faire* to modern Collectivism, and expressed the standard reservation that 'the experience of half a century would make us emphasize more firmly the degree to which the preservation of individuality depends upon the positive character of social control'; *Nation*, 28 Apr. 1923.

public discussion of social and economic questions.[56] Where *On Liberty* was still invoked, it was for its statement of the case for 'negative liberty'.[57] Its pervasive strenuousness and commitment to altruism passed largely unnoticed. The effective demise of the Liberal Party no doubt helped further to loosen the ties that bound Mill to contemporary political debate, and large-scale unemployment was not an issue upon which he could be deployed as an authority to much advantage.

'There is hardly a more striking example of the worthlessness of posthumous reputation than the oblivion into which my father has fallen among the world at large.' Thus wrote Mill in his diary in 1854, and so, wrote R. H. Murray in 1929, 'might have written any time the last thirty years those who recall the position which he [J. S. M.] once held. . . . He and his works have passed into the shade.'[58] Even at this, the nadir of his reputation, that shade was never quite as obliteratingly profound as the darkness which had earlier fallen upon his father's reputation. Apart from his continued life as a canonical text in economics and moral philosophy, he always occupied a prominent place in the various accounts of English nineteenth-century political thought written towards the end of this period. For the most part, these accounts placed Mill very much where Dicey had placed him. D. C. Somervell, for example, in his survey of *English Thought in the Nineteenth Century*, explicitly acknowledged his debt to Dicey and adopted his division of the century into three periods, treating Mill as the representative of 'the Benthamite Liberal orthodoxy' of the middle period.[59] The chief variation, especially in the 1930s, was to emphasize those elements in

[56] See above, Ch. 2, pp. 87–9, and Ch. 3, pp. 117–8.

[57] This emerges from the conscientious survey of Liberal political thought in the 1920s in Michael Freeden, *Liberalism Divided: A Study in British Political Thought 1914–1939* (Oxford, 1986), esp. 266–84.

[58] R. H. Murray, *Studies in the English Social and Political Thinkers of the Nineteenth Century*, 2 vols. (Cambridge, 1929), i. 429. Murray's book is yet another exploration, and celebration, of the distinctive qualities of English thought in these matters: 'The object of my history is to define the characteristics of English thinkers . . . by taking account of the cumulative effect of a lengthening past and showing how the current of English thought has gathered strength and depth from the gradual working out of the national adventure' (p. vi).

[59] D. C. Somervell, *English Thought in the Nineteenth Century* (London, 1929), pp. vi–vii. Crane Brinton slightly varied this threefold division, treating Bentham, Coleridge, and others under the heading of 'the Revolution of 1832', then Mill, Carlyle, and others under, somewhat incongruously, 'Chartism', leaving a longer list from Bagehot to Kidd to the section headed 'the prosperous Victorians'; Brinton, *English Political Thought*.

Mill's thought that made him a plausible candidate for the role of Founding Grandfather of English Socialism. Mary Hamilton presented such a Fabian portrait of Mill in the little book it still seemed worth devoting to him in 1933, while three years later Harold Laski, at the height of his Marxist phase and eager to distance himself from the evolutionary progressivism of the Labour Party, effectively pointed to the same connection, though viewed more hostilely, when he declared that English Socialism was 'a body of doctrine upon which the emphasis of John Stuart Mill's ideas was far more profound than that of Marx'.[60] The tendency of both accounts, of course, was to find in Mill a prime expression of those qualities which were taken to be distinctive of the national intellectual tradition.

VI

Herbert Butterfield claimed, in a now much-cited passage, that the Whig interpretation of English history had, by the end of the nineteenth century, become the 'national' interpretation; or, in other words, that what had once been partisan and polemical had mutated into a shared commonplace.[61] In similar vein, one might suggest that values and beliefs that had in the mid-nineteenth century been distinctively Liberal had by the 1920s become assimilated as part of the received political culture of the English educated classes.[62] A very minor consequence of this was to facilitate the depiction of Mill as an eirenic figure who embodied some of the most cherished dispositions of *the* English political tradition. What had, of course, to be played

[60] M. A. Hamilton, *John Stuart Mill* (London, 1933); see esp. 76–8 for her confident assertion that Mill would have elaborated a fully Socialist indictment of capitalism had he been alive in 1933. H. J. Laski, *The Rise of European Liberalism* (London, 1936), quoted in Freeden, *Liberalism Divided*, 309.

[61] Herbert Butterfield, *The Englishman and his History* (Cambridge, 1944), 79; cf. John W. Burrow, *A Liberal Descent: Victorian Historians and the English Past* (Cambridge, 1981), postscript. See also below, Ch. 9, pp. 350–1.

[62] A somewhat similar suggestion is put forward in Dennis Smith, 'Englishness and the Liberal inheritance after 1886', in Colls and Dodd (eds.), *Englishness*, 254–82. Much of G. M. Trevelyan's later work can be seen as blending Whig and Liberal legacies in a more encompassing 'Englishness', a conclusion that emerges from Joseph M. Hernon, 'The last Whig historian and consensus history: George Macaulay Trevelyan 1876–1962', *American Historical Review*, 81 (1976), 66–97. For an illuminating discussion of Ernest Barker's work along similar lines, see Julia Stapleton, 'The national character of Ernest Barker's political thought', *Political Studies*, 37 (1989), 171–87.

down along the way was his actual historical role as an outspoken critic of what he saw as the dominant political and intellectual tendencies of his own society. What he had derisively termed 'the Cimmerian darkness'[63] of English insularity had, arguably, not lightened very much in the first half of the twentieth century, and his complaints about English parochialism, philistinism, and complacency could have had no less purchase in the 1930s than in the 1830s. Indeed, it could be said that recruiting him to occupy a central role in what was now seen as the characteristic tradition of English thought largely served to bolster further the very habit of self-congratulation of which he had been such a vehement critic.

The extent to which, by the end of the period covered in this book, Mill had been absorbed into what one might see as the intellectual equivalent of the 'English Heritage model' of the national past can be neatly illustrated by his appearance in a collective volume designed to nurture and extend the pride in Englishness that was both needed and stimulated during the Second World War. *The Character of England* (which finally appeared in 1947), edited by Sir Ernest Barker, is celebratory, complacent, and a compendium of pious observations about the qualities of the English 'national character', whether displayed at Agincourt, on the cricket field, or on the magistrates' bench. The chapter on 'The individual and the community' (by the Right Hon. Richard Law, MP) actually begins with Mill's remark that in England 'nine-tenths of the internal business which elsewhere devolves on government is transacted by agencies independent of it', which is then made the text for a sermon on the virtues of *the* English tradition of individualism, free association, voluntary organization, and local self-government. (Mill's reservations about the English prejudice against state action are not mentioned.) It was enough that Mill could be recognized as the ideal spokesman for this national quality, someone perfectly suited to 'expressing, indeed, a truth which is fundamental to the English way of life and which differentiates it sharply from that of most other countries'.[64] In 1947, of all years, the identification of essential Englishness with a distrust of state action could hardly have been entirely innocent.[65]

63 John Stuart Mill, 'Coleridge' (1840), *The Collected Works of John Stuart Mill*, ed. John M. Robson, 31 vols. (Toronto and London, 1965–91) (hereafter *CW*), x. 140.

64 Ernest Barker (ed.), *The Character of England* (Oxford, London, 1947), 29–30.

65 It should be noted that Law, son of former Tory Prime Minister Andrew Bonar Law, was a prominent Conservative Party polemicist.

But for a more general re-making of Mill in the image of Englishness as it was officially conceived by the 1940s, we have to turn in the same volume to the chapter on 'Thought' by Basil Willey. One is tempted to say that the achievement of Willey's chapter is to make the phrase 'English Thought' appear to be an oxymoron. English thinkers, Willey is not displeased to record, stand to the 'peaks' of Continental speculation rather as the hills of the Lake District do to the Alps ('cosy' is the term Willey reaches for—and, alas, finds; it would be interesting to have the comments of Lord Brougham or Governor Eyre or Sir William Hamilton on this as the appropriate term with which to characterize Mill). In effect, Willey was at this point making an account of English intellectual history palatable by making it as little 'intellectual' as possible: the Lake District was not chosen on merely scenic grounds, for the celebration of English Romantic poetry, stripped of its overtly political and philosophical concerns, was a central element in this construction of the nation's cultural inheritance. In this context, the effect of portraying Mill as something of a cross between a 'matter-of-fact' Benthamite and a Romantic poet *manqué* is to make him into an example of just that spirit of 'practical empiricism' that he had devoted so much of his life to denouncing.[66]

The enormous growth of scholarly interest in Mill since 1945, and especially since the late 1950s, is beyond the scope of this book, though as I suggested above, it is arguable that he still retains a capacity to stir political passion, albeit in the curiously displaced form of conflicting scholarly interpretations. The tensions and ironies in this kind of press-ganging of past figures are nicely revealed in the way in which his alleged élitism and covert authoritarianism could be savaged by one kind of conservative, expressing the antipathy of old Toryism (and employing some of the high-handedness of the old *Quarterly*), while his individualism and libertarianism could be defended by another, speaking in the accents of the New Right, decked out with the technicalities of analytical philosophy.[67] That he should be thought to repay such investment

[66] Barker, *Character of England*, 321, 336–7.

[67] Cowling, *Mill and Liberalism*; John Gray, *Mill on Liberty: A Defence* (London, 1983). The political basis of Gray's selective reading of Mill is revealed very clearly in his more recent 'Mill's and other Liberalisms', in Knud Haakonssen (ed.), *Traditions of Liberalism: Essays on John Locke, Adam Smith, and John Stuart Mill* (Sydney, 1988); I am grateful to Donald Winch for this reference. Gertrude Himmelfarb, *On Liberty and Liberalism: The Case of John Stuart Mill* (London, 1975) is another work which shows its ideological hand pretty plainly.

suggests that as a political theorist, at least, he still enjoys some of the symbolic value of the third phase of response I identified earlier, and it is presumably safe to predict that if he is to have a claim on the attention of any but scholarly specialists in the twenty-first century, it will be on account of the continued vitality of a political theory calling itself 'liberal'.

How far he continues to be regarded as an embodiment of 'Englishness' will depend in part on the needs which such refurbishings of national stereotypes have to meet in the future. I have argued here that the late nineteenth and early twentieth century was a period which saw a particularly concerted construction of 'Englishness', as part of a more general 'nationalization' of English culture. The first half of the nineteenth century had witnessed some very deep conflicts in the nation's political and intellectual life, and for those thereafter who wished, not always consciously, to project a more emollient image of stability and consensus Mill was a useful figure who could be represented as combining, with characteristic native eclecticism, the best from several traditions of thought to produce a blandly acceptable and essentially untheoretical distillation of practical wisdom. The pressures likely to be felt in the future to explore and deal critically with somewhat different dimensions of Englishness may yet give a new and unexpected afterlife to Mill the relentless theorist, Mill the uncompromising partisan, and Mill the outspoken critic of English parochialism.

9

The Whig Interpretation of English Literature

Literary History and National Identity

I

Living largely in the imagination, we may begin by letting our minds play over two entirely imaginary episodes from an English history that never was.

The first is set in 1866, which, in this imaginary world, is the fiftieth anniversary of the Napoleonic conquest of Britain. The official language of government and education has now for two generations been French; the counties have been replaced by *départements*, and the real administrators are the *préfets*, appointed direct from Paris, though a regional assembly of co-operative notables has been allowed to stage a pastiche of Parliamentary debate in annual gatherings at Canterbury. But by the 1860s we have, as in so much of Europe, stirrings of nationalist discontent, and, as in so much of Europe, questions of language and literature and even philology are to the fore. Militant young members of the Guild of Wessex address each other in a laboriously learned version of Anglo-Saxon; meetings of the Early English Text Society are officially illegal, yet the recovering and re-editing of ancient English texts is pursued with patriotic ardour. Clandestine reprintings of a popular edition of Asser's *Life of King Alfred* can barely keep pace with demand. A dictionary of the English language on historical lines is planned, attempting to do for an imagined 'English nation' what had been done for Germany by her philologists and lexicographers in the previous generation and was being done by Hungarians and Bohemians in this.

Of particular significance for my concerns, one fruit of what was later to be known as 'the English Revival', is a proposal to publish a series to be called something like 'English Writers' or 'English Men of Letters', designed to subvert and eventually replace the official curriculum of Racine, Corneille, and Voltaire. Naturally, the discussions of this proposal become very heated: one group within the Early English Text Society insists that only authors who wrote in Old or Middle English are to be considered. Representatives of the League of St George, on the other hand, insist on the need to include authors who can stir the consciousness of the less scholarly classes: they regard the novels of Dickens as the equivalent of several regiments, and they engage one Frederick Elgar, whose son was to become an even more famous nationalist composer, to set some of Wordsworth's simpler lyrics to music. But eventually a compromise list is agreed, the basis for a literary education for properly patriotic Englishmen (and, suitably modified, for Englishwomen). The modern section begins, naturally, with Shakespeare; there was then much debate about Milton, finally rejected for republicanism, latinity, and excessive use of *enjambement*. Dryden and Pope are excluded as literary quislings, practitioners of a French aesthetic, just as, among contemporary poets and critics, greatest hatred is reserved for Matthew Arnold, whose literary toadying has recently been rewarded with election to the Académie Française. Others who have written in the English language, but who have expressed the consciousness of other peoples, are of course excluded: no Hume, no Burns, no Scott, no Carlyle, and no Swift, no Sheridan, no Goldsmith, no Burke. The premises where the Gibbon volume was being printed were attacked one night and burned when it was discovered that he had written his first book in French. But finally the flames of nationalist sedition were spread through Wessex and Mercia and the other ancient kingdoms by a series of inflammatory little books on Bede, Langland, Shakespeare, Camden, Dr Johnson, Wordsworth, and Dickens.

Now imagine a second, no less fictive but perhaps no less plausible, scenario. Here, the year is 1898, the centenary, in *this* imaginary world, of the (second) English Revolution, which had, like other revolutions, begun with mutinies in the navy in 1798, and been aided by the circumstances of war with a foreign power and intense economic hardship. Several republican regimes had succeeded each other in the first seventy years of the century, but then the army, the Church, and the landed classes had staged a successful counter-revolution and installed one of the least unacceptable descendants of George III on the throne. The arrival of the centenary of the Revolution, therefore, was bound to be a highly charged affair, marked by intense political and sectarian rivalry. Once again, questions of literature and the curriculum assume great political and nationalist significance. For the Right (a term, incidentally, used with as much familiarity by nineteenth-century Englishmen, in this account, as by any other European citizens), the pantheon of national heroes leans heavily towards soldiers, expansionist statesmen, Erastian churchmen, and court poets; the Left naturally favours republicans, anti-clericals, popular novelists, and professors of philosophy. Once again, there is a proposal to launch a series of volumes to be called 'the English Men of Letters', something that could provide the backbone of what the Right called the 'national' curriculum, a proper source of patriotic pride. But here the two sides are unable to agree a common list, and the Left, traditionally stronger (according to this fantasy) in London and the provincial universities, finally issues its own series to counter the official selection commissioned by the Right largely from Oxford and Cambridge (especially, perhaps, from All Souls).

The divisions are revealing. The Right propose, above all, court poets, dramatists, and wits such as Chaucer, Spenser, Dryden, Walpole, and Southey; among prose writers, those they would see read in every school in the land include Cranmer, Hooker, Lancelot Andrewes, Clarendon. Their list is a little weak on novelists, though they are prepared to include the series of novels that had been secretly commissioned by the aristocratic opposition in mid-century to idealize the traditional hierarchical relations of the English cathedral town, commissioned from a then little-known novelist called Trollope. The Left, whose series is called, inevitably, 'Writers of the English People', also have a strong list of poets, running, contentiously, from Marvell's Cromwellian odes to the work of Crabbe, Clare, and Shelley (proposals for a volume confined to the *young* Wordsworth were eventually dropped). But the great strength of their series is in prose writers, including Bunyan, Defoe, Paine, Dickens, and Hardy. Only one author is common to both series, namely Shakespeare, but whereas the volume commissioned by the

Right, and written by a young writer called Kipling, concentrates on the patriotism of the history plays and the reconciling message of the great tragedies, the volume commissioned by the Left—started shortly before his death by the aged William Morris, and finally finished several years later by a young and little-known writer called Herbert Wells—stressed instead the popular energies of the comedies and the subversive nature of Shakespeare's questioning of the limits of language. One could, of course, extend this story into the twentieth century, showing how the Right is finally brought down by its catastrophically incompetent conduct of the First World War, and how in 1919 the English Third Republic is established which, as well as dispossessing the Church of England and breaking up large landed estates, bans the use of the 'reactionary' English Men of Letters series in schools and universities. The whirligig of time, of course, brings in its revenges, and many decades later the greatest popularity among the rebelliously reactionary young is enjoyed, despite or perhaps because of official disapproval, by a new series called 'Old Accents'.

I trust that by now the point of both these imaginary accounts will be evident. To put it negatively, one could simply say that during the nineteenth century, 'the English' (I shall come back to that familiar metonymy later) did not undergo two of the most formative experiences of modern European cultural history. On the one hand, political, military, and commercial success insulated them from invasion, defeat, or the other common promptings to a self-conscious 'liberationist' nationalism and its associated imperative of political, cultural, or ethnic self-definition. And on the other hand, the relative internal stability and continuity of constitutional development since the end of the seventeenth century (or, in another idiom, the highly successful adaptation by the governing classes to changing social circumstances) meant that Victorian Britain was not marked by the kind of fundamental political and ideological division which, systematically and repetitively, makes all aspects of a society's life into material for partisan dispute. (Sporadic challenges from radical or working-class groups were another matter.) As a result, the dominant relation to the English past during this period, the intellectual and literary no less than the political and constitutional past, was experienced along the lines of what might be called, as I suggested in Chapter 8 above, the 'English Heritage' or 'National Trust' model, a repository of treasures which all members of a united nation can enjoy as part of their uniquely glorious heritage. The muffling inclusiveness of this view is beautifully caught in the almost liturgical cadence of a passage in Eliot's *Four Quartets*:

> These men, and those who opposed them
> And those whom they opposed
> Accept the constitution of silence
> And are folded in a single party.

And here the eirenic gentleness of 'folded', culpably disguising the violence of the actual processes by which conflict is rendered liveable, begins to suggest some of the tendentious purposes which can be served by this invocation of the encompassing membership of the national community, 'folded in a single party'.

These two absences, as I have characterized them, had a strongly re-inforcing effect on each other. The absence of challenges to fundamental moral and political legitimacy removed what would otherwise have been a major stimulus to defining the nature and limits of this 'national community'. Conversely, the absense of explicit (and thereby, inevitably, ideologically selective) definitions of the nation or the state removed what has elsewhere been one of the chief provocations to disputes over legitimacy. For these and other reasons, explicit nationalism did not become a prominent feature of public debate, with the result that to some ears there may still be a discordant oddity in speaking of 'English nationalism' at all. Certainly, the conventional view was for long that 'in England patriotism takes the place of nationalism'.[1] In part, this view rested on taking a rather restrictive view of nationalism itself: all the while it was defined as 'the reaction of peoples who feel culturally at a disadvantage',[2] the identification of its presence in modern English history would scarcely seem like an urgent task.

My own starting-point in this chapter is that, understood more largely as the dynamic or activating power of the assertion and confirmation of national identity, a power operating, often unobserved, across a wide range of political and cultural activities, *English* nationalism has in fact been a vast presence in *British* history of the

[1] H. M. Chadwick, *The Nationalities of Europe and the Growth of National Ideologies* (Cambridge, 1945), 3.

[2] John Plamenatz, 'Two types of nationalism', in Eugene Kamenka (ed.), *Nationalism: The Nature and Evolution of an Idea* (Canberra, 1973), 27.

last two centuries (that is surely the right relation between the two adjectival forms), even although it has largely not been recognized as such or systematically articulated. This suggests the need to explore in the light of the themes discussed in previous chapters, some of the sources and idioms available for formulating this sense of national identity in Victorian Britain. But, even more than in earlier chapters, the discussion will extend well beyond the narrowly political. For I want to propose that, since at least the late eighteenth century and in increasingly official form since the late nineteenth, a crucial vehicle for establishing and negotiating the relevant sense of national identity has been provided by that symbolic and emotionally charged selection of writing known as 'English literature'. I argued in the previous chapter that the late nineteenth century saw a process which may be identified as the 'nationalization' of English culture, that is, the softening of many of the political and religious divisions that had marked the first half of the century, and the deliberate creation or extension of national cultural institutions. (This development was further encouraged, one may suppose, by that sense of foreign competition and imperial rivalry which is such a marked feature of the pronouncements of the educated classes in the three decades before 1914.) I now want to suggest that the noticeably greater attention devoted to arranging and celebrating English *literary* history in the last few decades of the century, including moves to establish it as an academic subject, may be seen as part of this wider process of national self-definition. Indeed, the consolidation of a 'national' interpretation of England's political history in this period can be roughly paralleled in the celebratory accounts of English *literary* distinctiveness, to the point where we might get some illumination from referring to 'the Whig interpretation of English literature'.

The analogy implied by this phrase suggests a relation to the national literature which was celebratory and consensual, qualities much in evidence in the late nineteenth century. But in the course of the twentieth century this relation, while remaining culturally central, has become more divided, more combative, and more troubled, thereby contributing to the situation in which literary criticism in the broadest sense has been acknowledged as the chief idiom for cultural criticism in mid-twentieth-century Britain. (This is perhaps the unstated premiss underlying the common observation, usually given the form of a complaint, that much of the elaboration of moral and political values which has been carried on in some other European countries in a more explicitly theoretical vein has been conducted in Britain in the twentieth century through the medium of discussion of literature.) As part of this wider cultural activity, what developed as the academic study of 'English' was thus freighted from the start with an exceptional intellectual and even moral significance, a condition attested in part by the violence of so many of its ostensibly literary-critical debates. In particular, the question of sustaining, reworking, or challenging the central 'canon' of English literature has become a crucial mode of legitimation in the cultural politics of the mid- and late twentieth century, as well, of course, as an apparently inexhaustible source of rancour among those charged with the design or reform of syllabuses. I suggest that an important dimension in our understanding of these disputes will be missing until we recognize that what we are witnessing here is the disintegration of the Whig interpretation of English literature.

To understand how this has come to be true, however, we need to look well beyond the confines of the academic discipline of 'English' and to adopt a longer perspective than that provided by the profession's own much-publicized debates of recent decades. Accordingly, this chapter tries to sketch in the outlines of the so far unwritten history of English cultural nationalism in this period,[3] and to indicate the place of celebrations of the canon of English literature in it. My chief interest concerns the terms in which this literary tradition was characterized, though I also briefly point to a few of the changes which led, by the 1920s and 1930s, to the literary-critical engagement with that canon becoming one of the chief resources for conducting larger disputes in British culture, in the course of which the whole business of constructing genealogies of Englishness acquired an altogether less confident and more contentious dimension.

II

Almost any way of framing an enquiry about the identity of the 'English nation' before the end of the eighteenth century involves

[3] Cf. the opening (and in some ways most interesting) sentence of Gerald Newman's recent book, *The Rise of English Nationalism: A Cultural History 1750–1830* (London, 1987): 'It is strange to think how greatly English nationalism has eluded our scholarly attention.'

begging crucial questions. In this respect, the history of the national identity of the country which has allegedly not known nationalism in the modern period is full of paradoxes and contradictions. Admittedly, 'England' had had three of the defining characteristics of a stable national identity for longer than any comparable country. It had had a continuous and relatively stable political existence, unbroken by foreign conquest or loss of significant core territory, since the eleventh century. It had known an exceptional continuity of legal and administrative forms since at least the thirteenth century. And it had possessed a widely intelligible written vernacular language since the fifteenth century. From at least the seventeenth century onwards, these attributes, in various guises, provided the bases for celebrations of the distinctive continuity and good fortune of 'England'. Of course, the work of the antiquarians and propagandists responsible for constructing these narratives often involved the more or less conscious creation of fictions. The barons who signed Magna Charta, after all, neither spoke English nor thought of themselves as defending 'English liberties'; they were only retrospectively recruited as heroes of a subsequently unbroken constitutional development. More problematic still was the fact that the polity in question could only be defined in terms of the shifting fortunes of dynastic rule. 'England' (or, later, 'Britain') was at any given moment the realm of the monarch, and was not necessarily coextensive with the core of the territory in which English liberties or the English language were held to thrive. The awkward term 'the United Kingdom' still records a striking instance of this difficulty, a union of two crowns to make one 'country'. Moreover, not only did the boundaries of the polity frequently expand and, less often, contract, but the monarchs themselves were often of foreign origin, and not easily celebrated as incarnations of 'national' identity.[4]

But perhaps just because it has been difficult to hold on to any steady definition of the nature and limits of the *political* entity that is in question, more broadly *cultural* images of national identity have assumed correspondingly greater importance. (These play their part in sustaining the identities of communities everywhere, of course;

[4] It may none the less be a sign of the earlier absence of modern notions of 'ethnic' identity that the First World War seems to have been the first occasion when the 'foreign' provenance of the royal family was widely perceived as an embarrassment; see Benedict Anderson, *Imagined Communities: Reflections on the Origin and Spread of Nationalism* (London, 1983), 81.

the difference is one of degree, arising out of a peculiar history, rather than of kind.) There is now, presumably, no need to labour the tensions and contradictions that have been involved in using the term 'the English' to refer to the citizens, or more properly the subjects, of a doubtfully 'united' kingdom which was also throughout this period the nucleus of an empire. But it is also clear that there have in fact been certain core notions of 'Englishness' which have provided the dominant images and assumptions in relation not only to other parts of the British Isles but also within England itself, idealizing a rather vaguely located rural south—what has been aptly termed 'Deep England'.[5] There has clearly been work for notions of cultural identity to do here.

Quite where, if at all, in this development we first find that potent mixture of images, memories, and aggressions which we have come to term 'nationalism' is a more controversial question. One provocatively clear-cut answer would be that self-conscious English nationalism is first fully elaborated in the late eighteenth century as part of a largely middle-class, to some extent radical, and eventually Evangelical protest against the Francophile culture of a cosmopolitan aristocracy.[6] In this account, a sense of 'national character' is influentially adumbrated through the celebration, by Johnson, Warton, and others, of a distinctive English literary tradition, to set against the previously dominant models of French classicism. This leads to the highly contentious conclusion that what we know as 'Victorianism' is really the successful take-over of the wider culture by this initially oppositional 'nationalist' movement, as a result of which the English come to congratulate themselves on their unique blend of liberty, sincerity, and moral earnestness.

The question can be given a subtler and more restrained answer by attending primarily to the articulations of the Whig interpretation of the English past in Victorian historiography.[7] The sense of national

[5] Patrick Wright, *On Living in an Old Country: The National Past in Contemporary Britain* (London, 1985), 81; see also Alun Howkins, 'The discovery of rural England', in Robert Colls and Philip Dodd (eds.), *Englishness: Politics and Culture 1880–1920* (London, 1986).

[6] This is the answer proposed in Newman, *Rise of English Nationalism*, esp. ch. 6. I am not sufficiently familiar with the period on which Newman concentrates to be able to question his interpretation in any detail, but he does seem both to exaggerate the novelty of his enquiry and to press his case about a 'middle-class nationalist movement' a little hard.

[7] See J. W. Burrow, *A Liberal Descent: Victorian Historians and the English Past*

identity expressed in this literature rested principally upon the celebration of the way in which England's native genius for liberty and representative government had brought it a far more fortunate history than had been the lot of less happy peoples (again, the contrast with France is revealed as a crucial part of national self-definition). Of special interest here is the fact that this story proves to be in effect one of a growing consensus, in which what had begun life as a partisan account of, in particular, the constitutional and religious struggles of the seventeenth century, finally becomes accepted towards the latter part of the nineteenth century as the basis for what Butterfield later called the 'national' interpretation of English history. Even by the mid-Victorian period, however, it is clear that the two pillars of national self-definition (among the educated classes at any rate) were the sense of England's peculiarly happy political development and the related sense of a distinctive type of national character.

By the middle of the nineteenth century, of course, nationalism was already making its dramatic impact on the history and geography of Europe, and reflective minds in England could not remain untouched by this spectacle. Although it is obvious that Victorian England will hardly fit the classic pattern of nineteenth-century European nationalism, it was not entirely immune to the forces and impulses that fuelled more explicitly nationalist movements elsewhere. Consider, by way of example, a feature insisted upon in a recent synoptic account of the rise of nationalism, namely that the activities of 'vernacularizing lexicographers, grammarians, philologists, and litterateurs . . . were central to the shaping of nineteenth-century European nationalisms'.[8] Many such activities were, of course, pursued in mid-nineteenth-century Britain also, albeit without quite the same political resonances or sectarian functions as in my imaginary accounts. Germanic linguistic and historical scholarship, in particular, had sharpened the focus and extended the range of narratives of 'English' descent, as part of a wider Teutonic and, eventually, Aryan history. But even these enlarged scholarly perspectives assumed a peculiar form in the distinctive circumstances of British culture.

(Cambridge, 1981); although Burrow does not explicitly raise the question of nationalism in these terms, he makes clear that the historians he discusses were all concerned with 'an idea of England and the English' (2).

[8] Anderson, *Imagined Communities*, 69.

A good example of this is provided by the project of compiling a great vernacular dictionary on historical lines. I mentioned in the first of my imaginary accounts the nationalist and often oppositional significance that such an undertaking might possess (and did possess in Europe). In fact, the project that eventually issued in the *Oxford English Dictionary*, with its declared ambition to capture 'the genius of the English language', was not without its patriotic overtones, and it is not difficult to see how it might have corresponded to the European model. Indeed, in some ways, its moving spirit, James Murray, had the Identikit profile of a nineteenth-century liberal nationalist in its British mutation: he was a Nonconformist; he was an ardent Liberal; he was an admirer of Garibaldi; he enthusiastically welcomed Kossuth to Hawick with a banner written in Hungarian; and he named two of his sons Aelfric and Ethelbert.[9] In addition, he was, one might say, the Stubbs of English philology, charting with appreciative patience the slow, impersonal growth of the rich intricacy of the national vernacular. But the comparison with Stubbs—the Whig historian of ancient English liberties who voted Tory and gave up his Oxford chair to become a bishop[10]—also signals some of the complexity of the English case. It is not merely flippant to begin to indicate that complexity by pointing out that this great monument to Englishness was compiled by a Scotsman, who was knighted for it, and dedicated to a monarch of recent German descent. For these details not only indicate how far Murray's dictionary was from being an oppositional project, but they also suggest one recurring difficulty for any putative English nationalism in modern times, namely the absence of an easily identifiable or separable ethnic basis for the actual British polity—it has hardly been a pure example of the nation-state, after all.[11]

The complexity and ambiguities of the relation between the history of the 'British' state and the identity of the 'English' people may have increased the emphasis placed on the seemingly less

[9] See K. M. Elisabeth Murray, *Caught in the Web of Words: James Murray and the Oxford English Dictionary* (London, 1977). One indication of the fierceness of his Liberalism is that in 1910, following the Lords' rejection of the 'People's Budget', he wanted to see an English equivalent of the French Revolution (335).

[10] See the discussion above, Ch. 6, pp. 220–1.

[11] Some examples of the unsteady definitions of the *patria* during this period are given in J. H. Grainger, *Patriotisms: Britain: 1900–1939* (London, 1986), ch. 1. The more general problem of the changing limits of the British polity is interestingly raised in J. G. A. Pocock, 'The limits and divisions of British history: in search of the unknown subject', *American Historical Review*, 87 (1982), 311–36.

problematic unity offered by the English language and its literature. In the mid-nineteenth century 'the history of the language' developed as a scholarly field heavily invested with patriotic sentiment. There was evident pride in the tendentious claim that the English language was 'older than the majority of the tongues in use throughout Europe', and a revealingly insistent note in reiterations of its unbroken continuity: 'We have a continuous succession of written remains since the seventh century at least', and 'they afford us a record of representation of the English language in which there is no gap'.[12] Not surprisingly, the proper historical study of the national language could in these circumstances be envisaged as a 'monument of learning and patriotism', and the proposal that eventually led to the *OED* could similarly present the undertaking as a great 'national project'.[13] Arguably, the very project of an inventory of the 'standard' language acknowledged and encouraged a sense of greater national uniformity; the scope of the *English Dialect Dictionary*, which began publication in 1898, was defined by contrast as what was regional or not 'standard'. The same process was at work in the codification of 'Received Pronunciation', a further stage of 'nationalization' encouraged by universal elementary education and spreading literacy. But it was not only 'the' language (that is, a particular version of the language, 'standard' written English) which was elevated by the ambition of such a dictionary. Its compilation also involved an interesting symbiotic relation to the establishment of a 'canon' of English literature. The Philological Society's *Proposal for the Publication of a New English Dictionary* in 1857 had declared that a lexicon should contain 'every word occurring in the literature of the language it professes to illustrate', in effect presuming some working agreement on what was to be recognized as constituting 'the literature'. At the same time, the works consulted by the compilers thereby acquired canonical status, as was already suggested by the reference, in the 'preface' to the first volume, to taking the quotations from 'all the great English writers of all ages', just as references by other philologists to taking their material from 'the chief English authors' reinforced the process.[14]

[12] G. L. Craik, *A Compendious History of English Literature and of the English Language from the Norman Conquest; with Numerous Specimens*, 2 vols. (London, 1861), i. 30; cited in Tony Crowley, *The Politics of Discourse: The Standard Language Question in British Cultural Debates* (London, 1989), 46–8.

[13] See Crowley, *Politics of Discourse*, 39, 110.

[14] Both cited ibid. 117, 120.

In the course of the second half of the nineteenth century, language was increasingly overtaken by literature as one of the central symbolic expressions of the 'imagined community' of the English people. This process was heavily dependent on the sense that, with the increase in literacy assumed to follow from the expansion of education, there would be a large new audience needing to be inducted into the glories of the national literature. One of the most obvious ways in which the canon of English literature was given enduring form and disseminated widely during this period was through the production of 'primers' for the use of students at various levels. For example, Henry Morley's *A First Sketch of English Literature*, published in 1873, sold over 40,000 copies, but this was soon eclipsed by Stopford Brooke's *A Primer of English Literature* which sold 25,000 copies in the first ten months, and nearly half a million by 1916.[15] Similarly, this market was hungry for approved selections of vernacular texts, and the growing trade in anthologies of English poetry in the second half of the nineteenth century gave influential expression to what I am calling 'the Whig interpretation of English literature'. Perhaps the most notable example—certainly the most influential—was Palgrave's *Golden Treasury*, the first edition of which appeared in 1861. Palgrave's explicit purpose was to produce 'a true national anthology', though by the standards of the modern, post-Eliot, canon the selection appears highly idiosyncratic: Donne and Blake are absent and Herbert only gets 20 lines, whereas Walter Scott gets 345 and the comparatively minor Romantic, Thomas Campbell, gets no fewer than 400 lines.[16] The role of the later *Oxford Book of English Verse*, edited by Sir Arthur Quiller-Couch, would also repay investigation, particularly in view of the judgement that this anthology 'presides over the Great War in a way that has never been sufficiently appreciated'.[17] By 1939 Quiller-Couch's anthology 'had been reprinted twenty times and nearly half a million copies had been sold'.[18] Although in the reviewing of *new* works of

[15] On Morley's *Sketch*, see John Gross, *The Rise and Fall of the Man of Letters* (London, 1969), 172; on Brooke, see the editorial discussion of Matthew Arnold's review of the work in *The Complete Prose Works of Matthew Arnold*, ed. R. H. Super, 11 vols. (Ann Arbor, Mich. 1960–77), viii. 441.

[16] For details see Charles Morgan, *The House of Macmillan (1843–1943)* (London, 1943), 62–3.

[17] Paul Fussell, *The Great War and Modern Memory* (New York, 1975), 159.

[18] F. Brittain, *Arthur Quiller-Couch: A Biographical Study of 'Q'* (Cambridge, 1948), 39.

literature there were, inevitably, disputes on aesthetic and moral grounds between various schools of contemporary writers, the dominant relation to England's much-celebrated succession of poets and novelists in the past, at least as evinced by the most widely used accounts, seems to have been to accept that they could be 'folded into a single party'.

This was perhaps most evident in the actual 'English Men of Letters' series, launched by Macmillan's under the general editorship of John Morley in 1877. The advertisement for the series, reproduced in the early volumes, made clear that it was 'addressed to the general public with a view to both stirring and satisfying an interest in literature and its great topics. . . . An immense class is growing up, and must every year increase, whose education will have made them alive to the importance of the masters of our literature,' and so on. Needless to say, contingency played some part in determining the eventual range of both subjects and contributors: we know that the publishers tried hard but unsuccessfully to get George Eliot to do Shakespeare, for instance, and there were no doubt more stories, now unrecorded, of other big fish that got away.[19] Other kinds of pragmatic consideration are revealed by Morley's reflection that his provisional list 'would do for a launch provided we can get *one* recognized divine, Caird or Dean Church. We need that for respectability's sake.'[20] None the less, the series bore all the marks of a consciously designed national monument: the list is inclusive, unsectarian, and predictable. No restrictive view of the achievement of English letters is being pushed, though of course some covert criteria were operative, such as an understandable mid-Victorian prejudice in favour of the Romantic poets and their chief eighteenth-century predecessors. In the thirty-nine volumes published in the first series, eighteen were devoted to poets, seven to novelists, and fourteen to other prose writers. If one classifies by century, a certain bias towards the more modern figures emerges, in part, no doubt, for simple commercial reasons: there is one fourteenth-century author, two from the sixteenth century, five from the seventeenth, 16 from the eighteenth, and fifteen from the only three-quarters completed nineteenth century. In the twenty-six volumes of the

[19] Details of the unsuccessful wooing of George Eliot are given in Morgan, *House of Macmillan*, 115–18, which reveals that Arnold was another potential contributor who got away.

[20] Quoted ibid. 116.

second series, published in the first few years of the twentieth century, there were ten poets (or poet-playwrights like Shakespeare), six novelists, and ten other prose writers, and now fifteen of them came from the nineteenth century, many of the great Victorians having died in time to be placed in this national mausoleum. Unselfconscious inclusiveness of another kind is suggested by the fact that of the original thirty-nine '*English* men of letters' five were Scottish, four were Irish, and one American, while of the second series of twenty-six '*men* of letters' four were women.

Without claiming intimate acquaintance with all sixty-five volumes in these two series, it would be safe to say that the common format was very largely biographical: there was relatively little of what a more recent generation might expect by way of literary criticism, though a certain amount of what might more properly be called 'appreciation' makes a frequent appearance.[21] The tone in which these lives were for the most part recorded also suggests that the series embodied an assumption that, as I have already suggested, was common to much mid- and late nineteenth-century biography, namely a conviction that familiarity with the lives of outstanding individuals tended to have an inspirational effect, above all a morally elevating effect, as an incitement to the development of 'character'. The individual volumes were not, in fact, *all* written by Leslie Stephen, but he was naturally one of the most frequent, and characteristic, contributors, and of course the series spawned many imitators in the next couple of decades, similarly constructing genealogies of English achievement, including Longman's 'English Worthies', Scott's 'Great Writers', and on into the 1900s with Hodder's 'Literary Lives' and others. Edmund Gosse in effect succeeded Stephen as the leading journeyman of letters, contributing several volumes to these series—Gray for the 'English Men of Letters' in 1882, Raleigh for the 'English Worthies' in 1886, Congreve for the 'Great Writers' in 1888, Jeremy Taylor in 1904 and Sir Thomas Browne in 1905 for the second 'English Men of Letters', Coventry Patmore for the 'Literary Lives' in 1905, and so on.[22] At the

[21] There is a brief, perceptive discussion of the series in Gross, *Rise and Fall of the Man of Letters*, 106–8, including the judgement that 'no comparable series has ever come so close to attaining the rank of a traditional British institution'. There is an amusing parody of the somewhat predictable biographical format of the series in Stephen Potter, *The Muse in Chains: A Study in Education* (London, 1937), 81.

[22] For details, see Ann Thwaite, *Edmund Gosse: A Literary Landscape* (Oxford, 1985; 1st edn. 1984).

same time, a very important part of giving such a canon an effective existence lay in the greater numbers of cheaply republished editions of English classic authors for which the expansion in education in the last decades of the century created strong demand. The place of such enterprises in the larger national self-consciousness I am describing may be gauged from the way the most popular of these series of cheap editions—Cassell's 'National Library', under the editorship of Henry Morley—was prompted, as his biographer recorded, by 'an article in the *Daily News* in the summer of 1885, calling attention to the fact that we have nothing in England corresponding to the famous threepenny series in Germany'.[23]

The characterization of the achievements of English literature in compilations of this sort could be repetitive and clichéd, but clichés can be revealing of what a culture takes for granted. On this basis, the 'Whig interpretation of English literature' involved certain recurring elements. A native genius for individuality and sincerity made its appearance here, too, and the contrast with France was yet again a constitutive part of the self-definition, the role of the French penchant for the political dialectic of despotism and revolution being matched by the linked characteristics of formal artificiality and moral doubtfulness in French literature—indeed, all the qualities that can be ambiguously referred to as 'French polish'. Of course, such attempts to define the national literary character notoriously run the risk of circularity: only those authors who display the putative characteristics are recognized as authentically English, a category whose definition relies upon the examples provided in the literature written by just those authors.[24] In this respect it was always easier to find the approved qualities in, say, Johnson and Wordsworth than in Dryden and Pope. (Indeed, Leslie Stephen concluded his study of Pope with the stern judgement: 'Let us hope that it [sc. our final feeling about Pope] may be the pity which, after a certain lapse of years, we may be excused for conceding to the victim of moral as well as physical diseases'.[25]) But 'sound feelings' and

[23] H. S. Solly, *The Life of Henry Morley, LL.D.* (London, 1898), 356–7; quoted in Jo McMurty, *English Language, English Literature: The Creation of an Academic Discipline* (Hamden, Conn., 1985), 61.

[24] This problem is interestingly touched upon with reference to American literature in Russell Reising, *The Unusable Past: The Theory and Study of American Literature* (London, 1986), ch. 1.

[25] Leslie Stephen, *Pope* ('English Men of Letters') (London, 1880), 210.

'independence of mind' could, with a little ingenuity, generally be detected in any serious candidate for inclusion.

What is perhaps less obvious is the way in which the promotion of a certain conception of the distinctiveness of English literature reinforced the existing notion, subsequently much cherished, of the supposed English incapacity for systematic abstract thought. Pride in the national literature's special talent for expressing a rich diversity of life and feeling, symbolized not only by the essentially Romantic elevation of Shakespeare over Racine but also by the more recent acclaim for English achievements in the novel, easily shaded into self-congratulation that such fidelity to the complexity and concreteness of life should resist reduction to the abstract categories of a system. This in turn provided an important buttress for those soaring claims about how English individualism and its admirable respect for eccentricity had proved to be particularly favourable soil for the propagation of political liberty. This constellation of prejudices persisted, of course, well into the twentieth century, perhaps, in some quarters, right up to the present. In Ernest Barker's attempt to summarize the national character in the middle of the century, for example, we again meet the claim that although philosophy has proved 'outside the reach of the native genius' (or, in characteristic and unselfconscious hunting metaphor, 'the English mind has baulked and stumbled at the fence of philosophy'), this has more than been made up for by the glories of English poetry. 'There is a compensation in things; and the genius which denied England any great philosophy in prose may be said to have atoned for that denial by another and greater gift.'[26]

At the same time, one important effect of the scholarly Teutonism of the mid-Victorian decades was to link the narrative of English literary history, at least in its earlier stages, more closely to the actual Whig interpretation of English political history as that was in turn modified and extended by researches into Anglo-Saxon and ultimately Teutonic origins. The sense of excitement which the establishment of these links generated was alluded to by Sir Arthur Quiller-Couch, lecturing at Cambridge several decades later: 'Few in this room are old enough to remember the shock of awed surmise [*sic*] which fell upon young minds presented, in the late 'seventies or early 'eighties of the last century, with Freeman's *Norman Conquest*

[26] Ernest Barker (ed.), *The Character of England* (Oxford, London, 1947), 572. Note the 'greater': still cultural Top Nation, at least.

or Green's *Short History of the English People*; in which, as through parting clouds of darkness, we beheld our ancestry, literary as well as political, radiantly legitimized'. By 1915, Quiller-Couch could mock this enthusiasm, but it had by then played its part in helping to consolidate this sense of ancestry.[27]

A constitutive feature of the Whig interpretation of English political history was the insistence on unbroken continuity, and it is noticeable how strongly this same claim was pressed for the nation's literary past. Antiquarian piety and the sheer delight in establishing connections with distant centuries no doubt account for something, but continuity is a precondition of identity and hence of legitimate pride in earlier achievements. Uninhibitedly essentialist claims about the enduring spirit of 'English' writing abound in this period. The eminent textual scholar W. W. Skeat provides a representative illustration here when urging that the eyes of the English schoolboy

> should be opened to the Unity of English, that in English literature there is an unbroken succession of authors, from the reign of Alfred to that of Victoria, and that the language which we speak *now* is absolutely *one* in its essence, with the language that was spoken in the days when the English first invaded the island and defeated and overwhelmed its British inhabitants.[28]

Similarly, part of the case for preferring the term 'Old English' to 'Anglo-Saxon' was precisely 'that it makes prominent the continuity of our speech'.[29] In various forms, celebratory affirmations of the 'true continuity of spirit' of English literature and its 'unbroken line of development' continued throughout the first half of the twentieth century, though often now set against a more pessimistic sense of 'the power of the disruptive forces that threaten to break with our

[27] Sir Arthur Quiller-Couch, 'On the lineage of English literature' (1915), *Cambridge Lectures* (London, 1943), 22. This passage is also quoted by Brian Doyle, *English and Englishness* (London, 1989), 21, but he seems to miss the distancing irony of 'Q' here. The sentence occurs in a lecture which was a swingeing attack on the whole Teutonizing tradition; some indication of the lecturer's attitude is surely supplied by the fact that the sentence does not in fact end with the words 'we beheld our ancestry, literary as well as political, radiantly legitimized', but continues with: 'though not, to be sure in the England that we knew—but far away in Sleswick, happy Sleswick!'

[28] W. W. Skeat, *Questions for Examination in English Literature: With an Introduction on the Study of English* (Cambridge, 1873), p. xii; cited in Crowley, *Politics of Discourse*, 48.

[29] Thomas Lounsbury, *A History of the English Language* (New York, 2nd edn., 1894), p. v; cited in Crowley, *Politics of Discourse*, 48.

literary tradition'.[30] Once again, the relevant essay in *The Character of England* is almost an apotheosis of the clichés of the previous half-century. The essay by James Sutherland on 'Literature' affirms the enduring spirit of English literature, and insists that 'the English mind and character' may be known through its literature, especially 'Chaucer, Shakespeare, Dryden, Defoe, Fielding, Johnson, Wordsworth, Dickens, Trollope, Hardy' (a representative canon). It then, in effect, uses this 'heritage' as a stick with which to beat Modernist poets who, as a result of 'an abrupt break with tradition', now 'seem to be speaking only to themselves':

> The possibilities for the future are enormous, but unless the Englishman changes out of all knowledge, unless, in fact, he ceases to be English, he will not break entirely with the past. Yet the past can rarely have been receding more rapidly than it is today, and if there is to be no absolute break in the continuity of English literature and thought our writers must be content not to walk on too far ahead of their readers.[31]

A further important property of the type of narratives to which, generically, 'Whig' interpretations belong is that they can order the relevant past in terms of currently prevailing values. Thus, the characterization of the informing spirit of the national literature was subject to constant adjustment depending upon the particular scale of moral values to which it had to be accommodated, and it should be no surprise that in the late nineteenth century English literature was alleged to display precisely those values discussed in earlier chapters of this book: character, manliness, duty, and altruism. The fact that the following passage comes from Henry Morley's very popular *A First Sketch of English Literature*, published in 1873, indicates its representative status:

> The literature of this country has for its most distinctive mark the religious sense of duty. It represents a people striving through successive generations to find out the right and do it, to root out the wrong and labour ever onward for the love of God. If this be really the strong spirit of her people, to show that it is so is to tell how England won, and how alone she can expect to keep, her foremost place among the nations.[32]

[30] Quotations from Doyle, *English and Englishness*, 83, and Crowley, *Politics of Discourse*, 251.

[31] Barker (ed.), *Character of England*, 317–18, 319–20.

[32] The passage is quoted in John H. Fisher, 'Nationalism and the study of literature', *American Scholar*, 49 (1979–80), 107, who mis-attributes it to 1897, three

This is the sound of tribal pieties being incanted. The sentiment is commonplace: only the volume has been turned up a notch, presumably to justify the thump of the nationalist drum in the last couple of phrases. Other text-book writers substituted 'strength of character' or 'manly independence' or such-like for Morley's 'sense of duty', but they displayed a similar confidence that the history of English literature confirmed, rather than suggested any challenge to, the dominant ideals of their own time.

Nationalism requires that the base metal of the local and the temporary be somehow transmuted into the precious ore of the universal and the timeless. In this respect, affirmations of the distinctive moral properties of English literature provide another example of the pattern we have met so frequently in the different genres discussed in earlier chapters, whereby the values so strenuously insisted upon by Victorian moralists were implicitly presented as the self-evident truths of the moral sense or even of Reason itself, and hence as unproblematic, needing no historical explanation. Moreover, the benign conception of the relation between the emotions and moral action discussed above in Chapter 2 came into play here also, making it easier to justify the teaching of English literature as a contribution to moral education. A subject which promised simultaneously to 'sustain the spiritual side of life', to instil its students with 'a secure confidence in the ultimate triumph of good', and to 'promote a sense of national unity' clearly had a role to play in an expanding system of education.[33]

III

In earlier chapters, I have argued that there was no single pattern in the late nineteenth century to the 'professionalization' of various forms of intellectual enquiry as academic subjects, nor was the impact of such developments upon the kinds of 'voice' available to the public moralist by any means uniform. The institutionalization of 'English Literature' exhibited special peculiarities of its own, not least in the resulting discipline's continued engagement in, and

years after Morley's death. For a rather chatty account of Morley, Professor of English at University College, London, 1865–89 (and no relation of John Morley), see McMurty, *English Language, English Literature*, ch. 2.

33 See J. M. Newton, 'English literature at the university: an historical enquiry' (Unpublished Ph.D Diss., Cambridge, 1963), esp. 183.

overlap with, lay literary culture. The very fact of the ready accessibility to the non-professional of the subject-matter of English has surely contributed to the special prominence of academic literary critics in the wider cultural disputes of the twentieth century. Similar complexities are evident in the more immediate question of how the establishment of English as a discipline bore upon the contribution of literary history to the expression of national identity.

Initially, the prominence of philology within the newly established subject may have tended to limit the potentially parochial tendencies of the study of the national literature. Philology, especially when pursued in the comparative manner fashionable in the mid-nineteenth century, was inherently international: its practitioners were members of trans-national scholarly associations, devotees of a cosmopolitan science, and there was nothing improbable in becoming an expert on the philology of a language other than one's native tongue (many of the teachers of philology in late nineteenth-century British universities, for example, were German). Perhaps William Morris might be cited as one who did attempt to harness philological enthusiasm directly to an idealized conception of the English people, though the awkwardness was evident and Morris anyway remained far outside the circles of respectable academic philology.

Thereafter, it is clear that the very establishment of separate courses in *English* literature at the end of the century in part reflected an increased national self-consciousness. The general Victorian case for the value of literature, after all, had chiefly rested on the familiar Romantic grounds of providing a repository of aesthetic and moral values felt to be neglected or threatened by the operative forces of a commercial or industrial society. Such a case did not depend on assigning any special value to the national literature, nor was any such restriction implied in most of those classic nineteenth-century invocations of the value of 'letters', 'culture', or 'art'.[34] Similarly, many of the early proposals for teaching literature as an academic subject appealed to these larger moral justifications, and accordingly not all of them envisaged confining the syllabus to *English* literature.

In this respect, it can be particularly misleading to lump Matthew

[34] The classic account of this tradition is, of course, Raymond Williams, *Culture and Society 1780–1950* (London, 1958). It is arguable that since most of the 20th-century figures whom he deals with in the second part of the book *do* make a far greater appeal to the national literary tradition, this constitutes a greater discontinuity with the figures treated in the first half than his discussion suggests.

Arnold with later proponents of the discipline of 'English', as historians of the subject commonly tend to do. Not only did he frequently place English literature on a lower pedestal than French and regard both as inferior to the Classics, but he actually objected, when consulted near the end of his life, to the establishment of English Literature as an entirely independent subject within the university. In responding in 1886 to John Churton Collins's circular letter soliciting views in support of the proposal that a course in English Literature should be taught at the universities, Arnold at first replied: 'I should be glad to see at the Universities not a new School established for Modern Literature or Modern Languages, but the great works of English literature taken in conjunction with those of Greek and Latin Literature in the final Examination for honours in *Literae Humaniores*.' In the subsequently published version of his reply he wrote: 'I should be sorry to see a separate School.'[35] Moreover, he had also shown himself to be a little sceptical about attempts to infuse the treatment of literature with explicit patriotism: his one reproach to Stopford Brooke's otherwise excellent primer of English literature had been that it was all a bit 'too much to the tune of *Rule Britannia*'.[36]

On the whole, however, the realities of vernacular education encouraged an exclusive preoccupation with 'the national literature', and the institutional establishment of that mixture of historical, biographical, and philological enquiries that made up the study of literature in the late nineteenth century did not seriously threaten to disturb the complacent pieties of what I have been calling the Whig interpretation. Perhaps disturbance of any kind was hardly to be expected from convictions such as those expressed by Sir Sidney Lee (Leslie Stephen's successor as editor of the *Dictionary of National Biography*) in his Inaugural Lecture delivered at London University in 1913:

> There is no real difficulty in distinguishing worthless literature from that which for our purposes has some worth. Critics may differ as to the precise place that an author should hold in the scale of fame. But there comes a time

[35] The earlier reply was quoted by Collins in an article in the *Quarterly* in Jan. 1887, and the later one was published in the *Pall Mall Gazette* on 7 Jan. 1887; the latter is reproduced in appendix I (and the former cited in the editor's notes) in Matthew Arnold, *Complete Prose*, xi. 380, 501.

[36] Matthew Arnold, 'A guide to English literature' (1877), *Complete Prose*, viii. 240.

in the career of every book when a final decision is reached as to its general merit. The student will not wisely ignore any book which has been admitted by recognized authority within the charmed circle.[37]

Nor, more obviously, was 'disturbance' what most distinguished the fingertips-together style of aesthetic appreciation of the non-academic Edwardian bookmen. And any incipient tensions between the standards of professional scholarship and the requirements of moral or nationalist uplift were anyway deferred by the outbreak of the First World War.

The war encouraged, or even demanded, the expression of an aggressive nationalism (again overwhelmingly English rather than British or imperial), and the men of letters and the literary professoriat were not slow to make their contribution here.[38] The canon of English literature was mobilized to serve the nation's cause. Two remarks about the consequences of this are particularly relevant to my argument. First, far from revealing previously neglected *divisions* in the legacy of the nation's literary past, the war nourished the idea of a deeply *unified* literary tradition, predominantly pastoral in its register.[39] Stephen Potter later suggested that the nostalgia for an idealized rural England generated by the horrors of trench-warfare led many soldiers to 'retreat into the mental tent' of Barchester.[40] Indeed, it has been argued not only that the experience of the war was, to a very striking extent and for a surprisingly wide social range, mediated through a shared range of literary allusion, but that as a result the war may even have served to strengthen the position of literature as a privileged location or bearer of national consciousness.[41]

[37] Sidney Lee, 'The place of English literature in the modern university', *Elizabethan and Other Essays* (Oxford, 1929), 4.

[38] There is a growing literature on this. For the men of letters, see D. G. Wright, 'The Great War, government propaganda, and English "men of letters" 1914–18', *Literature and History*, 7 (1978), 70–100; and particularly Peter Buitenhuis, *The Great War of Words: Literature as Propaganda 1914–18 and After* (London, 1988). For the professors see Stuart Wallace, *War and the Image of Germany: British Academics 1914–1918* (Edinburgh, 1988). See also the sneering and too easily dismissive treatment of the jingoism displayed by Walter Raleigh, Professor of English at Oxford, in Chris Baldick, *The Social Mission of English Criticism 1848–1932* (Oxford, 1983), 75–80, and Terence Hawkes, *That Shakespeherian Rag: Essays on a Critical Process* (London, 1986), ch. 3.

[39] This emerges very clearly from Fussell's excellent *Great War and Modern Memory*, especially ch. VII. See also Fussell's observation that 'there were few of any rank who had not been assured that the greatest of modern literatures was the English and who did not feel an appropriate pleasure in that reassurance' (157).

[40] Potter, *Muse in Chains*, 243.

[41] Fussell, *Great War and Modern Memory*; this would not be strictly incompatible

Contemporary observers certainly believed that 'among the minor results of the Great War has been a revival in the interest taken by educationalists and by the general public in the historical study of English literature and of the English language'.[42]

Secondly, one casualty of the vehement anti-Germanism stirred up by the war was the tradition of Germanic philology and the emphasis on the common Teutonic roots of English and German literature (an emphasis which had already become rather dated by 1914). Part of the consequence of this was to shift attention away from philology and the earlier period of literature generally, a process reinforced by other pressures for a more 'relevant' or 'accessible' education after the war. Again there is a much longer story to be told here, one which would need to encompass the foundation of a distinctively modern English course at Cambridge in 1917. But the episode which has been taken by recent historians of the discipline to have given most concentrated and influential expression to the new ambitions for English was the publication in 1921 of the report of the committee, under the chairmanship of Sir Henry Newbolt, which had been set up by the Board of Education to consider the teaching of English in England.[43]

The Newbolt Report's almost artless concern that the shared experience of great literature should contribute to bridging 'the social chasms which divide us' has provided much quotable material for those who wish to denounce the class-bound assumptions alleged to have shaped the development of English as an academic discipline. But whatever impact the Report may have had upon the teaching of English in elementary and secondary schools, the claim that 'it can be said effectively to have shaped the nature of "English" as the academic subject we know today' seems a considerable exaggeration.[44] The judgement of one of the members of the

with Buitenhuis's (anyway disputable) claim that as a result of the willing participation of men of letters in the propaganda war, the prestige of that generation of writers was much diminished; *Great War of Words*, epilogue.

[42] R. B. McKerrow, *A Note on the Teaching of English Language and Literature*, English Association Pamphlet, 49 (London, 1921), 3; quoted in Crowley, *Politics of Discourse*, 231.

[43] *The Teaching of English in England: Being the Report of the Departmental Committee Appointed by the President of the Board of Education to Inquire into the Position of English in the Education System of England* (London, 1921).

[44] Hawkes, *Shakespeherian Rag*, 111. Cf. the improbable claim in Baldick's generally much soberer discussion: 'The report became a guiding influence upon the development of English studies, particularly in the schools, but also in the universities through the work of I. A. Richards' (*Social Mission*, 94). In the fullest and most recent

committee, John Dover Wilson, that its Chairman and guiding spirit, the poet, naval historian, and former barrister Sir Henry Newbolt, 'possessed little knowledge or sympathy with English scholarship or the teaching of the history of literature in universities'[45] is a better indication of the gulf between the approach of the Report and that of the newly professionalizing academic discipline. Rather than providing a manifesto for, or first instalment of, the 'critical revolution' of the 1920s, the Report in fact offers an eclectic mixture of familiar moral and historical assumptions. Indeed, given its conception of the relation between English literature and national identity, the Newbolt Report may be seen rather as an attempt to adapt the Whig interpretation of English literary history to the needs of the world brought into being by the Fisher Education Act of 1918.

Since Newbolt himself drafted much of the Report, it is scarcely surprising to find the prose marked by a tone of robust jingoism.[46] Passages such as the following amply illustrate this self-consciously nationalist note: 'It is only quite lately that we in England have begun to have the definite consciousness, which the French gained in the age of Louis XIV, that we have a great and independent literature of our own which need not lower its flag in the presence of the greatest on the earth.' Or again: 'No Englishman competent to judge doubts that our literature ranks among the two or three greatest in the world; or that it is quite arguable that, if not perhaps the finest, it is the richest of all.'[47] The contrast with France's explicit exploitation of its literary heritage for purposes of national unity recurs frequently—'Our language and literature are as great a source of pride and may be made as great a bond of national unity to us as those of France are, and have long been, to the French'—and the Report carried a separate appendix summarizing the steps taken in France since 1871 to make French (the language at least as much as the literature, apparently) 'an indispensable instrument of national culture'.[48] The chauvinist note is also evident in the insistence that English literature be recognized as genuinely *English*. The Report, and even more some of the individual witnesses whose comments it

account, however, Brian Doyle shows an admirable scepticism about these claims, and emphasizes the *failure* of the Newbolt Report to determine the subsequent professional development of English studies (*English and Englishness*, ch. II, esp. 41, 68–9).

[45] John Dover Wilson, *Milestones on the Dover Road* (London, 1969), 97.

[46] For an account of Newbolt's role, see ibid. 95–100.

[47] *Teaching of English*, 198, 200.

[48] Ibid. 202, 369.

reproduced, exhibited a full measure of the anti-Teutonism then at its height, and this coincided with the desire, to which that majority of members of the committee who were also members of the English Association were expressly committed, to dethrone the study of philology. The Report concluded its analysis of the evidence on this issue: 'We feel that under the influence of theories which assigned an almost exclusively Teutonic descent to English culture and institutions there has been an excessive concentration by students of the origin of our language and literature on the Anglo-Saxon elements.' Sir Walter Raleigh, Professor of English at Oxford and official historian of the RAFC's part in the war, who was the most outspoken of the witnesses cited, more pithily dismissed the philologists' concern with 'hypothetical sound-shiftings in the primeval German forests'.[49]

But the Englishness of English literature had, apparently, to be protected on other flanks as well. The committee noted that there could be advantages in studying Chaucer in relation to his Italian and French models, but they clearly feared that an important link in the nation's cultural heredity might thus be undervalued or lost sight of, for they offset this suggestion by urging a less comparative approach:

> But Chaucer is himself English of the English; and if we look for earlier appearances of the most permanent, at least of the deepest and most serious characteristics of our race, it is not in any Mediterranean books that we shall find them, but in things written in this island, connected though they be with Chaucer by the slenderest of links, in Beowulf and Alfred and Bede.[50]

The suggestion of rousing platform-oratory in the cadence of this sentence is inescapable, as it rises from the evocative but almost meaningless 'Chaucer is himself English of the English', through the clichéd patriotic references to 'our race' and 'this island', on to the dimissive sneer at 'Mediterranean books', and culminating in the roll-call of English worthies spaced out by unnecessary conjunctions. Its logic will not bear too much scrutiny: the derivation from Anglo-Saxon seems to return to favour here, for example. In effect, the passage was discounting the evidence of literary scholarship about actual textual and literary relationships in favour of a more intuitive grasp of 'the deepest and most serious characteristics of our race'—another invocation, in fact, of the 'essential spirit of English literature'.

[49] Ibid. 226, 218. [50] Ibid. 213.

The Report also conforms to the pattern discussed above in the way in which it suggests that the Holy Ghost of universal truth had somehow contrived to find its natural home in the established canon of works of English literature. 'It may be true that the story of the English people is best seen in English literature, but English literature contains much more than the story of the English people.' It contains a 'universal' element. This was sometimes thought to fall within the province of a rival subject, namely philosophy, but 'some might claim', the Report reflected disingenuously, 'that the truth of poetry is higher as well as far more permanent than that of philosophy'.[51] On this view, the study of English promised to be simultaneously a 'purifying of the emotions' and a 'School of national culture'; the possibility of conflict between these two goals was not addressed. Although there is much explicit and implicit Arnoldianism in its pages and although its frequently expressed concern to connect the study of literature more closely to 'life' is superficially similar to the later Leavisite creed, the Newbolt Report should not too readily be subsumed into a putatively continuous tradition of critical thinking about the cultural role of literature.[52] At many points its language is more Kiplingesque than Arnoldian, and its presuppositions indicate a far greater kinship with the world of the *Oxford Book of English Verse*, published twenty-one years earlier, than with that of *Scrutiny*, which began publication eleven years later.

IV

The story of the various ways in which the idiom and preoccupations of literary criticism have provided the chief medium for cultural criticism in mid-twentieth-century Britain lies beyond the scope of this book, though it is a story which still awaits its historian. In hinting at some of the leading themes of that story, however, we may take our cue from an interesting aphorism by Gustave Lanson, the doyen of academic literary study in Third Republic France, whose scholarly efforts had, for some two decades before 1914, been explicitly devoted to deploying the French literary past for nation-

[51] *Teaching of English*, 205–6. The Report also charged historical scholarship with neglecting literature's 'nobler, more eternal and universal element' (205).

[52] e.g., Hawkes, *Shakespeherian Rag*, 111: 'Its spiritual father is Matthew Arnold, its spiritual son F. R. Leavis'.

alist and republican purposes: 'Literary criticism divides; literary history unites.'[53] Like all aphorisms, this threatens to over-simplify, but certainly any adequate telling of the subsequent story would need to give pride of place to the successful promotion in the 1920s and 1930s of a demanding ideal of 'criticism'.[54] In its most militant form (and the increase in militancy is, of course, part of what is at issue), this notion of criticism promised not only a deeper intellectual and emotional engagement with works of literature, but also claimed to equip its practitioners uniquely well for the task of scrutinizing other areas of culture. At the same time, there was a sense in which it encouraged an exclusive preoccupation with English culture in a way that had not been true of the older philological or comparative approaches. Criticism in this sense does not travel well, certainly does not translate well, generating the problem of what might be called 'criticism in one country'.

But this development was related to at least two others of still greater magnitude. First, a major alteration in relations between academic criticism and the national literature was wrought by the advent of literary Modernism. In so far as the canon of texts and the underlying conception of the English literary character which was elaborated and refined in the nineteenth century had had its roots in Romanticism, it is hardly surprising that the great anti-Romantic shift of sensibility labelled 'Modernism' should involve some challenge to the received arrangement of the 'national literature', a challenge most notably exemplified, as well as theorized, by T. S. Eliot. In principle, the aggressive internationalism, or even anti-nationalism, of Modernism expressed a repudiation of the parochialism of pre-war English literary chauvinism. Whatever changes this may have signalled in creative writers' conceptions of their role, it had a more oblique impact on the place of critics in the wider culture. In practice the eventual form taken by the associated 'critical revolution' could be said both to have enhanced the role of

[53] 'La critique . . . divise; l'histoire littéraire réunit'; quoted in Antoine Compagnon, *La Troisième République des lettres: De Flaubert à Proust* (Paris, 1983), 142–3, where Lanson's aim is characterized as being 'fortifier l'unité de la conscience française'. Compagnon's book is a particularly rich source for instructive comparisons about the very different relations between politics and literary criticism in France during this period.

[54] According to Stephen Potter's (surely optimistic) judgement, the new intellectual strenuousness in criticism meant 'goodbye for good "the nature he describes is typically English in its quality"' style of belles-lettristic appreciation (Potter, *Muse in Chains*, 248).

literary critics as professional explicators of increasingly opaque texts, and at the same time to have contributed a more contentious note to English cultural politics than had been found in the earlier historical forms of literary study.

This was also the effect of the other large-scale development which must be mentioned here, that constellation of changes which prompted in many members of the educated class a profound cultural pessimism. Alarm at the power of the so-called 'yellow press' at the beginning of the century was extended in the next few decades by anxiety about the techniques employed in advertising, the potential power of new media like film and radio, and a wider unease at the cultural consequences of greater social equality. The importing into the language at this time of the terms 'highbrow' and 'lowbrow' indicates this perception not just of a gulf between the classes—that there had in some form always been—but of a sense (however well or ill grounded we might now take it to have been) that culturally the educated class were on the defensive. One common response to this sense was a conviction that a cultural heritage that was under threat or disappearing had to be rescued and made vital and effective in the present.[55]

A discussion of the sort attempted here obviously cannot have a 'conclusion' in any conventional sense, but I want to end with an expansive gesture towards some of the many possible ways of continuing. The issues I have touched on in this chapter provide one relevant framework in which to consider the cultural criticism of many of the figures who have been important in twentieth-century British intellectual history. The most predictable name to suggest at this point would, I suppose, be that of Leavis, though I think our sense of even *his* place in that history would benefit from a fuller understanding of just what view or views of English history and literature he took himself to be challenging, since his early work is these days rather too simply regarded as a familiar form of cultural conservatism, without its original oppositional and dissident, almost Dissenting, character being properly recognized. But a little less obviously, one might consider Eliot's revision of the canon,

[55] There is a useful summary of the diverse developments lumped together here in D. L. LeMahieu, *A Culture for Democracy: Mass Communication and the Cultivated Mind in Britain between the Wars* (Oxford, 1988). One particularly influential form taken by this anxiety is explored in Francis Mulhern, *The Moment of 'Scrutiny'* (London, 1979).

undertaken in the light not only of his own poetic practice but also of a conception of England's place in Christian Europe, and thus a means of criticizing a society he considered to be 'worm-eaten with liberalism'.[56] Or, less obviously still, we would find another literary definition of lineage at work in Orwell's attacks on what he derisively called 'the Europeanised Left intelligentsia' of Britain in the 1930s and 1940s, attacks partly conducted through essays on some of those earlier English writers with whom Orwell identified and who made up what has been nicely described as 'God's great awkward squad of unorthodox, dissident Englishmen'.[57] Or, bordering on the implausible, one might place Raymond Williams, too, in this framework as a reminder of the continuing centrality of attempts to appropriate and re-appropriate an enabling tradition of English literature even for someone hardly committed to promoting 'essential Englishness'. In each of these cases, it will be evident, the reordering of English literary history had an insurgent and oppositional character precisely because these critics believed that the dominant tendencies of contemporary culture represented a betrayal of an earlier England. That confident sense of historical possession, of mastering the times by successfully adapting to them, which was a constitutive element of a properly Whig account, is noticeably absent in such writing.

Extending this last point and ranging more widely still, one might also consider the ways in which the fond dwelling on England's 'incomparable' (and unrepeatable) literary heritage can be seen as a modulation of that pervasive nostalgia many observers have detected in English culture since 1918.[58] The tendency to cope with loss by resorting to elegy is surely deeply intertwined with the immense cultural presence of that particular body of writing, and writing about writing, that is known as 'English literature', with its varied and recurrent forms of pastoral, a genre predicated upon nostalgia. 'Nostalgia', the *OED* tells us, is 'a form of melancholia caused by prolonged absence from one's home or country'. Surely that 'England of the mind' which, in several of its twentieth-century forms, draws so heavily on images from 'the national literature' is so constructed that one only *can* be 'absent' from it.[59] What nostalgia

[56] T. S. Eliot, *After Strange Gods* (London, 1934), 13.

[57] Bernard Crick, *George Orwell: A Life* (London, 1980), 137.

[58] e.g. Geoffrey Hill who finds 'an elegiac tinge to the air of this country since the end of the Great War'; cited in a very perceptive article by David Gervais, '"Something gone": "England" in modern English writing', *English*, 158 (1988), 115.

[59] Cf. Seamus Heaney, 'Englands of the mind', reprinted in his *Preoccupations*

longs for, in English nationalist pastoral, is a time when one's relation to 'England' was not a matter of nostalgia. While reminding ourselves of that *OED* definition we ought perhaps also to remember that the same entry tells us the word originated as a term of what was called 'mental pathology'.

Finally, it is a truism to observe that the more troubled sense of English national identity evident in the late twentieth century has encouraged the search for other 'usable pasts' as alternatives to what is often hypostatized as the 'official' account. But in part this only involves a fresh adaptation of what is now an established tradition of cultural criticism, one that seeks its own legitimating ancestors and tries to constitute its own canon. Our heightened sense of inheriting a divided and contentious history may prompt us to look with new respect upon Eliot's teasing remark, made in 1947: 'The Civil War is not ended: I question whether a civil war ever does end.'[60] But if the spirit of that remark contrasts with some of the more blithely consensual assumptions I have been ascribing to the late nineteenth century, the fact that it was made in the course of a reassessment of Milton suggests one important kind of continuity, and reassessments of major authors have continued to provide some of the most highly publicized occasions for addressing questions of national cultural identity.

In more mournful (perhaps even elegiac) vein, it may seem that the chief manifestation of the increased sensitivity to questions of English cultural nationalism in Britain today is, alas, a rash of publications by academic historians and literary critics uncovering, with a mixture of scorn and envy, some of the ways in which our less self-conscious ancestors derived *their* identities from *their* less complicated relation to *their* chosen past. Still, there may be some unacknowledged continuities here, too, since the seductions of nostalgia are not altogether absent even in such reflections on a lineage twice removed. In other words, the scholarly study of 'Englishness' can, in some cases, be yet another way of perpetuating that fond absorption in the alleged distinctiveness of the English past which it ostensibly desires to criticize. But this sceptical observation

(London, 1980), 150–69; the particular case of Geoffrey Hill is perceptively discussed in Heather Glen, 'Geoffrey Hill's "England of the mind"', *Critical Review*, 27 (1985), 99–109.

[60] T. S. Eliot, 'Milton' (British Academy Lecture, 1947), repr. in *On Poetry and Poets* (London, 1957), quotation at 148.

does not entail the conclusion that we should regard the forms of self-definition discussed in this chapter simply as part of a world we have lost. If it does nothing else, the fact that 'our' recent Secretary of State for Education chose to promote his triumphalist version of 'England's' (predominantly military) history by publishing an anthology of English poetry[61] should at least suggest that the impulse, and perhaps the need, to address questions of national identity through the medium of literary criticism is likely to be with us for a while yet.

[61] Kenneth Baker (ed.), *The Faber Book of English History in Verse* (London, 1988).

INDEX